From Concept to
Wall Street

In an increasingly competitive world, it is quality of thinking that gives an edge—an idea that opens new doors, a technique that solves a problem, or an insight that simply helps make sense of it all.

We work with leading authors in the various arenas of business and finance to bring cutting-edge thinking and best learning practice to a global market.

It is our goal to create world-class print publications and electronic products that give readers knowledge and understanding which can then be applied, whether studying or at work.

To find out more about our business products, you can visit us at www.ft-ph.com

From Concept to Wall Street

Oren Fuerst
Uri Geiger

Special Advisors:
Chemi Peres
Davidi Gilo
Ron Lubash

An Imprint of PEARSON EDUCATION

Upper Saddle River, NJ • New York • London • San Francisco • Toronto • Sydney
Tokyo • Singapore • Hong Kong • Cape Town • Madrid
Paris • Milan • Munich • Amsterdam

www.ft-ph.com

Editorial/Production Supervision: *Kathleen M. Caren*
Acquisitions Editor: *James Boyd*
Marketing Manager: *Bryan Gambrel*
Manufacturing Manager: *Maura Zaldivar*
Cover Design Director: *Jerry Votta*
Cover Design: *Talar Boorujy*
Interior Design: *Gail Cocker-Bogusz*

©2003 Pearson Education, Inc.
Publishing as Financial Times Prentice Hall
Upper Saddle River, New Jersey 07458

Financial Times Prentice Hall books are widely used by corporations and government agencies for training, marketing, and resale.

For information regarding corporate and government bulk discounts please contact: Corporate and Government Sales (800) 382-3419 or corpsales@pearsontechgroup.com

Company and product names mentioned herein are the trademarks or registered trademarks of their respective owners.

All rights reserved. No part of this book may be reproduced, in any form or by any means, without permission in writing from the publisher.

Printed in the United States of America

10 9 8 7 6 5 4 3 2 1

ISBN 0-13-034803-1

Pearson Education LTD.
Pearson Education Australia PTY, Limited
Pearson Education Singapore, Pte. Ltd.
Pearson Education North Asia Ltd.
Pearson Education Canada, Ltd.
Pearson Educación de Mexico, S.A. de C.V.
Pearson Education—Japan
Pearson Education Malaysia, Pte. Ltd.

FINANCIAL TIMES PRENTICE HALL BOOKS

For more information, please go to www.ft-ph.com

Dr. Judith M. Bardwick
Seeking the Calm in the Storm: Managing Chaos in Your Business Life

Thomas L. Barton, William G. Shenkir, and Paul L. Walker
*Making Enterprise Risk Management Pay Off:
How Leading Companies Implement Risk Management*

Michael Basch
*CustomerCulture: How FedEx and Other Great Companies Put the
Customer First Every Day*

J. Stewart Black and Hal B. Gregersen
Leading Strategic Change: Breaking Through the Brain Barrier

Deirdre Breakenridge
Cyberbranding: Brand Building in the Digital Economy

William C. Byham, Audrey B. Smith, and Matthew J. Paese
*Grow Your Own Leaders: How to Identify, Develop, and Retain
Leadership Talent*

Jonathan Cagan and Craig M. Vogel
*Creating Breakthrough Products: Innovation from Product Planning
to Program Approval*

Subir Chowdhury
The Talent Era: Achieving a High Return on Talent

Sherry Cooper
Ride the Wave: Taking Control in a Turbulent Financial Age

James W. Cortada
*21st Century Business: Managing and Working
in the New Digital Economy*

James W. Cortada
*Making the Information Society: Experience, Consequences,
and Possibilities*

Aswath Damodaran
*The Dark Side of Valuation: Valuing Old Tech, New Tech,
and New Economy Companies*

Henry A. Davis and William W. Sihler
Financial Turnarounds: Preserving Enterprise Value

Sarv Devaraj and Rajiv Kohli
The IT Payoff: Measuring the Business Value of Information Technology Investments

Nicholas D. Evans
Business Agility: Strategies for Gaining Competitive Advantage through Mobile Business Solutions

Nicholas D. Evans
Business Innovation and Disruptive Technology: Harnessing the Power of Breakthrough Technology…for Competitive Advantage

Kenneth R. Ferris and Barbara S. Pécherot Petitt
Valuation: Avoiding the Winner's Curse

Oren Fuerst and Uri Geiger
From Concept to Wall Street

David Gladstone and Laura Gladstone
Venture Capital Handbook: An Entrepreneur's Guide to Raising Venture Capital, Revised and Updated

David R. Henderson
The Joy of Freedom: An Economist's Odyssey

Harvey A. Hornstein
The Haves and the Have Nots: The Abuse of Power and Privilege in the Workplace…and How to Control It

Philip Jenks and Stephen Eckett, Editors
The Global-Investor Book of Investing Rules: Invaluable Advice from 150 Master Investors

Thomas Kern, Mary Cecelia Lacity, and Leslie P. Willcocks
Netsourcing: Renting Business Applications and Services Over a Network

Al Lieberman, with Patricia Esgate
The Entertainment Marketing Revolution: Bringing the Moguls, the Media, and the Magic to the World

Frederick C. Militello, Jr., and Michael D. Schwalberg
Leverage Competencies: What Financial Executives Need to Lead

D. Quinn Mills
Buy, Lie, and Sell High: How Investors Lost Out on Enron and the Internet Bubble

Dale Neef
: *E-procurement: From Strategy to Implementation*

John R. Nofsinger
: *Investment Blunders (of the Rich and Famous)…And What You Can Learn From Them*

John R. Nofsinger
: *Investment Madness: How Psychology Affects Your Investing… And What to Do About It*

Tom Osenton
: *Customer Share Marketing: How the World's Great Marketers Unlock Profits from Customer Loyalty*

Richard W. Paul and Linda Elder
: *Critical Thinking: Tools for Taking Charge of Your Professional and Personal Life*

Matthew Serbin Pittinsky, Editor
: *The Wired Tower: Perspectives on the Impact of the Internet on Higher Education*

W. Alan Randolph and Barry Z. Posner
: *Checkered Flag Projects: 10 Rules for Creating and Managing Projects that Win, Second Edition*

Stephen P. Robbins
: *The Truth About Managing People…And Nothing but the Truth*

Fernando Robles, Françoise Simon, and Jerry Haar
: *Winning Strategies for the New Latin Markets*

Jeff Saperstein and Daniel Rouach
: *Creating Regional Wealth in the Innovation Economy: Models, Perspectives, and Best Practices*

Eric G. Stephan and Wayne R. Pace
: *Powerful Leadership: How to Unleash the Potential in Others and Simplify Your Own Life*

Jonathan Wight
: *Saving Adam Smith: A Tale of Wealth, Transformation, and Virtue*

Yoram J. Wind and Vijay Mahajan, with Robert Gunther
: *Convergence Marketing: Strategies for Reaching the New Hybrid Consumer*

This book is dedicated to our biggest investors,
backers and supporters, our wives Tzameret (Oren) and Karen (Uri).

Without your love and understanding for countless sleepless nights,
this book would have never seen the light of day.
Roy, Uri's newborn, is also thanked for his understanding.

We also dedicate this book to our parents,
Frida and Mordechai (Oren), Eliana and Roland (Uri),
as well as to our mentors,
Nahum Melumad (Oren) and Harvey Goldschmid (Uri)

CONTENTS

Foreword — xv
Preface — xvii
Acknowledgments — xix
About the Authors — xx

Chapter 1
Introduction — 1
    Book Structure 1
    Glossary 3

PART I
Establishment and Development of Ventures — 5

Chapter 2
Beginnings—Establishing a Venture — 7
    The Price of Success and Failure 7
    The Idea 8
    The Management Team 9
    External Advisors 11
    Incorporation 14
    Incorporation in Delaware 21

Chapter 3
Financial and Business Planning — 27
    The Company's Business Cycle 27
    Financial Statements 29
    Financial Projections 43
    Cost Structure Analysis and Forecasting 47
    Cash Flow Forecasting 51
    Market Analysis and Strategic Planning 53

Strategic Alliances 60
The Business Plan 64

Chapter 4
Employee Recruitment and Compensation 69

Employee Recruiting 70
Employee Compensation in the Technology Segments 72
Granting Options to Employees 75
Taxation of Stock Options 83
Performance-based Compensation 85
Incentives to Tie Employees to the Company 88
Considerations in Employment Termination 89

Chapter 5
Intangible Capital and Intellectual Property 91

Patents 92
Copyright Law 97
Trademark Law 99
Trade Secrets 99
Issues with Employees 101
NDA—Non-Disclosure Agreements 101
Considerations in the Granting of Licenses 102

PART II
Financing the Venture 105

Chapter 6
Milestones and Sources of Financing the Venture 107

Financing in Stages 107
Milestones in Venture Development 108
Scope of Financing and the Company's Value 109
Stages in Raising Venture Capital 111
Sources of Capital 116

Chapter 7
Practical Aspects of Raising Venture Capital   **123**

   Basic Terms 124
   Deciding How Much Capital to Raise 125
   Valuing the Company for the Purpose of Raising Capital/Determining According to Which Value Capital Will be Raised 126
   The Process of Raising Venture Capital 127

Chapter 8
Legal and Contractual Aspects of Raising Venture Capital   **133**

   Legal Restrictions on Raising Private Capital 133

Chapter 9
Valuation of Companies   **157**

   Methods Based on Multiples 158
   Methods for Discounting Cash Flows and Residual Income 162
   The Real Options Method 171
   Value to Investors or Strategic Investors and Buyers 174
   The Discount Rate Used by Venture Capital Funds 176
   Issuing Stock to Investors 178
   The Venture Capital Method 183
   Appendix—Basic Terms in Measurement 187

PART III
Venture Capital Investors   189

Chapter 10
Venture Capital Funds   **191**

   Private Equity Funds and Venture Capital Funds 191
   Venture Capital Investment Characteristics 194
   Venture Capital Funds and Their Investors 195
   Venture Capital Funds and Their Portfolios 196
   The Added Value of Venture Capital Funds 196

The Development of the Venture Capital Industry in the United States 201
The Venture Capital Industry at the Dawn of the Third Millennium 204
The Structure and Activities of Venture Capital Funds 211
Exit Strategies of Investments by Venture Capital Funds 219
The Return on Venture Capital Funds 220

Chapter 11
Other Venture Capital Investors — 223

Private Investors (Angels) 223
Corporate and Other Investors 225
Financial Institutions Which Invest Directly in Funds 227
Other Sources of Capital 230

PART IV
Raising Capital from the Public — 233

Chapter 12
Raising Capital from the Public—Introduction — 235

Deciding to Go Public 236
Preparing the Company for an IPO 239

Chapter 13
The Public Offering Process — 241

Stock Markets in the United States 241
Forming the IPO Team 243
The Process 247
The Underwriting Agreement 253
The Registration Statement 255
Liability under U.S. Securities Laws 257
Changes in the Registration Process 258
Following the IPO 258
Selling Shares That Are Exempt from Registration 261
Foreign Companies Raising Capital 262

PART V
Mergers and Acquisitions, Bankruptcies, and Dissolution   265

Chapter 14
Mergers and Acquisitions (M&A)—Introduction   267

The Scope of the Phenomenon 267
Types of Corporate Restructuring 268
Strategic Classification 269
Why Do Mergers and Acquisitions Occur? 270
Do Mergers and Acquisitions Create Value? 274
Sales and Mergers Versus IPOs 275
Case Study—The Sale of Chromatis to Lucent 277

Chapter 15
Conducting the M&A Transaction   283

Mergers 283
Sale and Acquisition of Assets 285
M&A Strategy 286
The Consideration in Mergers and Acquisitions 287
The Process 291
Tender Offers 292

Chapter 16
Additional Legal Aspects   295

Legal Rules Governing Mergers and Acquisitions 295
Merger or Acquisition Agreements 296
Antitrust Issues 297
Fairness Opinions 300

Chapter 17
Other Restructuring — 301

Other Types of Restructuring: Spin-offs, Split-offs, Carve-outs, and Letter Stocks 301
Equity Carve-outs (Spin-out IPOs) 302
Letter Stocks/Targeted Stocks 303
The Rationale of Separate Listing of Units 303

Chapter 18
Bankruptcy and Dissolution of Companies — 305

Legal Rules Governing Bankruptcy and Dissolution in the United States 306
Additional Issues Concerning Bankruptcy of Startup Companies 309

Glossary — 311

Further Readings — 319

Index — 323

FOREWORD

The venture capital industry went through a wild cycle in the late 1990s. Since its early beginnings in the 1950s, venture capital was really a cottage industry compared to investment banking, for example. There were only a relatively small number of firms devoted to early stage technology investments. The investment level, allowing for inflation, was stable.

The dot-com fever struck like a lightning bolt. The "new economy" revolution was on. If you didn't "get it" you would fall by the wayside. Money came pouring into venture capital and novices in the field created many new firms. Angel investors and Incubators became the rage.

To paraphrase Alan Greenspan, "irrational exuberance" prevailed. Then the bubble burst. Gone are the Angels. Gone are the Incubators. At Sequoia Capital, my partner, Michael Moritz, coined the term "B 2 N". We are all familiar with "B 2 C" or "B 2 B". "B 2 N" stands for Back to Normal. It will take some time for the excessive amounts of money raised to be invested. Unfortunately, much of it was used to shore up ventures that should not have been financed in the first place.

In 2002, many new firms (created in 1999 and 2000) are closing their doors and the trend is accelerating. We are also seeing established funds reducing their size from over 1 billion dollars to a more manageable $700 or $800 million. The same phenomena happened, on a smaller scale, in the mid-1980s.

"Back to Normal" has different meanings for venture capitalists and entrepreneurs. For venture capitalists, it means that the era of quick return is gone. Companies need to be nurtured, management teams must be assembled, and business plans and strategies must be developed. In other words, the business of venture capital is to build businesses and venture capitalists must go back to that first principle.

For entrepreneurs, it is important they understand that their interests are lined up with those of their venture investors. The goals are the same: build a successful company measured by revenue, profit, and cash flow. Eventually, the investment bankers will come knocking at the door.

This is why *From Concept to Wall Street* is an important book. It offers a wealth of information useful to the inexperienced as well as the experienced venture capitalist. The new entrepreneur will find it to be an indispensable tool at every stage of the company's development.

In my opinion, "venture capital", or, for that matter, "entrepreneurship" cannot be taught.

Successful venture capitalists go through an "apprenticeship." One needs experience to evaluate business plans, find the strengths and weaknesses of founding teams, build Boards of Directors, and participate in the development of the Company's strategy; in short, build an enterprise with the founders.

Entrepreneurship is not taught. One is either an entrepreneur or one is not. On the other hand, entrepreneurs need to inform themselves before and during the launching of their enterprise.

In both cases, this book will provide useful and thoughtful answers.

Pierre R. Lamond
Menlo Park, California, July 2002

PREFACE

Over the past decade, thousands of new ventures were established every year around the world, and tens of billions of dollars were invested by venture capitalists. Technological vision, an entrepreneurial spirit, and success stories of other entrepreneurs and investors have led many talented people to get involved in the technology-intensive, or high tech, industry as entrepreneurs, investors, or consultants. The far-reaching changes experienced by the global economy, and in particular, the introduction of the PC and the Internet, have dramatically accelerated the pace of development of new ventures, and their number. Furthermore, during the second half of the 1990s, the technological changes and vast resources invested in many high tech ventures, in both the private and public markets, have caused many to believe that the ratio of risk to return was never as low as during that period.

The unprecedented prosperity of the U.S. stock markets in the 1990s led to enormous financial investments in venture capital and in promising startup companies around the world. Such a volume of funds, unmatched in human history, supported thousands of new and existing ventures every year.

The severe economic crisis that befell the capital markets and started in the year 2000 symbolized, for many, the end of an era in capital markets and entrepreneurship. For us, this was an expected awakening after several years of euphoria in the market. We are confident the high tech industry will continue to supply the global economy with developments that will streamline business systems, decrease production costs, and improve the quality of life of citizens worldwide.

Despite the substantial slowdown in the capital market, technological changes have not come to a halt, and companies are being established, developed, and have raised capital. Technological progress is visible everywhere in fields such as communications, electronics, hardware, software, information technologies, biotechnology, genomics, and medical devices.

From Concept to Wall Street was written to fulfill the need for a central source of information for entrepreneurs, investors, consultants, employees, and anyone involved or interested in entrepreneurship and the venture capital industry.

In this book we combine our practical and academic experience, with the experience of leading experts in their respective fields, to communicate a mass of material in a manner that is as coherent and straightforward as possible, without sacrificing depth.

The book describes the lifecycle of the venture, from its establishment, though its various capital raising activities and its venture development process, including strategy formulation, business planning, and implementation, up to the IPO or acquisition by another company. The book addresses all the material aspects, theoretical and practical, of venture capital investment, venture creation and development, through the eventual investment realization.

The focus is on venture capital-backed companies (independent or part of larger organizations) and issues pertaining to their value maximization. At the same time, the book details the types of investors in those companies—their nature, method of operation, and the manner by which they are organized.

In the past few years, the venture capital process has changed dramatically, first with the dot.com explosion, again with the dot.com collapse, following by the collapse of the tech sector. These changes have underlined the importance of deep understanding of the venture process in order to guarantee the construction of economically solid entrepreneurial companies, leading to the successful fund raising for these firms, to their rapid and sustainable growth, and finally the success for their investors.

From Concept to Wall Street is the first book on venture capital and entrepreneurship to reflect these radical transformations and their impact on venture creation and development. Leveraging our experience and benefiting from the insights of countless experts, this book covers all you need to know to succeed in this industry—whatever your sector and whatever your role.

Dr. Oren Fuerst   Dr. Uri Geiger
New York, July 2002

ACKNOWLEDGMENTS

We wish to thank all those professionals who dedicated time to reading the book and who gave us helpful comments and guidance in their fields of expertise (the names are listed in alphabetical order):

Gil Alon (Partner, Heidrick & Struggles), for his comments on recruiting and remunerating employees; Tali Eitan, Advocate (Managing Partner: Eitan, Perl, Letzer, and Cohen-Tzadok), for her comments on intellectual property; Israel Eliyahu (CPA), for his helpful comments on valuation and capital markets; Avi Feldman, Advocate (Israeli Ministry of Industry and Trade); Avi Fischer, Advocate (Managing Partner: Fischer, Behar, Chen and Co.), for his insights; Ariella Lahav, Advocate (Partner: Goldfarb, Levy, Eran and Co.); Dr. Amikam Levanon (CEO: Asia Gate), for his comments on the perspective of a venture capitalist; Professor Nahum Melumad (chairman of the accounting division, Columbia University), for his mentorship and for his helpful comments, and in particular to the chapter on valuation; Dr. Avraham Ortal, Advocate (Partner: Zelermeyer, Pelossof), for his comments on raising capital; Enrico Friz, Advocate (Managing Partner: Walder Wyss and Partner, Advocates), for the information on capital raising; Ori Rosen, Advocate (Partner: Danziger, Klagsbald, Rosen and Co.), for his comments on legal and business matters; Benjamin Strauss, Esq. (Pepper Hamilton LLP), for his insights on Delaware law; Tzahi Yagur, Advocate (Partner: Shavit, Bar On, Inbar), for his comments on mergers and sales; Dr. Giora Yaron, for his assistance; Ron Zackay, Advocate (Yigal Arnon and Co.), for his contribution to the chapters on incorporation and mergers; and Dr. Ezra Zuckerman (Stanford University), for his helpful comments.

We owe special thanks to Raffi Gidron (the founder of Chromatis), for his contribution in general and his "insider" insights on the Chromatis-Lucent transaction in particular. Special thanks to Dr. Eyal Shenhav and Benny Kalifi, Advocate, for their knowledge of taxation; to Naomi Shenkar, Advocate, for her competent translation and editorial work, and to Gil Goshen, for his competent research work. We are grateful to Eviathar Matania (Managing Partner: Arcanum) for his insights and comments on the various drafts of the book.

Above all, we are grateful to our special advisors: Chemi Peres, the managing partner of Pitango Ventures, Davidi Gilo, the founder of DSPC and DSPG, and Ron Lubash, a managing director at Lehman Brothers, for their comments, insights, and support.

ABOUT THE AUTHORS

Dr. Oren Furst is the Managing Director of Strategic Models LLC, a strategic advisory focused on all aspects of venture development and venture capital investments in the technology and healthcare sectors worldwide.

Fuerst is also co-director of the Technology Valuation and Strategy Executive program at Columbia Business School, and lectures in the Executive and MBA programs on the topics of Technology Valuation and Strategy and Global Valuation. He was formerly on the faculty of Yale School of Management and served with the Capital Market Advisory Group of KPMG. He is also a featured financial columnist for leading financial newspapers, including the Financial Times.

Dr. Fuerst was also a commander in the Israeli Army's elite Technology unit. He received his master's and doctoral degrees from Columbia Business School (on the topic of International Securities Offerings), and his work is widely read in the academic and business worlds.

Dr. Uri Geiger is the co-founder and CEO of GalayOr Networks Inc., a developer of innovative micro opto-mechanical systems for applications at the core of next-generation optical networks. Formerly, he managed a U.S.-based private equity fund. He teaches venture capital and entrepreneurship topics at Tel Aviv University Business School. An experienced lawyer with leading law firms, including Sullivan and Cromwell, he specialized in securities offerings, M&As, and venture capital investments.

Dr. Geiger has vast experience in running technology-based and capital-raising projects, including founding and successfully selling an Internet-based jewelry company. Dr. Geiger is also a Captain (Res.) in the Israeli Air Force.

He received his master's and doctoral degrees from Columbia University Center for Law and Economics (on the topic of International Securities Offerings). His influential work has been published in leading law and economics journals.

1
Introduction

ABOUT THIS BOOK

This book, *From Concept to Wall Street,* was written to fulfill that need for all those entrepreneurs, employees in startup companies, investors, consultants, and anyone involved or interested in the industry of investing in startup companies in general, and in high tech startup companies in particular. The book methodically lays out the stages of the startup process, without oversimplifying the issues involved.

Book Structure

The book is divided into five Parts which address all the major issues related to startup companies and venture capitalists. The Parts are organized in chronological order, starting from the initial idea or concept, through the establishment of the company and the raising of capital, to the eventual IPO or sale of the company.

Part I—Establishment and Development of Ventures

Part I serves as a road map for startups. This part reviews the issues which the company must address in the early stages, starting from examining the idea and bringing the initial team together, through the establishment of the company and an examination of the sources of aid available to it in the preliminary stages, the corporate strategy and preparation of the business plan, recruitment and remuneration of employees, and ending in the registration of intellectual property and the economic ways of utilizing such property and realizing the economic benefits that it brings.

Part II—Financing the Venture

The sources of capital that are available to startup companies are limited. Entrepreneurs usually lack the capital needed in order to realize their ideas and therefore require external sources of capital. In the first stages of the development of a company, internal sources of finance are customarily used, as well as financing from private investors. Then, in most cases, the company soon turns to venture capital funds and other investors. Part II describes the stages of development of the venture, its cash requirements, the milestones of capital raising and capital sources, and provides a practical description of the process of capital raising. It also contains an in-depth discussion of the main contractual arrangements involved in a venture capital investment. Finally, Part II discusses the valuation of the company: The valuation of companies and projects is an essential component of each and every stage in the development of a startup, whether for purposes of calculating the feasibility of projects and investments, or in order to raise capital and debt. This discussion also includes a review of the established valuation models and of their relevance to various types of companies and various stages of capital raising.

Part III—Venture Capital Investors

Part III reviews the entities and institutions which invest in startup companies. The focus is on venture capital funds, which in the past few decades have constituted the most significant institutional segment of investors in startup companies. The discussion of venture capital funds also includes the funds' establishment, management, and liquidation mechanisms. A separate chapter is dedicated to private investors (Angels). A description of the methods of investment by corporate investors who, in addition to investing in venture capital funds, invest in startup companies directly or establish internal startup companies, is also included. Finally, Part III discusses direct investments in startup companies by investment banks and other financial institutions, and other sources of finance such as credit and leasing companies.

Part IV—Raising Capital from the Public

Once development is completed and sales have commenced (and at times even earlier), comes the stage when the company can raise capital from the public. From the company's point of view, raising capital from the public is not only a vast source of capital, it also constitutes a transition from a private company, in which far more is concealed than is known, to a visible public company that is required to meet high standards of disclosure and transparency. Part IV reviews the advantages and disadvantages of going public, discusses the question of choosing the location of the company's IPO, and describes the process of going public in the United States.

It must be emphasized that going public is important not only to the company itself, but also to investors and entrepreneurs. From the investors' point of view, this means bringing them closer to realizing their investment. In recent decades, the majority of venture capitalists profits was based mainly on the increase in the value of the shares, and not on the stream of payments from a company's cash flow (interest or dividends). Investors therefore demand contractual rights that will award them a certain degree of control over the process of realizing/exiting their investment. From the perspective of entrepreneurs, an IPO renders their holdings in the company more liquid, although various restrictions hinder the immediate realization of the shares.

Part V—Sale of Companies, Restructuring, and Dissolution

Part V focuses on mergers and acquisitions of companies, which are two of the main methods for realizing/exiting an investment and of the major factors underlying the technological revolution. The desire to be bought out by a leading company in the industry drives many entrepreneurs and companies, and allows for the financing of companies whose ability to exist independently in the long term is doubtful. The discussion in this Part reviews not only the phenomenon itself, but also the pros and cons of sales versus IPOs, as well as the main techniques used for mergers and acquisitions, including the contractual arrangements involved in merger and acquisition (M&A) transactions.

The last chapter in Part V discusses the dissolution of companies. With the collapse of technology stocks and the resultant blow to confidence in the venture capital market, an increasing number of companies are finding it difficult to finance their operations. Some of these companies merge with others, while other companies have no choice but to dissolve (either voluntarily or due to coercion by creditors).

Glossary

Naturally, the book uses many professional terms that are part of the common venture capital jargon. There are also terms that are used to signify several different meanings. For instance, the term **Venture Capital** (or VC) is used to describe the area of investments of venture capital in startup companies, but in many cases it also refers to Venture Capital Funds or to the people working in such funds. The purpose of the following short glossary is to create a uniform, basic, and common denominator for all readers (for a more comprehensive glossary, see Appendix B).

A **startup** is a company founded by **entrepreneurs** on the basis of an idea, the majority of its assets, termed **intellectual property (IP)** are intangible. Initially, the company's activity focuses on **Research and Development (R&D)**, in order to prove the feasibility of the idea and to develop the prototype/preliminary product.

Financing in the preliminary stage, or the **Seed**, is obtained in many cases from private investors, also known as **Angels**. These angels invest their personal funds in young companies in order to gain a high **Rate of Return**. Down the road, the company is financed in several **Rounds** by venture capitalists of various types, comprising the venture capital industry. The first class of investors is the **venture capital funds**, which specialize in high-risk investments and undertake such investments on behalf of several investors (usually **Institutional Investors**). The funds provide investors with screening and investment management services, and offer companies financing and assistance in business management and development. Other investors in startup companies and in venture capital funds are **Corporate Investors**, who typically invest in ventures in areas close to their lines of business, and other financial investors such as institutional investors who invest directly in companies. In consideration for their investment, investors receive part of the company's **Equity**, usually in the form of **Preferred Shares**, which grant the investors preference in dividends, and upon dissolution and sales, as well as other rights protecting the investment and its value. The main terms of the investment are fixed in the **Term Sheet**, after which a detailed investment agreement (**Stock Purchase Agreement**) is signed. In later stages, the company may also receive financing through **Debt**, or by a loan combining debt and equity (**Mezzanine Loan**).

Once the development has concluded and sales have commenced, the company can raise capital from the public through an **IPO**. Listing the company for trade also allows the investors in the company to make their investment more liquid, and after a **Lock-Up Period**, they can sell shares directly on the stock exchange or in the course of a **Secondary Offering**. The main **Exit** techniques are the sale of shares in an IPO, and, subsequently, a **Private Placement** or a **Merger** with, or **Acquisition** by, a strategic investor, in consideration for shares, cash, or a combination of the two.

PART I

Establishment and Development of Ventures

A long and winding path leads from a mere idea to ultimate success. Part I discusses the issues which entrepreneurs and companies need to address in order to transform an interesting idea or project into a valuable company. It emphasizes the practical aspects of establishing and building a startup, on the basic assumptions that an interesting idea is insufficient for success and that the execution of the idea is no less (or even more) important than the idea itself. The financing aspects of startups will be discussed in detail in Part III.

Startups are companies whose assets are usually primarily intangible. Although these companies engage in a variety of businesses, their common denominator is their reliance on the power of ideas. This is the focal point of companies representing the new economy, an economy founded mainly on intellectual property. Regardless of the company's line of business—be it biotechnology, Internet, communications, software, or otherwise—the value of these companies depends mainly on the intangible assets they create. These assets comprise, primarily, the company's manpower or human resources, as well as work methods, business models, algorithms, and production processes created by such manpower or bought or hired by the startup from others. Aside from the creation of intangible assets, the value of the venture depends to a great extent on the protection afforded to such intangible assets and on their introduction into the market.

A startup company is born from an idea which constitutes a solution to a problem arising or anticipated in an existing or future market. The idea is formed and consolidated by entrepreneurs, financed by investors, supported by consultants, and executed by entrepreneurs and employees. Another characteristic of most startup companies is their focus on R&D. Finally, there comes the stage in which the fruit of the idea is reaped, and all the persons involved realize their investment, whether such investment was made in the form of human or financial capital.

2
Beginnings—Establishing a Venture

CHAPTER OVERVIEW

This chapter reviews the various issues that require careful attention in the preliminary stages, before the company is established: a close scrutiny of the idea, its necessity and feasibility, forming the team, and incorporating the company.

The Price of Success and Failure

Every entrepreneur should know that the vast majority of startup companies fail. In most cases, the bulk of the returns on the venture capital investment portfolio is yielded by very few investments, whereas most of the portfolio is expunged. There is a high probability that the entrepreneur's company will comprise part of that component of the investment portfolio.

In addition, as an entrepreneur, one should be prepared for the fact that the financing of any particular stage of an investment does not guarantee an investment in future stages. The road to success is paved with obstacles, and the foundation of a new company often implies the dedication of nights and days, long periods of uncertainty, and severe fluctuation between moments of stress and joy. The price of failure may be relatively small (loss of time and some funds), but may also entail the loss of savings, of alternative promising employment, etc., as well as tension within the family. However, despite the possible high cost, many find that no career satisfaction is greater than establishing and developing a company.

With the increasing recognition that startup failures result from a variety of reasons, many of which are independent of the entrepreneurs, the latter are decreasingly deterred from re-embarking on new ventures, after the failure of ventures in which they took part. Furthermore, society no longer labels entrepreneurs whose ventures failed as "failures."

It is always important to keep in mind that many entrepreneurs who have failed once are later successful. In many cases, entrepreneurs choose to reinvest their human capital, while assuming that the probabilities of success and failure may work in their favor on one of such attempts, especially since prior experience is greatly helpful in improving the success-failure ratio.

The Idea

Not every idea or technology is feasible, and even if it is, it does not necessarily follow that there is a need for it. Sometimes an idea comes along which is both needed and feasible, but is nevertheless an inappropriate basis for founding a company. The idea must be a product or a process that improves on something that exists in the market, and whose financial value will yield a positive return on the investment. First, there are two basic tests which an idea must pass: the test of need and the test of technology.

- **Need**—There are many ideas that, although innovative, are entirely unnecessary. Moreover, many entrepreneurs believe that the key to success lies in recognizing a current market need and developing an idea to meet it. However, in many cases, a technologically feasible idea that meets a current market need is insufficient. It is highly likely that, if the need is genuine and visible, or the topic is "hot," dozens of other people will be addressing it at the same time. The best ideas are those that predict a need a few years down the line, and aim to meet such need.
- **Technology**—Even if a product is needed or is expected to be needed, its technological feasibility has to be verified. Technological feasibility should be checked at the practical, not the theoretical, level. A project that will cost vast amounts of money, will take long to develop, and end in a product that is not economical to produce, is inappropriate for the free market in general, and startup companies in particular will find it hard to finance. For instance, the development of an ability to fly to the moon, and even a satellite telephone system such as the Iridium (the failed satellite communications project that consumed more than 5 billion dollars), were proven to be technologically feasible, but uneconomical.

In addition, even if a project addresses a need and is feasible both technologically and economically, it does not necessarily justify an investment, given the limited amount of resources directed at venture capital investments. It is important to remember that, although the volume of resources allocated in recent years to this area has considerably increased, so has the number of projects seeking financing. The preference of one project over another depends on several factors that are not necessarily related to the technology. In the technological context, it is important to note that there are usually several solutions to the same problem (for instance, there are several protocols for the transmission of data on optic fibers, and there are several solutions for broadband connections). The company which anticipates the standard that will evolve in the market or, alternatively, develops the method most likely to become the standard, is the one that will gain the financing and reap success.

However, it is important to understand that a mere idea is insufficient, and that its execution is at least as important as the actual idea. Furthermore, over and above the need for perseverance and an ability to perform, an entrepreneur should assume that entrepreneurs with similar ideas have also started working on similar projects at the same time, and that therefore the manner of execution of the idea and its time to market are, in many cases, highly significant components of success.

In the next section, we focus on the most significant component determining the ability to execute the idea: the management team.

The Management Team

It is important that the founding team be staffed by people with experience in technology and business. This is one of the main reasons why success stories of companies established and managed over time by only one entrepreneur are rare. In most cases, even when the venture has only one entrepreneur, he quickly gathers around him a core of people in order to promote the idea from its initial stages. Investors regard the team as the greatest asset of a young company, and often prefer an excellent team with a mediocre idea, over a mediocre team with an excellent idea. If recruiting a full team in the preliminary stages proves difficult, it is possible to obtain people's consent in principle, to join the company, if and when it manages to secure financing or meets certain initial targets. Many investors understand and accept such agreements. It is also important that an agreement with respect to the division of shares in the future company—according to the anticipated added value that each founder will contribute to the venture—be reached in the early stages. It should also be kept in mind that investors may assist in completing the team, and their potential contribution to the consolidation of the team should be taken into account.

The composition of the initial team changes from one company to another, but such a team generally comprises the following positions:

- **Manager (CEO)**—The person who conceived the original idea is not always blessed with the skills required to run a startup. There is no shortage of examples of extraordinary entrepreneurs who ultimately led their companies to bankruptcy, because they lacked the ability to lead a large organization in the global market. Many management theories describe various blends of characteristics that are suitable for running companies throughout their life cycles, and only a few entrepreneurs fit these descriptions. It is important to find an experienced leader as early as possible, even if such a leader will not manage the company in the long run.

  On the other hand, an experienced CEO is not always essential in order to succeed. For instance, one of the most successful companies, Microsoft, was run for years by Bill Gates, one of its founders, who had no experience in managing a company.

Occasionally, one of the entrepreneurs can manage the company in its early days, but if the company grows beyond his managerial abilities, he must acknowledge this and step down. In addition, a talented outside manager will not normally join a very young company, but will do so after it has established itself somewhat, either by raising money or by developing its business. On the other hand, investors will not invest in a company that lacks a talented manager or, in many cases, will "penalize" it with a low valuation. The ability of one of the entrepreneurs to tackle the managerial position at the beginning, or, alternatively, the investors' faith in the company's ability to recruit talented and experienced managers, are therefore highly important.

- **Technological Leader**—If the venture is essentially technological, the founding team has to have at least one person with an acute understanding of the technology required in order to execute the idea. The presence of a technological leader on the team increases the chances that even if the original idea does not come to fruition, it will at least generate new and valuable technology. A technological leader increases the prospects of securing financing for the company; one of the main reasons for this is the fact that many companies start out by developing a product that was intended for a certain market, but ultimately succeed by putting their technology to other uses. The importance of a technological leader is usually crucial, and is naturally also conducive to garnering support from convincing potential employees to join the company.
- **Marketing and Business Development Manager**—From a historical perspective, most successful companies started by analyzing markets and engaging in business and marketing development already in the company's early stages. There are many advantages in engaging a person with marketing experience in the development stages, since such a person can influence the direction of such development and can create marketing channels concurrently with the development.
- **Production, Sales, and Financial Managers**—These positions are essential for the management and development of the company, although in many cases they do not form a part of the initial team. Such positions should be filled toward the end of the development stage, concurrently with the increase in the size of the company.
- **Coach**—A coach is an experienced outsider who can draw from his experiences to help build up the company and create the necessary connections in the industry and the capital market. Such a person on the Board of Directors, or as an investor, is an invaluable asset. For instance, it is doubtful whether Netscape would have been funded by Venture capital funds, and eventually sold to AOL for approximately $6 billion dollars, were

it not for the involvement of an experienced coach such as Jim Clark, nor is it likely that the company would have received financing in its various stages without his presence.

External Advisors

The engagement of talented consultants from various professional fields is essential to the success of the company. There are traditional areas, such as economic and legal matters, in which every company customarily hires outside advisors. But there are also professional consultants in other fields who may contribute to the company in its line of business or elsewhere, in order to accelerate the progress of the company and the time-to-market of its products (*accelerators*). Finally, there are numerous entities who offer companies all consultancy services in one package (*incubators*).

Financial Advisors and Management Consultants

The functions of economic consultants are very broad and include consultancy and guidance in a variety of areas, such as choosing the optimal channels for raising capital, drafting contacts with investors, and examining different directions of business development. Aside from functioning as independent consultants and strategic consultancy firms, many accounting firms now offer entrepreneurs various economic services. Economic consultants are particularly important for companies whose entrepreneurs have a deep technological background but whose managerial or business experience is lacking, or whose acquaintance with the capital market is sketchy. At times when the number of potential investments with which investors are faced is immeasurably greater than the number of ventures in which they are able to invest, the company's business design is already essential in the early stages of the venture, and the added value of prudent advice in this area to the venture cannot be overrated.

Legal Advisors

It is important to engage legal advisors who specialize in startups already in the early stages. Most law firms which work in this field now offer arrangements based on reduced payments (at times through sharing in the company's equity) that are appropriate for young companies. The role of the company's attorneys is crucial in determining the optimal form and location of incorporation in domestic and international tax planning, in preparing agreements among the entrepreneurs, employment agreements, employee stock options, and agreements with various suppliers. Naturally, they will also be responsible for the investment agreement with the investors. Finally, attorneys are instrumental in the company's IPO or sale. Except for legal work, attorneys with experience and contacts can advise the company on business decisions, and introduce it to sources of money or strategic partners.

Incubators

A veteran entrepreneur who is backed by an experienced team and independent sources of capital or many connections, usually does not require the extensive assistance provided by incubators and accelerators. At the most, he will utilize the connections of the fund who will invest in the company in its early stages. However, many entrepreneurs do not have the know-how, the experience, or the connections required to develop their ideas quickly and enter the market. Several solutions are available for such entrepreneurs.

Incubators are entities which specialize in cultivating the growth of new companies. Incubators provide (or at least profess to provide) much more than money; for instance, they may offer offices for the company, guidance and advice in development (and in some cases also managers), assistance in recruiting manpower, accounting and legal services, assistance in raising capital, contacts with strategic entities, etc. The experienced and well-known managers of an incubator could raise the value of an infant company by exploiting their know-how, and in particular their connections, in the relevant industry. Incubators are not a suitable solution for every company; they are appropriate mainly for young entrepreneurs or entrepreneurs who have no experience in management or project development. It is important to know that incubators demand significant portions of the company, usually between 20% and 50% of its equity, for the services they provide. That said, the entrepreneurs who apply to incubators are usually the ones most likely to significantly increase their chances of success through the added value provided by the incubators.

Many incubators are increasingly aware that focusing on a certain niche, although unwise from the risk-diversification perspective, significantly increases their ability to assist their portfolio companies, mainly due to the accumulation of knowledge and contacts on which the incubator's companies rely.

Many incubators have been operating in the United States for many years, and more still were established during the prosperous years of Internet startups. In 1999 alone, more than 200 incubators were established in the United States, and a similar number were established in early 2000. The incubator boom spread to Europe and Asia as well, and hundreds of incubators were established around the world during this time; only some of them were led by winning teams of experienced entrepreneurs, financiers, and managers.

Most of the incubators in the United States collapsed during the year 2000, concurrently with the collapse of high tech stock prices. The fundamental problem of most of them was their extensive reliance on the capital market. The incubators were required to make considerable investments within a short time frame in order to finance their high costs, and one of the obvious sources of such financing was the stock market. With the narrowing of the possibilities of raising capital on the stock exchange—for both the incubator itself and the companies held by it—and of exiting investments by selling held companies, the IPO dreams of some incubators shattered, and the shares of several American incubators which had already gone public, plummeted.

Idealab, for example, a company that focused on cultivating ideas that were born in the company itself, withdrew the prospectus it had filed with the SEC, only a few months after it had raised hundreds of millions of dollars in a private offering based on a value of more than $7 billion. The main problem that confronted the company was that its numerous previous successes (such as the establishment of the companies eToys, Tickets.com, and GoTo, and others, some of which even went public), lost their glamour after their stocks collapsed on the stock market. Although Idealab helped establish approximately forty companies, it stopped "supplying" IPO-worthy companies, at least for awhile, after a feverish period of rapidly taking its companies public. Like Idealab, the shares of other incubators, which were recently offered and already traded on the stock market, such as Divine Interventures, also crashed once the investors' hopes that the company would manage to take at least some of its investments public, evaporated.

More established companies which were associated with the incubator phenomenon also suffered a plunge in stock prices, even if they were fundamentally investment companies that exercised extensive managerial and operating involvement, such as CMGI and Internet Capital Group (ICG). This blow made it difficult for them to raise more capital on the stock market, and to attract outside investors to invest with them in their portfolio companies.

Although the investments in the incubators have not proven themselves so far on the stock exchange, incubators are beneficial to some entrepreneurs, as they offer an almost complete range of solutions to individual entrepreneurs with no entrepreneurial experience. In any case, before a decision is made to join such an incubator, it is important to check who is behind it and the nature of his experience and connections, and to make inquiries with other companies that have used the incubator's services. As the frequent establishment of incubators in recent years, and the fact that many of them were shut down, indicate incubators are often no more than startups themselves, and the large portion of equity they demand is often unjustified in view of the results they produce. One needs to remember that more than 80% of incubators do not achieve as much as a single exit.

Accelerators

Accelerators are persons or entities that specialize in technological, business, or financial areas that complement the skills of the company's internal team, and that share their know-how, experience, or connections with the company in consideration for equity and ongoing financial compensation. This is done with the purpose of accelerating the development of the company, raising its value and facilitating its entry into the market. The defining difference between an incubator and an accelerator is the stage of development of the companies they support and the measure of assistance they require. An accelerator usually works with companies that are slightly more advanced than those that use incubators, and almost always only with companies that already have a management team. Incubators are also prepared to accept projects that are just starting out, even before passing any feasibility tests, and without a proper management team. Furthermore, accelerators often do not provide a full package of services (offices, accounting and legal services, public relations, etc.), but rather focus on the professional issues in which they can assist the company. Also, the payment (in shares) to accelerators is usually not as high as that charged by incubators. The use of accelerators is also recommended for experienced entrepreneurs, if the accelerator's abilities genuinely complement those of the company. A shorter time-to-market is more important than the percentage in the company's equity.

Incorporation

Incorporation is the act of creating an artificial legal entity (usually a business entity—a company, a partnership, an LLC, etc.), that serves to fulfill the objectives of the persons establishing (organizing) it.

The Objectives of Incorporation

Whether incorporation is worthwhile, and the choice of the appropriate type of corporation (a company, a partnership, an LLC, etc.), depend on the purpose of the incorporation. The decision to incorporate should be based on many considerations, deriving from both the requirements of the members wanting to incorporate, and the legal and business environment, which may at times change, thus changing the considerations underlying the incorporation. The following issues may be listed among the considerations in favor of incorporating:

- **Limited liability**—The main advantage of incorporation for business and economic purposes is that it creates a separate legal entity which allows a separation between the acts of the corporation and the acts of the organs (either entities or individuals) composing the same, thus protecting such persons with limited liability. This principle, known as the "separate legal entity principle," determines that the corporation is a separate legal entity from its shareholders and, in principle, an act or undertaking performed by the corporation is not a personal act or undertaking by any of its members, who are therefore not personally liable for the consequences of such act or undertaking. In other words, as long as the employees, directors, and shareholders do not deviate from the rules fixed in the relevant laws of the state of incorporation, they will not be legally liable for the actions and debts of the corporation. Limited liability enables business initiatives that would not otherwise have been undertaken due to the risk involved in them, since private individuals would refrain from jeopardizing all of their personal property, and would seek risk-free investments. When liability is limited, the shareholders or partners risk only the part of the capital they invest in the venture, and not all of their capital. Several types of corporations allow the liability of members to be limited (such as a limited company and a limited partnership), the nature of which will be discussed below.
- **Separation between management and control**—Managing a business through a corporation allows the management to be concentrated in the

hands of a group of skilled managers, while dispersing its equity among many persons or entities.
- **Continuity**—The existence of the corporation (if it is a company) is independent of the existence of its member shareholders. Thus, the death or retirement of any of the members does not terminate the life of the incorporated business, and prior undertakings may continue to be fulfilled and future actions planned.
- **Separation between the property of the company and the shares**—Managing a business through a corporation facilitates complex actions such as the sale of shares in a corporation, as opposed to the sale of the corporation's assets individually. When the corporation is the owner of the rights and/or property that is to be transferred, a simple transaction of a share transfer suffices to overcome such procedural and substantive difficulties.
- **Instrument for raising capital**—The existence of the corporation enables the raising of capital by a variety of methods, such as the issuance of bonds and debentures, as well as public offerings and private placements, discussed below.
- **Tax considerations**—The tax paid by a corporation may be lower than the tax levied on individuals, and there are certain tax benefits that are available only to corporations.
- **Simplicity and certainty**—In short, incorporation creates a simple and efficient mechanism for realizing the business objectives of the company and the entrepreneurs. Corporate mechanisms should be simple and clear to the company's entrepreneurs, to investors, and to third parties dealing with the company. The business and legal environment should allow decision-makers to make correct business decisions with the knowledge of the legal consequences of such decisions, without fearing later intervention by the courts.

Types of Corporations

Among the many possible forms of incorporation available to ventures, this discussion will focus on the three that are most common at present: "ordinary" corporations, limited partnerships, and LLCs (Limited Liability Company). The manner and form of incorporation are determined according to the laws of the country and state of incorporation. However, there are certain principles in corporate law that are common to all countries belonging to the Anglo-American jurisprudence, including the United States.

- **Corporation**—A corporation is an artificial legal entity created to facilitate the incorporation of persons into a single, business-oriented economic body. As aforesaid, a corporation is a legal entity that is separate from its shareholders, who enjoy the protection afforded by the separate legal entity principle. The most common of these forms is the C Corp company, whose definition is derived from the arrangement whereby the liability of each member at the time of dissolution of the company is limited to the amount invested by him (or which he undertook to invest) in purchasing the company's shares. The term LLC (Limited Liability Company) is used to describe another type of corporation, to be discussed below.

- **Limited Partnership**—A partnership is a legal entity characterized by the fact that its members are personally liable to third parties, in addition to the liability imposed on the partnership itself. However, there are situations in which a partner is interested in limiting his liability (a limited partner). Such a partnership is a "limited partnership," since the liability of each of its limited partners is limited to the amount he invested, or undertook to invest, in the partnership. A limited partnership will include at least one general partner, who is liable for all its liabilities, and at least one partner who is liable for the capital he invested in the partnership (the limited partner). In practice, the general partner is usually incorporated as a limited company, thus limiting his liability as well. The main difference between a partnership and a company is that the partners are the ones who are levied with the tax on the partnership's profits, according to their share in it, and the partnership itself is not taxed separately (as distinguished from a company, which is levied with corporate tax). In other words, the partnership's profits or losses are personally prorated to the partners. The fact that general and limited partners operate together in a joint business framework creates significant differences between the partners' rights. Naturally, the limited partner will not be liable for the partnership's debts, but will also take no part in its daily management, whereas the general partner enjoys superior rights in the management of the partnership, but is also liable for its debts. The relevant laws are derived from this principle. For instance, a limited partner shall not participate in the management of the partnership's business, and is not authorized to bind it (and if he does participate in its management, he shall be liable for all its liabilities, as if he were a general partner).

- **LLC (Limited Liability Company)**—An LLC is a corporation deemed as a partnership for tax purposes: The company's profits or losses are attributed directly to its shareholders (or "members," in the language of the law), and the company itself is not subject to tax. In contrast with a partnership, the members do not forfeit their limited liability if they participate in the management of an LLC. All the affairs of an LLC are regulated in an operating agreement or LLC agreement (in the absence of which, the law provides a default). Due to various restrictions imposed on LLCs, it is not a common form of incorporation for startups, whose entrepreneurs do not invest the majority of their money in the venture. The following are the main restrictions imposed on LLCs: restrictions on the acceptance of new members, which restrictions hinder the allotment of options to employees;

restrictions on the lifetime of an LLC; the inability of an LLC to go public; and tax restrictions imposed on the conversion of an LLC into an ordinary corporation (a process that is required before an IPO). As a result of these restrictions, the use of LLCs in the venture capital industry is chiefly popular as a tool enabling shareholders in the company to decrease their tax liability, or as an investment vehicle (such as a venture capital fund), that allows the members to limit their legal liability, while enjoying the tax benefits of a partnership.

Incorporation Documents

The incorporation of a company is usually preceded by the actions of entrepreneurs/founders, who lay its business and financial foundations. Once these foundations are in place and the founders want to incorporate, they have to decide upon certain fundamental principles which determine the legal and business elements of the company and are expressed in its incorporation documents.

- **Normative Documents (required by law)**—The incorporation documents are the cornerstone of the incorporation of every company and in the United States include the Certificate of Incorporation and the Bylaws (for a more detailed discussion of incorporation, see the section, "Incorporation in Delaware"). The company's documents of incorporation constitute the normative framework that regulates the company's life and activities. Along with the documents of incorporation (see above), some companies have agreements among the shareholders (Shareholders Agreement or Founders Agreement). Alongside, and sometimes above, these agreements and documents are the laws applicable in the state of incorporation. The laws of the state of incorporation contain normative provisions that supersede any contractual agreement (and the documents of incorporation are essentially contractual arrangements), as well as other provisions that take effect when the parties have not fixed contractual arrangements of their own. In addition, the laws of the state of incorporation set forth procedural rules with respect to incorporation.

    The company's documents of incorporation contain the company's name, objectives, details of the company's equity, and details with respect to the limitation of liability. In addition, the founders may fix in the documents of incorporation the rights and obligations of the shareholders and of the company, various provisions pertaining to management, and any other matter which the shareholders deem fit to include in the documents. As aforesaid, the documents of incorporation and the agreements among the shareholders include, besides the mandatory technical details, provisions with respect to the relationship between the founders, and provisions

governing work procedures and various mechanisms for resolving problems in the company (for documents of incorporation in Delaware, see the subsection, "Organizing and Managing a Delaware Corporation").
- **Shareholders Agreement**—A Shareholders Agreement is a contract between the entrepreneurs (who may later be joined by other shareholders or investors) which regulates the contractual relationship between the shareholders. A Shareholders Agreement binds only the parties who signed it, in contrast to the organizational/incorporation documents that also bind shareholders who are not direct parties to them (in other words, who have not signed them), and sometimes also other entities which come into contact with the company (which is why they are usually filed with the authorities and are open to the public). Common provisions in Shareholders Agreements deal with the following issues: the composition of the company's equity, types of allotted shares, the composition of the Board of Directors, methods for appointing directors, the proceedings of the Board of Directors, signatory rights, matters required to be resolved by a special majority, a list of the rights attached to the shares, restrictions on the allotment and transfer of shares in the company, voting mechanisms and agreements, the company's activities and lines of business, confidentiality, and non-competition. Although these issues are often also regulated in the corporate bylaws, their inclusion in the Shareholders Agreement awards each shareholder a private cause of action to claim the fulfillment of such provisions from any other shareholder who is a party to the agreement.

The Corporate Organs

As mentioned above, the company is an intangible legal entity. It lacks the means to realize the company's policy and objectives or execute the wishes of its members. The company's organs are bodies or persons whose main duty is to serve as a medium through which the company can function. Modern corporate law recognizes three main organs: the shareholders (the General Meeting), who appoint the members of the Board of Directors and are required to approve acts of crucial significance to the existence of the corporation (such as mergers or dissolution); the Board of Directors, which directs the company's policy; and the company's managers, who translate the policy into practical action and run the company on a daily basis. It is important to understand that, although the powers of the various organs are fixed in the laws of the state of incorporation, such laws (as is the case in the state of Delaware) generally allow the organs to modify the balance of power among them. For instance, although the most important authority of the General Meeting is to appoint and terminate directors, the shareholders may decide upon other methods for the direct appointment of directors by the shareholders. Another example is when venture capitalists demand and receive the right to appoint a director or directors even though their holdings are insufficient to elect directors at an ordinary meeting.

- **Shareholders (the General Meeting)**—Shareholders who have voting powers (these are almost always the holders of ordinary shares, and in certain cases also of other types of shares) are entitled to participate in the General Meeting. Since shareholders have property rights in the company, they are entitled to control decisions pertaining to their property. Therefore, the General Meeting is defined as the company's primary body, responsible for appointing and terminating directors, changing the company's bylaws, and approving acts and transactions that require approval, either by law or the bylaws, including vital decisions such as the dissolution, sale, or merger of the company. In order to control the company's actions and policy, the shareholders convene for a General Meeting once a year. In special cases, a general or extraordinary General Meeting may be convened more frequently. In startups, it is customary to receive the shareholders' written consent as an alternative to holding meetings.
- **The Board of Directors**—Except for certain issues that are subject to the authority of the General Meeting, the management of the company is—according to the law in most countries—entrusted to the Board of Directors (with the General Meeting usually being authorized, as aforesaid, to appoint and terminate the directors). The following actions may be listed among the areas of responsibility of the Board of Directors: appointment and termination of managers/officers; outlining the company's action plans and the principles for their financing; examining the company's financial condition and the amount of credit it may undertake; determining the organizational structure and the compensation policy; preparing and approving the financial statements; reporting to the General Meeting on the condition of the company; and deciding to issue shares and convertible securities (within the framework of the company's equity). In order to adopt its resolutions and control the company's actions, the Board of Directors convenes periodically, at a frequency that changes in accordance with the character of the company and the issues on the agenda. In startups, this frequency is relatively high (about once a month). In many cases, meetings of the Board of Directors are held by telephone, and resolutions may also be adopted in writing.
- **Managers**—It is generally the case that the involvement of the company's General Meeting and Board of Directors in the daily running of the company is limited. A company cannot be managed by a body that convenes once a month (or less), and is not involved in the company on a daily basis. Therefore, modern companies operate mainly through professional managers, who are responsible for the daily management of the company's affairs, within the framework of the policy determined by the Board of Directors and subject to its directives. These managers are referred to as "executives," and among them are the General Manager or Chief Executive

Officer (CEO), the various senior executives such as the Chief Financial Officer (CFO), the Chief Operating Officer (COO), and the Chief Technology Officer (CTO), as well as other principal officers. The second line of management of the company is occupied by other managers, who are not executives. In startups, these are usually the Vice Presidents (VPs).

Corporate Capital

During its incorporation and thereafter, the company issues securities which award their holders certain rights toward the company and toward the other shareholders, in consideration for which it raises money. A security is an instrument that awards its holder an expectation or right to a future stream of payments, sometimes in addition to other legal rights (such as a voting right). In fact, it is a "standardized" contract that is also characterized by property rights. The basic types of securities are shares, preferred shares, and bonds.

- **Ordinary Shares**—A share is a personal property right that comprises a bundle of rights. These rights include the right to declared dividends and to assets upon dissolution, as well as the right to vote at the company's meetings.

    A company's capital stock is divided into several types. In this context, the following principle terms should be mentioned: **authorized** (or registered) **share capital** is the capital that the General Meeting has authorized to be issued; **issued share capital** is the share capital sold to investors; and **outstanding share capital** is the share capital held by investors. The outstanding share capital is smaller than the issued share capital when the company buys back from the shareholders some of the shares it has issued. The re-purchased shares are called **treasury stocks**. **Equity capital** is an accounting term referring to the balance-sheet value of the company's assets, less/minus its liabilities.

- **Preferred Shares**—According to traditional corporate law, a preferred share is a cluster of contractual rights, the most common of which is the priority in the receipt of dividends (both ordinary and upon dissolution). Preferred Shares are usually **cumulative** (in other words, if a dividend is passed in a certain year, the right for priority is reserved until the payment of a dividend, for all the years in which no dividend was paid) and **non-participating** (in other words, the holders of preferred shares are not entitled to partake in dividends together with the holders of ordinary shares after they receive their preferred dividend). Preferred shares may be **voting** shares (in other words, they may confer on their holders a voting right) or may be awarded without an attached voting right.

    Investors in startups are usually issued preferred shares that are convertible into ordinary shares, either at the investor's discretion or upon the occurrence of pre-determined events. Such shares are always voting shares, and they customarily entail priority upon liquidation or upon events deemed as liquidation, as well as other rights such as protection against dilution and a right to veto resolutions of the company. (See the section in Chapter 8 for the rights attached to convertible preferred shares received by venture capitalists.)

- **Stock Options**—An option is a right to buy (call option) or sell (put option) a certain asset, for the exercise price, in a pre-determined period. When the option holder wants to exercise it, he pays the exercise price to the issuer of the option and receives title to the asset.

  As far as startups are concerned, this is usually a right to buy a new share that is issued to the holder of the exercised option. This type of option is referred to as a **warrant**, mainly in order to distinguish it from other options that are based on monetary clearing, rather than by the issuance of new stocks. Such options are allotted to investors in many rounds of financing, as well as to the employees of the company.

- **Bonds**—These are securities that oblige the issuer to pay the holder pre-determined amounts on pre-fixed dates, or upon the occurrence of certain events. An issuance of a bond (or debenture) is, in fact, a loan that is taken from the buyer of the bond.

  The basic distinction is between a straight bond, on which interest is payable on pre-determined dates, and a zero coupon, on which no interest is paid but which is sold at a price lower than its par value. A bond can be **secured** (when the payment of the debt is guaranteed by certain assets that serve as collateral) or **unsecured**. The quality of the collateral, coupled with the anticipated stability of the business issuing the bond, determine the risk involved in the bond, and hence its price. Bonds issued by startups often include an option to convert the bonds into shares according to a pre-determined conversion ratio (**convertible bonds**).

Incorporation in Delaware

This chapter will examine why many companies choose Delaware as their state of incorporation and review central issues of the Delaware Corporation Law.

Background

The state of Delaware is known in the United States as one of the most attractive states for the purpose of incorporation. Since the Delaware General Corporation Law (DGCL) was enacted in 1899, the State of Delaware has offered a stable legislative framework that, on the one hand, allows broad flexibility and managerial discretion and, on the other hand, balances the interests of the various organs within the corporate world. The registration of corporations is performed by the Delaware Secretary of State automatically and quickly, with no bureaucratic delays. Business disputes are heard in Delaware in a special professional court (the Delaware Court of Chancery) that specializes in resolving complex business disputes without a jury. These principal considerations, in addition to further factors described below, are the reason that despite its small geographic size, Delaware has become the state in which most Fortune 500 corporations are incorporated, along with more than 50% of the companies listed for trade on the New York Stock Exchange (NYSE).

Organizing and Managing a Delaware Corporation

A Delaware corporation is organized by filing a Certificate of Incorporation with the Secretary of State. The organization of the corporation is performed by filing the certificate by fax or online, and in both cases the process is completed within minutes from the incorporator's filing of the signed Certificate of Incorporation. The registration of the corporation that is conducted by the Secretary of State, as aforesaid, includes only the name of the person or entity organizing the new corporation, and the corporation's registered agent in Delaware. According to Delaware law, the public information on the corporation need not include the names of the shareholders, the directors, or the officers.

The details that must be included in the Certificate of Incorporation are:

- The name of the corporation
- The name and address of the corporation's registered agent in Delaware
- The name and address of the incorporator
- The purpose of incorporation (it is sufficient to state that the corporation intends to engage in lawful activities undertaken by corporations)
- The registered share capital and the par value per share

Although Delaware law does not require any minimum number of shares, the consideration for the shares has to be at least their par value. It is therefore recommended to fix the par value of the shares in the Certificate of Incorporation at no more than $0.01, in order to give the Board of Directors the most flexibility in determining the consideration for the shares.

Delaware law provides considerable flexibility in determining the balance of power and the priorities among shareholders, in order to enable the broad variety of business and financial activities required during the course of the corporation's lifetime. The Certificate of Incorporation may also authorize the allotment of preferred shares, whose qualities may be determined by the Board of Directors from time to time.

Since the DGCL regards the Certificate of Incorporation as an agreement between the corporation and its shareholders, it may contain managerial provisions and directives, such as the limitation of the directors' liability and the granting of a preemptive right. The Certificate of Incorporation may be modified only by a resolution of the Board of Directors and a majority vote of the shareholders.

After the corporation is organized, the incorporator has to adopt bylaws that set out rules for the corporation's management and to appoint the first members of the Board of Directors. The first directors may also be named in the Certificate of Incorporation. Once the first Board of Directors is appointed, the incorporator's function is concluded, and its authorities over the corporation expire. The bylaws are not filed with any public authority and are consequently not a publicly available document. In order to complete the process of organization (or establishment) of the corporation, the elected Board of Directors has to appoint officers. Although the law does not set out pre-defined offices that need to be filled, the corporation has to appoint—according to common practice and an interpretation of the DGCL—at least a President and a Secretary, both of which may be occupied by one person.

Share Capital and the Shareholders

After its appointment, the Board of Directors has to allot the preliminary share capital. Subject to several exceptions, Delaware law prohibits shareholders from participating in the management of the corporation's business (which function is entrusted to the Board of Directors), and removes from them any personal liability for its debts. "Piercing the corporate veil" (i.e., attributing the company's debts to its shareholders personally) is a rare act in Delaware that requires an allegation of fraud or deceit.

The shareholders can function in annual and special meetings or through written resolutions. Written resolutions require the same majority required for the adoption of resolutions at a General Meeting, and become effective immediately upon the adoption of the written resolution by the required majority. According to an amendment made to the DGCL in 2000, the Board of Directors may approve the convening of General Meetings on the Internet.

The Board of Directors

A corporation's Board of Directors may comprise one member or more, as provided in the corporation's bylaws or Certificate of Incorporation. The Board of Directors may be classified into different groups of directors with different voting powers and terms of office (Classified Board). It is also possible to determine that one-third of the members of the Board stand for election every year, so that every member is elected for three years (Staggered Board). A simple majority of the directors constitutes the legal quorum, unless a different quorum is fixed in the corporation's Certificate of Incorporation or bylaws. In any case, the minimum majority for the Board of Directors' resolutions cannot be smaller than one-third of the Board. The Board of Directors' resolutions may be adopted at board meetings or by written unanimous resolutions.

The Board of Directors is authorized to establish committees for various matters, and certain committees are authorized to perform any act which the Board of Directors is authorized to perform, unless the Board of Directors or the corporation's bylaws provide otherwise. In any case, the committees are not authorized to perform acts that are expressly required by law to be approved by the shareholders in addition to the Board of Directors (mergers, sale of assets, and liquidation of the corporation). Nor are they authorized to change the corporation's bylaws.

Directors in a corporation owe special fiduciary duties to the corporation and to its shareholders, but not to creditors or third parties (except for cases in which the corporation is in the process of dissolution or is insolvent). These special duties include the duty of care, the duty of loyalty, and the duty of acting in good faith. The directors enjoy the presumption that they had acted properly and fulfilled their duties while managing the corporation's affairs, and the courts will not intervene in their actions, unless it is proven otherwise (the business judgment rule). In addition, Delaware law makes it possible to determine in the Certificate of Incorporation that the directors be exempt from the payment of damages for breaching their duty of care, unless they acted wrongfully or with bad intent. The law does not, however, allow directors to be exempted from the payment of damages for actions in which they had a personal interest that compromised their duty of loyalty. The law also awards corporations wide discretion with respect to retroactive indemnification for acts performed by the directors.

Mergers and Consolidations

Delaware corporations may merge with (or into) any company, whether registered in the United States or elsewhere. Usually, a merger of a Delaware corporation requires the approval of the Board of Directors and the affirmative vote of a majority of the outstanding shares. In triangular mergers, a vote by the acquiring company's shareholders is not required, since the acquiring company is not directly involved in the merger (see Chapter 17 for a discussion on triangular mergers). In addition, Delaware law provides a simple mechanism for mergers between affiliated companies (parent companies and subsidiaries). The fact that the merger of companies requires no regulatory approval or judicial intervention under the DGCL confers a significant advantage on the many companies that choose to incorporate in Delaware.

In order to avoid ordinary merger proceedings, Delaware corporations may change the legal entity they had decided to organize into a converted legal entity. The advantage of conversions over ordinary mergers is that in contrast with ordinary mergers, in which the target ceases to exist and is consumed by the acquirer, in conversions the target retains its legal entity, while modifying the legal form of its incorporation. This process is useful, and at times even necessary, when a company wants to merge but is bound by contracts or other undertakings prohibiting the assignment of rights or obligations.

Taxation of Partnerships, S Corporations, and Limited Liability Companies (LLCs)

Partnerships, S Corporations, and Limited Liability Companies (LLCs) are pass-through entities for tax purposes in the United States. In other words, these entities are not taxed at their own level, and their income and losses are attributed to the partners in the partnership or to the shareholders of the S Corporation or the LLC, according to their respective shares in the corporation.

S Corporations and LLCs are companies for all intents and purposes, and their shareholders can enjoy limited liability like any limited liability company. The tax treatment of S Corporations and LLCs is essentially similar, but S Corporations are subject to certain restrictions, such as a maximum of 75 shareholders, all of whom need to be local and nonincorporated residents. A similar consequence—having the income and losses attributed to the shareholders and the company regarded as a pass-through entity for tax purposes (including a company not organized in the United States)—may be achieved through the "Check the Box" rules in the Federal Internal Revenue Code.

From January 1997, the United States has allowed certain corporations to choose whether to be taxed as a company or as a partnership (each corporation marks its choice by checking the appropriate box on its annual income tax return). In other words, a company may choose whether to be a pass-through entity for tax purposes, so that its income and expenses will be attributed to its shareholders like a partnership, or to have its income taxed at the company level.

3
Financial and Business Planning

CHAPTER OVERVIEW

The business planning of startups is often summarized in a document called the business plan. However, it is important to understand that business planning is much broader than the business plan document. This chapter reviews the main aspects of the general business planning process, while emphasizing the factors that are important to early stage companies.

The first part of the chapter discusses the company's business cycle and the manner of presenting information in the financial statements. Understanding the principles underlying the financial statements, the manner of preparing them, and the presentation of the data is essential to anyone involved in the high tech industry in general, and to persons engaged in business planning in particular. The second part of this chapter reviews the main methods of financial forecasting. The last part of this chapter reviews other issues relating to strategic planning and reviews the business plan, which is one of the products of business planning.

The Company's Business Cycle

Understanding the company's business cycle is important for financial forecasting and for understanding the company's cash flow. Figure 3–1 presents the business cycle of a typical company: The company's equity providers or debt holders infuse money (in the form of capital and debt, respectively) into the company's cash account. This cash is used by the company to pay for services, salaries (human capital), and raw materials for the production process and to purchase production equipment. The human capital and the raw materials are used for the development and production (through means of production such as machinery and computers) of services and products. Products pass through the company's inventory and are sold to customers, and services are provided to customers directly. Customers either pay for the products or services in cash or receive credit from the company that is paid later. At the end of each period (cycle), any cash not returned to the company's debt holders is paid to the tax authorities, distributed to the shareholders in the form of dividends, or is re-invested in the company to allow further business cycles.

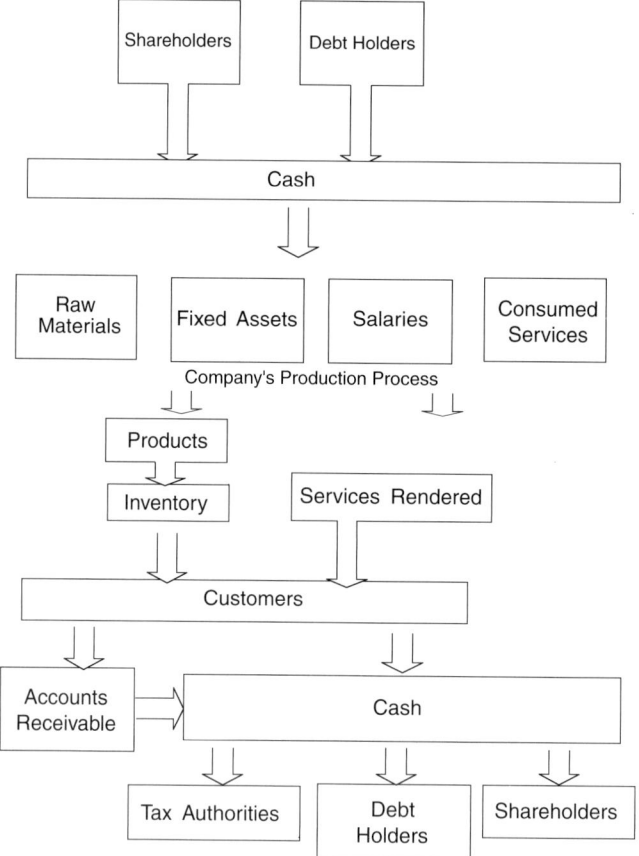

Figure 3–1 The Company's Business Cycle

Financial Statements

The company's business cycle is reflected in its financial statements; the main ones are the company's balance sheet, income statement, and cash flow statement. The company's financial statements provide information about its financial condition: The main purpose of the balance sheet is to describe the assets and liabilities of the company on a given date; the main purpose of the income statement is to describe the transactions and changes in the assets and liabilities of the company over a period of time; and the cash flow statement describes the changes in the company's cash flow over a period of time.

The company's financial statements are usually prepared in accordance with generally accepted accounting principles (GAAP). In most cases, the company prepares two sets of statements: One is used for reporting to the company's shareholders and debt holders, and the other, which is based on the tax rules governing the recording of transactions, is used for reporting to the tax authorities. Obviously, the statements report the same business results, but different rules used for different needs create differences between the reported results. The reason for the differences in most cases is the existence of specific directives for tax reporting, as opposed to other financial reporting principles that attempt to reflect the company's business condition in general.

In order to understand the company's financial condition and prepare financial and business plans accordingly, entrepreneurs need to understand the meaning of the different statements and the logic behind the reflection of the company's business cycle. The following explanation of the statements and their components is consistent with the customary reporting rules, but is based on the economic principles underlying them, rather than on the precise reporting rules.

Balance Sheet

The company's balance sheet reflects the company's overall assets and liabilities or, in other words, its financial condition at a given point of time. The balance sheet may be likened to a snapshot of the company's financial condition. It distinguishes among various types of assets and liabilities, such as cash held by the company or in its bank accounts, as opposed to inventories. The balance sheet also reflects the shareholders' equity, namely, the investment in the company made by the shareholders and the profits accumulated in the company (retained earnings). The company's total recorded assets are always equal to the sum of its liabilities plus the shareholders' equity (see Figure 3–2).

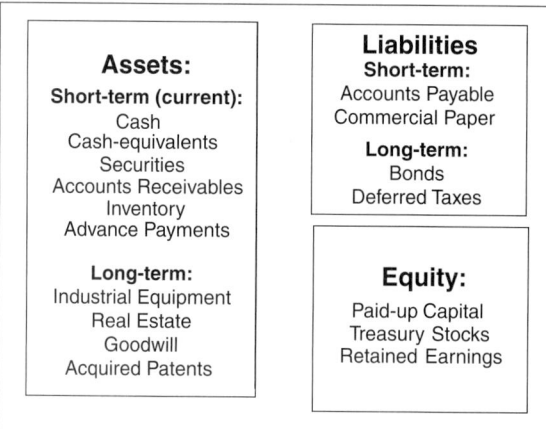

Figure 3–2 The balance sheet

According to the reporting principles, the company is required to distinguish between current assets and liabilities which may be liquidated or are due within one year or less, and other assets and liabilities, referred to as long-term assets and liabilities, whose life span is longer than one year. Assets are presented in a declining order of liquidity, i.e., the most liquid assets appear before the less liquid assets. The first assets presented (namely, the most liquid) include cash and traded securities, and the assets presented last are the company's fixed assets, such as industrial equipment and real estate.

It is important to note that the presentation of assets and liabilities in financial statements is guided by the principle of conservativeness: Assets are recorded according to their lowest reasonable value (in other words, they are not likely to be liquidated for less), whereas liabilities are recorded according to their highest reasonable value.

The main assets and liabilities appearing on the balance sheet (see Figure 3–2), are the following:

Assets

- **Cash, cash-equivalents and securities**—These are the first among the company's current assets. Cash, cash-equivalents, and securities include, except for the cash in the company's bank account, all short-term deposits owned by the company and traded securities, including treasury bills. The guiding principle underlying the classification of these assets is that they entail a relatively low risk in proportion to their value at the time of liquidation, and can be liquidated quickly (usually, within less than three months).
- **Accounts Receivable**—Since most companies do not receive payment in cash for all of their sales, almost every company that has reached the stage of sales has an Accounts Receivable (or Receivables) item. These are short-

term customer debts that the company records on its balance sheet after offsetting allowance for doubtful debts which it does not expect to collect. For example: a company by the name of Speed is owed $1,000 by its customers, but predicts that only $800 will be paid. The company will present in its balance sheet a net amount of $800 under this item, representing the portion of the debts that the company expects to collect. This amount is produced by deducting an allowance of $200 for doubtful debts from the gross debt of $1,000.

- **Inventory**—Inventories are assets in various stages of production that the company expects to sell as products. Inventories are divided into several types in accordance with their stage along the production process. Companies usually specify the types of inventories they have, since investors attribute a different value to different types of inventories. For instance, in most cases, an inventory of raw materials is easier to liquidate than an inventory of products in progress. A manufacturing company will generally have three types of inventories: an inventory of raw materials, an inventory of goods in process, and an inventory of finished goods. Inventories are estimated according to their cost, not according to the revenue they are expected to produce, unless such revenue is lower than the cost of production (in which case, the principle of conservativeness directs that they be recorded according to their net realizable value). The reporting of inventories in progress, as well as inventories of finished products, usually includes also allocated labor and overhead costs (such as electricity and some of the depreciation of the equipment used to manufacture them).

    When analyzing inventories, it is important to pay attention to the method of recording of the inventories, since a company selling products uses inventories of raw materials and finished products which might be recorded according to different prices. For instance, let us assume that Speed manufactures instruments that it combines with tractors that it purchases. In one month, the company purchased three identical tractors at different prices (according to the order of acquisition): $100,000, $120,000 and $115,000. At the end of the month, the company sold one set of equipment (a tractor on which the company's equipment was assembled) for $200,000. Obviously, the reported financial results reported by Speed will be affected by the choice of the tractor that constitutes a material part of the sold equipment. If the company uses an inventory method called FIFO (First In, First Out), then, assuming that Speed had no prior inventories, it will report an inventory of $235,000. $100,000 (the cost of the first tractor) will be reported as part of the cost of the equipment sold (see the next subsection for a further discussion of revenues and expenses). If the company uses the method of LIFO (Last In, First Out), then the company will report an inventory of $220,000. According to yet another method, the inventory (and the components of the cost of the goods sold) is calculated according to the average cost of the components of the sale. In our case, the inventory at the end of the period will be reported at: $(100{,}000 + 120{,}000 + 115{,}000)*(2/3) = 223{,}333.33$.

- **Advance payments**—Although companies usually try to defer payments, in many cases they pay in advance for services they will receive after the date of the balance sheet. For instance, companies often pay rent for several months in advance. The principle in the statements is to report expenses and revenues at the time of the economic occurrence of their underlying events. In other words, since the services will be received after the date of the statements, the expenses will be recorded concurrently with the receipt of the service. Therefore, the balance sheet will reflect an asset incorporating the cost for which the services or product was not yet received.

- **Long-term assets**—Assets that are expected to contribute to the production of revenues over a period longer than one year are referred to as long-term assets. They are divided into two main groups: tangible assets and intangible assets (intellectual property). Tangible assets include real estate, office equipment, production equipment, long-term financial assets, and stocks in other companies. These assets are usually recorded according to their historical value, i.e., according to the price of purchase, adjusted for depreciation.

    The term "depreciation" attempts to reflect the devaluation of assets over their economic life span or usage. The periodic depreciation of an asset is part of the expenses reflected in the income statement. There are various methods for calculating depreciation that are deployed in accordance with the character of the assets, the industry, and the company holding the asset. The most widely-used method is that of the "straight line": First, the asset's economic life span is estimated, and a proportionate part of the cost is recorded every year as an expense. For instance, if a car was bought for $20,000, and its economic life span is five years, then $4,000 are recorded every year as an expense, and the asset is reported on the balance sheet with a value that decreases by such amount every year. Another common method is that of the "accelerated depreciation," whereby the asset is depreciated more in the first years. This method reflects an accelerated depreciation in the first years of the asset's life. The value of a new car, for instance, is known to decline faster in its first few years.

    There are other depreciation methods, and in many cases the chosen method takes into account the amount of use made of the asset. For instance, consider the case of a factory where one million cars can be manufactured before it needs to be renovated. Obviously, it would be logical to express the depreciation of the factory over time as a function of the number of cars actually manufactured in it.

Assets appear on the balance sheet according to their historical value, less depreciation and any other devaluation resulting from a decline in their market value below their cost. In fact, the net fixed assets will be equal, at the end of each period, to the net fixed assets at the end of the previous period, plus new fixed assets acquired, minus the net cost of fixed assets sold and minus periodic depreciation and any other reduction in the recorded value of the fixed assets.

Where the statements of non-American companies are concerned, it is important to understand that in different countries the value of assets may be expressed differently, and in many cases assets may be revalued according to their market value at the time. Fixed assets may be revalued, for instance, in the United Kingdom and in the Netherlands. The principle in these countries is that assets are reflected according to the cost to the company of replacing them. In other words, if the car on Speed's balance sheet (which, for purposes of this example, will be reported according to British rules) is one year old, then, instead of reporting a depreciated value of $16,000 ($20,000 – $4,000), the cost of a similar used car on the market will be checked. If such cost is $21,000, then the car will be recorded in the balance sheet with this value. This change in value will concurrently be reflected under the item of the company's shareholders' equity. In all countries, if the market value of an asset considerably declined below its depreciated cost, and such devaluation is not expected to be remedied, then the value of the asset has to be reduced in the balance sheet by recording a loss as a result of the devaluation of the asset (since such devaluation is in lieu of future depreciation).

Intangible assets include items such as the cost of acquired patents, trademarks and trade names, franchises, and the cost of investments in other companies above the value of their tangible assets (goodwill). These assets also appear on the balance sheet and are depreciated in accordance with their expected life span, with certain restrictions (in accordance with the accounting rules applicable in each country) with respect to the manner of recording of various assets and liabilities. For example, if Speed bought a license to use a patent that will expire in ten years in consideration for one million dollars, then it will be depreciated over ten years, unless the patent is expected to become worthless after a shorter period of time, or is expected to continue being valuable after it expires.

Following an accounting rule change, effective from the year 2002, goodwill does not have to be depreciated if its value, as deemed by the company's management, has not declined.

Liabilities

- **Short-term liabilities**—This section includes overdrafts, commercial paper issued by the company, and any component of long-term debt payable in the coming year. This item also includes all short-term debts to suppliers of various services and products (accounts payable) and accumulated expenses (expenses accumulated but not yet paid), such as unpaid salaries and taxes not yet paid to the tax authorities.
- **Long-Term debt**—This section includes sub-items reflecting liabilities due later than one year after the date of the balance sheet. It includes, for instance, bonds issued by the company and deferred tax liabilities resulting from differences of timing between the recording of revenues and expenses for tax purposes and their reflection in the financial statements. Let us assume, for example, that the car bought by Speed for $20,000 may be depreciated for tax purposes over two years (namely, with an annual depreciation of $10,000). As mentioned above, for the purpose of the financial statements, a straight-line depreciation over five years was calculated (i.e., $4,000 per year). Since the difference between the two depreciation methods is $6,000, the company is deferring the payment of tax on revenues in the amount of $6,000. Assuming that the applicable tax rate is 20%, then the tax authorities are, in fact, lending the company $1,200 per year in the first two years, to be paid back from the third year forth. This loan from the tax authorities is itemized on the balance sheet as deferred taxes liability. This item includes differences of timing vis-à-vis the tax authorities under several items, and in many cases increases every year due to ever-increasing assets, assuming that the rates of depreciation for tax purposes are higher than the rates of depreciation in the financial statements. However, since these are timing differences, the company should record a deferred tax item on its balance sheet. Note that similarly, if the company accumulates losses over several periods, but forecasts profits amounting at least to these losses, then the company can record a tax asset in the amount of the tax it will not have to pay over the coming years due to its accumulated losses.
- **Equity**—The company's equity represents the value of its assets after deduction of its liabilities, and it belongs to the company's shareholders. This item includes the company's paid-up capital (namely, the amounts paid by the shareholders in consideration for their shares), the company's retained earnings and other items reflecting various reserves due to unrealized changes in the value of various assets and liabilities.

    Another important component of a company's equity is treasury stocks, namely, shares issued by the company but re-purchased by it. From the economic point of view, a purchase of the company's own shares constitutes an alternative to paying dividends, since the company is, in fact, spending money that is transferred to the shareholders, who may sell their shares to the company. From the taxation point of view, a re-purchase of shares is usually better for shareholders than the distribution of dividends that is subject to each individual shareholder's highest tax bracket (in the United States). A re-purchase of shares, on the other hand, affects the price of the shares but does not impose any tax liability on the shareholders, unless they choose to sell their shares (and even then they pay a capital gains tax, which, in the United States, is lower than the tax imposed on dividends).

Income Statement

In contrast with the balance sheet that reflects the situation of the company at a fixed point in time, an income statement reflects the company's activity over a period of time. The income statement presents the company's accounting revenues and expenses. A later section will discuss the difference between revenues and expenses and cash movements. The purpose of this statement is to present a summary of the company's activities over this period of time.

The principle guiding the reflection of revenues is that revenues are recognized in the period in which the transaction was made, when uncertainty with respect to its possible closing and to the payment therefore has been resolved. In other words, the transaction may be recorded in a different period from that in which payment therefore will be received. For instance, Speed will record the revenue from the equipment it sold when it closed the sale transaction, although the payment may actually be received later on.

Another important principle is the matching of revenues and expenses. According to this guiding principle, expenses incurred in the production of revenues from products and services are recorded in the same period as the revenues from the sale of such services or products. Thus, Speed will record the cost of the tractor as an expense in the above example only when it records the revenue from the sale of the equipment.

The expenses recorded in the statements reflect all the costs involved in deriving the company's revenues. Expenses are reported under various items in different parts of the statement and include, among others, the cost of materials, labor, marketing, advertising, research and development, and various administrative expenses.

An income statement comprises various items, including the following (see Table 3–1):

- **Revenues**—Usually, the first line of an income statement reflects the company's revenues. Such revenues may be recorded as gross revenues, in which case the expenses incurred in their production appear in the line "cost of goods sold"; conversely, the company can present the results on a net basis, in which case the first line will be calculated after deducting various costs relating to the sold goods. Amazon (the world's largest online bookstore), for instance, reports the entire turnover of goods sold by it, and records the cost of the books as an expense. eBay (the world's largest auction site) on the other hand, records as revenue only the commissions it receives on sales made through its site. The difference results from the fact that a company's revenue is tied to the transfer of principal risks and returns on the asset. In eBay's case, the company is not exposed to any risk resulting from the maintenance of inventories, and does not bear various risks of payment transfers and shipments. Consequently, it does not own the sold goods at any stage of the transaction. Amazon, on the other hand, bears the risk involved in the stocking of the goods it sells (including, in many cases, the maintenance of inventories), and therefore recognizes the sale and cost of the goods.

In many areas involving brokerage and production, lengthy, numerous, and deep discussions are held with respect to the nature of transactions, since these companies often sell products they do not stock. In such cases, a comprehensive examination is required in order to determine who bears the risk of stocking goods during the course of the transactions. In the aftermath of the collapse of the energy trading company Enron and the telecommunications company Global Crossing, issues pertaining to net versus gross recording of revenue are in the center of the public discussion. While there is typically no impact on cash flows from the transactions at different points in time, market participants tend to value firms based on revenue multiples (see Chapter 9 for further discussion), and hence these definitions become acute.

- **Cost of Goods Sold**—As mentioned above, costs of goods sold reflects the costs incurred in producing the service or product recorded as a revenue. The components of this cost vary from one company to another in accordance with the nature of the company. In retail companies, for instance, this cost is composed mainly of the cost of the goods themselves, whereas in software companies, the cost of goods sold is composed primarily of the employment costs directly related to the sale. The cost of goods sold will usually also include various components of depreciation, the value of which is loaded onto the price of the sold equipment or service.
- **Gross Profits**—Gross profits are revenues minus the cost of goods sold. The gross profits and their percentage of the revenues are two of the main parameters for estimating a company's performance. Investors often regard changes in the rates of gross profitability as an indicator of changes in the company's future prospects.

   Profit margins vary dramatically from one industry or market to another. The pharmaceutical industry, for instance, is characterized by a gross profit margin of up to 90%, whereas many retail chains are characterized by gross profit margins of below 25%.
- **Operating Profit**—The company's operating profit is calculated by deducting depreciation and amortization, general and administrative

expenses, research and development expenses, and marketing expenses from the gross profits. Operating profit is an indicator of the company's profit that is disassociated from the company's capital structure. In other words, this profit disregards the company's financing expenses. The assumption underlying the examination of operating profit margins is that the company's capital structure is a variable that depends on a mere managerial decision, whereas the focus on the company's basic data should be made without regard for the company's capital structure considerations.
- **EBIT—Earnings Before Interest and Taxes**—EBIT is calculated by adding additional items to the operating profit, such as the sale of assets outside the company's ordinary operating activities.
- **Net Income**—Net income is reached by deducting financing costs, taxes, and irregular items from EBIT. The net income is added to the shareholders' equity after deducting any dividends distributed to the shareholders.

Table 3–1 presents an example of an income statement. The company's revenues amounted to $1 million, and the cost of goods sold was $600,000. Consequently, the gross profit was $400,000. The company's other operating expenses were the salaries of research and development employees ($100,000), marketing and sales ($150,000), general and administrative expenses ($25,000), and depreciation ($50,000). The company's operating profit was therefore $75,000, and after deducting financing expenses of $20,000 and paying tax at the rate of 20%, the company's net income was $44. After distributing a $5,000 dividend to the shareholders, the company's retained earnings increased by $39,000.

Table 3–1   Sample income statement

Speed Inc. Income Statement for the twelve months ending December 31, 2001 (amounts in $000)		
Revenues:		$1,000
Cost of goods sold		600
Gross profit		400
Operating expenses:		
R&D	$100	
Marketing and sales	150	

Table 3-1 Sample income statement (continued)

General and administrative	25	
Depreciation and amortization	50	
Total		325
Operating profit		75
Special items		0
EBIT		75
Financing costs		20
Earnings before taxes		55
Income tax—20%		11
Net income (earnings after taxes)		44
Dividends		5
Balance transferred to retained earnings		39

Cash Flow Statement

Like the income statement, the cash flow statement also reflects changes over a period of time, rather than being a snapshot at a fixed point in time as in the balance sheet. This statement reflects all the movements of cash into the company (cash inflow) and out of the company (cash outflow) in a given period of time. This statement is essential for understanding the company's ability to survive over time. It is possible, for example, for a company to be profitable, yet to consume more cash than it has (for instance, due to a delay in receiving some of its revenues) and therefore to find itself in a cash shortage. (A later section on accounting revenues and actual cash flows will give a more detailed discussion.)

The cash flow statement is divided into three components describing the changes in the company's cash flows from operating, investing, and financing activities. We will first demonstrate how the cash flow statement may be constructed on the basis of the company's other main financial statements, namely the balance sheet and the income statement. We will then review the three components of the cash flow statement: the cash flows from operating activities, investing activities, and financing activities. The analysis proposed here is essentially economic, and although it is consistent with the accounting standards for the reporting of cash flows in countries such as the United States, it is not constructed according to such reporting (GAAP) standards.

The starting point for analyzing a company's cash flows is the cash item in the company's balance sheet at the beginning of the period, and the end point is the cash item at the end of the forecasted or analyzed period. The change in the company's cash positions is the difference in its cash between these two points in time. This difference takes into account all of the movements and transactions in which the company was involved. Therefore, this figure alone is insufficient to understand the company's cash needs, cash generation, and cash consumption over the period. Clearly, the value of cash infused into the company as a result of the sale of products or services is different from an inflow of cash to the company created by raising new capital.

The company's cash flow from operating activities is composed, in principle, of actions revolving the sale of products and services. Accordingly, expenses relating to the creation of such cash flows, such as the acquisition of raw materials, sale expenses, marketing expenses, and general expenses, as well as tax payments, are some of the components of the company's cash outflow resulting from operating activities.

The company's cash flow from investing activities is composed of actions such as the sale of real and financial assets or the repayment of long-term loans given to third parties. Accordingly, acts such as the acquisition of assets and investments in equipment and long-term financial assets are some of the components of the company's cash outflow resulting from investing activities, as are the receipt of dividends and interest from real and financial investments. The main component of the cash flow from investing activities is usually the change in the company's net fixed assets. As mentioned above, the company's net fixed assets at the end of a period are equal to its net fixed assets at the beginning of the period, plus assets purchased over the period, minus depreciation accumulated over the period and minus net sales of assets sold over the period.

Finally, the company's cash flow from financing activities is composed of shares and notes and debentures issued and long- or short-term loans taken. Accordingly, the re-purchase of the company's own shares, repayment of notes and debentures and other long-term debts, and the payment of dividends and interest on debts compose the company's cash outflow resulting from financing activities.

At this point it should be mentioned that there might be material differences between the classification of the cash flows for internal company analysis and the classification required by GAAP. The main differences typically relate to the company's financing expenses. In the above description, they are included in the cash flows from financing activities, whereas, according to GAAP, they are included in the cash flows from operating activities. The analytical difference between the two is that decisions with respect to the taking of loans are managerial decisions pertaining to the company's capital structure and should therefore be classified as cash flows from financing activities for an internal analysis of the business, as well as for free cash flow-based valuation (which is detailed in Chapter 9).

The Relationship between the Balance Sheet, the Income Statement, and the Cash Flow Statement

The company's balance sheet at a certain point in time is a reflection of the previous balance sheet, with the addition of changes in the company's business cycle that are reflected in the company's income statement over this period, and changes that are reflected directly in the balance sheet, such as loans and equity raising. Changes involving changes in cash will also be represented in the company's cash flow statement.

In most cases the change in the shareholders' equity from one period to another may be presented by using the following simple equation:

Shareholders' equity at the end of the period = shareholders' equity at the beginning of the period + profits earned over the period − dividends distributed over the period + capital raised over the period

The Difference between Accounting Revenue and Actual Cash Flows

There are significant differences between accounting revenues and profits and the company's cash flow. These differences may derive from several sources, such as the following:

- **Timing differences between sales and receipt of payments**—The main differences are the result of timing differences between when sales are made and when payment for them is received. Cash will flow to the company only when payment is received for a transaction it made, unless the company has made an agreement whereby it sold the debt related to the sale to a finance provider, who gave it cash in consideration for the debt.
- **Barters**—Besides the provision of credit to customers, another difference results from transactions in which the consideration is not given in cash. Such barters are far more common among high tech companies, and particularly startups, than in other companies. The reason for this is that in many cases neither party has the cash required to pay for various services and products it consumes. Therefore, they render services or supply other products, whose cost to the supplier is low, but that have a high market value, in consideration for products and services consumed by the company. The price at which such transactions are recorded is the subject of constant discussion by the authorities. Without going too much into accounting rules, the customary rule is that the price of barters must be based on the market price of similar transactions. One of the indicators of such price is similar transactions recently performed by the company in consideration for cash.
- **Accounting depreciation**—Another material factor that creates a vast difference between the revenue and the cash generated by a company's business is investment in fixed assets such as communication networks or

equipment. Although these assets may be paid for in cash, they serve the company over long periods of time. They will appear in the company's balance sheet and be reflected in the income statements only by depreciation over their expected useful life span, generally several years.

Let us assume, for example, that a certain software development company buys equipment which it can use for two years for $1,000. Therefore, every year $500 will appear as an expense in the income statement to reflect the depreciation of this asset. Let us further assume that the payment for the equipment was made in cash. In the year it bought the equipment, the company was still engaged in development, and incurred additional expenses of $2,000 for salaries. In that year, the company will report expenses of $2,500, namely the depreciation of the equipment and the salaries paid. The company's cash account, however, was reduced in that year by $3,000 for the same equipment bought and salaries paid. In the following year, the company finishes developing the product and sells it for $4,000, paid in cash, having incurred expenses of $1,000 for advertising (paid in cash), $2,000 for salaries and another $500 for the depreciation of the equipment. The company will therefore report a profit of $500, although its cash account increased by $1,000.

- **Leasing and relying on credit from suppliers**—Many startups significantly reduce their cash needs by making intensive use of leasing, i.e., receiving long-term credit (usually from the manufacturer or an entity specializing in this type of financing) to finance equipment that is received by the company immediately but is not legally owned by it. The manner by which such transactions are recorded in the income statement depends on many variables pertaining to the economic ownership of the asset. Another customary form of financing is relying on credit from suppliers, i.e., receiving credit from suppliers in order to pay for a purchase.

EBITDA and Cash Earnings

Many investors adjust the EBIT upwards by disregarding various deductions entailed by operating expenses, thus arriving at the EBITDA (Earnings Before Interest, Tax, Depreciation, and Amortization).

Changes in the company's capital structure naturally affect the rate of interest paid by the company and its tax liability, due to the tax shield afforded to interest paid on debts (interest is recognized as an expense for tax purposes). Therefore, the argument follows, there is logic in examining the profits produced by a company, irrespective of its capital structure, which are dependent upon managerial decisions.

Another argument in favor of focusing on this parameter is that depreciation and amortization are not a genuine expression of the devaluation of assets used by the company. The reason for this is that many assets may serve the company for years after they are fully depreciated. The use of EBITDA is common in industries with high levels of investment in equipment. However, it may also lead to erroneous conclusions since, as it does not take into account the level of investments required in order to preserve the company's operating condition, let alone improve it.

In recent years and particularly in view of a wave of mergers and acquisitions, the term cash earnings has become common usage. Many high tech companies now report this data, although it is not defined by U.S. GAAP (and consequently its composition may vary from one company to another). Like EBITDA, this figure refers to the company's pre-tax earnings, in addition to the various depreciations and amortizations included in the income statement. However, it too may misguide investors since not all companies include the required investments in equipment, the amount of which is supposed to be at least roughly indicated by depreciation. Nor does it reflect the company's cash flow with respect to the investments required by the company. In addition, it does not reflect changes in the operating capital required to support a growth of business.

Reporting Holdings in Other Companies and Consolidation of Statements

The company's share in other companies is reflected in the balance sheet and income statement in accordance with the nature of the holdings. If the holding is long-term and represents less than 20% of the control or capital of such company (more detailed tests lie beyond the scope of this chapter), the company will typically report the holdings according to its historical cost, unless their value has declined, in which case the company will recognize a loss equal to the decline in value (the lower of cost or market method).

Holdings exceeding 20% but awarding the company no control over the held company are typically reported according to the company's share in the held company. The guiding principle is that the cost is expressed after adjusting it to changes in the held company's shareholders' equity, changes that are affected by the profits of the held company and by capital raised by it (the equity method).

Companies controlled by the company will be reported in accordance with the equity method (while reflecting the appropriate rate of holdings). Alternatively, in the case of consolidated statements by the holding company, the controlled company's business assets, liabilities and results will be presented in the controlling company's statements. Appropriate items will be included in the balance sheet and in the income statement to reflect the minority interest in the controlled company. The balance sheet will include a liability reflecting the minority shareholders' interest in the controlled company, and the income statement will include a cost reflecting the minority shareholders' interest in the controlled company's profits over the period.

Financial Projections

This section reviews the main methods for financial projections. The review does not cover all the components required for meaningful forecasting, but provides the main tools used for such forecasting. It is difficult to overrate the importance of financial forecasting and its significance to investors, employees, suppliers, customers, and financial institutions. Many managers, for instance, lose their positions in companies due to their failure to meet financial forecasts; many companies are denied investments due to forecasts that could not be backed by reasonable assumptions; and yet other companies are denied from large contracts because customers who are considering these contracts and request long-term forecasts do not feel confident that the company will survive the period of the engagement and be able to provide various services also after its termination (such as customer service and spare parts).

The Purpose and Importance of Financial Forecasting

Correct financial planning is an important component of business planning, and too many entrepreneurs tend to underestimate its importance. Consequently, many startups run into financial difficulties which could have been predicted and even avoided by raising more money or reducing expenses. Financial forecasting can help investors in the company make more realistic estimates of the return on the venture. By using well thought-through forecasts, the company learns what resources will be required to be raised. The main objectives of financing forecasting are the following:

- **Forecasting the company's cash needs**—Forecasting the company's cash and financing needs is necessary to develop the company at the pace desired by the entrepreneurs and investors. One of the main issues confronting entrepreneurs almost daily is the issue of financing the company's activities. Correct forecasting of the company's financial needs in the short-, intermediate- and long-term involves an understanding of the management of transactions and a basic understanding of the concepts of revenues, expenses, and cash paid or received within them. Even for early stage companies, for which full-blown business plans may not even exist, no financial model and hence no forecasting regarding required capital can be prepared without making various assumptions with respect to the customer credit policy, the compensation policy, and other costs.
- **Valuing the company**—Which valuation is required in order to raise capital?. The financial model and discussion related to its underlying assumptions often serve as a basis for the associated investment contracts. See Chapter 9 for further discussion on valuation.
- **Comparing actual performance to forecasts**—Such comparison is important in order to amend forward-looking forecasts and to adjust them to reality, and for adequate control over the pace of outflow of expenses. Such a

comparison is important also to investors, since it can warn them of changes in the probability of the company meeting its performance milestones.

General Forecasting Issues

When forecasting the revenues and expenses of a company when it enters the market, it is important to rely on the statements of similar publicly traded companies, in order to examine their cost structure and profit margins. Such an examination is crucial, since it enables one to appraise the reasonableness and soundness of the assumptions underlying the venture's financial model. In addition, it enables one to examine whether the startup will be able to compete with such companies when it goes public. For instance, if the profit margins are low due to fierce competition among many players in the market, the startup will find it hard to break into the market, unless it can present a considerable improvement on the expected products of the existing and anticipated competitors in the market at that time. Sales volumes will probably derive from the size of the projected target market. Data on the target market at the time of product launch are available from many sources—some public and some in the form of reports published by research companies. In addition, in different cases, and in particular when the company is about to create a new market, tailored research that is conducted by or for the company should be used, in order to estimate the size of the potential market.

The data included in the statements of public companies should, however, be treated cautiously, since these are mostly companies that have already passed the test of investors before going public and therefore do not necessarily represent the average company in their field. Financial data and ratios may also be utilized—either from publicly available sources or from quotes for similar projects—with respect to employee compensation, project pricing, and so on.

Forecasting a company's scale of operations is complex, and in many cases companies will resort to technical and financial experts for such estimates. Even if the estimated market is large, and even if it is forecasted that the competitive situation of the market will not bite into the company's profitability, the company has to estimate the market share it can achieve and maintain. Determining the market share which the company can achieve is complicated, and setting targets such as "we will obtain 10% of the market" must be based on defendable assumptions. Otherwise, it will not be treated seriously by investors and, which is worse, could lead to erroneous strategic decisions by the company. A later section will discuss further aspects of market analysis.

Issues in Forecasting the Business Results of a New Company

There is no doubt that forecasting the business results of a company in its early stages of development is more of an art than an exact science. Nevertheless, financial forecasting at these stages is more important than for developed businesses. Given the scarcity of available sources of capital, the company must assess its business development decisions at every stage, while choosing the alternatives that will yield the best return for its shareholders (including the entrepreneurs). The main difference in comparison to a developed business is the level of uncertainty that may be addressed by examining different scenarios of parameters such as cost structures, market sizes, growth rates, and market profitability.

Companies must always examine scenarios that take into account the possibility of partial success. There is almost no greater hazard for businesses than managers who do not account for the possibility of partial success or failure of a project. Just like the preparation of strategy for war takes into account pessimistic scenarios such as accidents or defeat which would necessitate a retreat, companies too must prepare for scenarios in which not all optimistic assumptions materialize.

Sales Growth and Required Capital

An important component that affects a company's ability to raise capital, as well as to finance its development by using internal resources, is the growth of sales. However, it is important to understand that the substance of the growth in sales is more important than the actual pace of such growth.

Paradoxically, many companies which demonstrate a fast sales growth actually need more outside financing. The reason for this is that the company has to prepare for the increased sales by making considerable investments in equipment, manpower, raw materials, and inventory, which are made before the proceeds from the sales are received. Many entrepreneurs fail to plan their cash needs for accelerated growth and run into financial difficulties at times that are supposed to be good from the company's point of view. Although, as mentioned above, investors prefer companies with rapid sales growth, various factors could delay their investments, such as a forecast of a problematic situation on the capital market, or a projection that the pace of growth of an industry will not last much longer.

This dimension is crucial for attracting investments, as more and more investors prefer to "cut their losses" than to continue investing in rapidly growing ventures, whose future capital need on their path to profitability makes them too risky. For instance, during 2000 and 2001, many Internet ventures closed down. One of the most spectacular closures was perhaps the grocery and gasoline division of Priceline, in which more than $300 million were invested and that was shut down after less than one year of operations, as it was anticipated that hundreds of millions of dollars would have to be invested before it turned profitable, and the probability of raising this capital at a period of "hostile" capital markets was predicted to be slim. Along with companies in the public sector, there were also many spectacular failures in the public market, such as eToys, that consumed hundreds of millions of dollars before declaring bankruptcy. One of the reasons for this failure was that eToys was unable to secure additional sources of capital that would sustain it until it could (possibly) start generating net positive operating cash flows.

Utilization of Working Capital

A company's net working capital is an essential component of its operating needs. Working capital includes the company's cash, liquid securities, inventories, and short-term debt owed to the company, minus the short-term debt owed by the company. There is a natural connection between a company's working capital needs and sales since, as demonstrated above, companies must prepare for their expected sales growth by investing in equipment, inventories, or manpower, all of which require a substantial amount of cash. In addition, if the company extends credit to its customers, then the more its sales increase, so will its working capital, since the company has to finance the products it sells by its own resources or apply to outside sources for this purpose.

Companies will always try to obtain more favorable terms of credit in order to finance inventories. Thus, they reduce the need to freeze financial assets to this end. Many companies now manage to operate and grow with a net working capital that increases at a slower pace than their revenue, due to wise utilization of the cycles of accounts payable and accounts receivable, and are sometimes even able to operate with negative working capital. The computer company Dell, for instance, is often paid for the computer systems it supplies before they are even ordered from its suppliers.

Pricing and Credit Policy

An important factor in the company's business planning is estimates regarding the pricing of the company's products. Such decisions are essential as early as when the business model is structured, even before the company enters the market. In addition, the company has to update its analyses from time to time to accommodate any expected change in the competitive situation in the market, when the company's products are expected to be launched. The importance of such forecasts cannot be overrated, because no development decision is possible without examining the economic potential of such changes. Even meager changes can facilitate investment decisions.

A credit policy often seems irrelevant to companies that are not yet generating any revenues. However, determining such policy is highly significant, since in many cases it constitutes a material component of the company's business model. For instance, leveraging a model structured on production or assembly after orders are placed, enabled Dell to benefit from a steady competitive advantage in a market with narrow profit margins and intense competition. Dell's approach was to custom-build computers according to customer requirements, while relying heavily on a rapid decline in the price of components. Since the company did not stock large inventories, it was able to transfer to its customers part of the savings made from the falling prices.

Dividend Policy

In many companies, the dividend policy affects the company's cash balances. This is not the case in most startups. The principal portion of the returns earned by those who invest in the equity of high tech companies does not derive from the distribution of the company's retained earnings in the form of dividends, but rather from an increase in the value of the underlying asset, namely, the shares representing their stake in the ownership of the startup.

The reason for this is simple: Due to required heavy investments, startup companies rarely generate any earnings for a long period of time. Consequently, they have no profits and cannot distribute dividends. Alternately, even if the company could distribute dividends, in many cases the return which the company can gain from re-investing its surplus cash in the company is higher than the cost of its capital. In other words, it is better for the investors that the company will not distribute dividends. The company's value therefore derives from an estimate of its future profits (see Chapter 9 for a discussion of valuation), which value is manifested in a subsequent public offering or sale that rewards investors with revenues from the sale of their shares.

Cost Structure Analysis and Forecasting

Almost every business requires an initial investment before it generates revenues. In addition, some of the expenses in every period are independent of the scope of manufacturing or sales. In order to finance such fixed periodic expenses, the company needs to reach a certain minimum level of sales. For every unit sold at a price higher than the variable cost of its production (that includes, for instance, raw materials and labor), the company gains a contribution margin. The level of sales at which the total contribution margins from the company's operations equal its fixed costs is referred to as the "break-even point."

Analyzing the Break-even Point

An analysis of the break-even point usually assumes that the price and cost of each unit do not change with the increase in the volume of production/business, i.e., that the contribution margin of each dollar is similar. Clearly, this assumption is not necessarily realistic, and any analysis of the break-even point must include the appropriate formulas for the change in the contribution margin of each dollar of revenue.

The following example (in Table 3–2) presents a company that sells products with relatively low variable production cost. In fact, almost every product based on software or other information goods (such as downloadable music or movies) is characterized by such low marginal production cost structure. However, note that the assumption is that the overall marginal cost increases with the increase in the number of units sold, mainly due to increasing marketing costs per unit. This assumption represents the further assumption that the target clientele is exhausted in each stage, so that a larger overall expense per customer is required in the subsequent stages in order to convince them to buy the product.

Under the revenues item, the company receives $20 per unit for each 100,000 units. In other words, it earns revenue of $2 million for each 100,000 units.

Chapter 3 Financial and Business Planning

The situation is more complicated in the expenses item. The variable production costs do not change with the scope of production, and remain at $4 per unit. The marketing costs, however, increase from $6 per unit (for the first 100,000 units), up to $15 per unit, between the 350,000th and 400,000th units.

The company's fixed expenses are as follows: $500,000 for research and development (R&D), $500,000 for depreciation, $400,000 for fixed marketing expenses, and $400,000 for fixed general and administrative expenses (G&A).

As we can see, the company starts making an operating profit when sales exceed 200,000 units. Beyond 400,000 units, the contribution margin per unit is $0, since the marginal cost per unit is $20 ($4 for production, $15 for marketing and $1 for G&A expenses). In other words, there is no advantage in manufacturing beyond 400,000 units. However, the break-even point at 200,000 units includes the cost of depreciation, which is not a cash cost. Assuming that this cost does not require a recurring investment and that all sales are made for cash, the company turns cash-flow positive at under 150,000 units.

Table 3–2 The Break-Even Point

	Range	1	2	3	4	5
Revenue:						
Revenue per unit (in dollars)		$20	$20	$20	$20	$20
Maximum units (in thousands) in range		100	100	100	50	50
Revenue at full range (in thousands of dollars)		$2,000	$2,000	$2,000	$1,000	$1,000
Total Revenue (in thousands of dollars)		$2,000	$4,000	$6,000	$7,000	$8,000
Fixed Expenses (in thousands of dollars):						
R&D	$500					
Depreciation	500					
Marketing	400					
G&A	400					
Total	$1,800					

Cost Structure Analysis and Forecasting   49

Table 3-2   The Break-Even Point (continued)

Expenses:					
Variable production cost (in dollars per unit)	$4	$4	$4	$4	$4
Variable marketing cost (in dollars per unit)	$6	$6	$7	$10	$15
G&A Variable cost (in dollars per unit)	$1	$1	$1	$1	$1
Variable cost per unit in range (in dollars)	$11	$11	$12	$15	$20
Total variable cost in range (in thousands of dollars)	$1,100	$1,100	$1,200	$750	$1,000
Total expenses (in thousands of dollars)	$2,900	$4,000	$5,200	$5,950	$6,950
Total operating profit (in thousands of dollars)	-900	0	800	925	1,050

Summary:	Total number of units (in thousands)	Operating profit (in thousands of dollars)	Net cash flow (in thousands of dollars)
	100	-900	-400
	150	-450	50
	200	0	500
	250	400	900
	300	800	1,300
	350	925	1,425
	400	1,050	1,550
	450	1,050	1,550
	500	1,050	1,550

Forecasting Fixed and Variable Costs

It is also important to understand the links between various costs and the company's volume of business. Every sophisticated product requires a certain amount of manpower, but a certain amount of manpower is also required if no sales are made in the early stages, since the company must prepare for the possibility of future sales. As it is clear that every development person requires a minimum amount of equipment, so it should be understood that a material part of the company's cost structure includes, besides fixed components, variable expenses that change with the company's volume of business.

From the point of view of the cost structure analysis, the startup needs to estimate the cost structure it will have as accurately as possible. It is essential to understand the difference between a cost structure that includes components of high fixed costs, and a structure that includes mainly variable costs. In a power station, for instance, the cost of producing the final product—electricity—is low, since most of the costs are fixed: Some are financing costs incurred for the construction of the infrastructure and the building, and some are expenses incurred for maintaining the generators in proper working order. Similarly, the cost structure of hotels indicates that the cost of occupying an additional room is low, since the hotel employs a team that services other rooms. Hotel owners can modify their cost structures by engaging the services of an external company to maintain the hotel, in return for a percentage of the revenues (it is, in fact, customary for hotels to be run by such management companies). In other words, such outside companies reduce the fixed costs component upon themselves in consideration for a share in the revenues.

Outsourcing

By outsourcing, many companies are able to reduce their fixed costs. This is done, for instance, by hiring programming services (as in the ASP model) or hosting services instead of constructing and maintaining a server farm, and so on. Companies which sell products can similarly use other companies for shipping, customer service, and so on. Such services allow the company to focus on the core of its business without spending resources on activities that are less vital to the business. The strategic use of outsourcing enables startups and those who invest in them to reduce the risk involved as long as the company is still uncertain of its success (by cutting considerably on expenses at an early stage by hiring the service). Some of these services become too expensive and jeopardize the company's business, however, when the company grows beyond a certain level. The electronic retail company Amazon, for instance, earlier used Ingram as its outside warehouse and supply provider as long as Amazon was still a small to medium-sized company. However, at some point Amazon began developing its warehouses independently. This was done mainly to reduce the risk of dependency on an outside service supplier, which was then negotiating for its sale to Barnes & Noble, Amazon's competitor in the field of bookselling, on which Amazon was focusing at the time. Over the long run, Amazon was even becoming a provider of outsourcing services to other e-merchants.

The Costs of Market Entry and the Network Effect

Companies always aim at a cost structure in which every sale yields a positive contribution margin, in order to be able to finance its fixed costs. However, a company could clearly be prepared to execute transactions with a negative contribution margin for certain periods of time, even long ones, in order to penetrate into the market or start/ignite a network effect. The network effect is essential for a company to become differential in the market and to establish a user base that would make it difficult for competitors to enter the scene and compete against the company.

The basic principle in the network effect is that the value of the service to each user rises with the growth in the number of users of the service. Therefore, from a certain threshold number of users, the service becomes easier to sell, since there is already a base of users that makes the product highly valuable to new users. For instance, without a telephone on either side of every potential phone call, it would have been impossible to derive any income from telephone communications. If DVD players were not widespread, production companies would have no justification for releasing movies on DVD and vice versa—without DVD movies, people would have no reason to buy DVD players.

In the computer business, software engineers justifiably tend to first write programs for popular operating systems. Thus, even if the more popular operating system is technically inferior to an alternative system, users will tend to prefer the more popular system since it comes with wider technical support and a larger and more diverse selection of software.

On the Internet, software like ICQ (that essentially enables immediate communication between groups of users of the service without any charge to the users), Paypal (a service through which payments can be made among users of the service, usually without a per-transaction commission), and others would never have succeeded in breaking into the market were it not for the network effect. However, in many cases companies fall short of turning their user base into a source of revenues (or "monetizing" their user base), and may therefore be sold to companies that are better equipped to derive income from their users. ICQ, for instance, was acquired by AOL (America Online), which assumed that at some point it would be able to generate income from the ICQ users (for example, by advertising, direct sales, or cross sales of other services).

Cash Flow Forecasting

In order to build a healthy business, extensive capital raising is often required. The reasons for this are numerous: the recruitment of employees, the construction of a production, marketing, and distribution infrastructure, or the financing of large advertising budgets. Businesses are also often required to finance their customers by extending generous credit in order to break into the market. In the previous sections, we emphasized the importance of business planning and the structuring of realistic forecasts. This section will focus on a crucial issue facing every startup, namely, forecasting its cash needs. Even if a startup has a promising future, incorrect preparation for the various stages of the business could cause it to collapse due to a shortage of cash, and not necessarily due to an inability to meet its economic forecasts. On the other hand, entrepreneurs are usually not interested in raising too much cash at too early a stage, mainly due to the dilution entailed by capital raising. The objective of entrepreneurs is to maximize their share at the time of exit. It is therefore essential that the raising of capital be planned so as not to result in a significant dilution on the one hand (by raising too much capital), nor in a shortage of cash that would jeopardize the existence of the business on the other. For this purpose, it is important to focus on the various distinctions between cash flows and accounting revenues and expenses.

Cash Break-even Point

As mentioned above, when examining a company's profitability, it is important to check its cost structure and particularly its break-even point. The basis for the calculation is the company's fixed costs, divided by the contribution margin from the sale of a single product unit (i.e., the revenue per unit minus the variable costs per unit). However, it is important to distinguish between the profitability break-even point and the cash break-even point. There are several different definitions of cash break-even points, the most common of which is the FCF (Free Cash Flow). The FCF point is based on the operating cash flow, in addition to the cash flow components resulting from the investment activities required in order to allow the business to reach its goals with respect to its volume of business. Any cash beyond the FCF point may be distributed by the company among its shareholders and debt holders, in accordance with its chosen capital structure. Companies usually reach this break-even point when their growth rate slows down.

The Scale of Investment Required to Reach Profitability

In order to be able to use a break-even point analysis for financial forecasting, it is necessary to examine, beyond the actual level of operations at which the business becomes profitable, the scale of financing needed to reach such a point. In practice, this is the amount of cash required over the quarters and years leading to such a point. In addition, as may be seen in the decision tree example in a later section that includes possible scenarios, it is important to estimate the various scenarios and the business results of each one, and to attach probabilities to such scenarios. In this context, simulation tools may be used, as they enable assumptions to be made with respect to parameter distributions and to the various relationships between the parameters.

The most significant parameters relating to the uncertainty clouding startups in their infancy relate to the duration and cost of the product development stage. Delays in development could affect the expected revenues from the product, over and above its development costs, since the advantage of being "first to market" could evaporate, thus tightening the company's competitive situation. The timing of breaking into the market is related to the issue of uncertainty in the pricing of products, which itself is intimately connected to the forecasted competition in the market when the product is launched.

The costs of the products, and therefore the profitability of manufacturing them, are another contributor to uncertainty that needs to be addressed in the examinations made, since they will materially affect the company's cash needs until it becomes profitable. The company must further consider its market entry strategy, which has a dramatic effect on the amount of money that must be raised. For instance, in order to support an advertising campaign for the company's products, the company will need to raise a large amount of outside short-term cash, even if in the intermediate-term such amounts may be secured by large revenues.

Market Analysis and Strategic Planning

Introduction

Correct business planning starts with a market analysis, i.e., understanding its demands and examining the existing solutions, as well as the solutions that are expected to be in the market around the time when the company's products are launched. The role of the company's concept, the market, and the solution offered by the company were briefly discussed in an earlier section in Chapter 2. Any plan of the company's strategy must be made in consideration of the company's competitive position, as well as its development and sales potential, given the technology and production and managerial capabilities that are available to the company. A great risk is involved in decisions that are based on intuition only. Intuition usually expresses a decision process that takes place in the analyst's mind, but without any concrete quantification of the facts. In order to convince both outside and inside the company, it is important to quantify the decision-making process.

The bottom line of the market and strategic analyses is reflected in the company's business plan, the main components of which are reviewed in a later section in this chapter. This section will review various tools that may assist entrepreneurs in assessing target markets and the competition they should expect when the company enters such markets.

The Essence of Strategic Planning

A startup's strategic plan looks at the possibilities available to the company, identifies the preferred routes, and points to the path to implementing such recommendations. The analysis must be made in consideration of any existing and potential competitors, and of any response they may have to the startup's actions. When performing such planning, it is important to examine the cost to the startup of every possible route, both financially and from the point of view of the risks it poses. It should be understood that although many decisions are technically reversible, they are irreversible after implementation from the economic and competitive points of view. Let us assume, for example, that an entrepreneur invented a revolutionary algorithm for the efficient transmission of data that can be employed in numerous applications. However, due to budgetary and manpower constraints, the company chooses one of the possible applications and invests the majority of its resources in it. Although the company can technically go back and develop the other applications should the first one fail, it is possible that other companies that focused on such other applications have already achieved an unbeatable competitive edge. Furthermore, in contrast to large companies that have the resources to rectify erroneous choices and start new and different applications, a startup that makes an erroneous fundamental choice of application may not get a second chance.

Moreover, decisions with respect to the financing of the startup affect the manner in which it will be able to compete in the market. If the startup raises capital for a certain project that constitutes a material part of its activities, then a considerable amount is engaged in favor of the particular target market of such project, and it is entirely unclear whether financiers will be interested in investing in a different direction.

When performing its business planning, the company should examine decisions that could have a material effect on its flexibility. On the one hand, startups often want to preserve their flexibility in shifting between different areas. On the other hand, such flexibility, given the scarcity of economic resources, could result in a lack of focus and loss of all potential markets.

Analyzing Target Markets

In order to enable entrepreneurs to choose between alternative strategic paths, they must correctly assess the target market of their future products. Besides an analysis of the target market, it is important to assess the projected competitive situation of that market when it is entered into by the company. For instance, if several similar companies will be launching a similar product on the same market simultaneously, the company will obviously find it more difficult to take a significant share of that market than if it were operating in such a target market with no competition.

In many cases, and in particular when the target market is essentially technological, its size is difficult to quantify. Sometimes the target market does not yet exist or is still forming. Therefore, it is necessary to assess the scope of the market and the percentage of such a market that will require the solution provided by the company. The extent to which the company's products or services are capable of meeting such demands and the size of the relevant market should thereafter be estimated.

Every market analysis should address the basic components that will determine the future profitability of the industry. Material components are, for instance, the balance of power between suppliers and consumers in the target market, the expected competitive situation when the product is launched, and the availability of substitutes. A market analyst must examine developments of substitute technologies which, even if they do not currently constitute an alternative to the company's products, could become such an alternative in later stages of the product development. As mentioned above, market research can often characterize future market demands, according to which the company can choose its target market, direct the development of its products, and determine how they will be launched in the market.

In every industry there are many specific sources of information that the company can utilize. In addition, there are several major research companies that supply current reports on various technological industries, the projected scope of the markets, and the projected trends within such markets. Although the reports of research companies such as Jupiter, Gartner, and Forrester may provide an excellent starting point for market research in many fields, it should always be kept in mind that many competitors in the same target markets are using the same reports and reaching the same conclusions at the same time, thus reducing the value of the projects. In other words, when examining market analyses that are widely available to the public, it is essential that the reaction of potential competitors also be examined. Many sophisticated companies actually use such reports to identify smaller markets in which the company's competitive situation could be easier. Ultimately, it is not the size of the market in itself that will determine the company's future, but rather the potential for profit from the activities of the company. Such potential is a function of the company's market share in such target market and of its competitive situation. Paradoxically, from this perspective, a market in which there are no ready-made reports is often preferable, since the lack of readily available reports on such markets indicates, among other things, that the firm's competitive situation may be more favorable.

It is essential to examine different scenarios in which competing companies will be active in the target market when the company is about to launch its products. Many startups tend to examine the competitive situation when they start the development and ignore any developments that are made at the same time in other companies. For this reason, they might estimate their market share unrealistically. Likewise, many startups take into account the possibility of being bought out by a large company in the field, while disregarding the possibility that when their product is launched, other companies may offer comparable services that could also be of interest to such large companies.

Other than research companies, experts in the field should also be sought. These could be people who work in the field, analysts in investment banks who focus on public companies in the field, and so on. Over and above the information they can provide on the size of the projected market, such people can assist in analyzing potential competitors, in addition to providing contacts in the industry.

Naturally, Web-based research should be performed, including the use of industry-specific databases, some of which are available within larger databases such as Nexis or Dow Jones. In this area, those who compile data on the industries and markets in which the startup is interested are becoming increasingly important. Additional information is always vital to make informed decisions with respect to the startup's future.

While analyzing the target market, the company should examine not only the existing and projected competition in the direct target market, but also in close markets that could provide alternatives to the planned products of the company. For instance, if the startup will deal with broadcasting movies over the Internet, it should examine not only the projected competition in the same market, but also in alternative markets such as home movies, theatres, and movie theatres, and so on.

Real Options

An option is the possibility of making a decision in the future under pre-determined terms or a function of terms. In the capital market, for instance, if an investor holds an option to buy one share of a company for X dollars for one month, then he will exercise the option only if the price of the share during that month is higher than X.

Similarly, if a company has an option for one month to buy an inventory for $100, it will exercise the option only if, during that month, purchasing the same inventory elsewhere would be more expensive.

In any decision-making process pertaining to an investment, the company must examine whether it is creating new options for itself or rather realizing existing options and canceling others. For instance, the decision on the application of the algorithm, as explained in an earlier section on the essence of strategic planning, entailed the loss of the options for market entry in markets where the forecasted competition was strong.

Many companies in diverse industries utilize different techniques of real options in their strategic planning—in oil companies such as Mobil and Exxon, computer companies such as Apple, and industrial companies such as the aircraft manufacturer Airbus.

The importance of having options has a material effect on the value of companies in general, and of high tech companies in particular. One of the reasons for this is that decisions pertaining to investments of large amounts of capital may often be postponed until after different developments are completed or become clear. See Chapter 9 for a broader discussion of the importance of real options and their relationship to valuations.

Generally speaking, the value of an option is measured in accordance with the value of the underlying asset it is associated with, the degree of volatility of the asset during the term of the option, the current interest rate, and the investment required to exercise the option. There are various models for pricing options, but this book will discuss only the principles of such pricing.

Typically, price volatility in the target market has a positive effect on the value of options, since it raises the possibility that the value of the asset will rise during the period above the required investment. For instance, let us assume that a company has a one-year option to start manufacturing memory chips, and that the cost of production will be one dollar per unit, with a required investment of $2,000 to begin the production. Let us assume further that the company has no competitors in that market. Clearly, the decision to manufacture depends on whether potential users will be prepared to pay more than one dollar for the chip, and whether their number will justify the investment. Alternatively, if the chips are used by the company as part of a product, the company will examine if the cost of purchasing the chips from another source will cost more than to self-produce them. When will the company make the decision? If it starts manufacturing immediately, it will lose the value of waiting before starting to manufacture (for instance, until the market for the product grows bigger) that is incorporated in the option. On the other hand, it will start generating revenues from such production. These issues are analyzed by various option pricing models, some of which are discussed in Chapter 9.

Using Decision Trees for Strategic Decisions

Decision trees can dramatically facilitate the choice of the more favorable routes from among those available to the company. The decision-tree method provides a flow chart for the variety of alternatives available to the company and includes the company's projections in different scenarios. Hypothetically, every point of decision requires a separate evaluation and can be the subject of a separate assessment project. This would render the entire process impracticable, unless the number of decision points is not large, the assessment of the projects is not complicated, or accurate estimates are being used. Decision trees also enable various real options to be taken into consideration, as seen in an explanation of the real options method in Chapter 9.

For the sake of simplicity, let us assume that a startup, which had developed an innovative software tool, has raised capital and has two potential projects. The idea has already been developed, and the startup must now decide whether to penetrate the market with a large investment in production, marketing, and distribution, or to make a more moderate market-entry. In order to start producing at a high volume, the startup would need to invest $1 million, whereas a smaller capacity would require an investment of only $250,000.

The future situation of the market is unclear, and the startup estimates that the size of the market will be $150 million with a 30% probability, or $50 million with a 70% probability. If the company chooses the extensive investment, it will obtain a market share of 20% with a 50% probability, and a market share of 10% with a 50% probability. However, if the company chooses to penetrate the market cautiously, it will get a market share of 10% with a 50% probability, and a market share of 5% with a 50% probability. These two scenarios naturally reveal the correlation between the investment in entering the market and the results of such investment. Whereas no possibility is affected by the degree of penetration into the market, the different probabilities for the market shares are affected by the investment. For the sake of simplicity, we shall further assume that the company will reach its projected market share immediately and that the life span of the project is one year only.

The company forecasts that its gross profit margin will be approximately 60%. This high rate results from the fact that after the development stage, the company expects only installation costs to account for the majority of its expenses. Other than that, the company expects to incur other operating expenses of $500,000 if its entry into the market is aggressive and of $200,000 if it is modest. These differences reflect the intensive hiring of sales employees required to break into the market aggressively, which also involves higher accommodation expenses for its sales personnel.

After multiplying the projected revenues in every scenario by each of the forecasted market shares, each of the possible results is then multiplied by the gross profit margin in order to assess the gross profit in each of the four scenarios. Subsequently, the other operating costs are deducted, to calculate the forecasted operating profit at each level of investment and in each of the four possible pairs of the state of nature and the market share.

In order to choose one of the two paths, the startup must calculate its return from each of the two scenarios. The calculation is based on an examination of all possible scenarios, in accordance with the different options and the different levels of investment, and weighting the various results in accordance with the probability that they will materialize. With the larger investment scenario, the startup will have an NPV (Net Present Value), namely, the weighted average of all the different profit options according to the probabilities of their realization in excess of $5.7 million net of the investment. With the smaller investment scenario, the startup will have an NPV of approximately $3.15 million net of the investment. (See Table 3–3.)

It would appear that, in this case, the startup should clearly choose the larger investment, which is more profitable from its point of view. However, it should be noted that a startup will not always choose the route that is most profitable, both to itself and to the outside investors, if it implies an investment that would require extensive external financing for unfavorable prices that would substantially dilute the entrepreneurs' holdings (which is where conflicts between the best interests of the company and those of its entrepreneurs may come into play).

Table 3–3 Summary of NPV calculations for a given decision tree

			Large Investment	Small Investment
Required investment			$1,000,000	$250,000
Results, excluding investment:				
	(1)	High result	$150,000,000	$150,000,000
	(2)	Low result	$50,000,000	$50,000,000
	P1	Probability of high result	30%	30%
	P2	Probability of low result	70%	70%
	(a)	Large market share	20%	10%
	(b)	Small market share	10%	5%
	Pa	Probability of large market share	50%	50%
	Pb	Probability of small market share	50%	50%
Revenues:				
	(a)°(1)	Large market share and high result	$30,000,000	$15,000,000
	(a)°(2)	Large market share and low result	$10,000,000	$5,000,000
	(b)°(1)	Small market share and high result	$15,000,000	$7,500,000
	(b)°(2)	Small market share and low result	$5,000,000	$2,500,000
	GPM	Gross profit margin	60%	60%

Table 3-3 Summary of NPV calculations for a given decision tree (continued)

			Large Investment	Small Investment
Gross profit:				
	(a)*(1)*GPM	Large market share and high result	$18,000,000	$9,000,000
	(a)*(2)*GPM	Large market share and low result	$6,000,000	$3,000,000
	(b)*(1)*GPM	Small market share and high result	$9,000,000	$4,500,000
	(b)*(2)*GPM	Small market share and low result	$3,000,000	$1,500,000
	OOC	Other operating costs	$500,000	$200,000
Operating profit (OP):				
OP1=(a)*(1)*GPM-OOC		Large market share and high result	$17,500,000	$8,800,000
OP2=(a)*(2)*GPM-OOC		Large market share and low result	$5,500,000	$2,800,000
OP3=(b)*(1)*GPM-OOC		Small market share and high result	$8,500,000	$4,300,000
OP4=(b)*(2)*GPM-OOC		Small market share and low result	$2,500,000	$1,300,000
Probability table:				
	Pa*P1	Large market share and high result	15%	15%
	Pa*P2	Large market share and low result	35%	35%
	Pb*P1	Small market share and high result	15%	15%
	Pb*P2	Small market share and low result	35%	35%
		Total	100%	100%
Forecasted value:		**Required investment**	($4,000,000)	($250,000)
	Pa*P1*OP1	Large market share and high result	$2,625,000	$1,320,000
	Pa*P2*OP2	Large market share and low result	$1,925,000	$980,000
	Pb*P1*OP3	Small market share and high result	$1,275,000	$645,000
	Pb*P2*OP4	Small market share and low result	$875,000	$455,000
Net Present Value NPV			$5,700,000	$3,150,000

The guiding principle is that the results have to be calculated after every decision point and weighted according to the probability of their achievement. Since some of the decision points depend on situations that are independent of the company and some depend on decisions by management, calculations should always be made from the last decision node backward, i.e., the scenarios on each branch of the tree involving a managerial decision should be calculated first, while assuming that, given the information at that decision point, one of the branches will be chosen.

Decision trees are also helpful in examining possible reactions by competitors in the planned area of business. A correct strategic examination must be performed, one that will take into account all the main decision points and the possibility that the competition often makes the same calculations at more or less the same time. In these analyses, it is important to prepare decision trees also for the potential competitors in order to try to predict which alternatives they will choose. Clearly, the information which the company has with respect to its competitors is less accurate than the information it has about itself. However, valid conclusions may often be reached based on such partial information.

Such consideration of the competitors' reactions is vital, since without it a startup could choose investment alternatives that would appear illogical in hindsight because they did not account for potential competitors, who become quite real when the product is launched on the market. On the other hand, such analyses can explain why certain fields may appear to have no competition, although on the surface they seem profitable. In such cases, the reason could be the fear of potential contestants of the competition after the company invests in developing the market and clarifying its condition.

All of these analyses use various components of the mathematical branch called "Game Theory," but any detailed expansion of this issue lies beyond the scope of this book. The use of these tools is essential to understand the expected changes in the company's future target markets, from the points of view of both competition and the company's financial and strategic needs.

Strategic Alliances

In the course of the company's business planning (both in its early stages and as updates are made with time), the company plans in advance the most efficient way for reaching its goals. The company should take part in joint ventures or other strategic alliances if it finds that this would be a more efficient way of reaching its goals than a route in which the company independently invests the financial and human resources required to reach these goals. Alternatively, it should do so if it concludes that it will be unable to reach such goals independently. As an alternative to acting independently or jointly with another entity, the company can buy services from outsiders (otherwise known as outsourcing). This section will briefly examine when the company should opt for a strategic alliance and the best way of implementing it. This discussion is separate from that on mergers and acquisitions, an alternative to strategic alliances (see Part V), and from the discussion in Chapter 11 of the functions of strategic investors in the company.

The Advantages of Strategic Alliances

Many startups find that cooperating with stronger and better known companies can help them break into the market faster and secure less costly financing than would otherwise have been available to them.

In the past, joint ventures focused on the representation of companies in various countries or geographic areas. In the past decades, the phenomenon of joint ventures for pre-defined activities has become more prevalent. An alliance can impart to the company a relative advantage in size or an ability to learn the field faster, or provide a complement to areas in which it is lacking (for instance, an alliance between a startup with an advantage in development and production with a company with proven marketing skills). When the joint venture is performed in a formal manner, by establishing a separate legal entity for it (also known as the joint venture), it is similar in nature to a partial acquisition in consideration for shares (see Part V for merger and acquisition transactions). This is because the transaction creates an entity that combines the relative advantages of both parties and ties their futures together, at least with respect to the field in question.

The Disadvantages of Strategic Alliances

Alliances are costly, not only due to cash leaving the company's hands, but rather due to returns from which it could be denied. First, joint ventures involve the investment of managerial time resources in establishing the venture, managing it, and resolving possible conflicts of interest between the partners over the functioning of the venture. Even when a proper set of contracts, incentive schemes, and various transfer prices from the partners to the joint venture resolve most conflicts, almost no joint venture manages to entirely avoid conflicts between its respective parties.

Moreover, alliances can create indirect costs by blocking the possibility of cooperating with competing companies, thus possibly even denying the company various financing options. For instance, an alliance with Ericsson in the area of cellular communications could reduce the likelihood of contracts with Nokia, thereby putting the company at risk that if Ericsson is weakened, so will be all the companies that depend upon it.

Joint ventures also expose the company to its partners, and the unique technologies that it has are sometimes revealed to its partner company, which could later become a competitor or could utilize the fruits of the venture or the know-how better than the startup itself. In addition, strategic partners may often lead the company in directions that serve the partner company better than they do the company itself.

Although a material part of the costs of joint ventures may be forecasted during the negotiations for its establishment, in many cases the balance of power between the parties changes during the course of the venture's life, and the parties to it may have a change of mind. For instance, many joint ventures that were signed before the stock market crises of 2001–2002 between public companies and startups never materialized due to the drop in the stock prices of some such public companies. The fact that some of the private companies had meanwhile raised capital and actually had become stronger than the public companies, utterly changed the balance of power. Likewise, the non-raising of capital by the startup could motivate the public company to try to renegotiate the terms of the venture, while taking advantage of the startup's weakness. A change in the competitive environment in the field could also affect the alternative cost of the venture. For instance, if Nokia were to increase its share in the cellular market, then the alternative cost of the venture with Ericsson (namely, the economic value of the reduced opportunity to do business with Nokia) would be augmented over time.

Types of Strategic Alliances

In strategic alliances, at least two entities agree to combine economic resources—either financial resources, know-how, or material assets—in a contractual framework in order to achieve pre-defined strategic objectives. A simple arrangement, to be discussed in Chapter 5, is the granting of a license to use technology, within which one company provides the know-how and another company pays royalties in consideration for the know-how, either in the form of equity or cash, in amounts that may be conditioned upon performance or be fixed in advance.

Other setups combine in a single agreement an investment by one of the companies in the other, with the other company allotting equity in consideration for the investment, and providing know-how or products to be incorporated into the investing company's manufacture, production, marketing, or development systems. In such setups, it is often hard to evaluate each of the various individual components of the transaction. Such distinction is essential for the companies' financial statements, since many transactions combine capital components (i.e., an investment) with components in the income statements. For example, a transaction in which Amazon (the world's largest online bookstore) invested in drugstore.com (an online pharmacy) in consideration for equity, and drugstore.com bought advertising space on Amazon, raised the issue of the pricing of the different components of the transaction. In such a case, Amazon could ultimately gain more cash than it invested, while recording advertising revenues higher than its investment and recording an investment of the cash it put into the transaction. The Securities and Exchange Commission (SEC) often examines the manner of recording of such transactions and in many cases requires clarifications, and even changes to the way such transactions were originally recorded.

Arrangements that include components of an investment in equity have been highly popular in recent years and usually produce long-term alliances. In many cases, a new entity is created in which the companies invest money and know-how. For example, FDC, one of the largest companies in the world for money transfer services, established a new company for Internet-based payment systems, together with the investment bank Goldman Sachs and the venture capital fund General Atlantic, for a total investment in excess of one billion dollars. A main component of FDC's investment was its share in ventures in which it had invested beforehand. Such transactions are common when one of the parties to the transaction is not interested in diluting a stable and profitable company, but is interested in allotting shares in a new activity in which it invested, which could arouse investors' enthusiasm.

Cooperation arrangements bestow on both parties many of the advantages involved in mergers and acquisitions, without the need to bear the high premium entailed by a change of ownership. Such arrangements further provide the option to choose the essential components in the other party to the transaction, without the need to acquire and then sell the segments that are of no interest to the acquiring company. Furthermore, strategic alliances typically do not require the approval of the company's shareholders, and are generally welcomed by capital markets more than are acquisitions.

Various research has demonstrated that joint ventures are more successful when the management cultures of the partners are compatible and when the senior management of the companies is committed to them. In many cases, one of the parties invests more money if the other party agrees to run the business or, alternatively, transfers know-how to the business. In other cases, the partners take equal shares in the ownership but not in the management, and both parties have the right to veto various material resolutions, such as large transactions, the acquisition or sale of assets, and so forth.

Financial Reporting

An ownership interest in a joint venture that is formed as an entity is considered an investment in another company for reporting purposes. In other words, the principles of the cost method, of the equity method, and of consolidation are applicable here, too (see the earlier section in this chapter on reporting holdings in other companies and consolidation of statements). However, in many joint ventures the company uses the equity method to reflect its investment even when its holdings are smaller than 20%, since in most cases each of the companies has a material impact on the management of the venture.

There could be material timing differences between the financial reporting and the reporting for tax purposes, since the tax reporting will often be made according to the cost method, whereas the financial reporting will be made according to the equity method.

Antitrust Considerations

Like mergers and acquisitions, transactions that could affect competition in the market are subject to the scrutiny of the antitrust authorities. The examinations that are made are similar to those made in cases of mergers or acquisitions (see Part V). In recent years, many alliances have been exposed to scrutiny by the authorities. For instance, a joint venture of some large automobile manufacturers underwent intense scrutiny to examine its effect on the suppliers of these companies. As a result of the creation of many e-commerce platforms in recent years, various rules of reporting to the authorities were fixed for the establishment of such platforms.

The Business Plan

Introduction

The business plan is the document in which the company's business planning is summarized. Usually, the purpose of the plan is to describe the company and its products, while specifying the company's strategy and vision, as well as its operating, financing, and marketing plans. An additional purpose of the business plan is to serve as a tool for presenting the company to investors. This objective of the business plan attracted much attention for many years, but has lost favor during the "Internet bubble" years. However, it is highly important to understand that a primary reason for the loss of faith in business plans is the fact that business plans that were prepared by entrepreneurs were based on fixed templates and were not given the proper attention by the entrepreneurs. Such poor plans included extensive use of slogans and of unfounded projections. Above all else, they exposed the unprofessionalism of the entrepreneurs of such companies, and in many situations deterred investors, rather than recruiting them.

When a business plan is prepared properly, it can serve as the company's road map, showing the way from its establishment to its goals. In other words, this document is supposed to concisely reflect profound strategic thinking, while referring to both quantitative and qualitative data.

Every venture needs to identify a market with a demand and a solution for such demand. In other words, it must identify the opportunity, the way of realizing it, and the plan for maximizing the company's value. In addition, it must identify the way in which investors will both regain their investment and make as large a profit as possible.

Before preparing the business plan, and as described previously in this chapter, the company and its advisors need to gather and analyze information on the business environment, including the demand for the product, the market potential, customer characteristics, competition, and so on. Technically, it is possible to use software that facilitates the process by offering a format and drafting the plan, but it is important to understand that such software cannot substitute for in-depth investigations of the market demands and financial forecasts of the success of the product. The added value of such software is doubtful, since in many cases it lures the user into the format and slogan trap which, as mentioned above, deters most investors. Worse still, such formats can lead entrepreneurs to make erroneous managerial decisions with respect to the allotment of resources.

Pre-seed companies usually prefer to prepare a summary as a substitute for a full-fledged business plan. Such a summary should, however, refer as fully as possible to the competition on the market and should contain the main components of the complete business plan. In the early stages, particularly in high tech companies, entrepreneurs obviously lack a full picture of the future competitive situation of the market, as they do an understanding of the possibilities of pricing the company's products and services. However, it is always important to try to assess such parameters, since they must be used when investment decisions are to be made.

Business plans are written by startups for internal and external needs, but also by existing companies for the purpose of project financing. The most significant difference between the business plan of a startup and the business plan of an existing company is the fact that an existing and active company already has a setup of products, management and organization, and business results. Forecasts based on existing data and operations can naturally be more accurate. In order to overcome this tricky starting point, a startup is required to perform research and forecasts that will be as thorough as possible. Unfounded optimistic forecasts will drive investors to apply a higher discount rate to the forecasts, and cut the forecasts down in their calculations (see Chapter 9 for a discussion of the use of the discount rate for the purpose of valuation). Furthermore, the use of unfounded forecasts could indicate a lack of professionalism or credibility by the entrepreneurs.

The Structure of a Business Plan

The structure of the business plan is not fixed, but its main points are listed below. Attempts to write a plan according to a fixed format will reduce the value of the plan, since adjustments for the individual needs of each company will always be required. Beyond the internal considerations, one of the guiding considerations is the need to include within the business plan sufficient level of details to allow potential investors and strategic partners to make informed use of the plan for their investment decision. In addition, it is important to specify the assumptions underlying the significant data in the plan and the timeframes for the achievement of targets during the development and market penetration stages.

Executive Summary

The executive summary provides a brief review of the idea. Most executive summaries include the following items:

- **General description**—The business/field of activity, the product and the company
- **Business goals**—A statement of mission and the company's objectives
- **Product description**—A description of the product, the demand for the product, and its advantage over other products
- **Business opportunity**—The target market, the business opportunity, and the business model to benefit from it, including the exit strategy for investors
- **The team**—A brief description of the leading team and its skills
- **Current status**—The development stage, intellectual property protection such as patents, and so on.
- **Summary of financial projections**—Revenue, net profit, cash flow, and projected return in up to the next five years

- **Financial resource requirements**—Previous rounds of investments and what the company aims to raise in the current and planned rounds, as well as the items toward which the budgets will be allocated

Business Plan Headers

- **Company profile**—This provides a description of the company and of its activities from its establishment to the present day.
- **Market and competition analysis**—This is a general description of the market in which the company operates and a detailed description of its competitors. An in-depth analysis of obvious information that is common knowledge (for instance, that the number of computer users is expected to grow in the coming years) should be avoided. It is better, rather, to focus on a detailed analysis of the products or services that exist in the market and/or are expected to compete with the company and its products. The market description will include a description of the size of the market and the trends within it (both technological and financial), the market segmentation, the problems that exist in the market, the main competitors, obstacles to entering the market, and potential customers. This section of the business plan should include the results of detailed primary and secondary research conducted by the company with respect to the demand for its products. In addition, this section usually includes an analysis of the profitability of the industry and of legal and regulatory restrictions imposed in the field.
- **Vision and strategy**—In this part, the company should specify its vision and its strategy for realizing it.
- **Product or service description**—This part focuses on the solution proposed by the company, including a detailed description of the product and the technology, the company's intellectual property, competing products, and why the product is superior to them. The competitive advantage of the product proposed by the company over existing and potential competing products is presented in this part.
- **Development plan**—This part describes the development process, the current development status of each product and service, and the scope of the development team and budget.
- **Operating plan**—This part describes the company's organizational structure, such as the structure of the production setup, the costs of labor and materials, logistics and service, and a plan for acquiring the means of production and computers.
- **Marketing plan**—In this part, the company needs to specify, among other things, its objectives with respect to each segment of the target markets, the existing and planned marketing channels, the pricing of the products for

distributors and the structure of their remuneration, the advertising plan, and the incentives to be given to customers.
- **Management and ownership**—This part describes the management team, including brief resumés of the senior management. Management is probably the most material element in the investment decisions made by investors: Investors prefer to invest in a mediocre idea that is implemented by an excellent team rather than invest in an excellent idea that is not backed by the necessary high quality management. The structure of ownership of the company will also be described in this part.
- **Financial forecasting**—The forecasts need to be accompanied by full and detailed statements, and will usually include the projected operating budget (research and development, operations, general and administrative expenses, marketing), projected financial statements, economic analyses (return on equity, return on investment, and so on), and sensitivity analyses (the projected effect of any change in the various parameters on the forecasted business results). It is customary to include in the plan financial forecasts for a period of three to five years, with a quarterly or even monthly specification of the first years of the forecast. Many investors are deterred by assumptions that are not sufficiently supported, and consequently treat the entire plan with reserve. For this reason, many entrepreneurs avoid including detailed forecasts in investment rounds, especially in the early stages. However, even if such forecasts are not included in the plan, it is important that detailed estimates be available to the company and to the investors, upon request, so that decisions with respect to development and investments in various alternative schemes can be made in an informed manner.
- **Appendices**—Here will be found a specification of the expenses, table of comparison to competitors, full executives bios, letters from customers, and so on.

The order in which items are presented in the business plan and the degree to which various issues are emphasized change from one company to another in accordance with its field, innovativeness (for instance, a more detailed explanation of the product, as opposed to an emphasis on the description of the competitors), current status, and so on.

4

Employee Recruitment and Compensation

INTRODUCTION

The most important resource available to an emerging company is its human capital. Consequently, many managerial resources are dedicated to the recruitment of manpower. In startups that are constantly growing, the process of finding and recruiting employees is often performed under the pressures of tight schedules and uncertainty with respect to the company's future needs. In many cases, the company's organizational structure is still unclear and recruitment decisions are made on the basis of assumptions about manpower needs that are likely to change later on. Many managers assume that an excellent worker could have a role in the company even if his or her actual functions will be different from those designated for them at the time of recruitment.

The issue of compensating managers and employees is material, and becomes even more important in startups: How can good managers and employees, who are so essential to the startup's success, be compensated, while preserving the company's funds as much as possible? How can managers be encouraged to identify with the investors' objectives in both good and bad times? How can a comfortable family atmosphere be created, yet employees terminated when necessary? All of these are issues confronted by companies in all areas and managers in all companies. In startups, however, they are intensified. The timetables and the pressures, the scarcity of resources, and the uncertainty—all of these factors come together in startups and demand a management that will be excellent and unique, yet compensated in a manner appropriate for a company with no revenues, and certainly no profits.

This chapter reviews the main milestones in the recruitment process and provides a comprehensive overview of the components of compensation in high tech companies.

Employee Recruiting

Job Descriptions and Requirements

Many positions naturally demand certain requirements with respect to education, experience, and qualifications. For instance, it is customary for CFOs (Chief Financial Officers) to be qualified in accounting and finance and usually to have an MBA. However, in many cases, companies define prerequisites that are not essential to the nature of the position, but are rather the result of norms. In practice, many companies find that relevant experience, if it is accompanied by profound professional knowledge, may be preferable to this or to another degree in the relevant field. In any event, it is customary for companies to prepare job descriptions that are used to find the appropriate employees.

Extensive and significant experience is accumulated by working in the industry, not necessarily in the same position designated for the employee. A recruiter should always consider how important is the prospective employee's prior exposure to the particular industry in which the company operates, in comparison to his or her acquisition of work methods and managerial experience. For example, many consumer-oriented technology companies recruit senior employees from the institutional system of non-technology-based consumer products since, for many positions, the experience acquired by such employees in their previous jobs, as well as the work methods they learned and developed there over the years, could materially facilitate the establishment of an ordered managerial system—including processes such as marketing strategy and research—in the new organization. An example from April 2001 is the recruitment of the former CEO of the media company Universal Studios to manage Yahoo.

The personality and abilities of the candidate are naturally of material importance. If the candidate is being considered for a senior executive position, it is important to assess his or her decision-making and analytical abilities, creativity in problem-solving, and personality. A manager's leadership and interpersonal communication skills are priceless from the organization's point of view. Obviously, the composition of the necessary qualities changes from one position to another, and in many positions, leadership skills are less essential.

Headhunter services specialize in identifying many personal qualities in order to best match the employees to the right positions and companies. Such companies perform their initial screening mainly on the basis of prior relevant managerial experience (if the candidate is considered for an executive position), and the company interviews the employee later.

However, irrespective of the particular qualities required for each position, the employee's degree of motivation is essential for his or her performance. Motivation is composed of several elements, some of which depend on fixed factors, such as the amount of drive an employee has, and some depend on specific factors, such as the degree of interest the employee has in the position offered to him or her or in the company.

Finding and Screening Employees

There is a shortage of high-quality manpower in the world of high tech, and companies therefore compete vigorously for talented workers. Companies which specialize in recruitment have become a common phenomenon in recent decades in the United States. The high demand for highly skilled workers, managers in particular, resulted, in certain cases, in headhunters who recruit senior executives receiving not only commissions based on the annual salary of the recruited executives, but also receiving options based on the options awarded to the employee being recruited. The justification for this is economic—options constitute part of the compensation and provide a certain substitute for a salary.

In addition, many organizations offer monetary compensation to employees who introduce new employees to the company. Companies find that, in many cases, the mechanism by which the company's employees recruit personnel, besides being economically efficient, brings to the company more compatible employees in comparison to other alternatives (since the recruiting employees are more aware of the company's needs than any external body). In addition, the degree of loyalty of such recruited employees is higher, since they are usually brought to the company by their friends, who are the company's best advocates.

A traditional source of employees is classified ads published in newspapers. High tech classified ads have become a channel in which companies invest a fair portion of their advertising and recruitment budgets. In the case of private companies, a high correlation has been found between the number of positive mentions made of a company in the media (in such contexts as capital-raising, large contracts, and so forth) and the company's ability to recruit employees with better skills and at a lower cost, in comparison to other companies. In addition, companies which are backed by reputable investors and are advised by respected consultants find it easier to recruit employees. The reasons for this are clear—the process of employee screening is two-way, and it is important for employees to choose an organization that can provide them with stability and growth.

Once appropriate candidates are found, the company starts to interview them. Obviously, the interviewer's rank should correspond to the importance of the position. It should be kept in mind that employees are highly influenced by the level of management they perceive, as reflected in job interviews. In addition, clarifying in advance the possible promotion tracks is very valuable to potential employees. However, descriptions of possible promotion tracks are rarely incorporated into the employment contracts. Many companies require candidates (especially candidates lacking rich relevant experience) to undergo various compatibility tests, which may include psychological and graphological tests.

Employee Compensation in the Technology Segments

Introduction

One of the main objectives of companies in general, and startups in particular, is to navigate the company to a path of rapid growth that will enhance its profits and establish its financial stability. Since the development of products is based primarily on the human factor, the recruitment of talented employees and enhancing their bonding with the company are crucial elements on the road to the company's success. As in any field, companies, including startups, also seek to compensate their employees in order to bring out the best in them: industriousness, identification, loyalty, etc. The special nature of startups in the high tech industry sheds light on the unique trend created over the years to compensate employees in a different manner from that customary in other industries. In order to understand the different nature of such compensation, it is necessary to understand the unique environment in which startups operate, which creates different emphases in the compensation structure:

- Startups are usually not as cash-affluent as are established companies, and therefore find it hard to compensate managers at the levels customary in established companies. They make up for this by the generous granting of options in the company. Such options could turn out to be highly valuable if they succeed—maybe even more so than in established companies. Furthermore, by linking the remuneration with a salary and options that are vested over a period of time, the companies associate their success with the employee's remuneration to one degree or another, thus increasing his or her involvement and identification with the company.
- High tech employees are relatively well-educated and have high expectations. Therefore, it is natural for startups to give their employees generous social benefits and other indirect benefits, often much more than in more mature companies.

Methods of Employee Compensation

The forms of compensation are numerous and diverse. The principal ones are:

- **Cash**—This includes salaries, bonuses, social benefits, managers' insurance, and pension funds.
- **Stocks and options**—This is the customary form of compensation in growing companies, as discussed in further detail below.
- **Various benefits**—These include flexible hours, partial financing of tuition, participation in the cost of kindergartens and summer camps for children,

and often even the organization and management of such kindergartens and summer camps. In addition, most companies organize company outings and various services for employees such as messenger services and in-house gyms to save them from daily hassles. In many cases, the direct value of the benefits to the employees is higher than their cost to the employer.

Managers' insurance, pension funds allocations, and budgetary pension funds are customary components of employee compensation packages. Clearly, every such plan needs to be adapted to the worker's individual level of income, education, and age, as well as to the company's business condition. Such plans usually include the following components: life insurance (payment in case of the insured's death), compensation for occupational disability, pension annuities, and health insurance.

The contributions of employers and employees to pension funds are governed by regulations. Such regulations limit the amount of contributions employers can make without imposing a tax liability on the employees. In the United States, the vast majority of contributions defer the payment of the tax, but cannot provide a full tax exemption.

- **Non-monetary benefits**—These include promotions, improved work environments, and commendations.

Considerations in Planning Compensation Packages

In recent years, compensation packages have included many components which employers and employees need to take into consideration. Many startups grapple for a long time with the structure of the salary they will offer employees. Generally speaking, compensation is constructed of three components: a fixed salary, short-term variable compensation, and long-term compensation.

- **Salary**—The first element includes the employee's contractual salary and is independent of other factors. In most cases, the fixed salary includes two elements: the base pay, on which social benefits are paid, and the element of complementary salary, for which social benefits may not be paid (for instance, global overtime pay).
- **Variable compensation**—The second element is constructed of remuneration that is related to two elements: the amount of work invested by an employee (for instance, overtime pay) and the achievement of goals. The manner of calculation of the payment may be agreed upon in advance and may be included in the employment or other contract, or it may be concealed from the employee, who would be informed only of the amount of the compensation and not of how it was reached.

  Such bonuses may be affected by the volume of sales or production, customer satisfaction, etc. Obviously, the higher the employee's influence on the business results of the company or on the business unit, the more intimately will the employer want to tie the employee's compensation to the results. In other words, the ratio of the variable compensation to the fixed pay will be higher. Various components of the bonus may be based on the performance of the division or on the performance of the company as a whole. Mostly, it will be based on a combination of the performance of the company and the performance of the business unit (for a discussion on how to determine such a combination, see the later section on performance-based compensation).

In investment banks, for example, the annual bonus that is based on the results of the business unit may be up to ten times higher than the fixed-pay component. In high tech companies, it is not uncommon to find sales personnel whose sales commission is up to three times that of their base pay. In certain cases, the variable compensation is also given in the form of long-term compensation, as specified below. For example, the customary range for bonuses for CEOs and VPs in high tech companies can reach 50% of the total pay.

- **Long-term compensation**—The long-term compensation components are based primarily on payment in shares or in options, but may also include monetary compensation, as described below.

A correct balance between fixed pay, short-term variable compensation, and long-term compensation involves an analysis of the organization's overall objectives and depends on the status of salaries in the relevant field of activity and the startup's organizational structure. In the past, many startups belittled the importance of the structure of compensation. Now, many use outside advisors to plan the structure of their employees' compensation. For instance, complex issues arise when the startup is part of a large organization and some of its employees move to it from the larger organization. Other complex issues arise when the employees of the organization are located in different countries, and the comparison of the employees' salaries has to take into account differences in taxation and the cost of living.

Another important element in determining the compensation is matching the alternative compensation that the employee could receive elsewhere. Obviously, it is difficult to accurately assess the alternatives available to an employee, but they can be estimated by examining the compensation given to employees holding similar positions with comparable experience in similar companies. Accurate data on compensation are usually inaccessible other than through various research companies. In recent years, many databases have begun supplying free information via the Internet as a means of promoting the sale of their services. Both the employee and the company can obtain vast information about the customary pay in the market at any given time. However, the data often do not include details of the value of the option packages awarded to employees, since such details involve a valuation of the companies.

Granting Options to Employees

Introduction

In recent years, option rewarding has become an important component in compensation packages. Many companies establish their positions among other high tech companies from the point of view of employee recruitment by structuring generous and promising packages for their employees. Due to the high demand for employees in recent years, many companies offer to remunerate employees who bring new employees to the company, and in many cases this incentive too takes the form of options.

Currently, a significant proportion of employees in almost every high tech company holds options, and almost every company has a stock option plan for the company's employees and consultants, typically in the range of 20–30% of shareholders' equity. This form of compensation increases the alignment of interests between the employee and the company and creates a long-term bond between the employee and the company, the length of which depends on the number and vesting periods of the options. In addition, the allotment of options enables the company to save precious cash that is needed for the company's current operations.

On the downside, the effect which a decline in the price of the shares has on the morale of the employees and their loyalty to the company could be mentioned (see below for further discussion of this issue), and the dilution to other shareholders' holdings.

Stock Options Defined

A stock option enables employees to purchase shares of a given class in consideration for a pre-determined amount referred to as the exercise price. The employees profit from a rise in the price of the shares, since the exercise price is pre-determined, but they have not yet paid for the shares. Obviously, options already have an economic value when they are allotted, since they award employees the right to buy shares for a fixed exercise price, but they are not committed to such payment unless they choose to exercise them. The right to exercise options is tied to a contract and the vesting period changes from one company to another. However, a customary option vesting period is four years, with 25% of the options vesting at the end of the first year and approximately one quarter of the options of each subsequent year vesting at the end of every quarter thereafter. Many employment contracts provide for accelerated vesting if the company is bought out by another company. Once the options have vested, employees may exercise them over a period of several years, in accordance with the terms of the option.

Example: An employee is allotted 100,000 options for an exercise price of $1 per share. The vesting period of the options is four years. Two years later, the company goes public and the stock price is $20 per share. At that time, the employee can exercise one half of the options and sell them on the stock exchange (subject to the lock-up provisions of the prospectus and the securities regulations of the exchange in which the shares are listed). Let us assume that the employee exercises and sells all of his or her 50,000 vested options. He or she pays the company $50,000 and receives $1 million when selling the stocks (before commissions and taxes).

In many cases, the company or a trustee on its behalf performs these actions on behalf of the employees and transfers the money to them after withholding the required amount of tax. The terms of the options and the use of trustees have a significant impact on the tax consequences, as discussed in a later section of this chapter.

Advantages and Disadvantages in the Granting of Options

The granting of stock options in a company enables the employees to become part of the group of owners of the company. It is an exceptional instrument which creates loyalty and identification with the company's goals (as an owner), encourages employees to stay with the company for a long period of time (in accordance with the vesting period of the options), motivates excellence (with the aim of helping to enhance the company's profits), and all with a low cash flow. From the company's point of view, the advantages of granting options rather than shares lie mainly in the fact that unexercised options entail no voting rights or a right to dividends, and in the fact that if the employee resigns before the end of the vesting period, he or she typically forfeits his or her right to this benefit. A distribution of shares creates a reduction of capital that requires special legal and accounting treatment, whereas when options are distributed and the employee does not want to receive (or exercise) them, they expire and "disappear."

On the other hand, there are also problems in granting stock options to employees. For instance, a decline in the value of the options due to daily market fluctuations may lower the employees' motivation. In addition, the decision of who will be compensated may cause problems with non-compensated employees (including good middle management). In practice, almost all companies now grant options to all employees in managerial positions, and it is not uncommon to see companies in which all employees, junior and senior, receive options. In addition, some restrictions are imposed by the securities laws on the distribution of securities to employees, and the distribution of options or other securities to employees involves a registration procedure or the receipt of a special exemption. Furthermore, the investors in the company might object to the dilution in their holdings in the company that is associated with the exercise of these options.

Various studies have recently cast doubt on the effectiveness of compensation in the form of shares and options, as is offered today. From the employee's point of view, the allotment of options provides a chance to profit, but the employee and the company perceive differently the risk involved in holding options instead of cash. In practice, if we compare an actual valuation of employee stock options, with an estimate of the value of the options as perceived by employees, it appears that employees perceive the value of options to be approximately one-half that perceived by neutral valuation. The researchers Murphy and Hall, for instance, describe the allotment of options in public companies as an expensive and inefficient way of compensating employees. One of their reasons corresponds to the principle described in Chapter 9 which discusses valuations: Most of the managers' capital (both financial and human) is concentrated in the company they manage. Therefore, the portfolio of such managers is not well-diversified and, when evaluating the options allotted to them, they use a higher discount rate. Consequently, as a substitute for other compensation, they will require a larger number of options and shares than that called for by an evaluation made by the other investors in the company (by using models for the evaluation of options, discussed later in the section on stock option plans).

An alternative method for achieving the same targets—bonding the employee with the company for a long period of time and aligning the interests of the company and the employee—is a distribution of restricted shares within the framework of the employee's compensation package. These are shares that, like options, cannot be sold until after a certain vesting period, and enable employees to purchase a certain number of shares in each period for a price lower than the current market price. Since shares are less volatile than options, employees perceive them as being less risky and they are consequently cheaper to the company as a means of remuneration, although their economic nature is similar to that of options.

Stock Option Plans

The importance of the correct structuring of the stock option plan within the overall setup of employee and manager compensation cannot be overrated. An increasing number of companies add various components at the time of planning the options in order to best realize the organization's objectives. It is important to note that almost any element of compensation reached by structuring options may also be constructed by a combination of a salary and bonuses. When comparing compensation plans, one must examine all of their components and the relationships between them, as is presented later in the section on methods of employee compensation. As a simple illustration, a cash bonus that cannot be redeemed for a fixed period of time, but is based on changes in the price of the share, is similar in nature to options. This type of compensation is indeed nicknamed as "phantom stock."

- **Approval of stock option plans**—In most cases, options are distributed pursuant to a stock option plan (although they may also be distributed without any such plan). A general stock option plan is usually approved by the Board of Directors, and the managers are authorized to decide on an allotment of the options to the employees. In certain cases, the CEO retains the authority to set specific terms such as the vesting period of the options and the exercise price.
- **Exercise price**—The options are usually allotted with a fixed exercise price which is identical or below the price of the share at the time of allotment of the employment contact signing. When there are various classes of shares, options may be awarded with an exercise price that is lower than the price of

the shares in the last investment round, since employees are usually awarded options to buy shares that are inferior to investors' shares from the points of view of distribution at the time of the company's dissolution and their voting power. Therefore, it is logical that their price will be lower than the price of new shares allotted to investors. However, in various companies, particularly publicly traded ones, the exercise price of options is updated according to an appropriate stock index. The goal is to create an incentive to outperform similar companies in the field. The choice of shares used as a benchmark for the update is problematic, and it is usually made by the company's compensation committee, with the aid of outside advisors. In certain plans, the exercise price is updated with the rise in the price of the share, while others set a fixed exercise price. It is important to remember that options plans whose exercise price is constantly being updated could annoy the managers and increase the likelihood of their departure during long periods of underperformance, as the benchmark is rarely updated downward.

- **The number of options**—It is usually customary to allot a fixed number of options for each period of service. Alternatively, options can be allotted concurrently with the signing of the initial contract, yet be vested only after predefined periods of service. In practice, if the price of the share rises, the employee profits not only from the rise in the price of the options that were allotted and have been vested, but also from the value of any options not yet vested.

    Another customary plan is to award options annually at a certain pre-fixed value. For instance, every quarter over a period of four years, a manager will be issued options worth $100,000, with the value being determined every quarter separately. Thus, if the value of the company rises during that time, the number of allotted options will decrease. Such compensation naturally gives rise to the problem that as long as he or she is still receiving options, a manager who can influence the company's market value could have interests that are inconsistent with the best interests of the company. On the other hand, such plans allow the company to limit the cost of the managers they recruit. In addition, this method enables companies to periodically adjust the value of the options they award in accordance with what is customary in the market at that time.

- **Employee departure**—An employee who leaves the company is usually entitled only to the options vested up to the time of his or her departure from the company, although he or she might be entitled to exercise the vested options for a few months after the departure. Stock option plans often provide for a forfeiture of rights in the case of a criminal offense, or, alternatively, for a right to additional options even after termination of the employment relationship.

- **Restrictions on the exercise of options**—When a company is publicly traded, various regulations may apply to option holders with respect to the exercise of the options. Such regulations may result from legislation in the country in which the shares are listed or the company is registered, or from various managerial decisions designed to restrict the legal exposure of the company and its managers. For instance, many companies prohibit their employees from exercising options and selling shares at any time other than shortly after the publication of the company's statements, in order to prevent any allegations of insider trading by officers.

Valuation of Options

Employee stock options are similar in nature to call options. They award the right to buy an asset (in this case, the share), for a predetermined term (determined either as a fixed amount or calculated by using a formula). As mentioned above, options are often granted at an exercise price that is similar to the price of the share at the time the option is awarded. The transfer of the options to others is almost always restricted, they cannot be sold to third parties, and they must be exercised within certain time frames, usually less than ten years from the date of the grant. They are usually subject to a long vesting period, and in most cases are not protected against dilution resulting from the allotment of shares to different investors. A detailed discussion of the pricing of options lies beyond the scope of this book, but this subsection will review the fundamental principles of option valuation.

The customary model for option valuation is the Binomial Model, of which the Black and Scholes model is one version. This model, which was originally developed to price traded stock options that were not allotted by the company, provides in principle a good yardstick for valuating options, and its formula may be adjusted to account for the various terms of the options. In the case of employee stock options, the value of the options is substantially lower than that produced by the model without adjustments, due to the multitude of limitations imposed on them, mostly related to limitations on their transferability. According to various estimates, their value is on average less than one-half that produced by the Black-Scholes model.

The model prices the value of options on the basis of the following elements: the price of the share at the time of allotment, the risk-free interest rate at that time, the life span of the option (namely, the period in which the options may be exercised), the share's volatility (in the case of a closely held company, the data of similar listed companies are used after adjusting for the lower liquidity of the shares) and the dividend yield of the shares.

Paradoxically, the higher the share's volatility, the higher the value of the option. The reason for this is that the option holder will exercise it only if the price of the share is higher than the exercise price. Consequently, a higher volatility that may translate into a higher price per share (or a lower price per share, although this eventuality is irrelevant to the exercise of the option) increases the range of profits to the option holder. Obviously, this is not to say that the value of the option is not affected by a decline in the price of the share—the value of options drops faster than the price of the share when the latter declines.

In order to get a general idea of the value of options, let us look, for example, at an option that is exercisable over a period of ten years, with an exercise price identical to the price of the share at the time of awarding of the option. The annual share volatility is assumed to be 30% (which is more than the average volatility of large American companies, but is similar to a typical volatility of shares of established high tech companies) and no dividend yield. In such a case, the value of the option would be approximately 55% of the current value of the share.

The dividend yield has a dramatic impact on option holders since they are usually not compensated for dividend distributions, which signify the transfer of financial resources from the company to its other shareholders. Startups usually do not pay dividends, and therefore the significance of dividend payments is lower.

Responses to a Fall in Stock Values

As mentioned above, options became a material component of many compensation packages. Consequently, when stock prices fell, particularly in the second half of the year 2000 and during 2001, the value of such options declined dramatically. A plunge in stock prices has a severe effect on employee morale and on their loyalty to the company, since there is no point in waiting for an option to vest and become exercisable if the exercise price is higher than the market price of the share. In the past, companies in such situations have repriced the exercise price of the options, for instance, by issuing additional options with lower exercise prices to revive the motivational power of the options. This was done by the computer company Apple, the software company Netscape, and the electronic bank E-Trade. However, since the repricing of options infuriates investors in public companies, only a small portion of companies whose shares collapse indeed reprice their options. Repricing may cause severe accounting problems. The current rules require that if the exercise price of an option is amended downward, any upward change in the price of the share after the repricing be recorded as an expense in the financial statements. This has resulted in a smaller occurrence of repricing in the latest crisis compared to the scope of the phenomenon in the past. An alternative is for the company to cancel the exiting options and issue new options after more than six months, based on the prevailing market price at that point. Reporting rules do not customarily require the recording of the repricing value as an expense, since, in the interim, employees are exposed to potential changes in market prices.

Accounting Aspects of the Distribution of Options

The following discussion of financial reporting will be made according to U.S. Generally Accepted Accounting Principles (GAAP). In principle, under the current rules, if the price of exercise of the option is at least equal to the price of the shares at the time of awarding the options, then the cost of the options need not be recorded as an expense in the financial statements. A passionate and lengthy discussion has been conducted in recent years between high tech companies and the authorities with respect to a modification of the financial reporting rules governing the allotment of shares and options to employees. On the one hand, such compensation is clearly a substitute to a cash payment and is therefore justifiably recordable as an expense. On the other hand, the valuation of options is complicated and subject to various assumptions with respect to the company's operating data (such as the share's volatility) and the effect of various circumstances on the value of the option (such as restrictions on the transferability of options to third parties, restrictions on the exercise of options, and their inferior position compared to ordinary shares with respect to dividend distributions and voting rights).

Companies that choose not to report options as an expense are still required to report the value of the options while specifying the assumptions underlying such valuation. In addition, it should be noted that even if the company does not record the cost of the options as an expense in its statements, the per-share profit data under full dilution is still affected by the number of allotted options.

Issuance of Options Shortly before an IPO

As mentioned above, when a company is not publicly traded, options are often issued for classes of shares that are inferior to those of institutional investors from the points of view of voting rights, dividend distributions, and rights upon dissolution. Since the value of these shares is lower, there is usually no requirement that an expense be recorded for the difference between the exercise price of the options and the per-share price to investors in the most recent investment round. In addition, when the options are allotted long enough before an IPO, generally one year earlier, there is little chance that the difference between the price of the share in such an investment round and the exercise price will require the recording of an expense and result in a tax liability for the employees, i.e., that it be denied the preferred tax status of approved ISOs (Incentive Stock Options). As a rule, companies exercise more caution in awarding options as they near the date of an IPO. The "rule of thumb" is an allotment discount range of up to 25% of the IPO price for options allotted in the quarter immediately preceding the IPO, and approximately 75% when they are allotted at least three quarters before the IPO.

The Amount of Capital Held by Employees and Other Officers

An examination of private startups in the United States reveals that companies which raised more than $5 million usually allotted between 15% and 30% of the company's shares to the senior management team and to the employees. In many cases, the allotment to employees is even pre-arranged by creating a "pool" for employees in the investment agreement with institutional investors. Obviously, the structure of compensation and ownership-allocation is highly diverse and corresponds to the contribution made in the startup's early phases. On average, though, CEOs hold 10–30% if they are also entrepreneurs, and 5% on average if they are hired CEOs in companies that raised more than $5 million; hired COOs (Chief Operating Officers) receive holdings of 1–5%, depending on the company's stage of development and capital-raising; hired CTOs (Chief Technology Officers) generally hold 1–3%; a VP (Vice President) of Marketing would hold 1–2%; a VP of Sales would usually hold a little less than that; and a VP of Business Development would hold shares and options in the range of 1–3%.

A survey of public Internet companies conducted in 2000 by Mercer Consulting revealed that the total equity held by the CFOs of such companies was a little over 1% shortly before an IPO, of which approximately two-thirds took the form of options. COOs (entrepreneurs or otherwise) held approximately 1.5% of the equity, and Sales and Marketing VPs received slightly smaller allotments.

It is important to reiterate that the timing of employee recruitment is a crucial factor in determining the percentage of shares they will be allotted. For instance, a CTO joining the company after the first round of investment may get 3–5%, but less than 1% if he or she joins the company shortly before an IPO. Therefore, when comparing different companies and employees, it is essential that the employees' seniority in the company, and not necessarily their positions, be taken into account. It is also important to understand that the percentage allotted to an employee is directly related to the employee's reputation and the degree of confidence which the company and its financial backers place in him or her, and not necessarily to the company's current value. These are less objective factors which cannot be known to the employee with certainty.

In most cases, a small percentage is allotted to the members of the Board of Directors (who are often, in any case, the representatives of the investors), and additional options are allotted to various service providers of the company, such as selected advisors and important suppliers.

An examination of the number of employees who receive options upon joining the company reveals that close to 100% of VPs and directors receive them, and more than 60% of employees receive shares or options, a percentage that rises with the employee's rank. In addition, most companies make additional allotments of shares and options besides the allotments made to employees upon joining the company. Approximately 80% of officers and 50% of employees receive additional options on an ongoing basis after joining the company.

In addition to the ongoing allotment of options, which is usually associated with bonus plans, many companies have plans that allow employees to buy shares with a discount of up to approximately 15% off the price of the share. The amount of the shares depends on the employee's salary. Such plans, known as ESPPs (Employee Stock Purchase Plans), receive preferred tax treatment as described in a later section in this chapter.

Options and Shares in Spin-offs

In spin-offs, many companies come across the issue of options and shares that were allotted to employees of the parent company who are now working for the spun-off division. In addition, employees who remain with the parent company may demand shares in the spun-off division, like the employees who work for such a division. This demand is based on the argument that a material component of the value of their options was taken away from them since, as opposed to other shareholders, employees who hold options in the parent company do not always receive a direct share in the divisions. In most cases, employees who assisted in establishing the division will receive a stake in the spun-off unit, even if they do not become employed by it. Employees who move to the new division will naturally gain a share in it, which is supposed to compensate them also for a potential loss of pension, equity, and other rights in the parent company.

Taxation of Stock Options

Taxation of Incentive Stock Options (ISOs)

ISOs offer employees a very convenient tax treatment. If all the conditions for ISOs are fulfilled, employees are not taxed when they receive or exercise the options, but only when they sell the shares. When the shares are sold, employees are generally liable for a capital gains tax of 20% if the shares were held for at least two years from the date of grant of the options and at least one year from the date of exercise of the options (in any other case, employees are liable for ordinary income tax according to their respective tax brackets).

For an option to be recognized as an ISO, the following conditions have to be fulfilled:

1. The options have to be granted in accordance with a plan specifying the number of options and the employees or type of employees designated to receive them. The plan must be approved by the Board of Directors up to twelve months before or after its general adoption by the Board of Directors.
2. The options must be granted within ten years from the date of adoption or approval of the plan, whichever is earlier.
3. The options must stipulate that they have to be exercised within ten years from the date of the award.
4. The exercise price of the options must equal or exceed the market value of the share when the option is granted. This requirement is probably met if an honest attempt is made to value the shares at the time of the award.
5. The option terms must stipulate that they cannot be transferred, except in case of death.
6. The options must be granted to an employee of the company, a subsidiary of the company, or its parent company.
7. Before the date of award of the option, the holder of the option cannot have held more than 10% of the shares of the company, a subsidiary of the

company, or its parent company, either directly or indirectly. However, this requirement does not apply if the exercise price is at least 110% of the market value of the share and the options can be exercised pursuant to their terms within five years only.

It should be noted that there is a ceiling of $100,000 for ISO benefits associated with options which are exercisable within one calendar year.

The tax consequence of ISOs is that employees are liable, as mentioned above, for a capital gains tax at the time of sale of the shares.

If an employee sells the shares within two years from the date of award, or within one year from the date of exercise of the option (i.e., its conversion into a share), or if the employee ceases to work for the company, its subsidiary, or parent company during the period from the date of grant of the options until three months before the options are exercised (disqualifying exercise), the employee is then taxed for a portion of the profit as an ordinary income.

With ISOs, the company cannot record the benefit received by the employee as an expense. In the case of a disqualifying exercise of an ISO, the company can deduct the profit for which the employee is taxed as an expense for tax purposes, on the date of payment of the tax by the employee.

Taxation of Non-qualified Stock Options (NSOs)

If the conditions for an ISO are not met, then the options are deemed as NSOs. NSOs are generally awarded as a benefit only to employees and other service providers who cannot be given ISOs.

An employee who receives NSOs is taxed on the date of receipt or exercise of the options. If the market value of the share can be determined (for instance, if the share is publicly traded), then the employee is taxed at the time of receipt of the option. However, if the market value of the share cannot be determined, then the employee is taxed at the time of exercise of the option. In general, the employee is liable for ordinary income tax on the difference between the market value of the share and the exercise price of the option at the time of exercise. Any additional profit after the tax is paid is deemed as a capital gain and the employee is liable for the reduced capital gains tax.

The company may deduct the benefit received by the employee or the service provider, but only up to the amount of the employee's or service provider's ordinary income.

Taxation of Employee Stock Purchase Plans

An ESPP is a compensation plan which provides employees with a special mechanism for buying shares of the company. When the requirements fixed in Sections 422(a) or 423(a) of the Internal Revenue Code are met, the shares are subject to a favorable tax treatment.

In principle, an ESPP enables an employee who is interested in participating in the plan to notify the company to deduct up to 15% of his or her salary during the term of the plan. At the end of the term of the plan, the company buys shares for the employee with the amount accumulated, with a discount of up to 15% on the price of the shares on the date of share purchase, or the price of the shares on the date of commencement of the plan, whichever is lower.

The preferred tax treatment is that if the employee held the shares purchased for two years from the beginning of the term of the plan and for one year from the date of purchase of the shares, then the amount taxed as ordinary income will be the lower of the actual gain or the discount on the purchase price. That is, any increase in value from the date of purchase of the shares until the date of sale of the shares is taxed as a capital gain at the rate of 20%.

The following conditions have to be met for a plan to be recognized as an ESPP: The plan must be approved by the general shareholder meeting; its term cannot be longer than five years; no offeree may hold more than 5% of the share capital; an offeree cannot buy shares for more than $25,000 in one calendar year; the rights under the plan cannot be transferable; the offerees are all employees; and all of the company's employees have to be entitled to participate in the plan, although employees who are employed for less than two years, employees who do not work more than 20 hours per week, employees who do not work more than five months in a calendar year, and highly compensated employees may be excluded from this rule.

Performance-based Compensation

Introduction

Intuitively, it is natural to expect that the performance of an employee and the company affect managerial compensation. However, it is essential to understand that choosing the correct composition of the compensation package should be made while taking into account the existing risk associated with holding the company's shares, the current composition of the employee's equity holdings, and the degree of the employee's risk-aversion, which could be affected by his domestic situation, wealth, and lifestyle.

Compensation in the form of options assumes that the employee has a direct impact on the company's performance and on its market price. Compensation in the form of bonuses, however, is based on the actual performance of the employee, the officer, the division, or any other business unit influenced by the employee. The targets which the employee or officer have to meet are usually either set at the beginning of the period or result from a periodic performance assessment made by the employee's managers.

In most cases, the higher the employee's rank, the more explicitly will his targets be defined, either at the beginning of the period or even upon signing of the employment contract. The targets have to be based on a financial activity level, a market share, the profits of the division, or the employee, and so forth. The bonus itself may take the form of shares, options, or cash and can be conditional upon the targets having been met (i.e., a binary bonus that is either earned or not earned), or, alternatively, can be a function of the actual performance. For instance, if profits exceed $100 million, the CEO will receive 0.1% of the residual profits, up to a profit of $500 million (which will result in a bonus of $400,000).

The Financial Leverage of Compensation Packages

It is important to understand that the total economic value of the compensation package includes the current value of the shares and options already held by the employee, in addition to the net present value of expected salaries, bonuses, options, and the company's contributions to the employee's pension fund.

It is always important to examine the total financial leverage of compensation packages, namely, the degree of sensitivity of the value of the package to fluctuations in the price of the share. For instance, the financial leverage is 1 if the value of the total compensation package changes by 1% with every 1% fluctuation in the price of the share.

Calculating an employee's compensation leverage is complicated since the compensation package includes, on the one hand, components with a leverage that is close to 0 (for instance, the salary component, which is fixed) and, on the other hand, bonus and option components, whose leverage is greater than 1. The leverage of options changes in accordance with the price of the share, the date of expiration of the option, and the relationship between the exercise price and the share price. The higher the exercise price is above the price of the share, the higher its leverage on the value of the option. However, the leverage of most employee stock options is close to 1, since the exercise price is usually identical to the price of the share at the time of allotment of the options.

Since the salary is usually a dominant element in the compensation package, the leverage of the total package is usually lower than 1. In other words, the target of achieving an alignment of interests between the employees and the shareholders is not necessarily reached. An interesting method of achieving such alignment of interests is by giving performance-based bonuses that are credited to the employee's account in a "compensation bank" of sorts, which can be redeemed over a period of time. Bonuses can be calculated by using various formulas. One such customary formula is measuring performance by a decision on the operating unit to be measured, determining a cost of capital for that unit, in accordance with the unit's risk profile and comparing the division's operating profit to the equity "charge" resulting from multiplication of the unit's cost of capital, multiplied by the unit's capital base.

Performance Evaluation

Chapter 9, in which valuations are discussed, reviews the discounted residual income method which may be applied to the measurement of periodic performance, as illustrated above. In principle, it measures the residual income of the business unit, i.e., its operating profit after deducting the cost of any capital used by the business unit.

Performance evaluation may be made on the basis of the business results, reported in accordance with the company's reporting rules. It can also be based, however, on modified statements that reflect the activity of the business unit more realistically. For instance, the perceptible performance of a business unit which invests in R&D could be prejudiced due to accounting rules that require an investment in R&D to be recorded as a periodic expense. In such cases, R&D expenses should be treated, for the purpose of this calculation, as an investment in assets, depreciating over several periods. However, treating an investment as an asset increases the business unit's asset base, and hence the charge for the usage of capital. In some cases, adjustments are made to the rates of depreciation of the investment in the first few years. For instance, the investment may only be included in the basis in the assets two years after the investment is made, when it starts yielding fruit.

With the computerized systems that are now available for financial reporting, it is easy to make the required adjustments for different divisions, or even to measure the performance of different employees within each division. It is important to understand that the economic principles of performance evaluation are similar for different employees and different companies, but that their manner of implementation has to be adjusted to the circumstances of the evaluation. For instance, changes in the compensation parameters that depend on the residual income of the department managed by the employee will have a different impact on the behavior of a manager who has a large portfolio of company stock compared to the manager of a similar business unit who does not hold a similar package.

Types of Performance-based Compensation

- **Bonuses**—Bonuses are the most common method of performance-based employee compensation. If the bonus is based on performance that is measured by the residual income method, then typically the bonus components are a linear function of the residual income up to a certain maximum income. In some companies, the part of the bonus that corresponds to any residual income beyond this maximum is credited to the employee but cannot be fully redeemed in the same year. This "compensation bank" enables the fining of employees in subsequent years if they do not meet the targets fixed for such years. Thus, the employees' interests become identical to those of the shareholders even if the company's performance declines. The compensation gradients of officers should also be adapted to their other compensation parameters, as well as to the relationship between the changes in the residual income and the changes in share value.
- **Phantom shares**—Phantom shares are not actual shares, and are, in practice, an arrangement for monetary reward that is based on a direct change in the value of the company. Since it is a payment arrangement, it can be employed not only in listed companies but also in closely held companies. The price per share for the purpose of the calculation may be determined according to a formula that is based on the company's latest investment round or its financial results. For instance, it may be determined

that the value of the company for the purpose of the formula will be fifty times the company's profits in that year. Phantom shares usually confer no rights other than those related to the payment arrangement. The payment may be performed quarterly, annually, or only after a predetermined period such as three years or a predetermined event (such as an IPO).

Weighing the Relative Performance of the Business Unit

Almost every organization constantly debates the relative weights that should be applied for the benchmarks when calculating employees' compensation, namely, to what extent the performance evaluation should be based on the performance of the employee's business unit, and to what extent it should be based on the result of the organization as a whole. In many cases, the compensation is affected only by the performance of the business unit, and in other cases upward of 30% of the bonus is affected by the performance of the company as a whole. Obviously, the different weights given to the compensation components should depend on the position occupied by the employee. A bonus given to senior employees should have a larger component that is based on the performance of the company as a whole. However, such systems sometimes create motivational problems, since the performance of the business unit is often affected conversely to the performance of the company as a whole. Various methods of pricing intra-organizational business activities may solve such problems, but such methods lie beyond the scope of this book.

Incentives to Tie Employees to the Company

Over and above the monetary compensation, many companies invest considerable efforts in creating a work environment that will bond the employees with the company and encourage them to stay with it. Recruiting a talented employee is only the first stage in the battle to keep him or her with the company. In times of prosperity on the capital market the demand for good workers is high, thus increasing the turnover rate of employees. Companies are required to make significant investments to train employees for their positions in the company, and employees reach their maximum productivity only after a certain period of adjustment. Therefore, the departure of a skilled worker translates into a significant loss to the company, far greater that the loss resulting from a failure in recruiting new employees.

Many companies have been forced to increase their employees' compensation several times a year in order to keep them with the company. Option packages were an effective tool when companies managed to raise capital based on ever-increasing values. However, this effectiveness diminished when the value of the companies dropped during 2000 and 2001. Such impact was visible not only in startups, but also in more established companies. For instance, in late 2000 approximately two-thirds of Lucent Technologies' employees held options with exercise prices higher than the price of the share.

The importance of the alignment of interests between employees and the company and between them and other employees cannot be overrated. This unity alone is, however, insufficient—particularly in a market with excess demand for skilled workers. Employees need to feel that the company treats them as one of its important assets, not merely as a production mechanism designed to produce a higher yield than the cost of their salaries. Therefore, many companies offer various services to enhance the employees' and their families' quality of life. In the United States, for instance, it is customary to offer employees a contribution towards kindergarten and schooling expenses, or even to maintain day care facilities in or close to the company's offices. In addition, it is customary to organize various adventure outings for the company's employees and families, vacation packages, and holiday events.

In conclusion, from the points of view of the entrepreneurs and the investors, it is the effectiveness of the overall compensation package, which includes monetary and other rewards that is important. Every employee has different preferences regarding the monetary and non-monetary rewards that affect his or her decision to work with the company. It is the duty of the company's officers to put together a package of employee benefits that will attract the employees who match the profile of whom they want to recruit, that will enhance the productivity of such employees while with the company, and, of course, that will reduce the turnover rate of employees as a result of defection to other employers.

Considerations in Employment Termination

Alongside various means of bonding employees with the company, in both employment contracts and the company's procedures, attention should also be paid to the potential termination of the relationship between the company and the employee. For instance, various employment contracts often address the issue of non-competition. Any restrictions on competition have to take into account the laws of the state in which the agreement is applied, with respect to restrictions on employees' freedom of employment. Some states in the United States impose various conditions on the validity of various occupational restrictions.

Similarly, many employment contracts address the use which employees can make of the professional know-how they accumulated while working for the company. It is often only in legal suits against former employees that a discussion is conducted with respect to various distinctions between know-how pertaining to the industry in general (which is ostensibly the employee's property, even if it was acquired while working for the company) and know-how that is unique to the company and is a trade secret of the company (for further discussion of employment relations in the context of trade secrets, see Chapter 5 on trade secret laws).

Finally, many contracts address the options to which the employee will be entitled after leaving the startup. In many cases, employees are entitled to exercise the options that would have vested had they waited for the next vesting "milepost," even after leaving the company.

5
Intangible Capital and Intellectual Property

INTRODUCTION—TYPES OF INTELLECTUAL PROPERTY

Intellectual property has in recent years become one of the most important assets of companies in general, and is often the most valuable asset of companies in their early stage. The importance of protecting a startup's intellectual property and making the most use of it is therefore obvious.

A company's intellectual property derives from several sources, such as:

- Technology developed in the company or acquired by it, which may increase the company's revenues, save them costs, or confer other advantages on them.
- Unique and confidential information about customers or other contacts which could be valuable to other companies in order to increase their revenues.

Intellectual property retains its value only if the company diligently protects its rights to such property and if the rights to such intellectual property are commercialized in the best possible manner.

This chapter will review the main types of intellectual property and the means of protecting them. Particular attention will be paid to startups and to the various methods of extracting the highest return from such property.

Patents

Introduction

A patent is the protection afforded by the law to ideas. The protection of intellectual property is founded upon the need to balance among the inventor's right to his or her invention, the desire of the human society to encourage entrepreneurship and innovation, and society's need to use the invention for the common good. The inventor chooses to accept the protection of the law, and in consideration therefore is prepared to publish the details of his or her invention and to allow the public to use it once the patent expires.

Most patents are sought in order to prevent competitors from using the invention, or as protection in cases of legal action (as a means of filing a counterclaim). However, the registration of patents serves also as an instrument for generating revenues from intellectual property—by selling, leasing, or licensing it. Obtaining patents is significant also for raising capital, and startups often emphasize to investors that a patent application protecting their invention has been filed, that a patent protecting their invention is pending, and/or that a patent protecting their invention has been granted.

A vast number of patents are granted every year. For example, in 2000, more than 150,000 patents were granted in the United States alone, and the revenues generated in that year from the granting of licenses and the sale of rights to utilize patents exceeded $100 billion!

Aside from pharmaceutical companies, which have historically relied on patents to prevent competition and to protect the return on their large investments in developing products, a material portion of the value of many high tech companies is attributed to their patents. For example: In December 2001, Gemstar was traded according to a market value of more than $10 billion, mainly due to its patents for a method of recording television programs (for instance, the possibility of recording television programs by keying a code into the VCR) and for e-books. The company relied heavily on licensing its patents to other companies in order for the latter to integrate Gemstar's algorithms into theirs. Similarly, Qualcomm, the CDMA-technology patentee and a manufacturer of hardware for cellular phones and infrastructure, considerably reduced its manufacturing activities in recent years but has left its R&D center, and derives most of its revenue from licensing its patents in cellular communications, in the core of the company.

The courts (mainly in the United States) have made it clear in recent years that patents could be granted not only for technologies, processes, or uses, but also for "business methods." Amazon, for instance, uses a patent to protect its "One Click" technology, which effectively allows customers to make repeat purchases with one click of the mouse, without the need to enter their personal information again or to remember their user name and password.

Alongside the many advantages bestowed by patents, it should be kept in mind that seeking a patent carries certain disadvantages, primarily the need to expose the technology; the high cost of seeking and defending patents; the difficulties involved in enforcing patents globally; and the fact that they are only applicable domestically (i.e., applications have to be filed in every country separately). Moreover, where fast-moving technologies are concerned, there is often no point in seeking a patent since there is a possibility that it will no longer be relevant when the patent is granted.

Many companies have a strategy of obtaining as many patents as possible. I.B.M., for instance, has approximately 20,000 patents, and Intel has about 3,000. Other companies, on the other hand, prefer not to seek patents, the consideration being that the patent itself will be published and could enable its replication with a minor, though sufficient, modification of the technology. Such companies may prefer the protection afforded to trade secrets over the protection of a patent (see the upcoming discussion in this chapter on the trade secrets law).

Basic Principles

- **The use of patents**—In most cases, the patentee is not obligated to implement the patent as long as he or she keeps paying its maintenance fees. The law confers on patentees almost absolute freedom with respect to the manner in which the patent will be utilized. In other words, he or she can demand small or large amounts for using the patent, or decide to award no one a license to use the patent. Intel, for instance, does not customarily license patented technologies developed or acquired by it. Compulsory licensing is an exception to this freedom (see a later section in this chapter).
- **The period of protection afforded to patents**—A patented invention gives the patentee the rights to the patent for 20 years from the date on which the application is first filed, regardless of the date on which the patent is awarded. This period may be extended by five years if the procedure was delayed.
- **Provisional Patent Application (PPA)**—The U.S. patent law enables inventors to file provisional patent applications (PPAs). As opposed to a full-fledged patent application, a PPA is designed mainly to mark the initial date of filing, but cannot serve as a patent application in itself. As opposed to the broad disclosure required for receiving a patent (see below), only limited disclosure is required for PPAs and the information is kept secret. A full application has to be filed within 12 months from the date of the PPA. Many companies use PPAs as a tool for effectively extending the patent to 21 years, since the 20-year count of the patent's validity starts running only from the date of filing of the full application.

    Many startups use PPAs as a strategic tool when seeking financing, since the application is not costly but may still deter copying, and provide investors with at least some assurance that the firm's intellectual property is being protected.

- **Patent pending**—Once a patent application is filed with the Patent and Trademark Office (and in fact, also when a PPA is filed), it is pending. From that time forth, an inventor may state next to any description of the invention or on the product that a patent application has been filed and that the patent is pending. It is important to note that during the course of the process the applicant receives no protection and cannot prevent others from using technologies included in the application. On the other hand, so long as the patent is pending, its details are kept secret.

Prerequisites for Obtaining a Patent

In order to be patentable, an invention must meet three main criteria: usefulness, novelty, and non-obviousness.

- **Usefulness**—The inventor has to demonstrate that the invention is useful and that it may be classified within one of the existing patent families: useful art, machine, manufacture, composition of matter or plant. A patent application must also include a specification of the uses which may be made of the patent.
- **Novelty**—In order for an invention to meet this criterion, it must not be previously used by the public or be within the public domain. In addition, it must be the subject of no patent application which was filed more than one year before the date of filing in the United States, since such filing rules out the prior use principle, even if it concerns the same invention. Nor can the invention be included in any patent awarded or pending.

    If the invention was published before the application is filed, a patent application can still be filed in the United States within 12 months from the date of the first publication. This rule differs from the custom in other countries, in which any publication of an invention disqualifies it from being patented. However, if such publication is made after the filing in the United States (or in another member state of the international patent treaty), then the date of filing is based on the date on which the application was first filed.
- **Non-obviousness**—In order for an invention not to be deemed trivial, and therefore indefensible, it must contain elements of non-obviousness which will render it nontrivial to any person of average skills in the specific field. In addition, proof is required that a person in the field could implement the patent by following the instructions provided in it.

Patent Registration

Obtaining a patent usually takes over a year from the date of filing the application. The main factor that influences the length of the process is the number of applications filed in the same field. In recent years, the U.S. Patent and Trademark Office has been unable to keep up with the sheer volume of Internet and software patent applications, and the process could last even three years in these fields. When the application is granted, the patent protects the inventor against unauthorized making, using, or selling of the invention.

The most important part of a patent application is the list of claims—a concise description of the inventor's claims with respect to the novelty of his or her invention. Writing the claims is a highly professional task since, on the one hand, the inventor wants to include in them as many uses as possible so that the patent will encompass all the products that could be based on the same principles, while, on the other hand, he or she wants to avoid a disqualification of a claim by the Patent Office or the courts as being too sweeping. Let us look, for example, at the invention of the pencil and the drafting of one main claim. If the claim discusses a "writing instrument based on material which leaves markings and is encompassed in a wooden frame which allows material to project therefrom," then, although it is narrower than "a writing instrument based on material which leaves markings," it is broader than "a writing instrument based on a combination of lead and graphite which leaves markings and is encompassed in a wooden frame less than 0.5 mm thick, which allows material to project therefrom by sharpening the instrument." In practice, every patent application includes a body of claims, some more and some less sweeping. The art of choosing the claims and drafting them requires the careful planning and implementation of patent attorneys and advisors.

A patent application includes a description of the patent and drawings, if the latter are necessary to describe the claims (each claim must be supported by the description). In addition, the inventor is required to declare that he or she is the inventor.

When an application is received by the Patent Office, it is transferred to a patent examiner who is proficient in the specific field of the patent. The examiner analyzes the description and the claims and also what is already known in the field (existing patents in the United States or other countries, familiar products on the market, publications, or any other publicly available information). The examiner may ask various questions or make comments about the listed claims. The inventor and his or her representatives may dispute the examiner's objections, and the process may comprise several stages and take several years. As mentioned above, in an age of ever-increasing innovation in which the importance of protecting intellectual property is becoming increasingly important, the process of registration takes longer and longer, mainly due to a considerable shortage of manpower in the Patent Office.

Patents Outside the United States

Patent applications have to be filed in every country separately. The process is based on the Paris Patent Convention, namely the Patent Cooperation Treaty (PCT) and the European Patent Convention (EPC). A patent application filed in any one of the signatory countries of the Paris Convention (more than 130 countries), allows the inventor to file a similar application during the following year in every other signatory country, with the date of filing in the first country being deemed also as the date of filing in the other countries. In addition, the EPC process enables the saving of considerable costs in preparing the patent applications, since it is now possible to prepare one application for any member country of the European Community that will be valid in all EU countries. Such applications do, however, need to be filed in each country separately. However, it is important to note that the patent laws vary significantly from one country to another, and claims that are accepted in the United States may be rejected in other countries and vice versa. Business processes, for instance, are difficult to patent in countries outside the United States.

Patents for Business Processes

In recent years, many companies have started registering patents on business processes. Probably the first of such patents was a particular method of interconnecting information located in different bank accounts. Since then, many patent applications have been granted in the United States whose main claims include a description of a business process. Perhaps the most famous business process is that of "Priceline," which describes a specific conditional offer by a buyer to a group of sellers. Many components of the patent concern the algorithms of the encryption of the information between the buyer and the sellers. The core of the patent, however, is the claim concerning the actual business process, in which a buyer offers a maximum price for a product, which offer is backed by a purchase commitment (via a credit card). The offered price is transmitted to potential sellers, who choose whether or not to accept the offer. If the proposed price is accepted by any of the sellers, the buyer, who can no longer change his or her mind at this point, is informed of the acceptance of his or her offer.

Many people, including inventors who managed to patent business processes, have been claiming lately that the Patent Office is not keeping up with the technological innovations and is therefore granting patents that do not meet the requirements of the law, in particular with respect to their novelty and non-obviousness. Their claim is that the dynamic reality, particularly in the Internet area, demands a stricter scrutiny of nontriviality. In response to this claim, the U.S. Patent Office had announced in March 2000 that business methods will be examined more carefully than in the past.

Patents on business processes account for many legal suits between companies that have been filed in recent years to the courts. In many cases, it has been claimed that even patents which are not likely to win the protection of the courts may serve as an efficient weapon in competition-related battles. A company may often demand that the use of a product similar to a product protected by a patent it had obtained cease, even if the court ultimately decides that the patent is invalid. Amazon, for instance, is denying Barnes & Noble the use of a product which is contained in a patent it had obtained for its "One Click" purchasing process.

Compulsory Licensing

In certain cases, it is possible to compel a patentee to allow the use of a patent. Such compulsion will be supported by the courts if it transpires that the patentee is not utilizing the protected invention in a manner meeting the needs of the country which awarded it to him or her. The PCT recognizes the right of its member countries to limit the rights of patentees in cases of nonuse or abuse of patents.

This tool is rarely used; however, the responsiveness of patent authorities to compulsion requests differs from one country to another, and usually depends on the impact of the nonuse of the patent on the competition in the market. It is also possible that compulsion is rarely used because patentees who fear such compulsion, choose either to grant licenses to the parties interested in the patent—or at least to those who indicate that they will resort to coercion—or to use the patent themselves. In the United States, this instrument was common in the 1940s and 1950s in antitrust trials. Now, however, it is relatively uncommon and in the U.S. is almost always exercised within the Patent Misuse Reform Act of 1988, which examines the impact which the use (or nonuse) of a patent has on the competition in the market.

Copyright Law

Principles

The copyright law protects original works. Examples of such works are paintings, books, articles, speeches, study materials, songs, and software. Databases may also be protected by copyrights.

For a work to be defensible, it needs to be tangible. A speech, for instance, that is not recorded or otherwise documented cannot be copyrighted. The work must also contain an expression of an idea, since an idea in itself is not defensible under the law. For instance, formulas cannot be protected by the law (although they may be defensible under the patent laws). Another example is Shakespeare's Romeo and Juliet: The idea itself (the plot)—a love story between a boy and a girl from incompatible families which has a tragic ending—cannot be copyrighted (indeed, this idea has been often imitated as, for instance, in *West Side Story*). The particular words chosen by the writers of *West Side Story* to express the plot are protected however, and cannot be used without authorization.

The rights attached to a copyrighted work are the exclusive authority to duplicate, distribute, and perform the work. It is always important to examine whether the added value of the work cannot be protected by other means, since the law provides only limited protection to the information-content included in the work.

The measure of protection provided by copyrights depends on the nature of the work. Generally, the protection of a work is valid until the 75th anniversary of its publication or the centennial of its creation, whichever is the earlier. Copyrights originating from work performed by an employee or subcontractor belong to the company if the work was performed within the employee's duties in the company or within a contracting agreement which defines it as work that had been contracted for.

Any work on which the creator's name appears is protected by the copyright law, even if it does not bear the copyright symbol. However, many add the copyright symbol along with the year of creation (copyright John Doe © 2000). In principle, many companies add this symbol on many documents that leave the company.

Issues in Digital Media

The Internet created new issues that did not exist before, such as the broadcasting of works over the Internet and various peer-to-peer services. In 1998, a law was passed that purports to update the copyright law for the 21st century, namely, The Digital Millennium Copyright Act (DMCA). The main purpose of the act is to clarify the relevance of copyright laws to the technological advancements of the past decades. The act forbids the development and offer of any technology that enables access to copyrighted work. In addition, the act prohibits any manufacture, import, development, or marketing in connection with the offer of a product, service, or technology, which is essentially a means of breaching copyrights.

The act restricts the liability of Internet providers for violations committed by their customers, as long as the providers did not intentionally transmit information in violation of copyrights. If a provider becomes aware of a violation, he or she must stop it. The act imposes on Internet broadcast providers (such as Web-based television and radio stations) the same obligations with respect to the payment of royalties as are imposed on physical broadcasting stations.

Legal copyright suits have recently come into the spotlight that were filed against some Internet sites which enable the transfer of data files in a manner breaching their creators' copyrights (such as the Napster site, which allowed users to exchange music files). The main argument is that these sites enable the exchange of files, even if it is not the sites themselves which perform the actual copying. This argument is being examined from the year 2000 in the United States, and could have far-reaching implications on sites that rely on the sharing of information among users. One of the main arguments against Napster is that the site was used mainly to copy works which are protected by copyrights. The court ruled in 2001 that Napster must prevent the exchange of files of works appearing in lists provided by the holders of the copyrights to such works. Other sites, which do not maintain indexes of the files transmitted by their users, are still in constant litigation with copyright holders, claiming they are not liable for illegal use of their networks.

In practice, almost every Web site that engages in mediation, whether free of charge or for a fee, may be confronted with this issue. eBay, for instance, disclaims any liability for the sale of products in breach of their attendant copyrights, and takes many measures to minimize the number of cases in which counterfeit or copied products are sold in breach of copyrights. Clearly, sites whose core activity relies on the digital transfer of information among their users bear a higher risk of legal exposure if they do not make adequate preparations to address this matter, either by various means of control or by attempting to disclaim their liability from the outset (which attempts are usually ineffective). eBay, for instance, employs many workers in search of problematic products which could be sold through the site (such as human organs) and in search of stolen products or products which breach copyrights.

Case law in Europe has recently been stricter than in the United States. A French court, for example, has ruled that Yahoo must screen the material offered for sale via its auction service and is responsible for preventing the sale of Nazi propaganda through its site.

Trademark Law

Many items may be protected by the trademark law, mainly the company's logo, its name, product names, and various sales-promotion slogans.

The fundamental principle of the law is to assist consumers to distinguish between products. Trademarks are always associated with particular products. A trademark could be a name, a combination of a name with a mark, special packaging, or any other means that help consumers to identify the product or the service as being provided by the trademark holder. Trademarks are protected by case law, Federal laws, and state and municipal laws. No protection is usually afforded to a mark that symbolizes a phenomenon or simply describes the product. It is impossible, for instance, to trademark the word "television" as describing a television. Trademarks are automatically protected by virtue of being used, but may also be registered. When using a trademark, it is recommended that the symbol ® be used if the name is registered with the Patent and Trademark Office, and the symbol ™ if it is not registered.

Historically, high tech industries have not resorted to trademark laws to any significant degree. However, in recent years the industry has paid much attention to developing trademarks, which often underlie various legal actions. Intel, for instance, is known for promoting its registered name which appears on any computer containing processors manufactured by it ("Intel inside").

Trade Secrets

What Is Protected?

In principle, any information which does not need to be published or distributed to persons who are not contractually bound to keep it secret, may be protected as a commercial secret. Trade secrets need not be recorded or documented in writing. Such secrets may include customer lists, work methods which streamline production processes, production and distribution information, and information concerning R&D which is conducted by the company.

Main Elements

A trade secret is any instrument, information processing, or formula which enables the achievement of a competitive edge, be it as temporary as it may. Even information that is in the public domain, but whose utility in a certain field is unknown, may be regarded as a commercial secret.

The holder of a trade secret must prove that he or she took reasonable measures to safeguard such secret against disclosure. He or she has to point to the procedures maintained by him or her in order to keep the information secret and demonstrate that he or she indeed followed such procedures—for instance, a procedure whereby customer-related information is protected by passwords and is accessible only by the relevant persons, or a procedure whereby guests visiting the offices of the company are not exposed to confidential production processes and are escorted at all times.

It is always advisable to require potential customers and investors (especially strategic investors who are themselves active in the field) to sign a confidentiality agreement before disclosing to them trade secrets and patents of the company. Obviously, consideration should be given to the probability that such an agreement will be signed (many investors will refuse to sign such confidentiality agreements), and to the risk that an argument over such an agreement will cloud the actual transaction that is being sought (an investment or purchase of products).

The Protection of Trade Secrets

The protection of trade secrets is composed of many elements. This subsection will review only some of the methods used by companies to protect their secrets. It does not provide a comprehensive list, and specific procedures are always required for each company.

Many companies have their employees sign a confidentiality agreement whose components are similar to those included in confidentiality agreements with outsiders. A principal element provides that employees will not use trade secrets of the company outside their duties in the company. In addition, the agreements often contain provisions preventing employees from being employed by competitors for a certain period of time following the termination of their employment with the company.

Clauses of non-competition by employees (as opposed to non-competition clauses in agreements between shareholders, including entrepreneurs) might be deemed to be contrary to the public interest. The concept is that provisions in employment agreements which restrict competition are unlawful unless they are designed to protect "legitimate interests" of the employer. U.S. law in this matter usually differs from one state to another, and in states such as California, many non-competition clauses are not recognized as lawful by the courts.

However, even if the restriction of employment with competitors may be invalidated by the courts: it is important for companies to have their employees sign confidentiality agreements whereby information gathered by them in the course of their employment, which is a trade secret of the company, is the company's property.

In recent years, companies have frequently sued former employees for the disclosure or use of trade secrets in the employees' new jobs. For instance, the retail chain Wal-Mart sued Amazon, claiming that a senior employee of Wal-Mart who was recruited by Amazon to build a logistics system, used trade secrets which he had acquired in his previous position with Wal-Mart.

Many companies have procedures for compartmentalizing information which they share with their employees, if sharing such information with outsiders is perceived as risky. It should be taken into account that many fragments of information may be meaningless when viewed separately, but could become valuable when put together. In this context, industrial espionage is very common in the industry, and job interviews are used to gather information on competitors—both in the framework of attempts to recruit workers from competing companies and by sending employees to interview with competitors in order to elicit information on these competitors. Even classified ads seeking employees may at times disclose a company's development intentions when integrated with other pieces of information.

Issues with Employees

Many companies wage wars against employees who leave them for other companies or independent ventures if there is a good reason to believe they are utilizing proprietary knowledge developed under their previous job. This issue raises many questions, especially in the software field. For instance, routines developed by software engineers in one job may be later used for other software, and different schemes may serve various applications. Many employees tend to keep private copies of material they participated in creating in their previous jobs. Such copies may later serve as evidence against them in potential legal suits. Many other employees diligently prepare business plans in their new jobs, specifying new developments they intend to make, only to find out later that—to their surprise—their previous employer is sometimes entitled to claim ownership of such ideas and developments, since they fall in the realm of their area of activity in their previous job, or as their ideas were developed during the normal business hours.

Moreover, many entrepreneurs naturally want to recruit workers from their previous places of employment, partially because they are familiar with the recruited workers. However, such recruitments may not only violate their employment contracts, but may also provoke indignation in the previous employer over other issues to which he or she had chosen to turn a blind eye until then (for example, the fact that the new venture was planned when the entrepreneurs were still employees of the company).

NDA—Non-Disclosure Agreements

Many entrepreneurs are anxious about divulging the main ideas of their businesses. These anxieties are understood in certain cases, particularly when the ideas are new technological inventions. Such entrepreneurs may ask investors to sign non-disclosure agreements (NDAs). However, most investors refuse to sign such agreements. The main reason for their refusal is that investors are exposed to many similar ideas which are presented to them by different entrepreneurs within the numerous deals they are offered. In this state of affairs, even if they are discreet but invest in only one of the similar projects, the entrepreneurs of the projects which were not chosen may sue them for the divulgence of information, and the investors will be forced to prove in court what actually happened, while incurring costs and jeopardizing their reputation.

In order to overcome the unwillingness of investors to sign NDAs, entrepreneurs can file provisional patent applications, thus surmounting the obstacle of disclosing information (even partially) to investors.

Considerations in the Granting of Licenses

Licenses Defined

This section will review the main methods for pricing licenses to use intellectual property. It will focus on the granting of licenses to use technology in consideration for payment, as distinguished from licenses to use other information, such as customer lists. In many cases, a technology is leased or sold, in which case the difficult problem of pricing arises due to the complexity of the parameters involved. In practice, the legal and economic significance of the sale of software is the granting of a license to use the technology.

There are several methods for pricing the lease or sale of technology. One customary method is based on the payment that is common in the field. According to this method, which is undoubtedly the simplest to implement, the pricing is based on the accepted rate of royalties in the specific market and is adjusted to the expected return on the technology and to the current stage of its development. The contracts themselves will often be written based on the revenues or different profit measures, while taking into consideration the projected profit margins in the sale of the ultimate product or service. In the drug market, for instance, royalties in the amount of 15–20% of the sales are not uncommon, since drugs often carry high gross profit margins exceeding 80%.

Other than the projected volume of sales, the amount of the royalties depends on the degree of innovation of the patent. Royalties may be up to three times higher for innovative inventions than for similar inventions that are not equally innovative.

Sellers tend to perform the pricing based on the profit they deem reasonable in view of their total investment until such time and therefore often extremely misvalue their asset. In general, it is important to understand that pricing should not be based on the development costs incurred until a certain stage, but rather on the future return which the invention is expected to generate. A developer must always remember that any investment made until a certain point in time constitutes a premium on an option for success. If the development fails, then the investment is meaningless, and if the development is successful, then the return on it does not depend on the investment made until that time (except, of course, its significance as a barrier to rapid duplication by third parties).

In many cases, a lump sum or upfront license is paid in cash for the right to use intellectual property for a fixed period of time. In addition to this payment, there are usually other components, which essentially include payments for the period of use of the technology (time-based payment) and payments based on the success of the technology (success-based payments). Calculating the correct combination of the payment components, which may be made in cash or in shares, is an art that takes into consideration various elements relating to the identity of the owner of the intellectual property and of the licensee, the technological innovation, and the relevant field of activity.

Pricing a License to Utilize a Patent

The total payment for a right to use a patent may include a lump sum, commitments for future payments (certain minimum payments), an equity component, debt, and so forth. The components which have a material effect on the pricing of rights may be classified into several principal categories, each presenting many questions which need to be addressed. The following list does not purport to be comprehensive, and its sole purpose is to indicate the main considerations which need to be taken into account when negotiating a license to use a patent:

- **The quality of the technology**—What stage has the development reached? Is it a finished product or are there still uncertainties as to the applicability of the technology?
- **The market potential**—Has the existence of the market already been proven? What possibilities are available for shifting various production risks to the end buyers (i.e., what is their price sensitivity)? What is the size of the target market? Is the license being awarded for a certain geographic territory? If so, to what extent is this restriction enforceable? Is the license being awarded for a certain field of activity? If so, to what extent is this restriction enforceable?
- **The ability to protect the technology and the competitive situation**—To what extent can patent and trade secret laws be employed to protect the technology? What stage has the protection of the technology reached (are the patents pending or have they already been awarded)? What is the probability that potential competitors will circumvent the patent? Can clauses be included in the contract to reduce the buyer's risk (for instance, a downward adjustment of the price if principal claims in the patent application are rejected by the Patent Office)? To what extent is it possible to sue potential violators of the patent, and what is the projected cost of such actions? Who is the licensee—is he or she someone who breached the patent, with whom settlement negotiations are now being conducted, or is he or she an ordinary customer? How different is the technology from other technologies that meet the same needs, even if they do so by a different method?

- **Negotiation considerations**—How many competitors are seeking a license to use the technology? What is the likelihood that such competitors will resort to other technologies?
- **The added value of the licensee**—How strong is the licensee in the geographic territory and field of activity covered by the license? To what extent is he or she able to raise capital? How good is his or her technological ability to manufacture and market the product? Is the specific licensee the one who will make the optimal use of the technology in the said geographic territory or field of activity? Are there any restrictions on granting other licenses in the same area? Is there any commitment to remain bound by the contract even if either party's expectations are not fulfilled?
- **The profitability of the end product**—What are the expected gross and operating profit margins for the product? Does the contract divide the risk between the licensee and the owner of the rights (for instance, by deriving profit-based, and not revenue-based, fees)? What other economic costs are involved in launching the product on the market? Will the licensor be involved in such process? What cost structure will the product have, and will it be possible to affect such structure by using outside manufacture forces (outsourcing)? Will the choice between self-production and outsourcing affect the relevant profit rates with respect to the payment of royalties? Does the profitability of the product depend on the number of users or on increasing the revenues extracted from each user, and can a creative method of pricing be conceived, based on the number of users or on a change in the amount of revenues generated from each user?
- **Risks attendant to the technology**—Which party to the agreement bears the risk of third-party claims (such as product liability claims)? Are damages offset against the profit that serves as a basis for the calculation of the royalties? Could there be any legal restrictions, either at present or in the future, on the rate of the royalties (for instance, a restriction on the rate of royalties payable on drugs due to a medical reform in the country)?

PART II

Financing the Venture

Obtaining financing from outside sources is one of the most important and longest processes in the life of a venture, lasting until it gains financial independence. The issue of financing is, no doubt, one of the primary problems facing all businesses. In startups, however, which require large amounts of outside capital to develop their products and penetrate the market, and which generally have no revenues for long periods of time, this problem is multiplied and enhanced.

As opposed to mature companies which have "cash cushions" and can withstand periods of lack of funding, many startups go out of business because they lack financing, not because their products have failed. A startup's cash flow depends mainly on its ability to raise capital to meet ever-growing needs, typically more than on its ability to deliver its products to the market. An unfortunate timing in the capital markets can also thwart the successful launch of promising products.

This part of the book addresses all the aspects involved in financing the venture: why financing is conducted in stages and how it is done, the practical aspects of raising capital, the methods of raising capital, the contractual agreements involved in raising capital, valuation of startups, and so forth.

6

Milestones and Sources of Financing the Venture

Financing in Stages

Startups require outside financing for their activities throughout their life spans until they command sufficient financial resources of their own. Since almost no new startup is capable of raising capital by traditional loans (see below for detailed explanations of various methods of financing), they are required to do so by means of equity, i.e., by joining investors in their capital stock or by issuing convertible debt. Typically, only at more advanced stages can a startup combine investment rounds with financing by straight debt.

Startups almost always raise capital in several consecutive stages, according to values that are supposed to rise consistently (sometimes, due to difficult market conditions or internal problems in the company, the value of the company does not rise from one round to the next). The reason that investments are broken up into rounds is that the significant risk involved in investing in a startup decreases as the startup progresses and manages to prove its technological concept, develop a product, establish good management, market, and sell. The value of a startup increases with its development as a natural outcome of the company's progress and the decrease in the riskiness of the investment. With time, the startup's projected cash flows, both positive (inflows) and negative (outflows), can be forecasted with more certainty and, as a result of this diminished uncertainty, investors use a lower discount rate when valuating the company (see Chapter 9 for a discussion of valuation).

The process of financing in stages that are linked to the company's progress, the reduction of its riskiness, and the increase in its value operates in favor of both investors and entrepreneurs. Considering the many risks, investors are usually prepared to risk at first only a small amount of money and prefer to invest the rest as the project demonstrates visible progress. From the entrepreneurs' perspective, an investment that is very large in proportion to the company's (low) value at an early stage would cause an immediate and sharp dilution of the entrepreneurs' equity. They therefore prefer to raise only what is necessary for that stage, in addition to a certain margin of security, and to continue raising capital later on based on a higher value.

Milestones in Venture Development

Despite the vast differences between one startup and another, we will attempt to describe the main stages in the development of ventures, which are common to all startups. An understanding of these stages is vital for planning the capital-raising process, since they are intimately tied to the startup's cash burn rate, its ability to raise capital, its value, and the amount of capital it needs to raise.

The development of a startup may be tracked along four principal development dimensions. Its combined progress on all four dimensions determines the condition of the venture, its value, its cash requirements, and so forth.

The Research and Development Dimension

The importance of this dimension varies in accordance with the nature of the startup and the degree of emphasis its business model places on technology. The ability to prove a technology—i.e., to build a product that is suitable to the market and which meets all the international standards and tests—is a material and basic skill that all startups require. The main milestones which may be listed on this axis are as follows: proving the feasibility of the technology, if it is in doubt; building a prototype in the laboratory; building a full prototype (for field trials, or the alpha stage); building a prototype for a beta stage trial with customers; building a full product; creating versions of the products and upgrading it. These stages and the emphases within them may change from one field to another. Where medical products are concerned, for instance, feasibility is highly important, and tests performed on animals and human beings are crucial; where software is concerned, proving the algorithms in the early stages is different from facing a challenge in the system in the later stages of the prototype development.

The Managerial Team Dimension

The importance of the leading team to the existence, growth, and success of a startup is self-evident. An excellent development team, business leaders, and talented managers with international capabilities are perhaps the most important variables in a startup's success and hence in its ability to raise capital.

The Business and Market Penetration Dimension

A central component in turning a project into a valuable company is its business structuring: an overall understanding and analysis of the market, the need which is met by the startup's products, the competition and competitors, and prices; a clear definition of the product; the structuring and current updating of the business strategy; the preparation of marketing tools and methods; the marketing itself; sales, and so forth.

The deeper and more comprehensive is a startup's understanding of these issues, the better is its ability to develop the correct product for the correct market and to break it into such market, and the higher its value. Likewise, the better a startup understands its market and its position in it, the more confidence will its management and investors have in it, and the better will be its ability to raise capital.

The principal factors which may be listed on this dimension are as follows: understanding the size, form, manner of operation, and characteristics of the market; understanding and analyzing the competition and competitors (both direct and indirect); defining the product; structuring the business strategy; marketing and sales.

The Revenue Dimension

There is an important difference between a startup which sells its products and services and a startup that is not yet present on the market. This difference is clearly reflected in the startup's market value for the purpose of raising capital. The company's ability to make sales, the feedback received from existing and potential customers, and the ability to measure the sales performance in real terms and not based only on models are all important components in the development of a startup, and from the investors' point of view they eliminate important sources of uncertainty.

The principal factors which may be listed on this dimension are as follows: beta sales; initial sales; a sizeable penetration into a certain market segment; and penetrating additional market segments and other vertical and geographical markets.

Scope of Financing and the Company's Value

Demand—The Company's Capital Needs

In the first stage which most startups undergo, namely, research and development, the company invests in developing the product and usually does not yet invest in the expensive infrastructure required to implement it. At this stage, companies usually generate no revenues (unless revenues are generated by granting licenses to use intellectual property or selling rights for future developments). These companies' operating cash flows are negative, because they incur only expenses.

At the next stage, the company may buy or lease additional equipment to start implementing the results of its R&D. Since the investments in this stage are larger than those made in the first stage, the company's operating cash flow is now even worse. The increasing pace of employee-recruitment is another great contributor to the cash burn rate.

Next, assuming that all proceeds according to the plan, the company starts generating revenues. However, these might be at first insufficient to pay for the marginal production and marketing costs and hence cannot cover the costs of development. The reason for this is that the company is struggling to introduce its product into the market, is spending considerable amounts of money on marketing and advertising, and is sometimes forced to sell its product at low introductory prices.

If the company's business involves substantial investments in infrastructure, the company's profit for accounting purposes will be lower than its current cash flow due to the substantial accounting depreciation components it must bear.

At this stage, the company's revenue is growing at a rapid pace. The more favorably the company's products are received on the market, the faster will its revenues increase, alongside the growth in the revenues themselves. A main reason for this is that satisfied customers are an excellent marketing instrument and they accelerate the company's sales. In addition, the more entities the company recruits to market its products, the faster does its marketing potential grow. However, the paradox is that, at this stage, the more successful the product launch is, the more the company suffers from negative cash flows.

In order to finance its current negative cash flows, the company needs to raise capital at an accelerated pace. Paradoxically, investors now have to invest more money for their first investments to bear fruit. However, since more information is available at every stage from the market with respect to the feasibility of the project, investors are prepared to increase their investments at ever-growing increments.

The more the project advances, the higher the revenues and the lower the risk to investors. Concurrently with this development, more sources of capital become available to the company, such as loans and, ultimately, public offerings.

Supply—The Company's Ability to Raise Capital

Any attempt to force the various stages of a startup's financing into one standard mold is doomed to fail. There are vast differences among startups in a wide variety of issues, which have an immediate effect on the amount of money they can raise and their value at any given stage. However, some factors are always important:

- **The entrepreneurs' past experience**—The more experienced the startup's entrepreneurs and the more proven success in managing startups they can demonstrate, the easier they will find it to raise more money, according to a higher value.
- **The leading team**—The earlier a company can present an experienced leading team with diverse capabilities in development, marketing, and business development, the easier it will be to raise more money, according to a higher value.
- **The field**—There are significant differences in the type, scope, and structure of investments sought in fields such as advanced optical equipment or components to Internet companies (which are themselves divided into many subcategories) or to medical equipment or communications companies. Every field has different characteristics from the perspective of

the main milestones which the company has to meet, the timetables for progress and success, the anticipated exit, and the investors' current sentiment toward the specific field (many investors act according to the "herd principle," investing in fields that are considered "hot" at that point in time). Accordingly, the value of the assessed company and the amount of capital it could fetch will also be affected.

- **The maturity and current status of the technology**—Generally speaking, the more mature and less risky the technology, the easier it is to raise capital for it. However, some firms do enter highly attractive fields with experienced managers and investors and with a high value, although their technology has not yet been proven. This usually happens when the team and the management are outstanding and when success could revolutionize the field.
- **Understanding the market and the business planning**—The better the company's understanding of its market and competition, and the higher the level of its business planning, the more money it will be able to raise more easily and at a higher valuation.
- **Market penetration**—Usually, a company that has already established a presence in the market receives clear feedback from the market with respect to its products and has accumulated a visible mass of orders, is more attractive and entails a lower risk, and can therefore raise more money.
- **The situation in the capital markets**—The condition of the public capital market, which is the main outlet of investors, as well as the amount of money available to private investors (the supply of money), which also depends on the public capital market, considerably affect the amount of capital raised and its cost. At times when IPOs rarely exist, it is also difficult to raise capital in the private market.

Stages in Raising Venture Capital

There are several customary stages in venture capital investments, which will be discussed in this section. All of the stages are affected by several characteristics that change from one investment round to the next: the condition of the company, the sources of financing, the company's value, the amount of capital raised, the designation of the capital raised, and problems related to the specific stage of financing. Obviously, these are general characteristics that change from one company to another and also depend on the condition of the given market. For instance, the value of seed companies rose immensely in the years 1998–1999 and dropped sharply, beginning in the second half of the year 2000. It is also important to note that several rounds of investment are possible within one stage before the company moves on to the next stage.

Distinguishing among Preliminary Rounds of Investment

The distinction among the different rounds of investment at the first stage—pre-seed, seed, and first round—is not simple. There are many differences which are sometimes a little artificial. Nevertheless, we shall now attempt to explain these differences according to the development axes described above.

It is customary to use different terminology for seed and pre-seed investments according to the progress achieved in proving the feasibility of the idea. When the idea has not yet been proven, an investment is required to prove the technology (or even the existence of a market), and the company usually does not yet exist, the investment is considered pre-seed. If, on the other hand, the company plans on developing a product whose feasibility is proven, although the company itself may still be in its infant phase, the investment is considered a seed investment. Furthermore, a company in the seed phase is expected to be an actual company (even if it is just starting out) and not a project—a status which is perfectly acceptable for the pre-seed stage. What is meant by a "company" is more than just legal incorporation; mainly it implies the existence of a preliminary managerial team in the company as opposed to a single entrepreneur in the pre-company stage. In other words, the main differences between seed and pre-seed financing lie along the R&D axis and perhaps also on the leading team axis.

The main difference between seed financing and first-round financing is the progress of the company, mainly on the business axis, but also on the leading team axis. In the first round, the company will probably have a thorough familiarity of the market and its characteristics and the competition, an understanding and conception of its product with respect to its definition and market fit, as well as a visible management team, or even one significant leader.

It is quite possible for a company to go through all three stages of preliminary financing, or it could skip directly to the first round. A more detailed discussion of each of the three stages of preliminary financing, and of the subsequent stages of financing, now follows.

Pre-seed Financing

- **The condition of the company**—At this phase, talk of a "company" is still premature. What usually exists is an immature idea and an incomplete management team, and there is no guarantee that the idea is technologically feasible or commercially viable.
- **Sources**—The preliminary financing in the first stage is obtained from individuals who are close to the entrepreneur and know him or her personally (family and friends), private investors who are not organized in investing institutions, or incubators.
- **Use**—The money is needed to support the development of the idea in order to promote the product at least to the stage in which its feasibility is proven and to write the business plan.

Seed Financing

- **The condition of the company**—At this stage, there already is a company with a basic team of managers and/or entrepreneurs and possibly also a demo and a basic business plan.
- **Sources**—Once the feasibility of the idea has been proven, capital can also be raised from private investors (angels) who specialize in preliminary investments and from entities who invest in companies in their early phases, such as incubators and specialized funds.
- **The financing process and the investors' involvement**—The process of raising capital from private investors is relatively short, since private investors do not require more than several weeks to reach a decision. However, the entrepreneur should be prepared to present his or her project repeatedly since he or she must try to reach as many investor groups as possible, be they angel clubs, angel associations, or key persons who can influence other private investors because they have faith in the former's ability to screen investments. If the investors are funds or associations of investors, the process takes the form of institutional financing (see below), but this is still done in relatively short time frames. At this stage, investors are primarily involved in providing general advice.

    A large amount of capital is channeled to this field, although the amounts are much smaller following the decline in capital markets, but due to the multitude of new ventures, many investors find it hard to evaluate all the business plans that are sent to them, and without a good reputation of the entrepreneurs, or referrals and assistance by outsiders, a startup's chances of obtaining financing are slim.
- **Use**—At this stage, the money is applied toward recruiting a broader management team and employees, completing the business plan, and developing the product to achieve a beta version that will operate at a beta site (a working model at the customer's facilities) or at least an alpha version (a fully operative preliminary model).

First-stage Financing

As mentioned above, the focus of many funds on seed financing has blurred the distinction between seed financing and first-stage financing. We shall, however, attempt to point out several characteristics of first-stage financing.

- **The condition of the company**—The conditions for an investment are generally the existence of a functioning company with a reasonable understanding of the market and a product under development (at least a working prototype). In the past it was customary to expect a product that is

ready to be launched on the market, but in recent years this type of financing has been provided at earlier stages.
- **Sources**—The source of finance at this stage is usually venture capital funds.
- **The financing process and the investors' involvement**—An investment is usually made after a vigorous due diligence process, designed to corroborate the assumptions underlying the business plan submitted by the company, and after the signing of a detailed contract regulating the terms of the investment, the relationship between the shareholders, and the conditions of the fund's exit. On average, this process lasts between three and six months, and during its course entrepreneurs are required to dedicate many efforts to the capital-raising process while continuing the daily management of the company. At this stage, investors (most of whom are, as mentioned above, venture capital funds) make important decisions for the company, supervise the development activities and the recruitment of employees, and monitor the management's performance closely. These investments are also made in consideration for shares in the company (usually preferred shares which confer priority in distributions at the time of dissolution).
- **Use**—First-stage financing is used to complete the development and commercialization of the product, to expand the managerial team, and to commence the marketing efforts, including recruiting an initial marketing team and sometimes also a sales team.
- **Concerns**—Although the vast majority of the funds dedicated to venture capital investments are directed at first-stage financing, a company wanting to raise capital from venture capital funds for this stage still faces many problems:
    - Lengthy investigations—Since at this stage the company is still risky, venture capital funds perform lengthy investigations into the existence of a market for the product and into the company's chances of successfully completing the development of its products (most of the investment in this stage is dedicated to R&D and to preparing the ground for a managerial and marketing infrastructure). The entrepreneur is assessed at this stage on his or her ability to recruit employees, meet operating targets (he or she is usually not yet required to meet sales targets), and to present the company's vision.
    - Structural and expensive changes—The introduction of institutional investors at this stage usually results in a structural leap in the company's management, for example, financial reporting and a full-fledged board of directors. This transition, which is made during the course of the negotiations for an investment contract, is lengthy and requires considerable managerial resources.

Second- and Third-stage Financing

- **The condition of the company**—A company seeking this type of financing must demonstrate that it has a marketing system, solid management, and existing or pending sales.
- **Sources**—The investors are usually funds, institutional investors, and corporate investors who invest in companies whose business is close to their own.
- **The financing process and the investors' involvement**—Second-stage financing is usually a long and tedious process which requires considerable managerial attention. On average, it starts about one year after the first-stage financing and is followed by a reduced involvement by the investors in the daily management of the business (although they will still require the achievement of certain goals).
- **Use**—The money is used for working capital to enhance the marketing system, buy fixed assets required to support the growth of a company in the stage of active production, and to expand its sales and support teams. The ultimate aim is to reach the stage of sales and typically lead the company to profitability.
- **Concerns**—At this phase in the company's life cycle, it usually enters the stage of marketing and sales. These activities require vast financial and managerial resources that often exceed those available internally to the company. Companies therefore find themselves facing the need to raise more capital immediately, shortly after they finish their first-round financing. In this state of affairs, the company's value for purposes of the second-stage financing has usually not risen substantially, and the need for a large amount of capital may result in a considerable dilution of the existing shareholders, who would rather see a leap in scale in the value of the company.

Pre-IPO Financing

- **Sources and uses**—This round of financing is relevant to companies 12–18 months before an IPO. The amount raised depends on the company's needs until the IPO, and may range between several millions and tens of millions of dollars. The value of the company is derived from its anticipated value in the IPO. This round is usually designed to provide bridge financing until the IPO is completed. The investors in this stage are often passive investors who expect to sell their stakes after the IPO, and venture capital funds, which have already invested in the company. In recent years, they have been joined by private-capital divisions of large investment banks, mutual funds which also invest in the private sector, and other financial institutions such as insurance companies.

In the months preceding an IPO, many companies want to secure interim financing to reduce the uncertainty with respect to the timing of the IPO. Such interim financing, which is becoming more and more popular, reduces the company's dependency on the condition of the stock exchange when determining the timing of the IPO and allows the company to wait for the optimal timing. This interim financing allows investors who are deterred from investing in startups in their early phases to take part in promising private placements. This type of financing is sometimes provided by potential underwriters seeking priority or exclusivity in the role of underwriters for the company's upcoming IPO.

Along with direct investments in consideration for preferred shares, the private sector has in recent years exhibited a sharp trend toward issuing convertible debentures before an IPO. Such securities are issued both to groups of institutional investors and to commercial banks, which have recently been expanding their activities in this field (see Chapter 11 for a more detailed discussion).

- **Concerns**—Companies in need of bridge financing are companies which can demonstrate increasing sales and a well-functioning marketing system, but are not yet ready to go public for various reasons, such as the absence of past experience in a consistent growth in sales or unfavorable market conditions. However, these companies are growing and require ever-increasing investments to finance their high cash burn rate. In these situations, companies sometimes face the problem of having to raise capital with shareholders who object to being diluted other than according to a value that is close to the company's forecasted value in the IPO. Companies in this phase can sometimes receive financing from underwriters, with the disadvantage of having to make a long-term informal commitment in advance to a particular underwriter, thus losing their flexibility to choose the appropriate underwriter when the time comes to go public.

Sources of Capital

Introduction

Several relevant sources of capital are available to a startup in order to meet the company's needs in its various phases. Sources of financing are classified primarily into equity (usually in the form of shares), which is capital invested in the company in consideration for part of the ownership and debt. Many financial instruments are constructed from a combination of the two, such as convertible debentures, which combine debt and options for equity.

There is a direct link between perceived risks and required returns; the risk, the higher is the rate of return expected by investors. The risk incorporated in receiving equity in consideration for an investment is higher than the risk involved in debt (debentures), since shareholders receive only the residual claim, whereas debenture holders have a superior, contractual claim to principal and interest. The younger the company, the greater is the resemblance of any debt it issues to equity, since its debt offers no much better security for a return on the investment.

This section describes the various sources from which startups may obtain financing in the various stages of their development. The first sources will generally tend to invest in the company's equity. In practice, the securities which investors in startups receive are usually preferred shares that are convertible into ordinary shares.

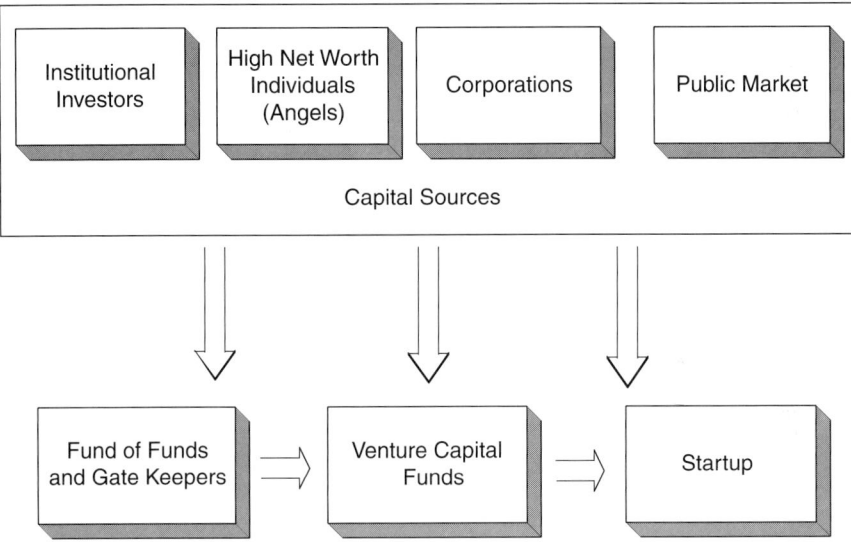

Figure 6–1 Sources of Financing for Startups

The main sources of finance which are available to startups (see Figure 6–1) are venture capital funds, various institutional investors such as pension funds and insurance companies, and private investors (high net-worth individuals, also referred to as "angels") who operate alone or together with others through investors' clubs and companies. The investments are made in three ways: directly in the startup; through entities which provide added value, such as venture capital funds which screen potential investments, make and manage them, and assist in managing the money of investors of different types; and funds of funds, which assist institutional investors in screening and dispersing investments among several venture capital funds. Obviously, public capital markets (particularly investors on stock markets) are another important source of financing for startups—both directly, by public offerings on stock exchanges, and indirectly, by investments in various investment funds.

Family and Friends

This is the first source of financing sought by most entrepreneurs after using their own funds. Investing personal funds or the funds of family and friends also serves as a signal to outside investors that the entrepreneur places great faith in the company.

Private Investors (Angels)

Private investors, also referred to as angels because of their concern for faithful but penniless entrepreneurs, are a common source of preliminary financing. A typical angel is a person who is familiar with the industry (such as an entrepreneur who "made it") and who contributes to the company not only money, but also added value and connections. There now remains only a vague distinction between an angel and a mere private financial investor.

Angels invest in startups in their early phases with the hope of receiving a high rate of return due to the high risk involved in the investment. In the last decade, many angel clubs have developed which bring together several angels to assess opportunities for investments and to aggregate the amounts of money required for them, thereby making the investment more efficient.

Seed and pre-seed investments are available both from individual angels and from angel associations. These investors typically allocate $10,000–200,000 per project, which are invested in the early phases of companies. There are considerable differences among different angels: Some are merely financial investors who are at times entirely unfamiliar with the startup's line of business, and some have vast experience in the company's specific field of activity. In the United States, angel investors contribute more than $15 billion per year to startups.

Information on angels may be obtained from other entrepreneurs, from attorneys and CPAs, and from Web sites which provide information on sources of financing. Angel associations may also be contacted for this purpose. For a further discussion of investments by angels, see Chapter 11.

Venture Capital Funds

In order to finance ventures after their initial establishment, entrepreneurs usually turn to bodies which specialize in high-risk investments. Venture capital funds concentrate capital which is designated for risky investments and provide their investors with investment-screening services in consideration for part of the profit they generate for them. For an in-depth discussion of the structure and manner of operation of venture capital funds, see Chapter 10.

Many venture capital funds now invest in companies in their early phases. Some of the funds also provide added value services similar to those offered by incubators. Nevertheless, it should be kept in mind that the investment process of venture capital funds is generally very long, and funds prefer to invest only after the business and technological models are clarified. Therefore, funds may prove a good source for seed financing, but not for pre-seed financing. Moreover, funds which declare themselves to be "seed investors" are not always capable of providing an infant company with the type of intimate support it requires.

Corporate Investors

Corporate investors have supported the development of business ventures long before the first venture capital funds were created. Even now, following the development of the venture capital fund, a substantial part of the investments in companies is made by corporate investors (either directly or by investing in funds). The investments are made in the development of new ventures inside the company or in new companies that develop promising technologies which complement the investing company's business (see Chapter 11 on corporate in-house startups and incubators). Some of the investments culminate in the acquisition of the company (for instance, the Chromatis-Lucent transaction, in Chapter 14).

Most of the direct investments made by corporate investors are not limited to mere capital, and are aimed at a strategic cooperation in the development of technologies and the acquisition of know-how or in the distribution of a product. This cooperation is often accompanied by the acquisition of 5–20% of the new venture, a level which does not require the investing company to report the investment using the equity method. Strategic cooperation can help new companies introduce their product to the market quickly. The position held by the strategic partner in the target market and its marketing channels can complement the technological know-how of the venture. On the other hand, caution should be exercised in the face of strategic partners who are more interested in gaining access to the technology than in seeing the company succeed by itself. In certain extreme cases, such partners would rather bury the technology than support its development in order to prevent competition with their own technology. Ties with a single strategic partner can also block opportunities for contacts with other players in the market.

In conclusion, cooperating with market leaders can bestow many advantages, but these advantages also entail many risks, and the partner's intentions and character should be carefully scrutinized before any technology is exposed to these potential partners. In addition, it is best to avoid giving the partner advantages over other potential competitors in the acquisition of the company, in case this issue becomes relevant (some companies condition their investment on clauses such as a right of first refusal to buy the company or a priority in the negotiations), to avoid shutting the door on future opportunities.

Other Venture Capitalists

In recent years, investment banks and many institutional entities have started participating in investment rounds, usually together with funds, and their readiness to join relatively early rounds has increased over the years (although most of the direct investments are still made in the later stages). Institutional investors seek opportunities to invest in companies which could provide them with a higher rate of return than that offered by the rest of the market. The phenomenon has become so prevalent that many institutional investors have started making direct investments. In many cases, a venture capital fund will suggest that its investors participate in the investment round independently, since the fund is either not interested in, or is incapable of investing very large amounts of money in, a single company even if it believes in the company's potential. Other venture capitalists that are particularly visible are investment banks that have created venture capital funds under their management. For a more detailed discussion of these investors, see Chapter 11 on financial institutions which invest directly in funds.

Financing by Debt

Beyond the initial stages, startups can resort to financing by way of debt. The term debt usually signifies a short- or long-term line of credit. The lenders can be banks, venture capitalists, or bodies which specialize in providing credit. The borrower receives the right to use the money for a pre-determined period of time in consideration for the payment of interest. The terms of the loan are set in the loan agreement. To guarantee the repayment of the debt and the interest, the loan is backed by the cash flow itself (an unsecured loan) or collateral (a secured loan).

An unsecured loan is given when the creditor ascertains that the company's cash flow will suffice to pay the interest and the principal. Common indicators for measuring the borrower's ability to repay the debt are his or her EBIT and leverage (debt/equity ratio). A secured loan is typically guaranteed by a marketable asset. Financing by debt (without an equity component) is usually inaccessible to early-stage startups, which are based on high-risk growth and which lack many tangible assets, unless their startups have a good chance of securing long-term contracts with customers. At later phases of the company's life cycle, it becomes easier to resort to financial instruments containing a significant debt component. The types of financing by debt that startups commonly use are as follows:

- **Mezzanine loans**—As mentioned above, startups face difficulties in securing traditional financing from banks. A popular solution is the "mezzanine loan." This type of investment lies between debt and equity (hence the name). The incentive for entrepreneurs to use this instrument could be their desire to avoid dilution, on the one hand, and an inability to obtain ordinary bank loans, on the other hand. From the investors' point of view, this loan offers a higher degree of security than an ordinary investment in equity since their right is senior to that of the shareholders.

    The main source for mezzanine loans are commercial banks, insurance companies, and specialized entities which are associated with banks, although mezzanine loans are also offered by several funds which specialize in this type of loan. Mezzanine loans are generally given only to companies that have already started or are about to start making sales, since the repayment of the loan depends on the company's ability to generate cash flows. The criteria used by lenders to screen investments are similar to those used by venture capital funds.

Generally, the securities issued in this type of investment are either high-yield convertible debentures or are accompanied by an equity kicker in the form of warrants. The rate of interest could be more than 10% above similar loans and range between 15% and 30% with the actual interest rate depending to a large extent on the equity component of the loan and naturally on the perceived risk of the loan. If the company is expected to have a negative cash flow in the first stages after the loan is granted, the payment of interest might be deferred for several years after the debenture is issued, with the interest accumulating during the first period. If the company defaults on its payments, the terms of the debenture could provide for changes in the loan terms. Such changes may include: accelerate the debenture's maturity; increase the interest rate; add warrants for additional shares (or a discount in the conversion price in the case of convertible debentures); add rights to control the board of directors, or add rights to force an issuance or sale of the company.

- **Bridge loan**—A bridge loan is typically a loan (for less than one year), designed to provide the company with sufficient funds to finance its current activities, pending an investment round that is expected to take place at a forthcoming time. Bridge loans are common at times close to IPOs from various financial institutions and are also common as a mechanism for funding between financial rounds, without the need to set valuation.
- **Other uses of debt**—In the various stages of a startup's life cycle, the company may use other sources of debt financing. For instance, many companies enable the long-term leasing of most of the equipment required by the company. The company may also obtain short-term loans for working capital needs, or obtain a line of credit from banks to be used as required.

7
Practical Aspects of Raising Venture Capital

INTRODUCTION

This chapter addresses the practical aspects of raising venture capital and the characteristics and the problems of each round of investments, starting from the contacts with the investors and ending in the receipt of the money. This chapter is aimed primarily at entrepreneurs who are raising venture capital for the first time and at others who have no experience in this field.

It is important to understand that the process of raising venture capital is complicated and that there are no guarantees of success. From among more than one million companies which are founded in the United States every year, less than 0.1% receive financing from the venture capital industry. Of every 100 business plans received by venture capital funds, fewer than five on average are seriously considered as candidates for investment and fewer than two receive financing. However, because entrepreneurs usually contact several sources of finance, approximately one-third of the companies which are initially rejected by venture capital funds ultimately find one source of financing or another. Moreover, it is usually a small number of companies from among those which receive financing from venture capital funds that generate the majority of the funds' return. As a result of the growing number of plans which are submitted to institutional investors, the process of raising capital after the initial rounds of financing could last many months and requires thorough preparations and groundwork.

Basic Terms

This section presents the basic terms with which companies raising capital need to be familiar. A more detailed discussion of the valuation of startup companies and various calculations in connection with these terms is given in Chapter 9.

Sale of Shares by Shareholders Versus Investments

The main difference between the sale of shares by shareholders (a "secondary offering")—a transaction to which the company is not a party—and raising capital for the company (i.e., importing money into the company) is that in the latter case the company allots new shares to investors (i.e., adds shares to the company's allotted share capital), against which it receives an investment, usually in cash which it can use for its business.

For example: Speed Ltd. has 3,000,000 shares that are equally divided between its two entrepreneurs. In other words, each entrepreneur holds 50% of the company's equity. If a certain entity were to buy 1,500,000 shares from one entrepreneur, the other entrepreneur would still hold 1,500,000 shares out of the 3,000,000 (50% of the company) and will not have been diluted at all. Ostensibly, the company's financial condition has not changed at all either, since no new funds were infused into the company. If, on the other hand, an investor invests money in the company, in consideration for which the company allots to him or her 1,500,000 shares, then, although each entrepreneur still retains 1,500,000 shares, these shares now constitute only one third of the company's equity. In other words, they were diluted by approximately 17%, or one third of their holdings (for an accurate calculation of the number of shares allotted in investments and the rate of dilution, see Chapter 9). However, in this case the company receives funds or other resources which it can use for its activities. This type of issuance is the most prevalent in early-stage equity private placements, since the main reason for raising capital is the need to infuse money into the company and not the entrepreneurs' desire to realize their investment.

Terms for Describing the Value of a Company

- **Share price**—The price of the share is the basic parameter for calculating the value of a company. Shares are the subject of the investment transaction and they are what changes hands from the seller to the buyer or from the company to the investor. Therefore, the price per share, multiplied by the number of shares purchased, is the gauge by which the value of the transaction is measured.
- **Fully diluted**—An investment in a company is usually made on a fully diluted basis. This means that the calculation of the investor's holdings is made based on the assumption that all the options and other rights to buy shares will be exercised. The dilution also often includes the equity (options) which the company intends to allot to employees. Obviously, when full

dilution is assumed, the number of shares from which the investor is entitled to receive a certain percentage according to the valuation of the company is higher, and hence the number of shares the investor actually receives is also higher (for a calculation of the number of shares allotted on a fully diluted basis, see Chapter 9 on issuing stocks to investors).
- **Pre-money value**—This refers to the product of the number of allotted shares before the investment multiplied by the price of the share. Alternatively, in preliminary investments this parameter serves as the standard for the degree of dilution, which is determined according to the amount of money invested.
- **Post-money value**—The post-money value of the company is its pre-money value, plus the amount of money invested. For example, if Speed Ltd.'s pre-money value is $3 million and it raises $1 million from new investors, then its post-money value is $4 million.

It should be noted that the price of the share just before and after the investment remains unchanged. Speed Ltd., for example, has 3,000,000 shares before the investment. Since its pre-money value was estimated at $3 million, the price of each share was $1. The company has now received an investment of $1 million in consideration for shares. Since the share price is $1, one million additional shares were bought and allotted. The total amount of allotted shares is now 4,000,000, i.e., the new investor holds 25% of the shares: 1,000,000 out of a total of 4,000,000, with the price of each share remaining $1.

Deciding How Much Capital to Raise

The first question which arises in the context of capital-raising is how much money should be sought. The company's ability to attract future investments is always uncertain, due to the volatility of the capital market, as well as the uncertain success of the company on its own merits. Therefore, as a rule of thumb, it is recommended the firm will raise capital, so that at any point, it has sufficient cash for at least 12 months. However, the amount of any potential investment is obviously always limited, as explained in the previous chapter, by the amount of money which investors are willing to risk at that stage of the financing process, and by the measure of dilution of the holdings which the existing shareholders are prepared to accept. The minimum amount which should be raised in each round is that which will enable the company to reach its next milestone, thus enabling additional rounds as well as the necessary time frame required to make such subsequent investment rounds (which could last many months). When making these calculations, the most pessimistic cash burn rate scenario should be used. A large round of investment enables the company to reach the market faster, to join a large number of investors who can contribute added value to the company and to pull through hard times. In that respect, a public offering is not necessarily the last capital raised before investment realization. Entrepreneurs should keep in mind that companies which are traded on NASDAQ were also afflicted with cash crises after the changes which became apparent in the market from the second quarter of 2000; their ability to raise cash on the stock markets was infringed, while their business plans called for ever-increasing cash investments (for a discussion of business planning and forecasting of expenses, see Chapter 3).

Valuing the Company for the Purpose of Raising Capital/Determining According to Which Value Capital Will be Raised

Whereas the amount of money required can, at least in theory, be calculated with reasonable accuracy based on the expense forecast, valuing the company for the purpose of capital raising is far more complicated and is one of the main issues faced by entrepreneurs, especially in the company's early phases. Entrepreneurs are usually not equipped with all the tools and knowledge possessed by investors (Chapter 9 reviews common methods of valuating startups).

Some entrepreneurs opt for the fastest financing, even if it is not based on the highest possible valuation, if they estimate that time is a crucial factor acting against them and the likelihood of success of their business. Other entrepreneurs, according to their character, choose to seek the highest possible price in each round, in consideration of the cost of diluting their holdings. Every startup and team of entrepreneurs take into account different parameters in making this decision. When deciding upon the timing of the financing in relation to the value, they are guided by considerations such as the identity of the investors, the degree to which the entrepreneurs are dependent on outside financing at each stage, and their assessment of the dilutions they expect to face in the future.

The average dilution in high tech companies is around 40–60% after the first round (including seed financing), 20–40% in the second round, and 10–30% from the second round until the IPO (in which 10–30% of the share capital is issued). Another 15–25% is allocated to employees. In other words, the group of entrepreneurs who starts out with 100% will hold approximately 40% after the first round of investment, approximately 25% after the second round, and approximately 15% of the shares before the IPO. These values tend to dramatically change when the round is done at a valuation lower than the previous round (down-round), as became common during the crisis of 2000. In a down-round, entrepreneurs' equity may be significantly reduced. To avoid such a situation, which could leave the entrepreneurs and top executives without incentives to continue with the company, investors tend to compensate the entrepreneurs with additional equity to maintain a minimum holding level (usually around 5% per entrepreneur).

Investments which are based on a high valuation may not only limit the amount of money invested (due to investors' refusal to take part in it), thus denying the company necessary funding, but may also cause friction between the company and its investors. Investors expect to see their investment increase in value from one round to the next. If a subsequent round of investment is made according to values similar or lower to those on which a current round is based, this could be interpreted as a failure, prejudice future investments, and cause tension within the company. Entrepreneurs need to understand that they will be diluted all along the way, and their only consideration should be to what extent any current round, and the dilution it involves, will generate a rise in the long-term value of their holdings. For instance, it is often preferable to raise capital from reputable investors for a relatively low price than from less reputable investors based on a high value.

Entrepreneurs are always subject to the whim of the markets, and sometimes it is almost impossible to raise capital for projects in fields which the financial community considers "cold." However, good projects and smart entrepreneurs may usually be displayed in the appropriate light, even if the company's business direction remains unchanged. As explained in Chapter 3 on business planning, a good managerial team and reputable financial backers and advisors are essential for raising capital, especially at times of crisis in the market for investments in the relevant field.

The Process of Raising Venture Capital

This section focuses on the process of raising venture capital from institutional sources or from organized angels. Investments made in the earlier stages (by family, friends, and small private investors) are not characterized by an orderly structure. Capital may be raised from institutional sources or from angel associations after the company is established and the business organization for raising capital is completed (including the business plan). This financing is usually founded on principles similar to those governing first-round investments, but at this stage entrepreneurs already have some experience and can also rely on the funds which were invested in the early rounds.

This section is aimed at novice entrepreneurs who have not yet experienced capital-raising personally.

What Interests Investors

Before approaching an investment round, it should be ascertained whether the company meets investors' standards. The main issues which interest investors are the following:

- **Management**—Almost all investors regard a team of entrepreneurs and managers capable of leading the company to success as the key to an affirmative decision. Investors expect to see teams whose aggregate skills turn them into a "commando" unit, capable of functioning under stress and finding creative solutions that will secure the company's anticipated success even in front of a tough environment. A good team includes managers, technology and business-development leaders, and advisors who complement the team in the field of finance and with contacts in the business world.

    Investors look for the entrepreneurs' commitment to their project. Jeff Bezos, for instance, the entrepreneur who founded the e-commerce company Amazon, demonstrated an exceptional degree of confidence and commitment by abandoning a promising career at an investment bank in favor of the new company and investing in it money from his own and his parents' savings. Investing in a working model of the product, preparing a technical specification, and other such factors which indicate the entrepreneur's commitment and investment, are always helpful in encouraging investors to make affirmative decisions.

Relevant experience in the field or other managerial experience is also helpful in attracting investors, but in their absence a company can still rely on the experience of others. It can recruit experienced experts from the relevant field to its management team or team of advisors, and their involvement in the project can contribute to the capital-raising efforts.

- **Market**—The existence of a large potential market, of which the company may gain a considerable share, is an essential and basic consideration which becomes more important as the company matures. For instance, institutional investors seek products with an annual sales potential of at least several hundred million dollars. Beyond a knowledge of the size of the market, investors need to assess the company's understanding of the market and be convinced that its proposed solution does indeed meet the future needs of that market. In most cases, the size of the market and the company's projected profitability are crucial factors in the company's potential, because even prudent managers and exceptional products cannot usually generate more than the maximum projected return, given the forecasted market data. Components which considerably affect a market's appeal are the impact of existing and expected legislation, either federal or local, anticipated demographic changes, tax consequences, projections with respect to the entry of potential competitors into the market, and the identity and nature of such potential competitors.

- **The company's relative long-term edge**—Investors seek out the product with a high added value to its target users that will become the sustainable market leader. For instance, a high tech startup has usually inferior resources at its disposal compared to high tech giants, and/or must therefore rely on visible technological depth and/or superiority of other domains. A major issue is the company's relative long-term comparative advantage over its competitors. A technological advantage is typically insufficient in itself, so the company must construct a "package" that is composed of a revenue model, a marketing model, a model for protecting its intellectual capital, and a set of schemes for cooperation. Investors will examine the components of this business model, and assess the chances of realizing the potential of the product or the service.

- **Synergism with investors**—Investors in general, and corporate investors and venture capital funds in particular, prefer combinations in which the

value of the investment will rise due to the investors' contributed experience and contacts. In addition, they may look for the added value of the company's products to their own offerings, or to the offerings of their portfolio firms.
- **Anticipated exit**—Over and above all of the issues mentioned above, investors obviously also examine the possible exits they will have to realize their investment, and the potential to achieve exceptionally high returns.

Preparing to Raise Capital

Contacting investors when the company is not yet fully prepared not only reduces the chances of an affirmative reply, but also diminishes the prospects of the company (and possibly also the prospects of subsequent ventures undertaken by the entrepreneurs) to secure financing in the future by giving an impression of imprudence. The more prepared and mature the company is when it approaches outside investors, the better its chances of obtaining the investment and at the value it hopes for. Venture capital funds are best contacted only after a company has a solid managerial backbone, a business plan prepared on the basis of thorough market research, and preferably also some product prototypes.

Choosing the Investors

First, a profile of the potential investor has to be drawn. There are many venture capital funds; some focus on a particular field or technology, others focus on certain stages of financing, and others have rules with respect to minimum and maximum size of investments. First and foremost, the likelihood of capital-raising is highly influenced by having pre-existing direct or indirect connections with the VC. However, beyond this pre-condition, the main issues which need to be examined are: (1) The fund's reputation in the market; (2) The experience it has and the investments it has made in the relevant field and in the stage reached by the company (relevant experience can help in contacts and even in development); (3) The fund's track record working with entrepreneurs; (4) The fund's contacts with bodies which can promote the company; (5) The fund's ability to take part in additional rounds and to recruit additional investors; and (6) The identity of the partner in the fund who handles investments in companies in the startup's line of business, because personal connections with the partner and his or her ability to contribute to the development of the company are crucial components in its success.

An entrepreneur could draw a matrix in which all of the funds are rated on the basis of the degree to which they meet basic criteria (field of investment, amount of investment, and stage of financing) and their "rating" in the issues listed above. At the end of this process, the company has to choose the most appropriate funds for an initial application.

Contacting and Meeting with Investors

Once the investors to be contacted are chosen, the company usually sends them a summary of its business plan with a cover letter. As mentioned above, whenever possible, this should be done with the backing of personal contacts, for recommendations, and/or the assistance of advisors who are "door openers." The chances for an "orphan" business plan to survive the initial screening process are slim.

A very small number of the companies which submit business plans to funds advance to the point of a meeting with the entrepreneurs. Only well-prepared companies which meet the criteria listed in the section above on what interests investors (and, naturally, which meet the fund's specific criteria) will reach the stage of a meeting. The impression created by the entrepreneurs in this meeting has a crucial impact on the fund's decision to invest. The fund does not intend to evaluate the technology during this meeting (it will engage experts for this purpose), but to gain a general impression of the entrepreneurs' ability to execute their vision. The entrepreneur must assume that the material he or she sent was not necessarily read attentively, and that in any case some people who are encountering the company for the first time will also be present at the meeting. The meeting will start with an introduction of the entrepreneur and his or her group and of the investor and his or her group. Afterwards, the entrepreneur will usually have an opportunity to give a short presentation about the company.

The presentation is a tool for communicating a message in a simple and efficient manner and is not a goal in itself. While it is important that the presentation should be vivid, it is also important to focus on the essence of the company and its offerings rather than on the presentation technology, as it may cloud the underlying message. The use of technical aids is not necessary at all, and when the group is small, some people prefer to just conduct a conversation.

Deciding upon an Investment

Based on the information furnished by the company (mainly the business plan), the meetings with the entrepreneur, and investigations which the fund will conduct with respect to the product and the team, the fund will decide whether or not to continue the investment process (see the next section on how venture capital funds work with respect to the internal decision-making process of funds). From the fund's point of view, the decision to continue the investment process involves the high cost of having experts in the field examine the plan and the company. In any case, the decision is subject to an agreement on the terms and to a due diligence process. If the decision is affirmative, a series of additional meetings will be held in which a term sheet will be drawn. The fund's signing of the term sheet is, in fact, the official seal of the fund's decision that it is interested in giving the investment serious consideration.

Furthermore, in order to be fair to the companies, funds try not to sign the term sheet unless they have reached a decision in principle to make the investment, subject to a due diligence process, and other specific examinations. This is because withdrawing from an investment after the term sheet has been signed could hurt the company, which has by then invested a significant amount of resources in working directly opposite the fund without pursuing other routes (including a customary exclusivity "no shop" clause undertaking in the "term sheet").

Due Diligence

During this lengthy process, the investor checks the company over from both the business and legal aspects in order to verify the facts presented to him in the business plan and the negotiations, and examines any material information which could affect the value of the company and the investment decision. This examination is usually performed by the lead investor in any given round. The process serves both the investors, as a means of getting to know the company better, and the company, by improving its acquaintance with the investors who could accompany it over several years.

The components of the examination and its emphases change in accordance with the phase in the company's development, but generally include the following main components:

- **A business investigation** of the technology, the market, the intellectual property, the assumptions underlying the business forecast, the revenue structure (if any), the expense structure, and the budget. A material part of this investigation is carried out before the term sheet is signed.
- **A legal examination** of the company's organizational documents, ownership structure, the resolutions passed by the shareholders and the board of directors, material agreements, the company's assets and liabilities, and ownership of intellectual property, including patents, the company's rights to its name and Web site (these issues are examined by attorneys who specialize in intellectual property), agreements with the company's employees, agreements with interested parties, proceedings opposite various authorities, and legal exposure.
- **An auditor examination** and analysis of the company's financial statements, taxation, and any liability. This examination is carried out by the investor's CPA.

8

Legal and Contractual Aspects of Raising Venture Capital

INTRODUCTION

This chapter addresses the legal and contractual aspects of raising capital for the firm from venture capital investors (a discussion of the relationship between the venture capital funds and their investors is presented in Chapter 10). The discussion is not limited to the technical legal aspects of investment contracts, but is primarily an extensive discussion of the manner in which the relationships between investors and companies are regulated, the parties' interests, and the manner in which they can be bridged. A brief discussion of the legal restrictions imposed on raising venture capital is followed by an extensive discussion of the main legal documents involved in venture capital investments: the term sheet, the investment agreement (which is, in fact, a share purchase agreement), and the registration rights agreement. It is important to note that some legal issues are also regulated in the company's organizational documents (see Chapter 2 on incorporation documents). The last part of the chapter briefly reviews some supplementary documents such as employment agreements for the founders, employee confidentiality agreements, and shareholders agreements.

Legal Restrictions on Raising Private Capital

Securities offerings are governed by the Securities Act of 1933 and rules thereunder. The relevant rules, with respect to a private offering of a startup, are those related to exemption from registration.

Legal Restrictions According to U.S. Law

According to Section 4(2) of the Securities Act of 1933, there is no need to register shares (or deliver a prospectus) in a private sale of securities. U.S. courts have laid down certain conditions for exempting private sales from registration. Generally, the following requirements have to be met for the exemption to be available: (1) the offeree receives or is given access to material information about the company; (2) the issuance of the securities is performed directly and not via means of mass distribution; (3) the number of offerees and buyers is limited; (4) the buyers will not act in practice as distributors of the shares (in other words, they will not purchase them with the aim of reselling them in the short-term).

Most investments of private capital in startups qualify for the exemption. However, it is still best to rely on clear rules such as those contained in Regulation D. Regulation D was promulgated by the Securities and Exchange Commission (SEC) in order to provide definite (although not exclusive) rules for exemption from registration. The rules in Regulation D exempt the sale of securities by companies from registration in one of three ways:

- **An issuance in accordance with Rule 504**—The sale of securities for a total amount of up to $1 million in a period of 12 months is exempt from registration with no other conditions.
- **An issuance in accordance with Rule 505**—The sale of securities for a total amount of up to $5 million in a period of 12 months is exempt from registration provided that all of the investors save 35 are "accredited investors" (i.e., 35 investors may be investors that are not accredited investors). This term generally refers to the following investors: banks, brokers, institutional investors, managers and directors of the company, or individuals with net assets exceeding $1 million or an income exceeding $200,000 per year ($300,000 per household/couple).
- **An issuance in accordance with Rule 506**—This refers to the sale of securities for an unlimited amount to "accredited investors" and to another 35 investors who are not "accredited investors." However, under this regulation, which does not limit the amount of the offering, the "non-accredited" investors are required to represent that they are able, either alone or together with their representatives, to assess the benefits and risks involved in the investment.

In order to meet the Regulation D rules, investors are customarily required to represent in the investment agreement that they are indeed "accredited investors."

How to Meet the Legal Requirements

As mentioned above, a private placement is subject to domestic and occasionally also foreign securities laws, as well as rules deriving from the law of contracts. The following discussion addresses both these sets of laws.

- **The number and identity of the offerees and buyers**—As a rule, securities should not be offered to a large number of offerees, who are not "accredited investors" under U.S. law. In any case, shares should be offered strictly to investors who are able, either alone or with the assistance of consultants, to understand the meaning of the investment and to bear the risk involved in such investment. This would also prevent claims by customers with respect to fraud or exploitation under contract law.
- **The offering document**—The document pursuant to which the securities are offered (usually the business plan or a PPM—Private Placement Memorandum) should include all the material information about the company. In addition, each document should be numbered and a record should be kept of the person to whom it was given, thus proving the number of offerees and that all material issues were duly disclosed.
- **Personal negotiations**—Negotiations should be conducted in person with each investor in order to eliminate the fear that the sale of the shares will be classified as a public offering requiring the filing of a registration statement. In addition, each investor should be given the opportunity to perform a due diligence process which would prevent claims of misrepresentations and claims under the law of contracts.
- **The investment contract**—Representations should be obtained with respect to (1) the investor's experience in investments of the type in question and his or her being an "accredited investor" for purposes of U.S. law; (2) the investor's ability to bear the risk and his or her understanding of the subject matter of the investment; (3) the fact that he or she had conducted a due diligence process to his or her satisfaction; (4) his or her understanding of the restrictions imposed on the sale of shares which are not listed for trade and his or her readiness to adhere to them (see Chapter 13 on selling shares that are exempt from registration).

The Term Sheet

The delivery of a signed term sheet to the company is a substantial milestone on the path leading to an investment. The term sheet is a legal document which is non-binding except for certain clauses specified below. It determines the main terms of the investment which are later expanded in the investment agreement and the documents attached to it. The document is not binding because the investor conditions his or her investment and the signing of the ultimate agreement upon a business, legal, and financial due diligence process. Nevertheless, the document is very significant because funds do not habitually sign term sheets and carry out expensive due diligence processes if they do not intend to invest in the company. The objective of the term sheet is twofold: As mentioned above, it serves as the basis for the investment agreement and addresses the main business issues. In addition, the "no shop" clause it contains enables the investor to proceed with the investment process, including completing the due diligence process and drafting the investment contract, knowing that the company will not, at this time, turn to other investors to improve its position. On the other hand, the importance of the term sheet must not be overrated, since it is only an intermediate step en route to the investment agreement, which is the document that fixes the terms of the investment.

Many investors have standard term sheets which they use. A term sheet may be one or two pages long and contain only the most basic terms, or it may also be a 20-page document, not easily distinguishable from an investment agreement. Since most of the clauses of the term sheet are incorporated in the investment agreement, we will now focus only on the issues that are unique to term sheets.

- **The legal status of term sheets**—As mentioned above, the term sheet is not legally binding on the parties. In most cases, the term sheet includes a specific stipulation whereby it constitutes a declaration of intent and is not legally binding except for certain clauses (no shop, confidentiality, and expenses), and whereby the signing of the investment agreement is contingent upon the satisfactory completion of the due diligence process, the drafting of an investment agreement on which the parties agree, and the approval of the investor's appropriate entities.
- **No shop**—The company undertakes not to seek out other investors for a pre-determined period of time (usually 30–60 days), during which the investor conducts the due diligence process and negotiations are conducted for the investment contract. This clause is the most important binding clause in the term sheet since all of the other provisions serve only as a basis for the future investment agreement.
- **Confidentiality**—Both the investors and the company undertake to maintain in confidence all of the company's secret information, as well as any information exchanged between them during the negotiations and the due diligence process.
- **Expenses**—If an investment agreement is executed, the company will reimburse the investor for his or her expenses, including legal expenses, up to a pre-determined amount. Sometimes, the reimbursement undertaking is not contingent upon the execution of an investment agreement.

Investment Agreements

Simultaneously with the due diligence process, the parties' legal representatives conduct negotiations for the conclusive investment agreement. The investment agreement is an agreement for the sale of shares in the company to the investors in consideration for a certain amount of money (the investment). Although the transaction appears to be a simple one (ostensibly nothing more than the sale of an asset for money, a transaction commonly made for thousands of years), an agreement for an investment in a startup company is a complex legal document which regulates many issues concerning the investment itself, and the future relationship between the company and the investors and often also with other entities such as employees, directors, and previous investors. These agreements are packed with professional terms, most of which are unclear to anyone not proficient in legal language.

There are several approaches to drafting investment agreements. The customary method is to include in the investment agreement all the issues pertaining to the investment, including the rights attached to the investor's shares and the balance of power within the company, issues which are usually regulated also in the company's organizational documents (the certificate of incorporation or the bylaws). The supporters of this approach emphasize the importance of creating one document which embraces all the relevant arrangements, even at the cost of having these issues repeated in other documents. Another advantage is the independent course of action afforded to the parties to the contract, as opposed to the situation in which these issues are regulated only in the company's bylaws, which creates a doubt as to an individual shareholder's right to sue the company alone. According to another method, the investment agreement should not repeat issues which are already regulated in other documents or agreements. Another advantage in creating separate documents is that whenever an investor joins the company, the bylaws need not be changed and it is sufficient to join him in existing agreements.

There is no uniform structure for investment agreements, but a typical structure would include the following components:

- **The transaction**—The material terms of the transaction (the sale of securities in consideration for an investment) are discussed. This chapter contains a description of the buyers, the purchased asset (securities), and the consideration (the price per share).
- **The company's representations and warranties**—This is usually the longest chapter in the investment agreement and the subject of lengthy discussions by the attorneys. "Reps and warranties" are designed to provide detailed information about the business and condition of the company and to enable the party relying on the representations to file a complaint if a representation is breached. However, where startups are concerned, as opposed to acquisition transactions involving giant companies, if a representation is breached and material damage is caused, the company will in any case not have the money required to compensate the investor. However, it is customary to require an opinion by the company's attorney with respect to certain legal representations, thus creating a "deep pocket" from which compensation can be sought in some cases, at least in theory. Over and above these representations, investors are protected against misrepresentations, fraud, or undue disclosure by standard provisions in the laws of contracts, torts, and securities. Section 10b-5 of the Securities

Exchange Act of 1934 provides protection in most cases against the breach of a representation in an agreement to purchase securities. A contractual representation is, however, still legally superior since a complaint can be filed due to the breach of a contractual representation even without the presence of a state of mind (such as knowledge) or negligence by the party who made the representation.

Another substantial advantage of reps and warranties is that they compel decision-makers to pay attention to and discuss all of the issues included in them. Bringing problematic issues to the surface enables the company to deal with them and enables investors to better quantify the risks involved in the transaction.

It is customary to provide reps and warranties on many issues: the organization of the company and its organizational documents, the authority to sign the investment agreement, the company's share capital and undertakings to allot shares, its financial condition, property, intellectual property, material agreements, legal proceedings in which it is involved, taxation, employees, debts, and other issues that are unique to the company or have surfaced in the due diligence process. From the company's point of view, it is best to qualify the reps and warranties, so that only a breach having a Material Adverse Effect (MAE) on the company will entitle the investor to a remedy.

- **The investor's representations and warranties**—Except for the standard reps and warranties with respect to the investor's authority to invest and his or her financial ability to do so, it is customary to request representations pertaining to the investor's experience in venture capital investments and to his or her status as an "accredited investor," as well as additional representations supporting the classification of the transaction as a private sale which does not require the filing of a registration statement (see the section on legal restrictions for raising private capital).
- **The company's covenants**—In contrast to representations and warranties which are a declaration of facts, a covenant is a promise to perform or refrain from performing certain acts in the future. There are two types of covenants: affirmative covenants such as an undertaking to provide financial information, and negative covenants such as an undertaking to refrain from performing certain acts without the investor's approval. The material covenants are reviewed in the section on the right to control and right to information.
- **Conditions precedent to closing**—There are certain acts which the company undertakes to perform by the date of closing: usually obtaining approvals and adopting resolutions, changing the bylaws, having employees and entrepreneurs sign employment agreements, and other undertakings. If these acts can be performed relatively quickly, a shortcut may be taken by

closing the transaction concurrently with the signing of the investment agreement, without holding a separate closing.
- **Closing**—In the closing, it is verified that all of the conditions precedent to closing have been met and that all of the documents which need to be delivered at the closing have been prepared. In some cases, there are several closing dates, either because the investment is made according to milestones or because additional investors are expected to join. In general, it is recommended that the transaction be closed as soon as possible without waiting for additional investors. Once the first investor is in, it is easier to attract more investors.
- **Indemnification**—It is customary for companies to undertake in the investment agreement to indemnify the investors for any damage they may suffer due to the breach of a representation or a covenant by the company. Although the parties and their attorneys dedicate much time to indemnification clauses, they are of little importance; legally, the investors are in any case entitled to a remedy under the laws of contracts or torts for the breach of a representation or a covenant. However, the company typically has no "deep pocket" from which the investors would be able to collect in case of such breach unless the company is about to make an IPO and has tangible assets and cash at its disposal. A partial solution is providing indemnification in the form of shares, not cash. From the company's point of view, it is best to try to limit, in the indemnification clause, the period of time in which a complaint can be filed for the breach of a representation. The statutes of limitation in most countries allow several years after the contract is signed, and in certain cases even after the breach is discovered, to file a contractual complaint. This exposes the company to a possible "retroactive complaint" by an investor who discovers after several years that his or her investment was unsuccessful and is looking for ways to collect his or her loss from the company. A possible solution is to limit the time frame for filing a complaint due to breaches in good faith.
- **Schedules and exhibits**—Two types of appendices are attached to investment agreements: disclosure schedules, which constitute part of the reps and warranties and provide information about the company; and additional exhibits, such as the organizational documents, employment agreements, and projected budget. Sometimes the company's legal counsel's opinion on legal matters is also attached to the agreement.

Main Issues in Investment Agreements

This section reviews the main issues addressed in investment agreements, the common practices in the market, the real meaning of legal terms which are usually clear only to attorneys who work in the field, and how to reach solutions which will meet the needs of both the investors and the company. Some of these issues are also regulated in the company's organizational documents, so that they will also be effective towards third parties who are not a party to the investment agreement. For features that are not presented in every deal, we have indicated how often they are seen in investment agreements and at what stage of financing (early or follow-up) they are being used.

Financial Matters

- **Valuation and the investor's holdings**—The investor and the company have to agree on the company's pre-money value, from which the price per share is derived, and on the amount of the investment. Value is calculated on the basis of models which are discussed in Chapter 9. Calculations of holdings are made on the basis of the value. Holdings and value calculations are usually performed on a fully diluted basis, i.e., assuming that all of the options and rights allotted to employees, directors, and shareholders are exercised.
- **Employee stock option plans**—The percentage (usually in the range of 15–25%) of shares set aside for employees stock option plans has a direct bearing on the negotiations for the value of the transaction. Obviously, the more shares which are set aside before the investor joins the company, the more shares he or she will in effect receive in consideration for his or her investment (or, in other words, a discount on the price of the investment). For a calculation of the number of shares allotted to employees, see Chapter 9 on issuing stock to investors.

    Example: A company's pre-money value is estimated at $4 million and the investor invests $1 million in the company. The company has 4,000,000 issued shares before the investment round. If no options are allotted to employees, the investor will receive 1,000,000 shares (at $1 per share), constituting 20% of the issued shares after the round. If it is determined that 20% of the company's shares before the investment should be allocated to the employee stock option plan, then the investor will receive 1,250,000 shares (20% out of a total of 6,250,000 shares after the round) in consideration for the same amount ($1 million), at the of $0.80 per share (for a further discussion, see Chapter 9 on issuing stock to investors).
- **Options for future investments**—Investors may ask for options to invest in the company in the future. Options are much more common in early rounds than in later stage ones. The use of options for future investment was a standard feature (more than 80% of the deals) in the first half of the 1990s. In the late 1990s, when money was chasing after companies, options have become less common. From mid-2001, the use of options has increased in popularity again and they are used in more than 50% of the deals. The terms of the option define the exercise price and the exercise date. Every option is,

in fact, a discount on the agreed price since the option has an economic value, although this value is hard to measure in private companies (for a discussion of the valuation of options, see Chapter 5 on stock option plans).

There is a disadvantage from the company's point of view in granting options, since an option dilutes the existing entrepreneurs and shareholders and is given at a price that is considerably lower than the true value at the time of exercise. Granting an option usually serves as a precedent for future rounds, and could cause the next investors to also demand options. On the other hand, options can also serve as an instrument for bridging gaps in value estimates, since they award the investor a discount on future required investments (the exercise price). In addition, an ostensibly high value can be displayed externally, since the discount component of the option is not necessarily reflected in the information given to the press and to outsiders. The same is true with respect to other terms concerning the allotment of additional shares in case of a failure to meet forecasts.

From the investor's point of view, an option constitutes not only a discount, but also an excellent means for receiving a high Internal Rate of Return (IRR). An option enables the investor to increase his or her IRR if the investment is successful and the option is exercised, since the investment will be made only if the option is "in the money." If options are issued, it is important to address several issues: the number of options (i.e., the number of shares to be received upon the exercise of the option), the exercise price, and the term of the option.

Venture capitalists are measured according to the IRR of their investment, but this measurement is based on their portfolio as a whole. In other words, in each individual investment, they also seek a high dollar return, and not only a high IRR. For instance, although a profit of $1 on an investment of $1 over a period of one year represents a return of 100%, investors may prefer, given the limited availability of opportunities and resources, a profit of $10 on an investment of $11, although the IRR of the former investment is higher.

From the entrepreneur's point of view, the number of shares (which dilutes the entrepreneurs and the other shareholders) is more important than the exercise price. The reason for this is that the company does not usually regard the cash flow received at the time of exercise as being important, since it assumes that the option will be exercised when the company has greater resources anyway. An illustration of the insignificance of this component may be found in the fact that in many cases the investor does not infuse new cash into the company at all when exercising the option, but rather "pays" with shares received upon exercise of the option (a method of exercise known in the market as "cashless exercise").

An option should state the number of shares—and not a percentage of the equity—which the option holder will receive at the time of exercise. The difference between the two can be enormous, since in the latter case the investor is not diluted until he or she exercises the option. For instance: A company which has 1,000 shares can give an investor an option to buy 10 shares (case "a") or 1% of the capital at the time of exercise (case "b"). At the time of exercise, after several rounds of share allotments, assume the company already has 5,000 shares. Whereas in case "a" the investor will still receive 10 shares (1% of 1000 shares), in case "b" he or she will receive 50 shares.

Since the longer the term of an option, the higher is its economic value, it is in the company's interest to keep the option as short as possible. On the other hand, a long term will usually ensure that it will be worth the investor's while to exercise the option. From a purely economic standpoint, it would appear that it is better for the company if the option is not exercised. However, an option which is not exercised by the investor and expires unexercised may have a negative reputational effect which could affect the company's ability to raise other capital. In any event, it should be ascertained that the terms of option end when the company is obligated to convert all of its equity into ordinary shares (usually before the company is listed on a stock exchange, or is sold).

- **Mechanisms for value adjustments (claw back or ratchet)**—When there are disagreements with respect to the value of the company, these often result from a disagreement on (optimistic) forecasts of the company. A mechanism can be added whereby the investor's holdings will be adjusted or he or she will be required to increase his or her investment if the company's actual performance is considerably worse or better than the company's projections. In most cases, it is preferable not to be dragged into such mechanisms since they complicate subsequent investments and may also cause a conflict of interests. On the one hand, the investor is interested in the company's success and progress but, on the other hand, a lesser success at the specified date would give him larger holdings. Such a conflict of interests could be a source of future friction. Due to the complexity and conflict of interest inherent in claw back, this feature is used in less than 20% of the deals and is more common in early rounds.
- **Using bridge loans**—When the parties cannot agree on the value of the company, the financing can be provided as a convertible debt which may then be converted into equity when capital is raised from another investor, according to the value set when the additional investor is introduced (usually with a certain discount). From the company's point of view, a bridge loan enables the company's value to be increased by the subsequent round and greatly facilitates the negotiations (since the value depends on the future investor). On the other hand, investors may fear being overly dependent on a future investor and receiving inadequate compensation for the risk they are bearing at present. The uncertainty embedded in such a mechanism makes it a feature that is used in less than 25% of the deals, both in early and late stage financing.

The Rights Attached to the Securities Allotted to the Investor—Protecting the Value of the Investment

The securities allotted to investors are usually preferred shares convertible into ordinary shares. Other types of securities allotted to venture capital investors are convertible debentures or ordinary shares. When preferred shares are converted into ordinary shares, usually before an IPO or a sale, the shareholders naturally cease to enjoy any special rights. The rights attached to preferred shares are also fixed in the company's organizational documents. These usually include all the rights attached to ordinary shares, including voting rights, as well as the following rights:

- **Preference in liquidation**—In liquidation, preferred shareholders are usually entitled to receive the amount of their investment, in addition to interest guaranteeing a pre-determined IRR, before any ordinary shareholder. Ostensibly, preference in liquidation is not very valuable, since when a startup dissolves it typically has no valuable assets except perhaps its intellectual property (which is, at times, subject to special arrangements). The reason for demanding preference in liquidation is that liquidation is often defined not only as actual dissolution or liquidation, but also as events that are deemed as liquidation. Such liquidation naturally includes voluntary dissolution, but also the sale of all of the company's assets, the sale of the company, a merger, restructuring, or any other act after which the current shareholders hold less than 50% of the company's shares. In such deemed-liquidation cases, the company may have many assets and funds.

    The reason underlying the preference in liquidation is composed of several elements. The investor, as opposed to the entrepreneurs, invests real money in the company and wants to have his or her investment repaid before profits are distributed among all the shareholders. In addition, preference in liquidation can increase the likelihood that the investor receives a minimum IRR when he or she exits the investment. Finally, preference in liquidation prevents the entrepreneurs from selling the company at a low price, which may be appealing to them, but does not signify success from the investor's perspective.

    In some cases, especially when the minimum IRR is not high, the preferred shareholders partake in another distribution together with the other shareholders, proportionately to the preferred shareholders' holdings (Participating Preferred Shares). In other words, the preferred shareholders enjoy both their preferred dividend and, together with the other shareholders, whatever remains. Such a distribution could cause directors to decline sale or merger proposals, since the share they would retain in the distribution does not provide them with a sufficient incentive. In order to prevent such an eventuality, it is customary to limit the right of preferred shareholders so that they do not enjoy a preference if their investment exceeds a specified return, typically a multiple of three to five over the investment. In other words, if the preferred shareholders would receive the minimum return agreed upon in an equitable distribution according to the holding ratios, then a single and equitable distribution will be made to all shareholders.

Example: An investor invests $1 million in a company according to a (pre-money) value of $4 million, and receives 1,000,000 class A preferred shares constituting 20% of the company's equity after the investment. The shares confer a right to a minimum IRR of 50%. Three years later, the company sells all of its assets (a deemed-liquidation event) in consideration for $10 million and transfers the consideration to the shareholders. In this state of affairs, the investor will, first of all, receive $3,375,000 representing an IRR of 50% per year on an investment of $1 million (i.e., more than one-third of the consideration even though he or she held only 20%); thereafter, the other shareholders will split the remainder of the consideration among themselves. Had the investor held participating preferred shares and had been entitled to take part in the distribution of the remainder as well, he or she would have received another 20% ($1,325,000) of such a remainder (i.e., he or she would have received, in total, approximately one-half of the consideration). On the other hand, if the assets had been sold for $30 million, the investor would have shared the amount equally with the other shareholders in proportion to his or her holdings and would have received $6 million.

- **Preference in the receipt of dividends**—Many agreements contain a requirement for preference in the receipt of dividends up to a certain rate of interest (preferred dividends). The interest is usually designed to ensure a return which will be a little above the prime interest rate. In most cases, the interest does not accrue before a dividend is distributed in order to avoid the recording of a contingent liability in the company's books, and this issue is therefore meaningless in startups which do not distribute dividends. If, however, the interest does accrue, it is added to the return on the investment as part of the preference in liquidation if the company is sold. In most cases, investors have no reason to ask for a dividend to be distributed in cash, since the main return they expect to derive from the investment results from an increase in the company's value. Any distribution of cash reduces this value since the return on cash which is invested by the company is higher than the return available in risk-free investment alternatives (otherwise, investors would not have continued to back the company). In fact, many venture capital investors demand a right to receive a preferred dividend only in order to reduce incentives for its distribution in the future.
- **Conversion**—Preferred shares may be converted at any time, at the investor's choice, into ordinary shares according to a conversion rate that is

adjusted to any changes in the company's capital and dilution. Such conversion takes place automatically (and involuntarily) at the time of a sale, or an IPO (usually, only an IPO or a sale which meet the conditions fixed with respect to the investor's minimum return). It is important to stipulate that a conversion can also be enforced at the majority decision of the shareholders in order to prevent "extortion" by a few shareholders when a transaction is on the table which requires a conversion but does not meet the threshold conditions for automatic conversion.

- **Preemptive right**—Originally, the preemptive right was a right which existing shareholders hold, that imposes on the company the duty, when allotting additional securities, to offer the securities to the existing shareholders according to their share in the company *before* offering them to outside buyers. The practical expression of this right in startups is the right of existing shareholders to buy shares in any future allotment proportionately to their holdings in the company, under the same terms and conditions at which they are allotted to the new investors, in a manner preserving their proportionate share in the company's equity (see an example of an allotment in which a preemptive right is exercised in the section on issuing stock to investors in Chapter 9).

  Preemptive rights exist in almost all investment agreements because they have an economic significance aside from the legal rights of control they guarantee. Preemptive rights provides investors with protection when the company wants to issue shares for a value lower than their economic worth in a manner which dilutes the investors. An issuance of shares according to a value lower than that according to which the investor joined the company is treated by anti-dilution rights (see below), but the company could still issue shares at a value higher than the previous investment, but lower than that which the investor perceives as economical. In this case, the investor can exercise his or her preemptive right and gain an economic benefit (or thwart the issuance in certain cases). Other than that, this right enables investors to increase the IRR of their portfolio by increasing their investments in successful companies.

  On the other hand, this right can create several problems for the company: If all or most of the existing investors were to exercise their preemptive rights, it would either be impossible to raise capital from new investors, or such investments would unreasonably dilute the shareholders who do not enjoy a preemptive right—usually the entrepreneurs. In addition, awarding a preemptive right to all the investors involves bureaucratic problems (the need to ask all the investors for a waiver in each new round of investments) and legal problems (if the right is awarded to more than 35 investors who are not defined as classified investors under the Securities Law, a prospectus will have to be published in every investment round made by the company, discussed in the section on legal restrictions on raising private capital).

Therefore, an attempt is sometimes made (only with respect to private investors) to limit this right to one round. In other words, the investor will be entitled to maintain the percentage of his or her holdings in the round following the one in which he or she invested, but not more than that. A more customary limitation on the preemptive right is that each shareholder is entitled to preserve his or her holdings only, so that if another shareholder waives the right, the other shareholders may not exercise his or her right in their favor. Another limitation is granting a preemptive right only to investors holding more than a certain percentage (for instance, 5%) of the company's equity. The goal of all of these mechanisms is to enable the company to introduce new investors into the company in the future.

- **Anti-dilution protection**—As mentioned above, preferred shares are convertible, at the investor's demand, into ordinary shares according to a pre-determined conversion rate. The conversion rate is usually 1:1 and is adjusted to any changes in the company's capital and dilution. From an economic perspective, long as the company does not raise share capital at a price lower than the conversion price, and does not allot stock options with a low exercise price, the investors are not diluted economically, although their share in the company could be diminished since the total value of the company's assets increases.

In order to prevent dilution, investors typically include anti-dilution, or ratchet, mechanisms, in the investment contracts. It is customary that shares offered at a discounted price to employees, directors, and advisors do not activate the anti-dilution mechanism. There are two customary mechanisms, full and weighted ratchet, with the former being used almost exclusively in situations with distressed companies and the latter one being more common.

- **Full adjustment of the conversion ratio (full ratchet)**—The conversion ratio is increased in accordance with the lowest price at which an ordinary share is sold (i.e., as if all of the investor's shares were bought at the lower price). In this manner, even if only a few shares were sold at a lower price and the economic dilution is not material, the existing investor receives a substantial adjustment to his or her percentage of the company's equity.

The formula for calculating the new conversion ratio is as follows:

$$\frac{\text{Original (or adjusted) price}}{\text{Price at which the diluting shares were allotted}} = \text{New conversion ratio}$$

Example: The investor invests $1 million according to a pre-money value of $4 million (the company had 4,000,000 shares before the allotment) and received 1,000,000 preferred shares (i.e., 20% of a company now worth $5 million) which he or she is entitled to convert into 1,000,000 ordinary shares at the rate of $1 per share. The company needs additional financing and, due to the conditions in the market, is forced to raise $250,000 according to a price per share of $0.50 (i.e., to allot 500,000 additional shares). The new conversion ratio is therefore 1/0.5=2, and the first investor can convert his or her shares into 2,000,000 regular shares, which would constitute more than 30% of the company's equity (2,000,000 out of 6,500,000 shares after the new allotment and the conversion of the shares). The investor has gained a windfall due to a small investment which did not materially dilute him.

- **Adjustment of the conversion ratio according to a weighted average (weighted average ratchet)**—The conversion ratio is updated according to the decrease in the weighted average of the price of all the shares after the issuance of shares at the lower price (the diluting issuance). For the purpose of the calculation, all of the shares issued before the diluting issuance are deemed to have been sold at their adjusted conversion price (the conversion price after adjustments to previous diluting events, if any).

In order to avoid a situation in which the entire diluting effect will be borne by the founders, it is possible to require that the number of shares used to calculate the average be on a fully diluted basis, including common shares (broad based weighted average). In this manner, the dilution effect will be spread over a larger number of shares. This calculation is the proper one from an economic perspective, since the preferred shares were allotted to the investors on a fully diluted basis from the outset.

The formula for calculating the new weighted price is as follows:

$$\frac{(\text{current price} * \text{new shares}) + (\text{previous price} * \text{previous shares})}{\text{new shares} + \text{previous shares}}$$

The new conversion rate is therefore calculated as follows:

$$\frac{\text{Original (or adjusted) price}}{\text{New weighted price}} = \text{New conversion ratio}$$

Example: Using the data of the previous example (with respect to the full ratchet mechanism), the weighted price is 0.954, and the new conversion ratio will be 1.05 and the investor will therefore be compensated for the diluting issuance by receiving only 50,000 additional shares.

If a full ratchet mechanism is nevertheless fixed in the contract, it is customary to limit the protection provided by this mechanism to a pre-determined period of time, after which all of the investors will bear the risk according to the weighted average ratchet mechanism. This intuition of this restriction is fairness, because if a diluting issuance does indeed take place after the investor has been with the company for a long time, and therefore had an opportunity to influence the direction taken by the company and the value of the investment round, he or she should share the impact of dilution with the other shareholders.

Investors in early phases who invested according to low valuation often agree to waive the ratchet clauses. Investors in later stages, however, who join the company based on a higher value, usually demand this mechanism, since at these stages there is a higher risk that the company will have to raise capital based on a lower value.

- **Right of redemption**—Some (less than 20%) investment contracts contain clauses which entitle investors to sell their shares to the company (in practice, put options) if the company fails to meet certain targets. In practice, the right to sell the shares to the company is rarely exercised, since in most cases the investor is entitled to sell his or her shares to the company under the terms of the put option only when the company fails to meet certain targets, in which case the company is unable to pay for the shares. Nevertheless, it is common to see clauses dealing with pricing adjustments on the conversion prices of the preferred shares.
- **Group voting**—In most cases, it is possible that waivers or group decisions will be required of the investors. A clause should be drafted whereby an appropriate majority of the investors (a special or a simple majority, in accordance with the resolution) may waive or exercise rights afforded to investors, thus avoiding bestowing a veto power on individual investors. Without delving into strategic issues from game theory, which are beyond the scope of this book, group-voting mechanisms can become complicated and are also affected by the number and character of the investors. The fewer and more sophisticated the investors, the less is the need for complex voting mechanisms.
- **Prohibition of sales**—Founders are almost always subject to a full or partial prohibition from selling shares for a fixed period of time (referred to as "lock-up;" see the section below on founders and managers). In addition, the organizational documents usually prohibit shareholders from selling shares to competitors of the company without the approval of the board of directors.
- **Right of first offer**—The right to be the first to whom an offer to sell shares will be addressed. Strategic investors sometimes demand this right in order to be able to buy the company before their competitors do.
- **Tag along**—Most of the deals have a provision to the effect that if one shareholder sells his or her shares to a certain buyer, the other shareholders may join him and sell shares to the same buyer, proportionately to their holdings in the company. Investors usually demand this right in order to prevent the entrepreneurs from exiting the company and leaving the investors without the company's main asset (namely, the entrepreneurs). The rationale underlying this demand is that an investment in the company is an investment in the entrepreneur and, therefore, if the entrepreneur has

found a way to maximize his or her investment in the company, he or she must share it with the person who financed it.
- **Bring along**—Most corporate state law has a provision that enables a majority of shareholders selling their shares to compel other shareholders to join them. The right is designed to enable a sale to be forced upon an extortionist minority. In some cases, there is a contractual provision under which a supermajority consent is required for a sale to be forced on other shareholders. In addition, investors may demand that a forced sale be allowed only if the sale achieves a certain pre-determined minimum return on the investment.

Right to Control and Rights to Information

Over and above creating an equity structure designed to bring the interests of managers and investors closer together, investment agreements provide several mechanisms designed to give the investors a certain degree of control over the company. These means include representation on the company's board of directors and the granting of voting rights and rights of control. In addition, investment agreements include an undertaking by the company to provide the investor with a multitude of information and financial statements and to seek the investor's approval before undertaking certain acts. In many cases, these rights expire with the IPO.

- **Using the investment consideration and milestones**—Investors will usually demand that the agreement specify to what use the company will apply their money. When the amount of the investment is considerable, or the uncertainty is high, the investment is sometimes not made immediately upon the signing of the investment agreement, but rather in stages defined in advance by the company and the investor (staged pay-in). This mechanism provides the investor with the ability to control the use of the money and the company's progress. The milestones can relate to development (for instance, completing the development of a beta version), management-recruitment (for instance, the recruitment of a VP of Marketing), regulatory approvals (customary in the medical field), commencement of sales, or any other issue which is important to the investors.

    These mechanisms are typically not recommended, because they not only encumber the company's activity by forcing it to adhere to an action plan which could become irrelevant with time, but also place the investor in a conflict of interests. On the one hand, the company's success is important to the investor but on the other hand, he or she would "profit" from a failure to meet a milestone, since it would enable him to pressure the company into increasing his or her holdings for a lower valuation. Even when the investor acts in good faith, friction could be caused due to the fear of a conflict of interest. These drawbacks make the use of milestones by experienced investors less common at times of flourishing capital markets, and rather common during difficult times in the market.

- **Voting rights**—It is customary that preferred shares confer the same voting rights as ordinary shares, with the number of shares being calculated on a converted basis (see earlier section for a discussion of conversion rights). In some situations, preferred shares confer enhanced voting rights, for instance, when the company fails to meet pre-determined targets.
- **Representation on the board of directors**—The composition of the board of directors usually changes after the investment, in a manner reflecting the new ownership structure. By being represented on the board of directors, the investor can monitor the company's activity and contribute to it from his or her experience. Venture capital funds ascribe much importance to being represented on the board of directors, not due to aggressiveness and a desire to control (since the fund will almost never control the board of directors), but usually due to an honest desire to take part in what goes on in the company, to help the management lead the company forward, and to monitor management. Broadening the board of directors by boosting it with knowledgeable and reputable persons is important to the company and contributes to its growth. The holding of regular meetings of the board of directors, in which an in-depth discussion is conducted on the central issues concerning the company should be viewed favorably and not as a formal nuisance. In many cases, it is determined that the entrepreneurs will remain members of the board of directors regardless of their holdings and that the investors' right to appoint a representative to the board of directors will, on the other hand, be according to their holdings.
- **Veto rights**—Investors demand a right (either on the board of directors or as shareholders) to veto certain resolutions of the company in order to protect their investment against resolutions which may prejudice them. It should be taken into account that managers of startups are sometimes inexperienced in making decisions in the management and financing of large-scale companies, and it is understandable that investors want to monitor their decisions. It is important to remember that a single investor rarely controls the company and the veto rights are usually used, among other things, to protect the minority.

The scope of the issues in which investors have veto rights is different from one company to another and depends on the phase at which the company stands (the more advanced the company in its development, the less do investors tend to intervene), its managers' experience, the investors' policy, and so on. The issues on which investors may demand veto rights typically include: a change in the organizational documents; a material change in the company's business; the approval of annual plans; share allotments; a merger or sale of material assets; large investments; large loans; encumbering the company's property; distributing dividends; dissolution; the appointment of directors; transactions with interested parties; the appointment of an attorney and a CPA; rights pertaining to an IPO, such as the right to prevent such an issuance below a certain value; and influencing the choice of underwriters.

There are two types of veto rights. On the one hand, there are rights to veto minor issues (such as expenses above a certain amount, or the authority to open lines of credit in the ordinary course of business) which may disrupt the proper management of the company and impose liability on the investor as a manager of the company (as opposed to the diminished liability imposed on shareholders). On the other hand, there are veto rights over material issues such as additional investments in the company (any additional allotment) and mergers and acquisitions (M&A). The company usually objects to giving investors these rights, claiming that they are already protected against subsequent investments by the preemptive right and the anti-dilution mechanisms. As for vetoing sales, investors are in any case entitled to a minimum return on their investments by virtue of the preference in deemed-liquidation events. Investors believe, however, that events such as soliciting investments and sales have a crucial impact on the value of their investment in the company, and therefore demand an ability to monitor them. It is possible at times to take a middle course between the two perspectives in the form of a veto right which is limited by the value of the investment. For instance, the investor would be entitled to veto an investment or a sale at a value lower than three times the value according to which he or she joined the company. Giving such veto rights to reputable venture capital funds does not pose a problem. The interests of such funds are similar to those of the company, and in any case they would be unlikely to act in an opportunistic manner since they have a reputation to maintain in the market. It is far more problematic to give such rights to unsophisticated private investors who may use them to blackmail the company later on, or to strategic investors whose interests may not be identical to those of the company.

In any case, it is important to limit the veto rights until the IPO, since such rights are unacceptable in public companies (due to market perception and various SEC rules).

- **Rights to information**—Investors will demand to receive detailed information which would allow them to better monitor the company. Except for the annual and quarterly statements, which are reviewed or audited by an independent CPA, the investor will demand that the company give current reports to the board of directors, present a budget, and allow him or her to

monitor the degree of adherence to such budget. Investors will also demand access to the company's documents and regular visits at its place of business.
- **Right of first negotiation**—Strategic investors demand priority in negotiations for the sale of the company.

The Founders and the Managers

- **The importance of the founders' holdings**—The founders, at least initially, are the company's most important asset. Some investors tend to forget this fact and are tempted to take advantage of the fact that they own the capital to appropriate large shares of the company at the founders' expense. It is important to leave sufficient holdings in the hands of the founders to motivate them to develop the company. On the other hand, it is important for investors to fix arrangements which would guarantee the founders' commitment to the company and would solve the agency problem between the founders and the investors. The "agency problem" reflects the conflict of interests inherent in any relationship in which a representative manages the affairs or the money of another; in this case, the entrepreneurs and directors manage the investors' money. Some of these arrangements are fixed in the investment agreement and others in the employment agreements between the company and the entrepreneurs, the signing of which is usually required as a condition in the investment agreement. These arrangements are described in this subsection.
- **Reverse vesting**—When the investment is made at an early phase, the investors usually require that the founders' right to their shares vest over a certain period of time (usually around three years). To this end, it is required that the employment contract of each entrepreneur include the company's option to buy his or her shares for no consideration, or for a price significantly lower than the market price, in case he or she departs the company. This mechanism addresses two problems: First, it provides an incentive to the entrepreneur to continue working with the company (despite the existence of an employment contract, the entrepreneur cannot be coerced to work for the company, not even through the courts); second, if the entrepreneur leaves, his or her shares may be used to compensate the substitute managers who will replace him. It is also possible to consolidate the founders' right to their shares based on performance (performance vesting), i.e., depending on the achievement of pre-determined goals.
- **Earn-up**—This is an arrangement which entitles the managers to increase their holdings if the company's performance exceeds a pre-defined threshold. Similar to claw back, such clauses are rare.
- **Lock-up**—In almost every deal, there is full or partial prohibition of the sale of shares by the founders for a fixed period of time. However,

entrepreneurs are sometimes allowed to sell a certain amount of shares every year without any restrictions on such sale in order to provide them with a certain degree of liquidity. There are also other sale restrictions, as discussed in the section on protecting the investment.

Registration Rights Agreements

Almost every investment agreement with an institutional entity is accompanied by a registration rights agreement of one sort or another. A registration rights agreement enables the shareholders to force the company to make a public offering in which the investors' shares will be sold or, alternatively, enables the investors to sell some of their shares in a public offering made by the company. Most registration rights agreements refer to the U.S. market as the target market, although the same principles apply, with certain modifications, to other markets as well. It is important to know that, in practice, registration rights agreements are almost never enforced by investors since a successful public offering is impossible without the genuine cooperation of the company's managers. Furthermore, these agreements usually change when an IPO is performed at the demand of the underwriters.

The Need for a Registration Rights Agreement

The need for a registration rights agreement is derived from the fact that it is illegal to sell securities to the public in the United States (except for some exemptions granted to private sales) without registering the securities with the SEC. Since venture capital investments are usually made with an eye to exiting the investment within several years, and since only the company can decide to make an IPO or a secondary offering, it is important that the registration rights agreement determine the investor's rights with respect to the registration of his or her shares in a manner enabling him to exit the investment. It is important that the company will have only one registration rights agreement to which all the investors will join. The existence of several registration rights agreements which are signed separately with each investor creates inconsistencies and may impose a double burden on the company. Registration rights are applicable only after an IPO. In the U.S. market, there are restrictions on the sale of securities bought from the company or from an affiliate of the company other than in a public offering (which is mostly the case with respect to shares bought by the fund). The sale of such securities in the secondary market without registration can be made either in a private sale which is exempt from registration, or in a sale outside the United States (pursuant to Regulation S) or in a sale subject to the restrictions of Rule 144 promulgated under the Securities Act of 1933 (see Chapter 13 for a discussion of sales which are exempt from registration).

Types of Registration Rights

There are three types of rights which investors customarily seek:

- **Demand registration right**—The investors' right to demand registration imposes a heavy burden on the company since every registration involves significant expenses and requires a considerable investment of time by the company's management. This right is usually limited to no more than twice (for all investors together) and it is required that at least one half of the persons entitled to the registration ask for it. In practice, this right is almost never exercised since there is no practical way of forcing a company's managers to conduct a registration process against their will.
- **Piggy-back registration right**—This is a right granted to shareholders to sell additional shares when the company is in any case registering shares for itself. This right does not impose a particular burden on the company, and the main restriction is on the number of shares which the shareholder will sell so as not to "flood" the market and prejudice the offering.

Restrictions on Registration Rights

The company will usually require that the registration right be limited in several ways: (1) The right will not exist before an IPO is performed (in other words, the company may not be compelled to make such an IPO); (2) Restrictions on the period of time in which a demand registration right may be exercised and the number of times this may be done; (3) A requirement of a minimum percentage of investors for demand registration; (4) A restriction on the number of shares to be sold, as determined by the underwriters (the underwriters will refuse to commit to selling a very large number of shares which could cause the price of the share to decline) and the fixing of an arrangement according to which the shares will be sold; (5) Other restrictions required by the underwriters, such as a prohibition of the sellers to sell shares (lock-up) for 90–270 days following the public offering.

Other Matters Regulated in Registration Rights Agreements

Registration rights agreements regulate several additional issues, principally the following:

- **Indemnification**—Registration rights agreements contain mutual indemnification clauses. On the one hand, the company is required to indemnify the shareholders due to damage they may suffer as a result of misrepresentations in the registration statement. On the other hand, the investors are required to indemnify the company for damages it may suffer due to incorrect information provided by the investors.
- **Expenses**—This is a provision specifying that the company will bear the costs of the offering.

- **Transfer right**—This addresses the question of whether the registration right is transferred with the shares if the investor sells his or her shares.
- **Choice of underwriters**—Investors may demand the right to choose the underwriters in the case of demand registration.

Other Arrangements

There are several other issues which are regulated in the investment agreement or in the supplementary agreements.

Other Matters Regulated in Investment Agreements

- **Confidentiality and non-competition**—Both the entrepreneurs and the investor undertake to maintain all of the company's secret information in confidence. All of the company's employees are usually also required to sign confidentiality agreements. Sometimes key employees are required to sign non-competition clauses, preventing them from competing with the company for a fixed period of time after their departure from the company.
- **Intellectual property**—The founders are required to transfer to the company all of their rights to the product. All of the company's employees are required to sign agreements whereby any intellectual property developed while working for the company belongs to the company. Investors may also require a right of first refusal for buying the intellectual property in cases of liquidation.

Employment Agreements

Investors will usually require that the founders sign an employment agreement fixing the entrepreneurs' rights and obligations (position, salary, benefits, managers' insurance, etc.) and regulating issues such as: justified causes for termination (usually criminal convictions, misuse of the company's property, and recurrent breaches of orders given by the board of directors), advance notice of the non-renewal of the contract, severance pay, restrictions on occupation and competition (prohibition from competing with the company for several years after ceasing to work for the company), intellectual property rights, and buyback in case they leave the company (the entrepreneurs are required to sell their shares to the company at a discounted price if they breach the employment agreement). Where a clause of non-competition by entrepreneurs is concerned, it should also be ascertained whether such non-competition obligation is not prohibited by the antitrust laws or by state law.

Shareholders Agreements

In some cases, issues relating to the relationship between the shareholders such as restrictions on sales (see the section on protecting the investment) are separated from the investment agreement and regulated in a shareholders agreement. So long as these issues are also regulated in the company's organizational documents in order to make them effective against third parties who are not a party to the contractual set of agreements, it is inconsequential whether their regulation in the context of the relationship between the investor and the company is made in the investment agreement or in a separate shareholders agreement (for a further discussion of shareholders agreements, see Chapter 2 on incorporation documents).

Employee Stock Option Plans

Investors may demand that the company adopt a stock option plan granting employees shares in the amount and under the terms determined in the investment agreement. It is usually customary that 10–25% of the company's shares are set aside for employees who are not founders (for a discussion of employee compensation, see Chapter 4).

9

Valuation of Companies

INTRODUCTION

The company recruits employees, calculates the feasibility of projects, and raises capital and debt in consideration of the company's value and the value of its growth opportunities, and hence valuating a company has a crucial impact on the venture development.

Market price can provide a basis for valuing public companies. The valuation of private companies, however—particularly startups—is more complicated. The main reason for this is that startups are plagued by more uncertainties: By definition, startups are in an earlier phase of their life cycle than are public companies, and therefore the uncertainties clouding the technological feasibility and managerial abilities of the companies and the existence of a market for their products are higher.

This chapter briefly presents the main methods for valuing companies. These methods are commonly used among investors—either private investors, venture capital funds, or companies—but they are certainly not the only methods for valuating companies. The appropriate model should be chosen carefully, since specific adjustments are always required in accordance with the characteristics of the valued company. In any case, a company should be valued using several methods to enable comparisons among the results of each method.

Obviously, a valuation performed without an in-depth analysis of the company's technology, managerial abilities, access to markets, and competitive situation is meaningless. Since these issues are addressed in other chapters, the methods presented in this chapter are based on the assumption that such an in-depth analysis has already been performed. The models are presented based on the assumption that the investor is a financial investor, i.e., an investor who values the company according to the direct financial cash flows he expects to derive over time from his/her holding of the company's shares. This presentation is followed by a description of the adjustments made by strategic investors to the models.

Ostensibly, one would expect all financial investors to reach the same valuation upon concluding their calculations. In practice, different investors will usually reach different valuations because, among other things, they use different models and rely on different assumptions. While in theory most of the models are supposed to yield the same result, but different assumptions used by the investors with respect to parameters required by the models will typically cause a difference in the implementation of the different models, even when these valuations are conducted by the same people.

Although valuations produce numerical results, no exact number can represent the "true" value of a company at any given time. Value is almost always subjective, since different investors attribute a different value to the same asset (in this case, the company). For instance, from the standpoint of some investors (namely, strategic investors), an investment in the company carries additional value, such as direct contact with innovative technology. Likewise, a company would sometimes be prepared to admit such investors based on a low value, since they bring an added value to the company such as ties with potential customers. This is another example illustrating a main point in valuation of emerging companies, and in particular in the context of capital raising: From the entrepreneurs' perspective, the ultimate objective is to maximize the value of their share in the company in the long run and not to maximize the value of the company at any given point of time.

Methods Based on Multiples

Principles

Valuation methods which are based on multiples of projected financial data are easily applied—in theory. The guiding principle is that multiplying projected financial data which are directly or indirectly related to the future profitability of the company, by a number which is the multiple by which similar public companies are traded, or according to which similar private companies have raised capital, provides a scale for valuating the assessed company. The method identifies a set of companies that is comparable on various dimensions, such as area of operation, the maturity of the company, and its size. It looks at the set of appropriate variables for comparison and then compares the ratios of market valuation to these variables. The ratios are then applied to the parameter values of the valued company.

The best-known multiple is, of course, the earnings multiple (namely, the ratio between the price of a share and the earnings it yields, otherwise known as the price/earnings, or P/E, ratio). For example, assuming that Speed, Inc. generates current annual earnings of $10 million, and that similar companies are traded on the stock exchange according to an earnings multiple of 40, then the value of Speed Inc. (without taking into account other data) is $400 million.

Analysis based on multiples typically relies on the peer group's current results and forecasts made by market participants such as equity research analysts. However, it is important to understand that valuation based on multiples is meaningless if the variables used for comparison do not reflect the ability of a company to create value for its shareholders.

In market sectors that have little history, selecting appropriate parameters is difficult and market participants tend to change from time to time their perspectives on such multiples. As a result, many investors use parameters that seem to explain the market valuation of other companies in the sector, sometimes with disregard to their economic link to future profitability.

In most cases, therefore, we do not prescribe multiples as a central mechanism for valuation. Regardless of the explanatory power of a multiple for pricing at a specific time, unless the multiples are logically and economically related to the future profitability of the company or to the way potential buyers of the company value it, they are meaningless. History shows that periods of incorrect valuation can last for a long time and naturally lead to opportunistic behavior by companies. For example, in many industries, such as the construction business, companies are valued by future revenue multiples. That may give companies incentives to sign money-losing contracts before trying to raise capital, even at the expense of future profits.

Supplementary information on the financial stability and the prospects of a company can be derived from balance sheet multiples, such as enterprise value-to-total assets, or equity market value-to-equity (market-to-book ratio). These ratios are highly relevant in mature industries. However, in growth industries relying mainly on intellectual capital, they may distort analysis unless the asset base or equity is adjusted for the pitfalls of some accounting rules. For example, the value of intangible assets, which may have been written off, may make these ratios seem out of context.

In practice, the method requires the careful identification of companies whose business resembles that of the valuated company as closely as possible, determining an appropriate operating multiple for the valuated company, and multiplying it by the company's projected operating data. It is also important to remember that the operating data used for the valuation must be genuinely and logically related to the company's future profitability and hence to the earning or cash flows it will generate.

The main advantage of the multiple method is the fact that it is based on market data, i.e., the company is assessed according to the value of similar companies. Obviously, this is also the main disadvantage of the method: In times of economic euphoria, the valuation of companies may include parameters which are not likely to be sustainable for long. For this reason, many investors are skeptical about valuations made in times of booming stock markets on the basis of projected operating multiples.

- **Determining the group of comparable companies**—When making valuations on the basis of multiples, the multiple has to be determined in accordance with a profile of companies which is as similar as possible to the valuated company. When looking for companies to provide a comparison, the selection process is crucial. Leading companies in an industry may receive a premium in the marketplace, reflecting the premium pricing they can charge or the increased profitability (due to economies of scale) they may achieve. In addition, the financial leverage and equity risk differences associated with factors such as the companies' cost structure could explain differences in multiples.

It should also be kept in mind that the companies traded on the stock market are the successful companies in each field. In other words, there is a selection bias, and the operating profile of the representative group of companies is not necessarily similar to that of the valuated private company.

- **Determining the relevant parameter and its values**—Once the group (or groups) of companies comparable to the valuated company has (or have) been chosen, the parameter for comparison, such as earnings or sales, must be selected. Several parameters should usually be chosen, rather than relying on a single variable. In addition, it should be determined whether current or projected data will be used. Most parameters, except for earnings per share and sales, are not predicted by market analysts. Therefore, only historical and current information is used and is compared to the predicted parameter values for the valued firm at a stage of maturity that is similar.

  In most cases, multiples should be based directly on profitability. This can be measured as the ratio of enterprise value (that is, the market value of equity plus debt) to EBIT (earning before interest and income taxes) and price to earnings per share; or operations, such as price to sales, whether these ratios are based on current or forecasted values. Other ratios may need to be used, typically where the industries under examination have not shown meaningful reported profitability because of their early stage of development. Large investment can also adversely affect reported profitability as well as lack of meaningful revenue (in which case measures based on revenue are meaningless as well).

  However, investors should be wary of measures that do not refer to the cost of obtaining future profitability, for example, ratios based on simple EBITDA (earning before interest, income taxes, depreciation, and amortization). Multiples that incorporate the cost of the capital and the required capital expenditures are useful in this context. Such adjusted mechanisms, which are based on current and forward-looking adjusted income measures, are applicable in most situations involving publicly traded and private companies. However, these measures are not always adequate by themselves in very early-stage industries where revenue is scarce, and should be used with other tools.

  It is hard to overrate the importance of choosing parameters which are highly correlated to profitability in the future. In other words, it is important that the parameters constitute a material gauge of the companies' future profitability. Also, when comparing firms on parameters that are not

financial, it is crucial to understand the differences in the relevance of a parameter across firms.
- **Allowing for the risk factor**—When performing valuations on the basis of multiples, it is important to make allowances for the specific risk factors of the comparable companies. Since the valuation of every company is based on the discounted financial flows of the company, it should always be kept in mind that companies will be traded according to different multiples in accordance with their projected flows, as well as the level of uncertainty (or riskiness) associated with these flows. Therefore, when determining the multiple, the relevant parameters of the peer companies should be carefully examined. Such parameters include profit margins, the rate of tax to which they are subject (which naturally affects the net future flows), and the degree to which debt is used to finance the company's activity.
- **Multiple compositions**—The relevant parameters which are used as a basis for multiplication by the industry multiple are unique to each field. Therefore, the value of companies operating in several industries should be calculated based on a sum of the values of their business divisions, while applying the relevant industry multiple to each division.

Customary Types of Multiples

- **Net earnings multiple**—Using the companies' net earnings is the simplest. However, these data are affected more than many other parameters by the company's capital structure. Since this structure is almost always subject to change, this multiple reflects the company's operating results less effectively than some other multiples. Furthermore, the company's net earnings are affected to a large extent by one-time profits, which may be substantial in high tech companies (for instance, profits resulting from dilution due to investments made in held companies). In other words, it is important to establish that the earnings used as a basis for determining the multiple represent earnings that will recur in the future.
- **EBIT-based multiple**—The logic underlying the use of multiples which are based on EBIT is that these earnings are less dependent on managerial decisions with respect to the company's capital structure and on the effect of taxation on its activity. Multiples which are based on this parameter are indeed better focused on the company's operating profitability and on the risk entailed in obtaining them, since they are less affected by the tax shield which the companies enjoy (factors not associated with the company's operating cash flow, such as the recognition of depreciation and interest expenditures for tax purposes, provide companies with a tax advantage or a tax "shield").

- **Book value-based multiples**—A market to book multiple reflecting the ratio of the company's market value to its net book value. In the most simplistic manner, the company's market value reflects the market value of all of the company's assets minus its liabilities, i.e., the amount which would be divided among the shareholders if the company were to dissolve after selling all of its assets and paying all of its debts.

    Most public companies are traded at a market to book value multiple which is much larger than 1. Even after revaluating the tangible assets of public companies in order to establish their market value, not their recorded cost, the ratio between the market value and the reappraised asset value is higher than 1. In practice, this phenomenon is explained by the value of the companies' intangible assets. These assets include the value of patents, managerial abilities, and brand value (goodwill). In the case of startups, the majority of whose assets are intangible and therefore are not reflected in the company's balance sheets, the method becomes meaningful only after many adjustments, such as capitalizing amounts invested in R&D, depreciating them over several years—similarly to other tangible assets—and multiplying them by a representative industry parameter.

- **Other multiples**—Other common multiples are multiples of other operating data of companies, such as revenue multiples and multiples of the number of subscribers. In any case, the multiple method is meaningful only if the multiplied parameter is meaningful to the company's future earnings-generation ability. For instance, valuations based on the number of users of a software or other service which is given free of charge is meaningless if the number of users cannot be translated into future earnings ("monetized"), either in the way of revenues from subscribers, revenues from advertising, or other revenues. However, it is important to remember that a large user base could be meaningful to a strategic buyer even if it is meaningless to the company itself. For instance, when Microsoft acquired Hotmail, a company which provided free electronic mail services, the main motivation for the acquisition was to establish a user base for Microsoft's portal, which generates revenues from other services. Later on, Hotmail had also become a per-fee service for its advanced features.

Methods for Discounting Cash Flows and Residual Income

Principles

Perhaps the most common valuation technique is the free cash flow method. The starting point is based on forecasting the company's free cash flows available for shareholders or to its entire set of capital providers. These include earnings, adjusted for expenses and income that are not in cash (for example, depreciation), and adjusted for required investments and changes in working capital. The series of forecast free cash flows is then brought to current values by discounting it using the company's cost of equity or overall cost of capital.

A conceptually equivalent method, the residual income method, is based on forecasting the company's excess earnings (essentially, net income after charging for the cost of the capital employed to achieve it). Similar to the free cash flow method, the series of forecasted excess earnings is then brought to current values by discounting it using the company's cost of equity. Here, investors use the intuition that a company is creating wealth only if it provides earnings that more than compensate capital providers for the risks they take. The method, which we can trace back to its origins a century ago, is widely used in academia as well as in business circles and appears, with different flavors, under names such as Economic Value Added (EVA), Super Profits, and Abnormal Earnings.

A full valuation model would require a forecast made of every income flow and balance sheet item in perpetuity. Clearly this is impractical, so the valuation process is split into two components. The first component reflects the value of the company over the forecasting period. For that period, we derive the stream of annual residual income, or free cash flows, based on detailed forecasting of revenue and expense items, as well as the balance sheet items.

The second component is analyzed by assuming some permanent (or decaying) growth rate of the forecast item (that is, residual income or free cash flow) in the last detailed forecast year and capitalizing this item. Alternatively, an expected multiple is assumed for the main estimated parameter. For example, a P/E multiple may be applied to the forecasted net income at that period. This would be based on the anticipated prevailing multiple at that point for similar companies, taking account of the company's expected ability to grow and maintain its competitive position over the long term. Note that while it is normal to have positive growth rates for other forecast parameters such as earnings, it is rare for firms to retain an ability to obtain positive residual income for long periods of time. Therefore, investors should be very careful when determining these growth rates beyond the forecasting horizon.

Naturally, the more value beyond that detailed forecasting period, the more the forecast is subject to estimation error. However, as the raw data for this second component (typically labeled as the "Terminal Value") relies on detailed analysis of earlier periods, the longer and finer the forecasts are in these periods, the better the estimate will be for the second component and therefore for the entire valuation.

Estimating the Value Component during the Projected Period

The quality of the valuation according to the DCF method basically depends on the quality of the projections of the company's future cash flows. In startups in particular, changes in the assumptions used in the financial model with respect to the company's first years of activity which seem negligible, may have a critical effect on the company's value. For instance, if you conducted a valuation of Cisco in the year 1995, a change of 1% in its projected growth rate for the next 5 years would have resulted in a difference of hundreds of percents in the company's value. Since most of the value in the valuation of companies in their early phases of development lies beyond the projected period, small changes in each of the early years (which affect the periodic cash flows after the projected period), as well as small changes in the assumptions made about the growth rates after the projected period, could have an immense effect on the outcome. Because the terminal value is based on the forecasted period, the thorough analysis of the forecasting is very important.

When forecasting the company's cash flows, it is important to examine the logic underlying the model. Arbitrary assumptions with respect to growth rates, which are dissociated from the expected growth rates in the industry in which the company operates, may sometimes lead to scenarios in which the company's share in the target market is assumed increase to a disproportionate size.

To bring the series of free cash flows (or residual income) to current value, we need to determine the proper interest rate for discounting them. This cost is the rate of return investors require for investment in a project with similar risk characteristics. That should be the cost of equity (if we forecast the series of streams for equity holders) or the weighted average cost of capital (if we forecast the series for the entire capital base).

There are many ways of estimating the cost of equity. However, it is typically derived using a combination of methods, taking into account the stage of development of the company, the industry in which it operates, and the stage of development of the industry as a whole.

Perhaps the most commonly used method for estimating the cost of equity is the Capital Asset Pricing Model (CAPM). Under this model, the cost of equity of the company (r_e) is the sum of the risk-free interest rate (r_f) and the risk premium for the market portfolio, which is then multiplied by the company's "beta" (β), which reflects the relative sensitivity of the company stock return volatility to the market returns variability. The risk premium is the required additional return for holding equity the market stock portfolio (r_m), rather than risk-free assets such as government bonds.

$$r_e = r_f + (r_m - r_f)\beta$$

If the company is financed by equity (E) and debt (D), with corresponding interest rates of r_e and r_d, then the Weighted Average Cost of Capital (WACC) is:

$$\text{WACC} = [D / (D + E)] * r_d(1-t) + [E / (D + E)] * r_e$$

The cost of capital of the company's debt is the rate of interest on the company's debt (r_d) after tax (the rate of which is signified by the letter t).

The cost of capital is weighted according to the market value of the company's equity and debt. In the case of private companies, the calculation is made according to the financing composition by the company. However, in most cases, the entire financing of startups is based on equity. Given their high risk profile, even debt for startups could be handled as equity in most situations for valuation purposes, as it carries similar risk characteristics (and hence required return) of equity.

- **Risk-free interest rate (r_f)**—This is the rate of interest paid on risk-free investments such as treasury bonds. This rate of interest is composed of the projected inflation and of the return that compensates investors for the long-term use of their capital. In practice, the risk-free interest rate that is customarily used for the valuation of long-term projects is the rate of return on government bonds with maturities of 10 years.
- **Equity risk premium ($r_m - r_f$)**—This premium indemnifies investors for the systematic risk of equity holdings. That is, this is the risk which cannot be diversified away by holding a diversified investment portfolio. In practice, the term refers to the difference between the expected returns on the equity market portfolio and on risk-free bonds. Although this parameter is supposed to be objective, different investors assume different premiums, usually between 6% and 8%, according to the perspective which one takes on the historic return differences, and the expected ones.

The difficulty of estimating the equity risk premium has been debated at length. To illustrate the divergence of opinions, the average historic (in the last 60 years) equity risk premium in the United States has been about 6%. However, some analyses suggest that the correct measure should be based on the expected risk premium as measured at each point in time, rather than on the actual, realized risk premium. Using the former method yields a value of about 3%. Assuming a risk-free rate of 6%, this means a difference of 50% in the estimated cost of equity for the average company in the United States.

In deriving the beta for the valued company, we need to consider that the capital structure of such companies is different from that of the measured company, and we must therefore adjust beta to the company's equity without debt, since beta changes in accordance with the company's capital structure. We would therefore examine the capital structure of all comparable companies and calculate their beta without financial leverage by adjusting the leveraged beta observed in the market (b_L) to the company's capital structure:

$$\beta = \beta_L * E / (E + D)$$

Deriving beta requires the firm to be publicly traded. In the case of private companies, it is therefore customary to assume a beta of similar public companies in addition to a premium due to the illiquidity of an investment in a private company.

When a startup is being valued, it is often difficult to find a public company which resembles it. In such cases, we would use various simplifying assumptions with respect to beta and examine the sensitivity of the results to changes in beta values.

In addition to issues of estimating the equity risk premium, the actual validity of the CAPM model has been debated, and under other models, such as the Arbitrage Pricing

Theory (APT), the cost of equity also considers the exposure of the company's stock returns to additional macro-economic or companies' characteristic factors.

Another delicate issue is the time-varying discount rate of companies, in particular in their early years of development or in the early stage of development of their industry. The sensitivity of companies to market conditions may change over the years, not only because of changes in the environment, but also due to the age of the company and its size in its industry. Altering the discount rate could have a dramatic effect, in particular for companies where most of their valuation stems from the far future. Simulation tools can help here.

Estimating the Value Component after the Projected Period

Even after the cash flows projected during the period of assessment are understood, the valuator must make many assumptions about the pattern of such cash flows in subsequent periods. The value is usually calculated for the end point of the projected period, based on assumptions about a fixed future growth rate (or a formula with some other pattern of growth or decline rates).

As we mentioned above, a careful derivation of this "Terminal Value" is crucial, as it is typically responsible for a large portion of the overall value of the company. It is also important to reiterate the fact that the parameters for the "Terminal Value" are based on the detailed forecasting period. The more refined the detailed forecasting period is, the better the "Terminal Value" forecasting will become, and the better the overall valuation.

Following is a simple formula for estimating such terminal value, based on the company's projected data in the last year of the projection (FCF_T), and assuming fixed future growth:

$$\text{Terminal Value}_T = \frac{FCF_T * (1+g)}{r-g}$$

where *FCF* is the free cash flow, *g* is the company's projected fixed future growth rate, and *r* is the discount rate.

In practice, this formula—like other similar formulas—applies a multiple to the free cash flow in the last year of the projected period. This value often constitutes a material component of the company's value, at times even 80–90% of the value of a startup, which lacks almost any positive free cash flow during the projected period. Nevertheless, often little attention is paid to the calculation of this value.

The terminal value of the company may also be calculated by another method based on the company's projected earnings multiple at T, the end point of the detailed forecasting period. This multiple may be assumed based on multiples which currently exist in the market for companies in similar phases of development as those in which the company is expected to be at the end of the projected period.

Example

CellBill Ltd. is planning to manufacture revolutionary equipment which will substantially streamline the billing methods of cellular companies. The required initial and only investment is $150 million. After a detailed analysis, the entrepreneurs prepare a projection of their revenues and expenses over the next five years. They expect the expenses (as a percentage of revenue) will decrease over time, reflecting improvements in production efficiencies. The company will be liable for income tax at the rate of 40%. In addition, the company's depreciation expenses will be the same as the investment required to maintain the company's production capacity (capital expenditures), and are described in Table 9–1. For simplicity, we are ignoring tax deductibility of depreciation. The entrepreneurs forecast that their required working capital will increase every year by 15% of the increase in sales. The entrepreneurs therefore calculate the company's free cash flows for each of the coming years. They then forecast the terminal value beyond five years, and predict that the company will continue generating a free cash flow at a growth rate of 8% per year. Note that this is a high expected growth rate, and a careful selection of the growth rate should be conducted after a thorough analysis of the growth opportunities of the firm over the long run. In the example, we also assume only expenses in the aggregate, but naturally a full analysis should be conducted one line item at a time.

The risk-free interest in the market is 6%, the risk premium for investments in stock (see the discussion on the discount rate used by VCs) is 7%, and the company's beta is 2. Therefore, the company's cost of capital (the company is financed entirely by equity) is $7\% \cdot 2 + 6\% = 20\%$.

As can be seen in Table 9–1 below, the free cash flow in the fifth year is $50 million, and therefore the free cash flow for the first period beyond that year is assumed to be $54 million $= 50 \times (1 + 8\%)$, and the terminal value is therefore $54 / (20\% - 8\%) = \$452M$. The discounted value of the terminal value is $452 \cdot (1/(1 + 20\%)^6) = 151M$. Note that we are assuming here that the beta of the company will not decline although the firm is expected to grow over time, and hence is likely to converge to its industry beta, which is typically lower than 2.

Discounting the free cash flow series and the terminal value using the annual discount rate of 20% results in a present value of $200 million. Note that the terminal value reflects more than 76% of the total discounted FCF (154/200), even though the company is profitable during most of the detailed forecasting period. After taking into account the required investment of $150 million, the value of CellBill (assuming the described activities represent all of CellBill's activities, and the firm had no other assets), is $50 million.

Chapter 9 Valuation of Companies

Table 9-1 An Example of the Valuation of a Company by the DCF Method

CellBill Ltd.— Sample Valuation (figures are in $ millions)	Year 1	Year 2	Year 3	Year 4	Year 5
Revenue	100	130	145	155	180
Assumed expenses (as % of sales)	90%	85%	70%	60%	50%
Expenses	90	110	101	93	90
EBIT	10	20	44	62	90
Tax rate	40%	40%	40%	40%	40%
Operating profit	6	12	26	37	54
Depreciation	10	12	15	17	20
Capital expenditures	10	12	15	17	20
Changes in net working capital	15	5	2	2	4
Free cash flow (FCF)	-9	7	24	35	50
Discounted FCF	-8	5	14	17	20
Total Detailed Period FCF:	$49				

Terminal Value (TV):
    Representative FCF:
    Terminal Value (TV):
    Discounted TV:
			$50*(1+8%)=$54
			$54/(20%-8%)=$452
			$452/(1+20%)^6=$151		

Total Value:
    Detailed Period Value:
    Terminal Value:
    Required Investment
    Pre-Investment Value:
			$49
			$151
			($150)
			$50		

Table 9-1 An Example of the Valuation of a Company by the DCF Method (cont'd)

Assumptions:	
Beta	2
Equity Risk Premium	7%
Risk Free Rate	6%
Discount Rate:	6%+2°7%=20%
Growth beyond 5th year:	8%
Working Capital Requirements (as % of sales):	15%

Valuation According to Discounted Residual Income

As mentioned above, residual income is another alternative which might offer a better solution for the valuation of early-stage companies. As discussed above, it is common to find that within the forecasted period, a company's free cash flow is negative or low because the firm is still in the investment phase and most of the value lies in the terminal value.

The Residual Income model works well in most situations and with certain adjustments can help with technology-related companies in particular, as well as with other companies that have significant components of intangible assets. It incorporates available information reported by the company and market participants, as well as the characteristics of companies in their earlier years of development. The amount of income, after a charge for the cost of capital, reflects the net value created for shareholders during the period (if the measurement is based on adjusted income available to shareholders), or the value created for all capital providers (when the measure is based on adjusted operating income).

The intuition of this method is simple—a company creates value if it earns more than the cost of the capital invested in it. For the purpose of the calculation, we have to examine the earnings generated, the cost of capital, and the capital invested in the company. The capital invested every year is the equity, plus changes due to investments made in the company, minus any dividends distributed, plus capitalized expenses (namely, items deducted from the income statement and added to the balance sheet as an asset). Ostensibly, the company could have operated in another field with the same financial resources, and the company's shareholders could have invested their capital in a different investment alternative bearing the same risk but yielding an appropriate return. Therefore, the real profit generated by the company is that part of the profit that exceeds the cost of the capital.

The Adjusted Residual Income (ARI) method is a refined version of the traditional residual income method. The method, described in Fuerst and Melumad (2001a, 2001b), adds important adjustments to all of the measurements of net income and invested capital. These changes turn the general model, which was conceived primarily for companies operating in traditional industries, into a model that works particularly well for knowledge-based industries and companies.

The starting point for this calculation is adjusted net income. The adjustments are mainly related to items which were included in the financial reports (or excluded from them) in a manner inconsistent with their underlying economics. For companies that rely on intellectual property, one of the main components is the adjustment for research and development investments. Under current accounting rules, this item is typically charged as an expense in the year incurred. The ARI approach is that because R&D investments greatly affect future profitability, they should be treated for valuation purposes as assets whose value depreciates over time, based on analysis of the company and the characteristics of its industry. The valuator should therefore determine the expected life of these assets by measuring the effectiveness (in short, productivity and profitability changes) of R&D in that industry or similar industries (in many industries, R&D assets tend to have a life of three to five years). Naturally, the process impacts the income figures as well as the balance sheet.

The next step in deriving the ARI is to charge for the use of capital, based on the company's cost of equity, multiplied by the adjusted equity or the weighted cost of capital, if the measures are based on net operating income and correspondingly, the total adjusted asset base. This measure gives a series of forecasts that can be discounted to current values. The sum is then added to the current equity (or total asset) base to yield the valuation.

The result of the adjustments is that a fast-growing company, which every startup aims to be, whose R&D expenses are consequently also fast-growing, will reveal its real condition, i.e., the creation of long-term value for its shareholders. For instance, assuming a capitalization of the R&D and marketing expenses of the company Real Networks from the mid-1990s forth and depreciating them over 3–5 years, reveals that the company had already then created a residual income for its shareholders, although it reported profits only about 5 years later. However, if we use a sufficiently long projection period (such as 10 years), we will often find that a valuation using the ARI method—with or without the adjustments mentioned above—does not materially affect the valuation. This results from the mechanism of the model, which neutralizes the effect of the timing at which the company's business actions are recorded. For example, according to the same principle, recording a revenue earlier will increase the capital basis, since it will increase the profit which is a component of the capital for the next period, and hence indirectly the annual charge of capital in future periods.

The adjusted residual income measure can also be used for several analyses, for example, by comparing the ratios of market value to adjusted residual income or adjusted capital, as in the above example.

The terminal value derivation is made in a similar fashion to the DCF method, except for the reliance on the residual income of the last year for the projected period. Economically, over time, it is hard to find companies which earn more than the cost of their capital indefinitely. Intuitively, the more profits a company accumulates above the cost of its capital, the more companies will enter its field and reduce the profitability of the industry. On the other hand, high tech provides broad possibilities for creating niches which may be protected over time, such as Microsoft, which has been earning more than its cost of capital for years (even after capitalization of its R&D and marketing expenses). However, this is a rare case, and it is customary to assume that the growth rate of the residual income will be negative, i.e., that the adjusted residual income will be reduced to zero several years after the projected period.

Is ARI different from methods involving free cash flows? Not conceptually. Both approaches come from the same formula that states that a company's value equals the sum of its discounted expected dividends and should yield the same results. However, in practice, often there would be significant differences in valuation between the results of these models. These differences have to do with the implementation effects of the models: the information requirement for estimation, the forecasting period chosen, and the company's managerial discretion over the forecasted items.

The Real Options Method

Introduction

The main methods used by managers and investors to analyze projects and companies—the DCF method and the residual income method—are based on the discounting of forecasted cash flows from existing and projected project baskets of the company. In practice, when the company examines the feasibility of projects, it analyzes the net present value of each project (or, in the case of a company valuation, the value derived from the models in comparison to the price of the company) and invests in the projects which demonstrate a positive present value. Using an excessively high interest rate in the discounting process results in many projects being mistakenly seen as uneconomical. In addition, the projection of cash flows from projects (or a company) is exposed to mistakes in the projection, which again may cause many projects to be rejected although they may create positive value. Furthermore, in many cases, when the analysts use the traditional projection methods, they do not give due consideration to the effect of the examined project on other projects (synergies) or to the fact that such projects *could* affect the company's growth *possibilities* even if they do not directly affect the growth of the company.

The basic assumption in models based on discounted cash flows (or residual income) is that the level of such cash flows is uncertain. Therefore, the discount rate is determined in a manner which "indemnifies" the investor for the risk entailed, from his perspective, by such uncertainty. The problem with this method is that it does not relate to the possibilities which are opened to the managers after the investment, namely, to the changes in the system of possible investments and sources of revenue, which become clearer after a certain period of time. The company and its investors always face different options, and the most basic among them is the option which most investors in the company benefit from: the possibility of investing based on the company's development. In other words, investors could decide to discontinue the financing the company if they are not pleased with the interim results. This is an example of what is called real options.

Valuations could incorporate these real options facing the company, which are usually not fully addressed by the traditional valuation methods. This underpricing is particularly evident in startups, especially those operating in high tech fields.

Types of Real Options

- **Options to switch**—These are options to use the company's tangible and intangible assets for other uses than those represented in its current line of products. For example, options can change the blend of raw materials or the blend of products as a response to changes in market conditions or divert the use of a technology to another field.
- **Options to abandon**—These are options to abandon an investment which turns out to be uneconomical before it consumes all of the resources needed in order to launch the product on the market. For example, an investment in an R&D project may be terminated based on its results, without bearing the costs of market penetration and production if it is clear at that time that the product is likely to fail.
- **Options to delay**—These are options to change the timing of necessary investments or of the implementation of irreversible decisions in accordance with changes in market conditions. For instance, if the launching of a product can be postponed until such a time that the price of the product will economically justify its production, such delay would significantly reduce the risk entailed by just assuming that launching the product regardless of the prevailing market price for it at the launch time.
- **Options to scope and scale**—These are options incorporating the probabilities for higher-than-forecasted growth rates, which enable the investment to be increased or the company's fields of activity to be broadened while utilizing the company's existing infrastructure or technology. For instance, a company may increase its investment in a chip factory it owns and increase the volume of production two years down the road, in accordance with the demand for such products over the course of the coming year.
- **Options to stage**—These are options not to commit to invest all of the necessary amount at once, and constitute in fact a series of options to abandon an investment. These options actually represent the venture capital industry on the whole. Investors are always examining the cost involved in a smaller investment pending the meeting of certain milestones, opposite the prospects presented by a larger investment at an earlier stage.

Pricing Real Options

Real options may be priced by using models from option theory while taking into account specific parameters of the company and of the industry in which it operates. In many cases, customized models are used to price each real option individually, and the resultant values are then summed. It is important to note that the arbitrary use of commonly used models, such as the Black-Scholes model or the binomial option pricing model (explained below), may at times produce meaningless results since the model is fundamentally unsuited to the examination of investments when the possibility of creating similar investment portfolios synthetically (which is an underlying assumption in most of these models) is limited. Furthermore, the Black-Scholes model assumes a possible price distribution which does not necessarily correspond to the distribution of the results of each project. That said, almost any option which is desired to be taken into account may be priced by various algorithms based, among other things, on the use of simulation tools.

In practice, all option pricing methods inherently assume decision trees that are based on a succession of binominal decisions, and the quality of the computation is dependent only upon the scope and accuracy of the information available to the valuator. Binomial models (of which the Black-Scholes model is a case in point) assume the ability of short selling of the asset under examination, and of sales or purchases of risk-free bonds. Consequently, the models assume that any distribution of possible results may be reconstructed by stock and bond portfolios whose composition is changed from one stage to the next in order to provide the investor with a risk-free portfolio. This is not to say that projects' forecasted cash flows should be discounted with risk-free interest, but rather that in the structuring of the pricing model, stock and bond portfolios are constructed in a manner that creates an environment where anticipated cash flows should be discounted with risk-free interest.

In many cases, the value of real options—despite the complexity of their computation—is so crucial that ignoring them and making exclusive use of models such as discounted future earnings or cash flows models, may produce a valuation that is dramatically lower than the company's true underlying value. Over and above the deficient valuation, disregarding real options incorporated in a technology could cause an investor to decide not to invest in a company, whereas their inclusion in the valuation process would have presented the startup in a more favorable light.

Usually, the real options facing entrepreneurs and investors are too complicated to describe by a series of options which are priced by the model. Simulation methods are therefore the most efficient and useful tool for estimating and pricing such options.

Value to Investors or Strategic Investors and Buyers

Introduction

Financial investors value a firm based on the direct cash flows arising from the investment (e.g., in the form of dividends and capital gains). Strategic investors are those who derive additional expected cash flows from the investment in the firm (for example, the products of the firm can enhance their own product offerings marketability), or investors whose investment brings additional value to the firm (in terms of reputation, sales capabilities, etc.). Companies are typically worth more to strategic investors than to financial investors. On the other hand, the value of one investor to the company may be higher than the value of another investor. Therefore, although the company's value to a particular investor may be higher, the company may agree to an investment by another investor according to a low value since such investor is expected to better enhance the company's value than other investors. The company must always remember that its goal is to raise its value over the long run and not in any specific round of investment. The reasons for a company's being worth more to some strategic investors than to financial investors are varied—starting with the fact that the company's customer base could be better exposed to sales of other products by the strategic investor and ending with the possibility that the products developed by the company in which the investment is made will fit into the mosaic of products manufactured and offered by the strategic investor to its own customers.

Let us assume, for instance, that Radio Ltd. has developed an algorithm for compressing vocal information which makes it possible to broadcast to a thousand listeners at a bandwidth required by other technologies for broadcasting to a single listener. The value of the company will naturally be derived from the fact that it opens up possibilities to save substantially on broadcasting costs and to expand the station's audience without changing its infrastructure. However, obviously such or another type of cooperation with one or more Internet radio station infrastructure suppliers will raise the company's value considerably, since it will enable an integration of the product into the products of the infrastructure manufacturer.

Real Networks, which sells infrastructure for radio stations, will be interested in purchasing the company (or investing in it) in order to improve its ability to benefit from the company's developments and to influence the company not to cooperate with its competitors. Therefore, the company's value to the infrastructure manufacturer is higher than its value to other investors, and the value of the manufacturer as an investor is higher from the company's standpoint than the value of many other investors. Without going into the expected results of the negotiations between the parties—which may be forecasted according to the competitive positions of Real Networks and Radio Ltd.—Radio Ltd. obviously has a weighty interest not to frustrate the investment negotiations, although the company would possibly be better off by signing a cooperation agreement without an investment (since such an investment could "label" the company vis-à-vis other potential partners, for example, Microsoft).

Components in the Value to Strategic Investors and Buyers

An extreme case of valuation for strategic investors is the case of valuation by a strategic buyer. The value of a company to strategic buyers is the company's value to a financial investor (namely, its value as an independent company), plus the value of the synergy between the company and the strategic buyer, minus a component representing the independence value which will be lost as a result of the acquisition. In the example given above, if Radio Ltd. is bought out by Real Networks, the chance that stations using competing technologies will use Radio Ltd.'s products will clearly decline. However, integrating Radio Ltd. into Real Networks may increase the growth rates of Real Networks, thus considerably raising its own value.

Historically, companies which buy other companies tend to overvalue the synergy with their business, as is visible from the market reactions to announcements of such acquisitions. Companies which declare substantial acquisitions usually suffer a neutral or negative market reaction. This phenomenon is prevalent mainly in industrial sectors in which a slight change in growth rates does not materially affect the value of the company. In high tech or fast-growing industries, the "defensible" synergy component is larger, and payments reflecting a high acquisition premium in proportion to the value of the company to financial investors are therefore more likely.

The Importance of Potential Strategic Buyers to Financial Investors

Strategic investors each make individual specific estimates of a company's value to them. However, when valuating a company, it is desirable and even essential to try to estimate the possibilities of exiting the investment via an acquisition. In the late 1990s, more than five acquisitions of high tech companies took place for every IPO. This figure clearly reveals the importance of a valuation of the company to potential buyers.

Statistical data of acquisitions in related fields, which usually indicate the various multiples according to which acquisitions were made, may facilitate an estimate of the company's value to strategic buyers. For instance, many independent Internet Service Providers (ISPs) in attractive locations are valued according to the value-per-subscriber in similar acquisitions, and not the value-per-subscriber of public companies. One of the reasons for this is that this field is highly sensitive to economies of scale, and using the value-per-subscriber of public companies could therefore lead to unreasonably high values.

When there are not many potential buyers, separate valuation should be made of the companies which may purchase the company, in an attempt to assess the effect of an acquisition, if made, on their value. Let us assume that the value of Real Networks will rise by $100 million if it were to buy Radio Ltd. In such a case, it may be expected that the maximum price which Real Networks would be prepared to pay for Radio Ltd. would be this amount, if it does not fear the damage it may suffer if Real Networks' greatest competitor, Microsoft, buys Radio Ltd. If Real Networks is convinced that Microsoft will buy Radio Ltd., as a result of which Real Networks' own value would decline by $50 million, then the maximum price which Real Networks would be prepared to pay for Radio Ltd. would rise to $150 million, since the acquisition would increase its value by $150 million as compared to a situation in which Radio Ltd. is bought by Microsoft.

After assessing the company's added value to potential strategic buyers, the probabilities of such a scenario materializing should be assessed and priced according to the value to financial investors. It should always be kept in mind that exiting an investment via an acquisition provides a cash flow to the financial investor, which is similar in nature to cash flows obtained by him or her from the company through other channels (such as dividends or sales of his or her shares following an IPO), but with a different risk profile.

The Discount Rate Used by Venture Capital Funds

Introduction

In principle, in every valuation method based on discounting future anticipated flows of free cash flows, earnings, dividends, or residual income, the discount rate has a crucial effect on the derived value and may determine the fate of investments, since a change in the interest rate used for discounting may stamp a project as unprofitable. Obviously, the discount rate used by venture capital funds to discount the future value of cash flows also has a crucial effect on the value of the assessed company and hence on the percentage of ownership which the investors will require.

Historically, the discount rate by which venture capital funds calculate the value of companies lies in the range of 20–80% per year, depending on where the company stands in its lifecycle. This rate is materially higher than the customary discount rate for equity investments or for investments in other traded securities, even if the latter are very risky.

This section reviews the reasons which drive venture capital investors to use such a high discount rate. See Figure 9–1.

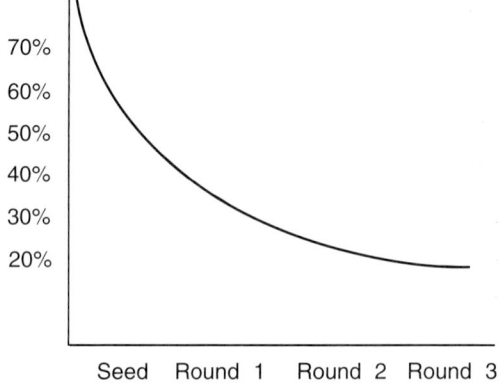

Figure 9–1 The Discount Rate Used by Venture Capital Investors in Each Investment Round

Why VCs Use a Higher Discount Rate

Following are several possible reasons why venture capitalists usually use a much higher discount rate than the rate derived from the CAPM model described earlier:

- **An inability to hedge the risk**—In venture capital investments, the overall risk, both systematic and specific, is very high. Venture capital investments obviously entail a very high specific risk, which includes the risk involved in the technology and in its prospects of becoming commercial. By creating a highly diversified investment portfolio, most of the specific risk may be hedged at the level of the fund, which invests in a large number of investments (although these are often concentrated in a single industry), or at the level of the investors in the fund, namely, the large institutional entities which make many different investments. However, since the fund cannot usually hedge all of the specific risk of each individual investment, since the portfolio of the fund itself, particularly industry-specialized funds, is not well diversified, fund managers use a higher discount rate, although the investors in the fund who have a well-diversified portfolio should use a different cost of capital to measure the performance of the fund itself.

    In addition, a venture capital investment is also exposed to a large extent to the systematic risk (market risk). For instance, the terminal value of an investment greatly depends on the level of prices on the market several years down the line. The fund is usually unable to exit its investment before an IPO or a sale of the company. Furthermore, market risks could cause an investment never to mature or meet projected returns. High tech companies, especially small companies with no resources, are very much exposed to changes in the market and to recessions. A recession, and/or a significant decline in the stock market, usually also translate into a slack IPO market which does not allow capital to be raised for other companies in the fund's portfolio and burdens the fund with their financing needs.
- **Illiquidity premiums**—The discount rate used by venture capital funds also includes a premium for illiquidity (liquidity is defined here as the ability to exchange an asset for cash at its full value within a reasonable period of time).
- **Projection errors and information gaps vis-à-vis the entrepreneurs**— A high discount rate compensates potential investors for errors in forecasting the company's future cash flows. As opposed to objective valuators who are equally likely to err upward or downward in their projections, the cash flows projected by entrepreneurs as presented to the investors are naturally inclined toward optimism. Therefore, an assessor relying on such figures may cut down the flows forecasted by the entrepreneurs and discount them with a reasonable rate of return, or increase the rate of return and use it to discount the projected cash flows.

Theoretically, however, the correct manner of treating this issue would be to examine several scenarios while attributing probabilities to their respective likelihood of materializing and then discounting them according to the correct rate of return for cash flows carrying a similar level of risk (which is rarely more than 30% per year).

- **Premium for the added value of venture capitalists**—A high discount rate may also constitute a mechanism by which companies pay a premium for investors who can contribute added value to the company. According to this theory, the company pays investors who can contribute added value with part of the return it generates. This added value is calculated directly in the form of a premium on the discount rate, which reflects an additional rate of return required in order to indemnify the fund managers. Venture capital investors are often active and involved in the company's decision-making processes, in the hiring and termination of managers, in directing the management, and in cultivating their investment in general. For instance, the fact that a certain investor or fund has invested in a certain company assists in opening doors, attracting customers, and facilitating the raising of additional capital.

Changes in the Discount Rate over Time

Investors lower the discount rate they use as the company matures. The reason for this lies in several factors. One could argue that the bigger the company, the smaller is its systematic risk since its growth rates are more moderate and its expenses lower in relation to the turnover. In addition, the investment becomes more liquid as the company grows and succeeds since there are more potential buyers for its stock. Furthermore, as the company develops, it hires its own skilled management team and is less dependent on the assistance of venture capitalists. Therefore, the payment for the added value contributed by such investors is reduced. In addition, the uncertainty with respect to the company's terminal value also decreases as it develops and accumulates an operating history, which may be used to judge how far it meets targets stated in the business plan.

Issuing Stock to Investors

Venture capital investors valuate a company according to one or more of the models mentioned above, while using the discount rate required by the company's risk level. The result is the company's post-money value, based on the assumption that the company managed to raise the capital it needs to implement its plans. Post-money value makes it possible to calculate pre-money value, namely, the company's value after the investment minus the amount of the investment. The share which the investor will demand in the company's equity is also derived from the amount infused by investors into the company and from the company's post-money value.

Following is an example of an ordinary issuance (see the section on the number and price of the shares allotted to the investor), followed by an example of an investment made with the allocation of a pool of options and shares for employees (see the section on investment rounds with a pool of employee stock options). Investors usually require at the time of the share issuance that the calculation of the value and the number of issued shares be made on a fully diluted basis. Although the options are not allotted to the employees at the time of the issuance, a pool of options (15–25% in the early phases) is reserved, thus assuring investors that they will not be diluted in the future due to the allotment of options to employees. Since the entrepreneurs bear the cost of the pool, such an allotment may be seen as a "discount" of sorts on the price given to the investors. This is because they receive more shares for the same investment so that their share after the investment round and the allocation of the pool is identical to the share they would have received had they been promised that no diluting issuances would be performed in the future.

The section on the effect of pre-emptive rights presents a scenario in which a new investor enters a company in which the investor from the previous round has a pre-emptive right, i.e., the right to preserve his share. In this scenario, we will calculate the number of shares which the existing investor is entitled to purchase when required to invest according to the price given to the investor in the current round.

The Number and Price of the Shares Allotted to the Investor

The number of shares which are allotted to an investor is a function of the share to which he is entitled according to his investment and the valuation:

$$\text{Required ownership percentage} = \frac{\text{Investment}}{\text{Post-money value}}$$

The number of shares allotted is determined in accordance with the existing number of shares:

$$\text{Number of new shares} = \frac{\text{Existing number of shares}}{100\% - \text{Required ownership \%}} - \text{Number of existing shares}$$

The price per share is, of course, a direct function of the variables calculated above:

$$\text{Price per share} = \frac{\text{Investment}}{\text{Number of new shares}}$$

Let us assume, for instance, that investor X is interested in investing $15 million in Speed, Inc., a company with a pre-money value of $100 million. We shall assume that the company has 20 million shares, i.e., the value of each share is $5. The investor will therefore be allotted 3 million shares, constituting 15/(100+15) of the company's shares, i.e., approximately 13% (see Table 9–2).

Table 9-2   Allotment Example

	Dollars (in millions)	Shares (in millions)	Price per share (in dollars)
Pre-money	100	20	5
Investor X	15	3	5
Total		23	
Percentage ownership	13.04%		

Investment Rounds with a Pool of Employee Stock Options

The basic formula for deriving the share to be received by investors in consideration for their investment assumes that such share will be preserved until they exit the investment. In other words, the formula does not account for future investment rounds which will require an additional investment by the investors or will dilute them, nor does it account for an allotment of shares to employees or the management team. Any future allotment not incorporated into the valuation translates into a dilution of the investor's ownership percentage, and it is therefore essential that it be addressed at the time of the investment. Consequently, investors require a higher rate of initial ownership in order to secure the ultimate ownership percentage they desire.

In order to calculate the share to be received by each investor in the current round, the company's value is usually examined based on the assumption that it will raise all the outside capital it will require (i.e., the value incorporates the amounts to be raised in the future, discounted to present values). Thereafter, it is necessary to assess the stages in the company's development at which it will raise outside capital, and the company's value in each one of these stages. It is also necessary to estimate the ownership percentage which the entrepreneurs and the company's employees will hold. It is then possible to calculate the number of shares which will need to be allotted in each of the next investment rounds, and to estimate the allotment of shares required in the current round according to the expected dilutions.

Many investment rounds take into account the allotment of a pool of options and stocks for employees, with an exercise price lower than their price in the investment round. In practice, the cost of the pool is usually borne by the entrepreneurs, and in some cases by investors from previous rounds.

Since the options are usually long-term and are given either for no consideration or at a substantial discount off the market price, they are counted as shares for the purpose of calculating the value and the number of shares, but the proceeds anticipated from their exercise are usually disregarded.

For the sake of illustration, we shall continue with the previous example, but shall assume that investor X requires that a pool of options be set aside for future employee recruitments at the scope of 20% after the investment. We shall further assume that until now all of the shares were held by the entrepreneurs.

At the end of the allotment process, on a fully diluted basis, the investor will have—after the round—the same share in Speed's equity, i.e., 15/115 = 13.04%. This figure reveals the entrepreneurs' holdings on a fully diluted basis as part of the equity after the investment: 100%–13.04%–20% = 66.96%. It is now possible to calculate the total number of shares after the investment (including the pool for future allotments): 20/66.96% = 29.87M. From here, it is easy to calculate the number of shares which will be set aside for the employees' option pool: 20%*29.87 = 5.97M, and the number of shares which will be issued to the investor: 29.87-20-5.97=3.9M.

Since the pool is not issued at the time of the investment, the investor's initial share in the equity is obviously higher than in a scenario without an employee option pool and is initially 3.9 / (20 + 3.9) = 16.3%. The amended required ownership percentage may be described by the following formula:

Amended required ownership percentage = Required ownership percentage * dilution factor

Where:

$$\text{Dilution factor} = \frac{1}{1 - \text{the percentage of the employee option pool}}$$

In the above example, the investor's share in the equity will be 13.04%/(1 – 20%) = 16.30%.

The price per share is an immediate result of the number of shares: 15M/3.9M = 3.85. The results are summarized in Table 9–3.

Table 9–3 The Effect of an Employee Option Pool

	Value (in $ million)	Number of shares (in millions)	%	Price per share (in dollars)
Pre-money	100	20	66.96	
Investment	15	3.9	13.04	3.85
Employee option pool		5.97	20.00	
Total (on a fully diluted basis)		29.87	100.00	
Investor's current ownership		16.30%		

The Effect of Preemptive Rights

Let us assume that the only financial investment in the company was made in the past by investor Y, who has a stake of 25% in the company, i.e., 5 million shares, in consideration for his investment. Based on his or her investment agreement, the investor is entitled to preserve his or her share in the company, and he or she wants to exercise this right. The company's pre-money value is, as before, $100 million, i.e., the allotment price is $5 per share, and we shall assume that no future dilutions are expected (in other words, this is the first scenario). Also, assume there is no requirement for an employee option pool.

The calculation of the number of additional shares to which investor Y is entitled is based on the fact that his total number of shares must constitute the same percentage (25%) of the company's total number of shares after the investment, which includes the shares of investor X (to whom shares are allotted at $5 per share), the founders' shares (who usually do not enjoy a preemptive right), and the new and existing shares of investor Y himself for which he would pay $5 per share. In other words:

New Y shares + Existing Y shares = Ownership percentage * (Founders' shares + X shares + New Y shares + Existing Y shares)

Simplifying the equation enables us to find the number of new shares which investor Y will be entitled to buy in order to preserve his share:

$$\text{New Y Shares} = \frac{\text{Ownership \% * (Founders' shares + X shares + Existing Y shares) - Existing Y shares}}{1 - \text{Ownership percentage}}$$

Investor X is allotted 3 million shares, and investor Y will invest $5 million in order to preserve his share, in consideration for which he will be allotted 1 million new shares. At the end of the process, investor Y will hold 6 million out of 24 million shares, i.e., exactly 25% (see Table 9–4).

Table 9–4 The Effect of a Preemptive Right

	Pre-investment				Post-investment			
	Shares (in M)	Shares (in %)	Value (in $M)	Investment (in $M)	New shares (in M)	Total shares (in M)	Ownership (in %)	Value (in $M)
Founders	15	75	75			15	62.5	75
Investor Y	5	25	25	5	1	6	25	30
Investor X				15	3	3	12.5	15
Total	20	100	100	20	4	24	100	120

The Venture Capital Method

Introduction

Underlying this method is the desire to project the company's value based not on a forecast of the cash flows it is expected to generate, but rather on an estimate of the company's terminal value (TV) at the time of exit, which is the number regarded as relevant for the investors. The present value of the company is subsequently calculated. The result is the present value of the company after the investment (i.e., post-money).

While the determination of the terminal value of the company can be done using any of the methods described in this chapter, the most common method VCs use is the multiples model, primarily due to its simplicity, and that VCs are typically interested in the general range of values the company could fetch at an IPO, where it is typically valued by market participants based on industry multiples. As described earlier in this chapter, there is no one parameter or a set of multiples that are always used, as these will vary from one investor to another, and particularly from one company to another. In addition, the more mature, advanced and well known the company, the more accurate and detailed the process will be, and the closer it will become to traditional valuations.

We note, though, that following the decline in the stock market in recent years, we already observe more extensive use of the other traditional methods of valuation described in this chapter, as well as usage of other advanced methodologies, such as option pricing and simulation tools.

The Venture Capital method is composed of several stages, the ultimate goal of which is to determine the share in the company that the venture capital investor will demand for his investment.

We will now detail the process and illustrate it using a medical technology firm as an example:

Stage 1: Analyze and Identify the Type and Time of the Exit

In the first stage, the fund attempts to weigh the risks involved in the investment against the chances of success. The fund examines the management, market, product, and business model. In this process, the fund manager is required to use intuition and experience; the product of this process is not necessarily one figure, but rather a range of values the company will be worth at approximately the time of the desired exit. The VC is looking at the value ascribed to similar companies, the competitive environment in which the company operates, and the sentiment in the market toward companies in the particular field—as well as estimating the chances of an exit by selling the company to a strategic entity, and the company's value to such an entity.

The VC tries to identify the possible type of exit from the company in the range of three to five years, which is the time frame preferred by venture capitalists, who are required to return all of their investments within seven to ten years. It is worthwhile to note that if the possible foreseeable exit is more than five years away, then only some investors will be suitable for such an investment. Such longer-term exits are appropriate for venture capital funds with a long-term outlook (i.e., funds that operate in areas with long-term exit-horizons, or funds that are just starting out investing for their current fund) or for strategic investors.

The investor tries to estimate which type of exit from the company will be feasible: an IPO, a sale, or a merger. If he or she thinks that a sale or merger is conceivable, he or she examines who the potential buyers are.

Mini-Case Study: Medica—Stage 1

We shall assume that Medica (a fictitious company) has achieved a revolutionary development in the medical diagnostics market, which could be used as an add-on to the CT scanner, a field over which medical equipment giants such as GE Medical, Philips, Toshiba, and others are competing.

Medica could potentially sell its products to all of the manufacturers, to be bundled in their products, or sell the products to distributors of these systems, to be marketed as an add-on. However, given a thorough analysis of the competitive environment, the VC realizes that it is likely that Medica would not be able to achieve substantial sales on its own, and an exit via an acquisition by one of the manufacturers would be the preferred alternative. The giant companies are already well established in the market, and have experienced, global, visible, and proven marketing and sales forces, as well as a customer base.

It therefore follows that the company's value in a sale to one of the giants, which could use the add-on as a tool for obtaining a competitive advantage, would be derived from the synergy in sales of the larger CT machines. The value will be determined based on the value for the large company itself, as well as from the perceived threat of Medica's acquisition by one of the giant's competitors.

We shall assume that the VC decides that he or she is interested, in principle, in investing the required $10 million in the company (I=10 in Table 9–5). For the analysis in the next steps, the VC assumes the exit would be in the form of an acquisition by another company, which will take place in four years time, when the development and testing of the tool will be completed (t=4 in Table 9–5).

Stage 2: Estimate Terminal Value (TV)

In the second stage, the VC tries to estimate what the company's value will be three to five years after investment in the company. For this purpose, the investor uses one of the methods reviewed above: the market value of comparable mature companies, the company's sales or earnings multiple, and so on. Due to the great sensitivity to underlying assumptions, the investor does not work with only one number. In other words, he does not use a working-point, but rather a working-range.

Mini-Case Study: Medica—Stage 2

As discussed above, the company's value in a sale to one of the medical equipment giants could be derived from the value which the large company calculates for itself, and from the threat it perceives in the acquisition of Medica to one of its large competitors, which could increase their market share with the technology. In our example, the VC analyzes the potential contribution of the add-on to the value of the potential acquirers. Without going into too many details, we assume that after a careful analysis, utilizing the methods described in this chapter, the VC determines that the sale could be expected to yield $300–$500 million (TV= 300 in the lower valuation in Table 9–5, and TV=500 in the higher valuation).

Stage 3: Determine the Discount Rate (r)

At this stage, the investor needs to decide upon the minimum return he will demand for his investment. As discussed earlier in this chapter, this rate is affected by the main risks involved in the investment, such as the company's developmental phase, existence of sales, risk involved in the development, entrepreneurs' experience, quality of management, market and field, competition, and so on. All of these factors, even if they had already been analyzed and accepted by the investor when deciding to actually make the investment, must be weighed again in the context of their impact on the value according to which he or she will join the company.

The rates that VCs apply are typically much higher than those applied by investors in the stock market, or those that would have been anticipated using the standard models (such as CAPM) for determining the discount rate. Venture capitalists are interested in achieving annual returns of 20–40% on their investments. Because some of their investments will be lost, or may not succeed at the anticipated level, investors aim to only make investments that could potentially earn them very high rates of return, namely 50–100%. This reflects both the need to indemnify unsuccessful investments and the internal risks which could cause a delay in performance, and hence in the exit as well.

Experienced venture capital investors will try to take combined action. On the one hand, to they will make "conservative" investments in advanced startups that are close to an exit and are led by experienced and well known teams, in which they will make do with returns of 40% or less but have a good chance of succeeding. On the other hand, they will make earlier and riskier investments, in which they will demand a return of up to 100%. See the section on why VCs use a higher discount rate than the rate derived from models for detailed discussion of the reasons mentioned above, as well as other reasons.

Mini-Case Study: Medica—Stage 3

The investor has tremendous faith in Medica and its management team, but based on his or her past experience of investing in other firms in the sector and the relatively early development stage of Medica (which involves risks associated with potential delays in the development, testing, and regulatory approval of the tool), the VC decides that the discount rate to be used is 75% per annum (r=75% in Table 9–5).

Stage 4: Estimate Additional Required Investment

At this stage, the investor tries to estimate how much money the company will need to raise in the future and according to which value, based on its needs and capital-raising options until the planned exit. This stage is important in order to estimate the dilution the investor is expected to experience if he or she does not exercise his or her pre-emptive rights to preserve his or her percentage of ownership by joining the next rounds.

Mini-Case Study: Medica—Stage 4

The VC and the company believe that until the exit, Medica will require an additional $20 million over and above the current investment (I2=20 in Table 9–5).

Let us assume the investor estimates that the additional investment will be raised in a single round in about two years, based on a (pre-money) company value of $80 million (V2=80 in Table 9–5). The VC does not plan to not take part in that round, and thus expects his or her holdings to be diluted by about 20% (D=I2/(V2+I2)=20% in Table 9–5).

Stage 5: Calculate the Range of Values for Investment

At this stage, based on the company's range of values at the time of exit, the time range until such exit, the expected dilution, and the discount rate, the investor will calculate what the company's range of values is at the time of investment. Based on the results of the valuation, the investor will negotiate with the company to determine the actual value according to which the investment will be made. Dividing the desired investment by the company's present value produces the equity share that the investor will demand in the company.

Mini-Case Study: Medica—Stage 5

The resultant range of values for the investment is $32–$55 million without dilution (PV=TV/(1+75%)^4 = $32 using the lower value, and $55 using the higher value in Table 9–5). Taking into account the expected dilution, the derived range of values is $26–$43 million (DPV=PV°(1-D) in Table 9–5.

The investor will therefore require 23–39% of the company in consideration for the $10 million investment.

Table 9-5   Illustrating the Venture Capital Method

Medica Example (all figures in $ millions)		Lower Value	Higher Value
Value at Exit	TV	$300	$500
Time to Exit	t	4	4
Discount Rate	r	75%	75%
Additional Raise	I2	$20	$20
Value at 2nd Round	V2	$80	$80
% dilution	D=I2/(V2+I2)	20%	20%
Present Value	PV=TV/(1+r)^t	$32	$53
PV with Dilution	DPV=PV*(1-D)	$26	$43
Investment	I	$10	$10
Required %	S=I/PV	31.26%	18.76%
Required % with Dilution	I/DPV	39.08%	23.45%

Appendix—Basic Terms in Measurement

The purpose of this section is to review and recall the basic terms in the measurement of returns and statistics which are used in valuations.

Basic Terms in Returns Measurement

- **Net Present Value (NPV)**—NPV is the sum of all discounted flows (both positive and negative) from a project. NPV is used as a gauge for measuring the advisability of an investment; an investment is only worthwhile if NPV>0.
  Example: We are contemplating investing $100 in the present ($C_0$) and expect the investment to yield (C_n) $110 one year from now (n=1). We shall assume that the investment is "risky" and that the appropriate interest rate (k) is therefore 15%. Inserting these values in the formula reveals a negative NPV—i.e., the investment is not worthwhile.

$$NPV = (-100) + 110/ (1 + 15\%) = -4.348$$

- **Rate of return**—The rate of return on an investment is the profit or loss made on the investment over the period of the investment, as a percentage of the initial amount invested. The rate of return is measured by dividing the sum of the cash flows (both positive and negative) by the amount of the investment. The rule is that an investment is worthwhile only when y>k, i.e., when the rate of return on the investment (y) is greater than the market return on such investment (k).

$$y = (C_0 + C_n)/-C_0$$

In the case of an initial investment (C_0) of $100 and a return ($C_n$) of $110, the rate of return is:

$$y = (-100 + 110)/100 = 10\%$$

If the appropriate interest rate (k) for an investment with such a risk profile is 15%, then the investment is not worthwhile.

- **Internal Rate of Return (IRR)** –IRR is defined as the discount rate at which the NPV of the investment is zero.

$$IRR = (C_n/C_0)^{1/n} - 1$$

For example, in an investment of $100 now which is expected to yield $200 five years from now (n=5),

$$IRR = (200/100)^{1/5} - 1 = 14.9\%$$

PART III

Venture Capital Investors

The first two parts of the book focused on startup companies—their nature, establishment, development, and other relevant issues. The discussion in the third part focuses on the entities which finance ventures—the venture capitalists.

Within this framework, we review the issues related to venture capital investors while differentiating between venture capital funds (Chapter 10) and other venture capitalists (Chapter 11). An in-depth discussion is dedicated to each type of investor, its role in startup financing, how it operates, its structure, and its distinguishing characteristics. Understanding these issues is essential for anyone involved in the venture capital industry, whether he or she is an investor, entrepreneur, or an advisor. For example, such an understanding could enable ventures to contact the investors most suited to them, to conduct a more knowledgeable and comfortable dialogue with them, and to upgrade their work together.

10
Venture Capital Funds

INTRODUCTION

The sources of capital which are available to startups are limited. Entrepreneurs usually lack the capital required to realize their ideas and must therefore seek outside financing. Capitalists, on the other hand (mutual funds, pension funds, trusts, etc.) lack the time and know-how required to make direct investments in new companies. Traditional sources of finance, such as bank loans or raising capital from the public, are not accessible to new companies. It was the meeting-point between the need to raise capital and the desire to achieve high returns from investing in private companies which led to the creation of venture capital funds. They serve both as an investment-management vehicle for the persons who invest in them (see the section on venture capital funds and their investors), and as financiers and added-value providers for the companies in which they invest (see the section on venture capital funds and their portfolios). The term venture capital fund refers mainly to an entity which raises capital for investments in private companies on an equity basis and which is managed professionally by a management company. This chapter describes their background, history, characteristics, and main methods of operation.

Private Equity Funds and Venture Capital Funds

Introduction

Venture capital funds are an important segment of the private equity fund sector which invests in the equity of private businesses and the securities of public companies. The financial activities of private equity funds are spread over a variety of fields, including derivatives, real estate, commodities, and emerging markets. Conservative estimates indicate that more than $100 billion are invested annually by private equity funds registered in the United States. While the numbers declined sharply in 2001, they are still above the amount in the years prior to 1999. It is important to point out that the figures are only approximates, since funds are not subject to public disclosure requirements with respect to their private equity investments. Some funds may choose to publish their investments and size in order to demonstrate their own financial ability and to enhance their own ability to raise capital, and gain access to attractive investments. Other funds, on the other hand, prefer to stay away from the limelight.

Private equity funds usually have a pre-defined model of their field of investment. For instance, many funds specialize in investing in companies which are experiencing financial difficulties by buying the securities of such companies (distressed securities); various hedge funds invest in securities, commodities, and/or currencies, often through financial leverage (i.e., using debt to "leverage" the equity).

As mentioned above, venture capital funds are part of the private equity fund sector. It is interesting to note in this context that with the development of the high tech industry in recent years, many private equity funds which were once identified with other investment fields, started investing considerable amounts in fields which are associated with "classical" venture capital funds. Kohlberg, Kravis, Roberts and Co. (the KKR fund), for instance, which was known for years for its investments in leveraged buyouts (LBOs) and in companies undergoing restructuring, has in recent years been investing considerable amounts of money in high tech companies.

The Main Types of Private Equity Investments

Although the different fields of activity of private equity funds do overlap, they may be classified into several main categories, according to their specialties.

- **Venture capital funds**—A venture capital fund is an entity which amasses money from investors in order to invest it in companies which are in the early phases of developing their products or services (startups). An investment in a startup is made in several stages, starting in the seed stage and ending in the last stages before the IPO. The investment is usually made by buying preferred shares which are convertible into ordinary shares, shares which provide some protection in the form of preference in the distribution of dividends and upon dissolution. The main method by which venture capital funds exit their investments is by selling shares after the company in which they invested goes public or is bought out by another company (for a discussion of investment milestones, see the section on stages in raising venture capital). Venture capital funds often define their area of activity for their investors, as well as the profile of the companies in which they intend to invest. The entities which invest in such funds are

usually various institutional investors, corporations, and high net-worth individuals.
- **Leveraged buyout and merchant banking funds**—These funds invest in acquiring all or most of the shares of different companies, usually in financial distress. Such acquisition is usually made by a company which is established for this purpose, with the funds investing some of the capital, and the majority of the acquisition being financed by loans, many of which are provided by the funds' institutional investors. Historically, the companies bought by such funds were companies which had demonstrated economic stability in the past but found themselves facing operating difficulties at a certain period of time, particularly companies in areas which could generate stable free cash flows. Following operational improvements, the companies are able to derive cash from operations and that cash is used to pay the interest on the large debt undertaken by the companies to finance the acquisition (known as "serving the debt"). The acquisition is often made in cooperation with the company's management, which gains a substantial part of the equity of the new company.
- **Hedge funds**—The term "hedge" is derived from the original goal of these funds: to generate risk-free returns by buying assets (long positions) by using proceeds from the sale of assets carrying the same return profile (short positions) and which, according to the investors' estimate, will bear a lower return. In other words, these funds aim to hedge the risks involved with holding the assets and retain the difference between the projected returns on these similar assets. However, over the years, most of the funds in this category have become funds which have net positive position and are not necessarily maintaining a non-exposure (i.e., hedge) status.

    Hedge funds include various types of funds which usually define their field of activity for their investors. In practice, hedge funds operate as mutual funds, but they are not subject to the reporting and management rules which apply to mutual funds, particularly the obligation of disclosing their investments, and the prohibition of receiving revenues which are contingent on profits. Hedge funds usually make extensive use of loans to leverage their returns. They are active in all fields in which mutual funds operate, alongside fields which are almost free of mutual funds, including fields such as (1) financial derivatives, i.e., investments in options and financial contracts while taking advantage of projected return differences between similar assets; (2) investments in shares and debentures of companies which are expected to be bought out, and the sale of the shares of the companies which are about to buy them (risk arbitrage funds); and (3) investments in commodities and currencies (commodities and currency funds).

    One of the most famous hedge funds was Long Term Capital Markets (LTCM). This fund was managed by a team of famous experts, including

Robert Merton and Myron Scholes, Nobel Prize laureates in economics. LTCM received broad attention from the media due to its remarkable success, as well as its collapse in 1998. A main component of its business was the investment in and sale of bonds while taking advantage of small interest gaps between similar assets and using highly leveraged investments. Successful hedge fund managers, such as George Soros and Michael Steinhardt, frequently appear in the media even though the investments made by their "macro funds" (funds investing in a broad selection of securities) generally remain concealed. Many of the hedge funds had invested in startups and, in particular, technology startups in the last few years, but significantly reduced the level of investment in the area from mid-2000.

Venture Capital Investment Characteristics

Venture capital investments almost always involve investments in assets which cannot be liquidated immediately and the return on which is highly uncertain. Venture capital investments also have several significant characteristics.

- **The investment process**—The investment process of venture capitalists is longer compared to most other investors and includes a close scrutiny of the product, the technology, the market, and the management.
- **Involvement in the company after the investment**—Venture capital investors, as money managers, are usually much more actively involved in the management of their portfolio firms than most investors in capital markets.
- **The investment objective**—A venture capital investment is made with the declared intention of exiting it within a fixed period of time.
- **The types of companies in which the capital is invested**—Venture capital investments are usually made by purchasing the equity (either ordinary shares or preferred shares which are convertible into ordinary shares) of companies in the private sector, as distinguished from buying and selling traded securities.
- **The risk of and return on the investment**—In venture capital investments, the chances of an investment losing value or being lost altogether are high. Therefore, investors in venture capital funds expect a significant compensation for the risk involved in their investment. Where investments in startups are concerned, the risks involved in the investment are typically higher than in investments in more marketable assets. First, an infant company is more exposed to changes in the market and to recessions. It does not usually generate revenues which enable it to survive on its own resources, and it is therefore more dependent on raising external capital, the availability of which depends to a great extent on the condition of the capital market. In addition, since the company places most of its hope in products

not yet fully functional, there is a risk that the products will not function or sell as anticipated, that the young and inexperienced management will not succeed in driving the company forward, or that another competitor will overtake the company in conquering the relevant market (for a discussion of the IRR required in investments in startups, see the section on the discount rate used by VCs).
- **The human factor**—A venture capitalist will prefer, more than in other types of investments, to invest in a company which has a good management team in which he believes, than in a company with a more promising product and target market but with a management team in which he has no faith. A weak management team could cause the entire investment to be lost or require the investor to dedicate much time to managing and monitoring the investment. Due to the illiquidity of investments of this type, an exit is usually not readily available, and the investor must therefore carefully consider whether he is prepared to join the company for several years.

Venture Capital Funds and Their Investors

Venture capital funds are intermediaries between investors and companies. On the one hand, funds provide professional screening services and scrutinize promising investments as well as provide a means to invest in portfolios of ventures, and on the other hand, funds amass capital and attract a large number of investors to invest in companies. Funds also provide investors with management, reporting, and monitoring services with respect to the portfolio companies and provide portfolio companies with added value (see the section on the added value of venture capital funds). From these respects, venture capital funds improve the investment process and reduce its cost and the investors' exposure to risk, in consideration for which they are compensated by the investors in the fund with annual management fees and a portion of the future profits.

Private equity funds in general, and venture capital funds in particular, give investors an alternative to investing in traded securities and debentures. They offer investors a diversified portfolio with the chance of increasing the risk adjusted return on their investment (see the discussion on investment theory in the section on the venture capital method). Venture capital funds are an efficient platform for these alternative investments, and they remove the need for establishing an in-house department for this purpose. However, many large technology companies have in recent years established investment arms which focus on identifying investment opportunities which are close to their fields of activity. For instance, Nokia, Intel, Time Warner-AOL, and many others also make considerable direct investments in startups, besides their investments in venture capital funds.

Venture capital funds use various control tools to provide their investors with monitoring and supervision services. These services are founded on the experience of the fund managers, as well as their ability to supervise portfolio companies by determining procedures and targets for them. Naturally, the larger the information gaps between the investors and the managers of the company, the more valuable are the controlling entities. Since venture capital funds provide investors with the means of control, they understandably focus on areas in which there are large information gaps, such as in many areas in technology which require a high level of expertise, and in companies in the early stages of development (see the section on the means by which venture capital funds oversee their investments for a discussion of funds' control tools).

Venture Capital Funds and Their Portfolios

The development of the venture capital industry, spearheaded by the venture capital funds, was and still is central and essential to the development of technology companies. The prolific and developing world of technology would probably not have reached such a high and advanced stage of development, in which entrepreneurs and companies literally change the world economy, without venture capital funds.

The uniqueness of venture capital funds as the most natural and suitable partners for startups stems from the fact that they usually have no extraneous interests which can clash with the company's interest: The main interest of the venture capital fund is that the company in which it invests will develop in the quickest and best manner into as valuable a company as possible. As such, the venture capital fund is the ideal partner of entrepreneurs in building up the company. While many if not most private investors have no extraneous interests either, their strengths and the assistance they can offer emerging companies are usually considerably inferior to those which venture capital funds can offer.

This is not to underestimate the importance of introducing other partners to the company such as strategic partners and large companies in the field, whose assistance in building up the company, including its marketing facilities and credibility in the market, is very important. However, it should be kept in mind that in contrast to venture capital funds, strategic entities have other interests which may at times not coincide with those of the company. Therefore, their involvement as partners should be conducted with caution.

The natural partnership between venture capital funds and entrepreneurial firms has created an integrated world in which the two industries are interlaced and mutually dependent: To be successful, funds need a wide variety and large number of promising startups; startups, in their turn, need experienced financing partners who have connections in the market, are ready to take chances, and whose interests overlap those of the company.

The Added Value of Venture Capital Funds

A good venture capital fund is not only a source of financing for a startup, but is also a financial partner with connections in the capital market and experience in building up companies. The added value of venture capital funds is expressed mainly by having the funds' partner-managers serve on the boards of directors of portfolio companies, as well as by the ongoing consulting to and guidance of such companies. A good venture capital fund can assist its portfolio companies in the following aspects:

- **Money**—First and foremost, a venture capital fund offers high-risk money which it is prepared to invest in companies in which it believes in consideration for a percentage of their equity. This investment is made without additional guarantees aside from the companies' resources (which are limited) in a very well-informed and sophisticated manner which has evolved over the years. This readiness should not be slighted; most financiers are deterred by such risky investments, even in euphoric times such as the years 1999–2000.
- **Financial backing**—Good funds do not abandon their portfolio firms in times of crisis, but rather tend to support them until additional resources may be engaged, even when the process takes longer than expected. This is true as long as they believe in the company, its entrepreneurs and managers, and in their ability to pull through the rough times and recover from them. For instance, after the crisis in the capital market started in 2000, many funds continued investing considerable amounts of money in their portfolio companies, even though their original plans were to solicit financing from the public or by private placements. Companies which are not backed by funds with strong financial resources are less likely to survive in times of crisis on the capital markets.
- **Credibility**—The introduction of a substantial fund into a startup requires the company to manage its affairs properly and to keep them in good order. Moreover, other investors and entities seeking cooperation usually like to see a substantial venture capital fund in the company, since such presence affirms the propriety and high standards of the company and its entrepreneurs. The existence of a reputable fund among the main investors in a company also facilitates the recruitment of senior employees for the company, since potential workers are favorably impressed by the fact that the company has passed the fund's screening mechanisms and can rely on the fund's know-how, experience, and connections.
- **Connections in the financial community**—Successful venture capital funds are well-connected in the financial community, both with other venture capital funds and in the broader community which includes, among others, investment banks. These connections are highly beneficial for the company's future investment rounds. Funds tend to work with one another, and a company referred by an esteemed fund stands a better chance of securing an investment from the fund to which it was referred. Furthermore, in later stages, the presence of funds and other institutional investors among a company's investors provides the company with additional support which facilitates the raising of capital from the public and, consequently, engaging underwriters for the offering.
- **Strategic connections**—The managers of venture capital funds are usually well-connected in the business world, either directly or through their

acquaintance with their own investors. Connections in the industry can significantly facilitate a company's securing of strategic alliances, as well as business deals. This issue is particularly important when the company's clientele are not end consumers, but rather the business community itself. In such cases, fund managers help to open doors to potential customers and tie deals with the investors in the fund and the companies which its managers know, as well as promote investments by various strategic investors.

- **Considerable assistance in recruiting top management**—An excellent management is crucial for leading a company on the road to success. Leading venture capital funds have reserves of and connections with managers who possess the potential to manage different companies, and the funds help to bring them to the company. Fund managers may also assist in screening and interviewing candidates. Furthermore, as mentioned above, senior executives prefer to see a leading venture capital fund as a partner in the company because such partnership indicates that serious outsiders have invested money in the company (i.e., the risk is lower than the risk involved in anonymous ventures) and guarantees that the company has stable financial backing, at least initially.

- **Managerial and operating know-how and experience**—Throughout the development of a venture, particularly in its early stages, the managerial know-how and experience with which the managers of a good fund are equipped are important. At times, fund managers are former entrepreneurs or people who managed companies before becoming venture capital fund managers. In addition, fund managers have accumulated experience in investing in and guiding many companies, and have therefore confronted various managerial situations and mistakes which are characteristics of new companies. Such prior experience enables them to give timely warnings of incorrect developments and choices and to propose practical solutions.

- **Assistance in forming the business model**—Many companies start out by developing a product for a particular market, but later decide to change direction. Experienced fund managers can also assist companies in identifying other markets in which their existing technological potential can be applied. The identification of applications which are not in the focus of the entrepreneurs' initial business plan does not necessarily involve the use of more advanced technologies.

  An example of this is the well-known story of Hotmail, the company now owned by Microsoft and one of the largest providers of free e-mail in the world (in fact, Hotmail was one of the first to offer this product). The company was bought by Microsoft for the large amount of approximately $400 million, although the company's original business model did not include any material element of revenues from users. Nor did the company receive any significant amount of venture capital financing. Originally, the company focused on creating a site for developers in the Java programming language, and many funds which saw the company's business plan and its managers turned it down immediately. Help came to the company from one of the leading funds in the United States, Draper, Fisher, Jurvetson (DFJ). It was actually the free e-mail service, which the company had created as a service for their users, which excited the managers of the fund. This supplementary service became the cornerstone of the company's action plan and was the main reason for the fund's investment. The company reached more than 10,000,000 users before it was acquired by Microsoft for more than $400 million.

- **Constructing a balanced and contributing board of directors**—The board of directors is involved in strategic and material decisions and complements the company's management team with its experience. The fund leading the financial round will usually appoint at least one representative to the board of directors and may also help in recruiting talented and experienced persons to the board to the company's advisory board. It is hard to overrate the importance of an advisory board staffed with reputable and well-connected persons. A company's success depends to a large extent on its ability to build a network of investors, customers, and other companies in the field.

In conclusion, having venture capital funds join a startup is a considerable event in the company's life, which testifies that it has achieved a certain degree of maturity, and the more prominent the fund in the market (in its size, connections, financial abilities, understanding and level of management), the more significant will be the event to the company.

The Means by Which Venture Capital Funds Oversee Their Investments

As investors, venture capital uses various supervision mechanisms to ensure that their investments in their portfolio companies will yield the highest return possible. The need for different supervision tools results from the uncertainties which face any investor in a company, but particularly investors in early stage companies. These result from information gaps between the company and the investor and from the "agency problem" which exists between principals (in this case, the shareholders), and their representative agents (in this case, the company's management). The "agency problem" is driven by the fact that a manager who is not the full owner of an enterprise may act without proper supervision to maximize his own benefit by engaging in activities which promote his wealth, rather than the investors benefits. For example, if he or she chooses only high-risk projects, the investors are the ones who bear the full financial risk of the project's failure. If the project succeeds, however, the manager shares the rewards. Due to such potential conflicts of interest, the readiness of investors to finance the company is reduced, and consequently the investments are also smaller or, alternatively, are made according to a lower valuation, since investors require a premium for the risk involved in the representative's opportunistic behavior. Therefore, both the manager and the investor would rather have the manager supervised, which would reduce the investors' uncertainty and therefore raise the level of their comfort with the investment.

We will now review the main monitoring tools used by funds to reduce the cost of uncertainty and to alleviate information asymmetries with managers (for a discussion of the legal aspects of the control mechanisms, see the section on the main issues in investment agreements).

- **Investing in several rounds**—The first main tool used to reduce the risk and increase the ability to control a company is investing in stages. An investment in a startup is usually made in several rounds, not all at once. This is the most effective tool for reducing the investor's risk, as well as the strongest means of control which an investor can exercise over his portfolio companies. By investing in stages, the investor can re-examine the investment, and he is not committed to any additional investment unless the company meets the targets determined as a condition for the continuation of the investment. Naturally, the closer are the investment rounds to each other, the more effective is this means of control, but it also reduces the managers' freedom of action in a manner which could prejudice the company's current activities and impose too heavy a burden of control on the investors. Venture capital investors take the cost of such control into account and ensure that the investment stages are determined in accordance with the need to re-examine the company's progress. This is one of the reasons why investment rounds are larger and less frequent when the R&D stage is lengthy, since the probability that any considerable change will occur in the short term is low. However, if the business environment in which the company operates is dynamic and fast-moving, then a constant evaluation of the company is crucial to ensure that the company is indeed on the track which will yield the returns hoped for by the investors in the previous round.
- **Syndication**—Venture capital funds tend to enter investment rounds together with other investors. Syndication enables venture capital funds to hedge risks by investing smaller amounts of money in many companies. In follow-up financial rounds, this also enables each fund participating in the round to signal its commitment to the firm. Typically, a lead firm is responsible for monitoring the due diligence and investment contracts, but it is commonly one of the new investors in the round. This also provides an efficient manner to reduce duplicative due diligence costs.
- **Ongoing control**—From the venture capital funds' point of view, the cost of control by investing in stages is high, since the examination of the investment requires resources, which could otherwise have been spent identifying and

examining new potential investments. In addition, if the financing rounds are frequent, they may entail burdensome transaction costs. Consequently, between rounds, the leading investor in the latest round monitors the company constantly, and the other investors receive reports from him and from the company. Such control includes, among other things, representation on the board of directors, the receipt of current reports and financial statements, and the right to veto certain decisions (for a further discussion, see the section on the main issues in investment agreements).

- **Compensation of entrepreneurs and managers**—Compensation methods which are based on options and on performance assessments contribute to the alignment of interests of the investors and the managers (see the section on the methods of employee compensation). Long vesting periods, as well as various stipulations in the investment contracts with respect to continued employment with the company, ensure that the managers will remain with the company and will dedicate all of their energy to it.
- **Geographic preference**—Venture capital funds enjoy broad representation on the boards of directors of their portfolio companies in particular, in its early stages, and are often also involved in the daily management of the company. When a company is undergoing a crisis, additional representatives of the venture capital fund join the board of directors, and there is a tendency to replace managers. Such managerial involvement by venture capital funds, and the vast time-resources it requires, explain the preference exhibited by funds to invest and exercise managerial involvement in companies which are in geographic proximity to their offices. Indeed, it has been documented that the probability that a venture capital fund will appoint a representative to the board of directors of a company declines with the increase in distance between the fund and the company.

The Development of the Venture Capital Industry in the United States

Beginnings

The venture capital industry has developed in the United States over the last few decades, and U.S. funds now manage more than $100 billion. While private and corporate investors have financed ventures in the United States for many years, the first U.S. venture capital fund (ARD—American Research and Development) was founded only in 1946 after World War II by Professor Carl Comton, President of the celebrated Massachusetts Institute of Technology (MIT) and Professor Doriot of Harvard University. With the help of several local financiers, ARD started financing ventures which were based, among other things, on inventions developed for the U.S. Army during the Second World War, particularly developments made at MIT. The investments of this venture capital fund fit what had subsequently become the norm among venture capital funds: a small portion of the investment portfolio yielded the lion's share of the fund's return during its lifetime. The fund's investment in Digital, for instance, in the amount of $70,000, yielded approximately one half of the fund's return (the value of the investment rose to more than $350 million).

When the fund was first founded, institutional investors shied away from it, and it was traded on the stock exchange as a closed-end mutual fund. Its main shareholders were private investors. More venture capital funds were founded in the 1950s, but they too raised money mainly from the public, and were traded as closed mutual funds. The first known fund which was organized as a limited partnership for venture capital investments, was the Draper, Gaither and Anderson fund, which was established only in 1958, and signaled the beginning of a phenomenon which became more prevalent in the 1960s and 1970s. Nevertheless, most of the funds in these decades were still closed mutual funds traded on the stock exchange, or small business investment companies which received loans guaranteed by the U.S. government to encourage investments in small businesses.

At first, most of the funds were founded in the Boston and New York areas. A little later, starting in the late 1950s, similar funds started appearing in California. In the 1960s, funds became organized as limited partnerships, but these funds constituted a small percentage of funds until the 1970s. Although now it may seem puzzling, the investments in those decades were only on the scale of hundreds of millions of dollars per year. It was not until the late 1970s and 1980s that the venture capital industry started raising large amounts of money. The turning point in the volume of money raised may be attributed to the 1979 amendment of the regulations governing the investments of pension funds in the United States. Until then, restrictions were imposed on the amount of money pension funds were allowed to allocate to high-risk investments. The amendment enabled such funds to invest in high-risk capital, known today as "alternative investments," which also include investments in the venture capital fund industry. From that point on, a constant increase has been visible in the resources directed by pension funds to venture capital investments. Thus, the share of pension funds in the venture capital money invested in the industry grew from approximately 15% in the late 1970s to more than 50% at the turn of the 21st century.

The 1980s

One of the most important phenomena in the venture capital industry, which began in the early 1980s, was the investment which large venture capital funds made in companies in earlier stages than was customary until then. That resulted in the investment requiring more resources in each company. In addition, although the funds preferred to dedicate their managerial attention to a relatively small number of companies, the amounts of money which they started managing were larger than before. This substantial transformation created more flexibility for funds to specialize in investments in early-stage companies, as well as private investors.

At the same time, many advisors started assisting pension funds and other institutional investors in screening and selecting investments in venture capital funds. These consultants (known as "gate keepers") helped pension funds and institutional investors to create a portfolio which was spread across several venture capital funds. Pension funds were thus able to achieve the diversification they sought and reduce their exposure. In the late 1990s, more than one-third of the money which pension funds undertook to invest in venture capital funds was managed by such gate keepers, who usually manage "funds of funds" for institutional and other investors.

The share of pension funds in the resources of venture capital funds rose to approximately 50% of the funds' money. Other large investors who invest in venture capital funds are corporate investors, whose investments account for approximately 30% of the money invested in venture capital; high net-worth individuals, whose investments account for approximately 10% of the investments; and not-for-profit organizations, such as university funds which receive many endowments, whose investments also constitute approximately 10% of the money raised by funds.

In the 1980s, due to the multitude of venture capital funds established and the vast amounts of money they raised, the returns on their investments declined. The surplus money raised the investment prices, which in turn reduced the IRR. This phenomenon slowed the pace of investments funneled to venture capital funds and reduced their volumes. The returns achieved by venture capital funds declined dramatically, not necessarily because of a decline in the returns on the stock exchange, but rather due to the excessive amount of investments made in limited areas of the high tech world (for instance, an absurd investment in an unprecedented number of companies manufacturing computer hard disks) and due to the establishment of new funds led by managers who had no relevant experience in the field and hence were bidding up the prices of private firms, causing returns to decline. For instance, the average annual return by funds rose in 1982 to 32% and declined in the following decade to a low of approximately 8%.

The 1990s until the 2000 Crisis

As a result of the deceleration in the pace of investments in the late 1980s, together with the eruption of the communications and Internet revolution, the returns started rising again, and funds were once again raising ever-increasing amounts of money. The huge prosperity of the stock market in the 1990s also contributed to an unprecedented infusion of money into private investments in startups. In the first three quarters during the year 2001 alone, venture capital funds raised more than $50 billion, a process which came to a near standstill in the fourth quarter of 2001 (see the section on the venture capital industry at the dawn of the third millennium for a discussion of the venture capital industry today).

The venture capital industry of the 1990s was characterized by changing trends which reflected changes in the expected returns in various fields. For instance, B2C (Business to Consumers) companies, which flourished in 1999 and in early 2000, receive almost no financing at all from venture capital funds following a significant decline in returns expectations in the area. On the other hand, investments in biotechnology became more fashionable from 2000.

Additional characteristics of the venture capital industry in the late 1990s were:

- The immense volume of money which is managed by venture capital funds approximately $100 billion in the year 2000.
- The establishment of mega-funds, including some funds commanding more than $1 billion.
- The unprecedented returns on investments. According to the trade journal *Venture Economics*, the average return of U.S. VC funds in 1999 was approximately 160% (for a further discussion of venture capital fund returns, see an earlier section in this chapter).
- The entry of many entities into venture capital investments, including private equity funds which had previously invested in other fields, as well as operating companies.
- The increase in the compensation of fund managers. As a result of the remarkable performance demonstrated by funds, some fund managers started charging up to one-third of the profit after reimbursement of the investment ("carried interest")—far above the 20% which had once been the industry standard (see the section on distribution of profits and compensation of fund managers for a discussion of fund managers compensation).
- The global basis of fund investments, as well as the establishment of separate funds for investments in different continents (see the section on the characteristics of the venture capital industry today for a discussion of globalization).

The crisis which befell the capital markets in the fall of the year 2000 has many implications on the industry. These implications are discussed below.

The Venture Capital Industry at the Dawn of the Third Millennium

Introduction

As mentioned above, the venture capital industry is completely intertwined with the technology industry in general and the startup industry in particular. The main characteristics of the venture capital industry and the changes it is undergoing are, first and foremost, a result of the corresponding characteristics and processes experienced by the technology industry. Even typical local variables, such as political instability, have only a minor effect on this industry.

The 1990s have been characterized by an exceptional window of opportunity in the communications and Internet fields and in the industries which support them. This opportunity came from new technological capabilities in these areas which advanced the world in quantum leaps. These possibilities, which were not previously utilized by industry giants, created a large vacuum which naturally drew in entrepreneurs and technologists who established many companies, some of which became new global giants over the years (such as Cisco and AOL).

At present, it is unclear whether the pace of technological advancement and its embracement by consumers will persist in a manner enabling an accelerated growth of the technology industry as was demonstrated in the past decade. As a result, these are significant changes that the financial backers of the technology industry are going through.

The Impact of the Crisis in the Capital Markets on the Industry

Figure 10–1 illustrates the tight relationship between public capital markets and the venture capital industry. This relationship can be used to describe the main impacts which a crisis in the capital markets would have on the venture capital industry.

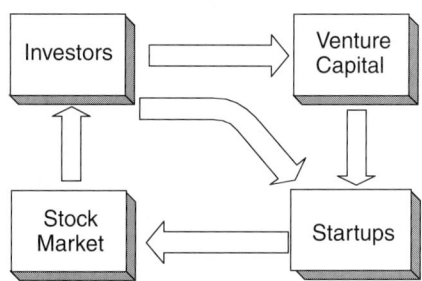

Figure 10–1 The Relationship between Public Capital Markets and the Venture Capital Industry

- **The Impact of the VC-Market Cycle**—There is an intimate connection between the prices of publicly traded stocks and the amount of capital raised and invested by venture capital funds. Successful exits through the stock market by way of IPOs, secondary offerings, in which shareholders sell shares to the public, or by selling shares released from lock-up or, alternatively, acquisitions by public companies at high prices, provide investors with enhanced incentives to invest in venture capital funds. Since most of the funds raise substantial amounts of money when there are many successful exits in the market, additional investors invest more in the companies directly, and since the number of potential investments does not rise proportionately, then naturally the returns in the subsequent periods are lower. It is indeed projected that funds will not be repeating the returns they demonstrated in the years 1999–2000 (see the section on the return on venture capital funds) and, consequently, their ability to raise capital will decline. Less money will be invested in funds also because investors in funds prefer, in times of crisis, to invest in investments carrying a lower risk. That, in turn should improve the returns in the following years, assuming the market will return to a growth path.

Small and mid-sized funds with short investment records are hit the hardest. Well-established funds still manage to raise capital in bad times.

Support of this phenomenon may also be found in the behavior of some funds. Even funds which can raise a large amount of capital may decide not to pursue this course of action in times of crisis because they do not anticipate high returns for their investors. The Crosspoint fund, for instance, decided in 2001 to cancel a scheduled investment of $1 billion in a new fund it was planning to establish even though the fund had already received commitments from investors. The reason given by the fund was that the fund managers did not foresee in the near future sufficient likelihood of yielding the returns to which investors in the previous funds had become accustomed. Other leading funds, including Benchmark Capital and Kleiner Perkins, reduced the size of their new funds. The upside is that since in times of crisis less money is invested in funds and consequently in startups, the funds' returns typically rise in subsequent years. However, this time, it seems the U.S. market suffers from an economic recession, which may impact the prospects for such returns.

Numerically, after record-breaking quarters in the amount of capital raised by funds and companies, the growth rate of capital-raising and investments slowed from the third quarter of 2000. This did not prevent U.S. funds from raising approximately $90 billion in 2000 and investing over $100 billion. In 2001, the capital raised by U.S. venture capital funds declined to less than half of that, and the investments made by U.S. venture capital funds also declined to approximately $30 billion, as compared to approximately $100 billion in the previous year.

- **Directing fund investments to portfolio companies**—Another phenomenon which is noticeable in times of crisis is that venture capital funds invest more in their portfolio companies than in new companies. Thus, out of the total amount of capital invested in the United States in 2001, only about $10 billion was invested in new companies, and the remainder was invested in portfolio companies in more advanced financing stages. This phenomenon is to be expected, given that in times of crisis the chances of raising capital from the public on the stock exchange or from new investors are low. Since the companies' financing needs are not diminished, they rely on private investors and the previous investors are a natural choice. The combination of a reduced availability of outside capital with valuations lower than would have been projected based on past data, drives funds to invest more in their portfolio companies at this stage. If, in the past, funds used to rely on their portfolio firms new investors, they are now compelled to persevere in supporting their companies. This process leads to a reduction in the number of new companies in order to sustain the greater support of each portfolio company over time.

- **Providing added value services**—Leading funds now emphasize more the value added services (see the section on the added value of venture capital funds) they provide to their firms. The cost of expanding the service package should always be measured by its impact on the fund's return, either by persuading entrepreneurs to work with the fund or by its direct and indirect effects on portfolio companies' achieving their goals. We expect this trend will continue, although it might be in the form of services for reduced fees, rather than services offered for free to the portfolio firms.
- **Investment rounds based on lower values ("down-rounds")**—In many cases, the valuations used for new investments are lower than those used for previous investment rounds. Starting in fall 2000, the market value of public technology companies, and hence of companies in the private sector, considerably declined. For instance, in 2000 and 2001, many companies which raised capital at the height of the capital market's prosperity were forced to raise capital according to valuations which were at times dozens of percents lower than their previous value (down-round) despite the progress they had made during this time in developing their products.

In 2001, the average value of companies which had performed private placements in the United States with the involvement of venture capital funds was approximately $15 million. Although this figure represents a considerable rise compared to the average value in the years prior to 1998, it is significantly lower than in 1999 and 2000. This represents a sharp decline in the value of the companies in conformity with the sharp decline in the value of traded companies.

Emotional considerations have always played an important role in the valuation process, and in 2001 it appeared that investors had despaired of the technology market. However, there is also an optimistic aspect to this phenomenon, since companies are now once again being valued based more closely on the fundamental economic prospects in their business models, rather than based on "bubble-prices" of 1999–2000.

It is important to remember that, despite all the talk about a "new economy," the basic principles of company-valuation have remained the same, i.e., the company's value should reflect the present value of the cash flows it will generate for its owners. Such cash flows are composed of direct cash flows which the company will generate in the form of operating and financing profits, as well as additional cash flows which the company or its owners will gain, such as the projected cash flows from selling shares on the stock market while possibly utilizing any higher favorable valuation which may exist at that time. It is these principles which ultimately determine the value of a company and the "bubble-prices" observed in the market prior to the decline drive many investors and entrepreneurs to believe their companies could benefit from exits at price levels which proved to be unsustainable (for a further discussion of the valuation of companies, see Chapter 9).

Furthermore, in times of crisis, the importance of the size of the investment round is greater than ever. In prosperous times, companies can be selective and choose to have smaller investment rounds to avoid dilution, assuming that additional financing will be readily available in the future; in times of crisis, however, they are compelled to increase the investment rounds due to the great uncertainty clouding the availability of future financing. In other words, the considerations remain unchanged, but the weights attributed to the parameters at the time of valuation are different.

- **Closing down and mergers of startups**—In times of crisis on the capital market, an increasing number of startups are denied additional financing, since the typical exit—IPO or the sale of the company—appear less realistic. At such times, investors, and particularly venture capital funds, usually sift through their portfolios to separate the wheat from the chaff, a task that would not necessarily have been undertaken with the same intensity in other times. As a byproduct of the uncertainty in such times, many companies with excellent products and promising target markets are also closed down. Sadly, while in times of prosperity even failing companies sometimes can raise capital and make it to an exit, hard times are also difficult for good companies (for a discussion of the dissolution of startups, see Chapter 18).

  Companies that cannot yet demonstrate revenues are entirely dependent on the infusion of capital by investors (in most cases) or by future customers who are prepared to pay in advance for future developments (rarely). In addition, when the possibilities of raising capital on the stock market are more limited and the speed at which capital is raised has also slowed in the private market, the importance of orderly business planning is greater than ever, and funds and other investors will demand that their portfolio companies observe tight control measures.

  Many companies conclude that in order to survive they need to join forces with other small firms to augment their power in the market and to reduce costs. Sometimes it is the investors themselves who push in the direction of mergers, and funds may even encourage mergers between their own portfolio companies, in order to increase the likelihood of their survival, by combining their financial and managerial resources, while eliminating redundancies.

- **Closing down and mergers of funds**—In difficult times in the capital markets, many funds which did not manage to raise capital before the crisis, close down. Other small funds tend to merge in order to increase the amount of money they can manage and support their portfolio firms. Many newly established funds and incubators were closed down in 2001 and there are funds who suffer from the departure of partners, mainly new ones, who do not foresee high likelihood of large profit-sharing.

- **Establishment of specialty funds**—During the crisis, investors started voicing complaints that some funds had ventured into areas in which they had no comparative advantage. It appears that the coming years will bring a phenomenon of funds specializing in narrower areas, similar to the phenomenon which took place in mutual funds in the last decade. An increasing number of institutional investors will channel investments to specific areas and compare funds with similar investment profiles in order to choose the most promising funds. These specialized funds may be managed by the same large VC fun management companies, but we'll address specific niches. This pattern is similar to the one observed in the mutual fund industry during past decades.

  Moreover, the differences between experienced and large funds and less experienced funds will become more evident. Experienced funds, which usually also command more resources, often focus in times of crisis on cultivating and investing in their portfolio companies, either by providing financial resources or by vigorous assistance in the search for strategic partners which could assist, or even buy, the companies. Smaller funds with fewer resources have a limited ability in these areas, particularly in difficult times.

- **Globalization**—In the late 1990s, U.S. funds have expanded operations overseas (mainly in Europe and in the Far East) and European funds were expanding operations to the United States. Most of them have done so to assist in the business development of their portfolio companies and to better support them.

  The reasons for the shift to global investments were clear. The technologies used around the world are similar, and the educational systems around the world allow innovative technologies to be created almost anywhere. In addition, communication networks have created a situation in which the entire business world is run on a global basis. The cooperation among venture capital funds operating in different countries is expected to grow tighter. Since venture capital activity does not, in itself, require highly staffed establishments in each country, there is justification for opening separate branches as part of a single fund or as part of funds having a specific geographic destination. This is in contrast to networks of attorneys or CPAs which constitute, in practice, a network of independent offices under a single marketing and direction umbrella, or that are serving multinational clients.

  The phenomenon of establishing separate funds for investments in different countries is inconsistent with the globalization phenomenon.

However, it is important to understand that in many cases, the separation of the funds was a result of investment restrictions imposed on the entities investing in the funds (for instance, restrictions on some institutional investors with respect to investing outside their native countries). The trend of global expansion and the proliferation of country or region-specific funds had almost completely stopped in the years 2001–2002, but we anticipate that the leading VC funds will continue to search for investment opportunities on a global basis. This pattern will further widen the differences between these leading funds and the funds with weaker resources.

- **A decline in investments by angels and operating companies**—In times of crisis, the share of professional investors who specialize in venture capital investments increases. Angels, particularly those who are not familiar with the industry, steer clear of venture capital investments after being discouraged by the decline of the public market and seeing their hopes for a fast exit drift away. Operating companies also focus more on their main business and less on venture capital investments at these times. Only venture capital funds, whose entire existence revolves around venture capital investments, remain in the market.

An Analysis of the Phenomenon and an Outlook to the Future

It is important to keep in mind that, despite the crisis in the capital market, an unprecedented technological revolution has been taking place in recent years. The changes which the Internet has brought about and is yet to bring, as well as the far-reaching changes in the communications and biotechnology markets, will have a dramatic impact on the business world for decades to come. We cannot ignore this fundamental economic phenomenon due to a stock market slump following a period of euphoria.

From the economic viewpoint, is it really surprising that the majority of companies in these infant technology fields have either disappeared or plummeted? Looking at the early 20th century, we may see that at the beginning of the revolution which accompanied the first motor vehicles, hundreds of automobile manufacturers emerged, each backed by the venture capital investors of the time. Most of these companies crashed within several years and some merged. Consequently, the American automotive industry is now represented by three important manufacturers, each created by dozens of mergers over the years. It should be kept in mind that these are only U.S. manufacturers and that the industry is far less innovative than most of the technology fields with which we are familiar today.

Whenever a new technology creates new markets or changes existing ones, many competitors emerge in the first stages of the industry's development. It takes several years for the industry to undergo the process which reveals who is to survive and which companies do not offer a package of added value sufficient to justify their existence. For instance, does anyone still use an Osborne computer? Osborne was one of the first companies to offer laptop computers and was deemed as the pioneer of the mobile computing concept. Yet, the company could not survive the steep competition in the industry. On the other hand, can we envision our lives today without laptop computers?

The communications and Internet industries developed much faster than other industries; it is therefore not surprising that many companies in this field crashed so quickly. When the pace of innovation is so high, the identity of the victors is revealed much sooner. In addition, the existence of new competitors in the market, backed by huge venture capital resources, has created the existence of many companies without any economic justification. Once more, the principles of economics prevail: When companies resemble one another and there is a sufficient number of competitors, the projected competition erodes any possible profitability which justifies investing in companies at high prices. Therefore, investors demand that the prices of companies be adjusted downwards and prefer to focus only on the companies which are expected to lead the industry. This is also why it is increasingly harder to secure financing for companies whose plans do not include a realistic expectation of gaining a substantial share of their defined target market.

The process is one of painful disillusionment. The technology industry and the investments in it will not disappear. The value of companies will be lower at the time of financing rounds, since any decisions on investments and valuations will be based on established economic models and not mainly on the euphoria in the public capital market or on market trends. Similarly, the returns of venture capital funds are expected to go back to their normal level of 20–25% per year after profit-sharing. In addition, the anomaly of an employment market with high and fast salary increases will cease to be, and the loyalty of employees to their employers will rise again. At the end of this process, we expect that the technology industry will emerge stronger and more mature.

The Structure and Activities of Venture Capital Funds

The Organization of Venture Capital Funds

The basic principle underlying the structure of venture capital funds is the creation of a distinction between the passive investors (the limited partners) and the fund managers (the general partners and the management company). The actual structure of the funds is determined according to the identity of the investors and the specific legal restrictions to which they are subject.

A venture capital fund is usually a private corporation organized as a limited partnership, or a company taxed as a partnership, such as an LLC (limited liability company) (see Chapter 2 on types of corporations for a discussion of the nature of LLCs). Being organized as a partnership excludes taxation at the level of the fund in the form of corporate tax, enables the partners to offset losses incurred against their capital gains, facilitates the dissolution of the partnership from the points of view of corporate and tax law, and protects the limited partners against legal liability.

Some of the funds are now registered as partnerships, usually in Delaware. Others organize several partnerships in order to meet the tax needs of the investors in the funds, who come from different countries and are subject to different tax liabilities (some are exempt from tax in their respective jurisdictions of incorporation). The investors in the fund are the limited partners (LPs); the general partner (GP) is a separate company (often an LLC), which is usually the fund's management company (the fund managers).

In other cases, the managers organize another company which is defined as the fund manager or investment consultant and receives some of the fund's income. The separation between the management company and the general partner is made when the general partner comprises other entities besides the fund managers (in some cases leading, value-adding investors are joined as general partners and not only as limited partners). The general partner and the management company are organized to enable the daily management of the fund to be performed in return for the management fees. This arrangement also facilities the distribution of the fund managers' profit-sharing component.

Figure 10–2 presents the typical structure of a venture capital fund. For the sake of simplification, the diagram presents the structure of a single fund, although funds usually manage several parallel funds with different legal structures and methods of management in order to meet the needs of different investors from the legal and taxation points of view.

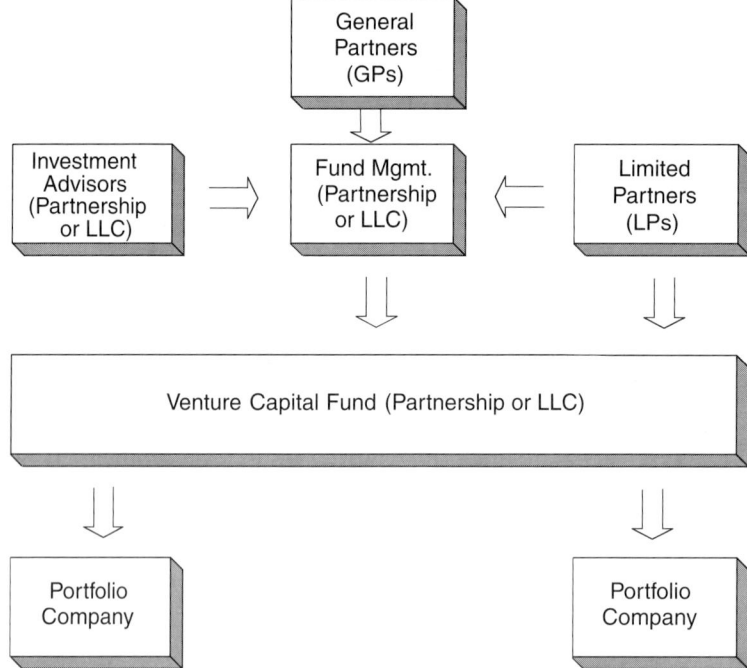

Figure 10–2 Typical structure of a venture capital fund

The legal significance of the fact that the investors are limited partners of the venture capital fund, whereas the general partner is (or may be) the fund manager, is that although the profits of the fund are distributed among all the partners, it is only the general partner whose legal liability is not limited to the capital invested in the partnership. As demonstrated below, the management of a venture capital fund involves many strategic and managerial decisions which are much broader than the decisions involved in the management of a mere traded-securities portfolio. Therefore, the fund manager is also far more exposed to the risk that decisions will be regarded as incorrect in retrospect.

As mentioned above, in order to minimize its liability, the general partner usually protects itself by being organized as a limited company. In other words, the general partner and the fund manager will themselves be companies, thus limiting their liability. Although venture capital funds have only rarely been sued, some recent cases have included venture capital funds which invested in companies that were a party to the complaint. For instance, the Hummer-Winblad fund is a party to the complaint filed by music companies in the United States against Napster, the company which enables the transfer of duplicated music files in violation of their creators' copyrights. In loose terms, the claim against the fund was that it financed a company whose core business involved the violation of copyright law and that since this activity was known to the fund, it was an accomplice to the crime.

Raising Capital for Venture Capital Funds

The main sources of capital for venture capital funds are large institutional investors such as pension funds and insurance companies. Most institutional entities in the United States and a large part of corporate investors invest in venture capital funds, as do high net-worth individuals. As discussed above, in the last decade, pension funds have constituted the largest group of investors in venture capital funds, with a share more growing to be higher than 40%. Another 30% is invested by operating companies, 15% by private investors, 10% by not-for-profit organizations such as universities' endowments), and 5% by foreign and other investors.

As opposed to other investors, many of the institutional investors are suitable for venture capital investments since their investment horizon is relatively far. The obligations of pension funds, for instance, extend over many years, and they can dedicate a material component of their capital to long-term investments. Because they are not that concerned about short-term illiquidity, investments which offer high returns in the long-term, albeit volatile and illiquid in the short-term, appeal to them.

The share of universities in the mass of investments has been on the rise in recent years, and large universities invest up to around 20% of their endowments in private equity funds, including venture capital funds. In principle, universities are an optimal source of venture capital investments since their investment horizon extends further than that of any other institutional investor. They usually do not utilize the actual endowments (the principal), since they are typically limited to using only a certain percentage of the return they yield. Therefore, investments bearing a high long-term return, and which lock up the money for several years, are suitable for this risk profile. The universities with the largest endowments such as Columbia, Yale, Harvard, and Stanford are also the ones that invest larger percentages of their money in venture capital.

Money is usually raised by way of private placements, although some funds have also raised capital from the public. Capital-raising is made pursuant to a PPM (private placement memorandum) or offering circular, since a private placement is not required to be registered with the SEC. Funds are investment companies, as defined in the Investment Company Act of 1940, that are subject to the rigorous registration and reporting requirements imposed by this law on financial holding companies. Fund managers are therefore required to obtain an exemption from these requirements. Usually, a special exemption given to private equity funds whose securities are held by no more than 100 investors (the Private Investment Fund Exemption) is used, or an exemption given to institutional investors or high net-worth individuals (the Qualified Purchaser Fund Exemption). A fund manager is also required to obtain an exemption from the requirements imposed on investment advisers under the Investment Advisers Act of 1940.

According to the fund's partnership agreement, the investors undertake to invest money in the fund (*capital commitments*). The capital which is actually invested in the fund by the investors is known as the *capital contribution*. According to common practice, the investors provide the money for each investment pursuant to a "capital call" made by the fund manager. In this way, investors' capital is not frozen as long as it is not needed for investments.

According to the partnership agreement, the capital received from the investors is used by the general partner for its investments in companies, and a pre-determined percentage is used to finance the current expenses incurred by the management of the fund.

How Venture Capital Funds Work

There are various types of venture capital funds which are distinguishable by several characteristics, such as the type of companies in which they invest, the stage at which the investment is made (i.e., the early or late phases in the company's life), and the degree of their involvement in the management of the company.

A fund's *modus operandi* is affected not only by its own characteristics, but also by the business environment in which it operates and by the composition of its investors and management team. For example, some funds tend to choose certain industry segments in which they are interested in investing and actively search for companies which suit that profile. This mechanism is known as theme investment, and it differs materially from the more passive mode of investment used by funds which invest in broad fields from among the deal flow of investments they are presented with. In addition, considerations of taxation and restrictions on the investments stipulated in the fund's investment guidelines (see below), limit different investors to certain funds. For instance, many pension funds in the United States are not allowed to invest in non-U.S. companies.

As mentioned above, venture capital funds are often organized as partnerships; their organizational documents regulate not only their methods of operation, but also the relationship between the limited partners (the investors) and the general partner and fund manager. The partnership agreement is founded upon the desire to ensure that the manager will dedicate the better part of his time and expertise to the fund's benefit, and will attempt to avoid conflicts of interests between his activity within the fund and other activities (sometimes as the manager of previous funds). The fund's organizational documents regulate the following principal issues:

- **The period of time fixed for the fund's existence**—A typical venture capital fund is founded for a period of seven to ten years. Usually, the fund invests in companies in the first third of its lifetime, nurtures them in the second third, and uses the remaining time to exit the investments. Once the investments have been exited, the fund dissolves.
- **Investment decision-making**—Decisions to invest in companies are made in accordance with the fund's investment charter, as defined in the fund's investment guidelines. When capital is raised for the fund, the fund managers present investors with a profile of the investments on which they intend to focus according to the fund's investment guidelines, which are similar to the investment guidelines of pension funds or mutual funds.

    The fund's management company (the fund manager) examines investment opportunities received by the fund. It is entrusted with screening the investments, scrutinizing them, managing the investment process, and monitoring and supporting the investment after it is made. The internal mechanism for making investment decisions differs from one fund to another, but it usually includes receiving the investment committee's approval for each investment made by the fund.
- **The measure of involvement of the limited partners**—In a limited partnership (as opposed to an LLC), the limited partners refrain from getting involved in the management of the partnership in order to avoid personal liability and enjoy the tax benefits of a limited partnership. Consequently, the involvement of the limited partners in the daily management of the fund is formally limited to representation on the fund's advisory board. In practice, fund managers often consult with and update the investors. The contact with investors is based not only on the desire to maintain good relations with them, since such investors may also invest in follow-up funds of the fund managers, but also on the recognition of the value which such investors can provide to the fund and to its portfolio companies. Therefore, the investors in the fund may be large financial entities which could help portfolio companies with future financing; they may be large companies of strategic significance, which may cooperate with or buy portfolio companies; and they may be private investors, well-supplied

with money and connections, who may assist in various ways. Therefore, despite the investors' limited legal status, their involvement in and ties with the fund may run very deep.

- **The ability to dissolve the partnership**—The partnership agreement sometimes addresses the right of the limited partners to dissolve the partnership in the case of a material change in the composition of the management company or the general partner, or in the case of poor performance.
- **The maximum investment in any single company** –Limitations are usually imposed on the maximum scope of a single investment or several investments, in order to reduce the risk of a sweeping failure if such company sinks.
- **Use of debt**—Venture capital funds are usually limited in leveraging their investments (in other words, they cannot borrow money or use the fund's investments as collateral in order to invest in additional companies). The reason for this is that it is the investors who need to decide upon their level of leverage in their investments, which naturally increases the risk in the investments. Given such a decision, the fund managers are supposed to invest the money in the field with which they were entrusted and for which they were appointed.
- **Re-investment of profits**—The general partner may at times have an incentive to invest the fund's profits rather than distribute them, since investing the profits could yield another distribution of profits (although it also postpones the distribution of profits to the general partner). An investment of profits usually requires the approval of the limited partners' advisory board, and is sometimes prohibited after a certain amount of time or after a certain percentage of the capital has already been invested. Sometimes the fund's regulations allow a re-investment of funds which were gained by a fast exit (for instance, an investment in a company which was bought out one year after the investment, with nine years remaining until the dissolution of the fund).
- **Private investment by the general partner**—In many cases, the general partner is interested in investing his own money together with the fund in a certain investment. This may give rise to the fear that the general partner will use the fund's money to cultivate the private investment, and will dedicate a large amount of time to the particular company in which he has a private interest. In many cases, the private investment is limited in size (1% of the fund's investment) and may require the approval of the advisory committee. An alternative method is to require that the general partner invest together with the fund, i.e., make a proportionate investment in all of the fund's investments in order to prevent him from choosing only the best investments (known as "cherry picking"). Another method of overcoming conflicts of interest is having the general partner invest in the fund itself (usually 1% of the fund).

- **Future raising of capital by the general partner**—After the majority of the fund's money has been invested, the general partner may seek to establish a new fund. The general partner is obliged to continue managing the fund in accordance with the customary professional rules. The partner will therefore be allowed to raise additional funds only if he can guarantee that the previous funds will continue to receive the required level of attention. In many cases, this matter is handled by defining a certain percentage of the fund's money, and only after investment of this money is the manager allowed to solicit additional money.
- **Investments with other funds of the fund manager**—Some fund managers manage several funds, the capital of which was raised at different times. In order to prevent a situation in which the manager will tend to invest in companies in which he had already invested, although the investment is not sufficiently attractive objectively, the approval of the advisory board is often required before a fund can invest in a company in which a previous fund of the manager's had invested.
- **Other occupations of fund managers**—Partnership agreements may contain terms and conditions limiting the scope of the fund manager's business activities outside the fund. These restrictions are relieved after a substantial part of the fund's capital has been invested.
- **The addition of other general partners**—The approval of a majority of the limited partners is often required for any material change in the identity of the partners managing the fund, be it the replacement or the addition of partners.
- **The fund's management fee**—Funds customarily charge annual management fees of 1.5–3% of the size of the fund. The definition of the size of the fund varies from one agreement to another: In many cases, it refers to capital commitments, in others to actually invested capital, and in others to the value of the managed portfolio, which naturally changes as a result of capital-raising rounds in the portfolio companies. Often, the initial definition of the management fee is valid for 3–5 years and is based on the capital commitments until the end of the period during which the fund is supposed to invest the money. In some cases, uncalled capital commitments and capital actually invested in portfolio companies are weighted at different rates. Later on, the management fee is based on the capital under management (in other words, exits made by the fund which are allocated to the limited partners reduce the basis for the calculation of the management fee). Management fees are usually collected at the beginning of each quarter. Since a venture capital fund closely monitors its investments until it exits them, management fees continue to be collected in the years following the full investment of the fund's money, but are almost always reduced, reflecting the reduced required efforts in screening investment opportunities.

- **Exit**—Another important component of a fund manager's work is his responsibility for deciding upon an exit for the fund's investments. Venture capital funds exit their investments by selling shares in initial or secondary public offerings, selling the company, or distributing the shares among the investors in the fund. In recent years, many funds have chosen to distribute shares among their investors instead of selling them and distributing the sale proceeds.

Distribution of Profits and Compensation of Fund Managers

The mechanism of compensating venture capital fund managers is designed to tie the manager's compensation to the fund's performance over time and to indemnify him for the effort exerted in the daily management of the fund. As mentioned in the previous subsection, the compensation of fund managers is composed of annual management fees which are usually measured as a percentage of the fund's capital and are used to cover the fund's expenses, and of a certain percentage of the fund's profits after reimbursement of the investments (*carried interest*). The measurement of performance is typically based on the cumulative return on all of the fund's investments, and not on any individual investment.

The definition of the basis on which performance-based compensation is distributed is usually founded on the capital invested in the fund (capital contribution). Such distribution is often made after the investors are guaranteed a certain minimum return. This minimum return is usually determined as a function of the return on government bonds. Also, the management fees are often deducted when the profit for distribution is calculated. The measurement of the return is based on the return accumulated over time, which includes the profits earned by actual exits from the fund's investments, in addition to the unrealized profits distributed among the fund's investors by way of traded shares (payment in kind). It is important to note that the general partner is often also an investor in the fund and thus enjoys also a share of the profit as an investor as well. If, for instance, the general partner invested in the fund 1% of its capital, and the compensation is 20% of the accumulated profit, then the general partner will receive 20%+80%*1% = 20.8% of the fund's profits.

This explanation is given at the level of general principles, and it should be noted that return arrangements often incorporate other calculation components which address, for example, cases in which the fund distributes profits over the years. It is common to provide the fund managers with some or all of their share in profits from exits that are distributed to the investors over the lifetime of the fund, and it might be the case that such profits will eventually exceed the compensation the fund managers are entitled to. Such a pattern is observed in 2002, with funds who raised capital in the 1990s had some phenomenal performance in their early years, and hence provided their managers with high cash compensation, yet later on had poor performance, and therefore the fund managers might be required to return some of their earnings.

The fund manager usually receives at least 20% of the fund's net cumulative return, namely, the return received from exits after all capital investments are returned to the limited partners. In fact, it is well documented that approximately 80% of funds give their managers a share of 20–21% of the return after the return of the capital invested and minimum return arrangements, as determined in the fund's partnership agreements. In the late 1990s, an increase has been visible in the percentage of the profit which remains in the hands of the managing partner. When the investors in the fund are guaranteed a high minimum return, it is customary to determine a scaled profit distribution to fund managers, the actual rate of which may even be higher than the said rates. However, following the rude awakening era of 2001 and 2002, the rate of profits allocated to the funds' managers is reduced back to its historical norm. Furthermore, some of the leading funds had even reduced the management fees they charge.

The management of venture capital funds involves high current expenses which include, besides the payment of salaries to the employees and general partners, legal costs, travel and convention costs, and payments to outside advisers. In addition, considerable costs are associated with each specific investment. If the transaction materializes, the company in which the investment is made usually indemnifies the fund for its direct costs, but the fund bears the costs of transactions which are not consummated, and of course costs which cannot be directly attributed to a specific deal. The management agreement between the investors and the entities involved in the management of the fund determines which expenses are included in the management fees and which costs are reimbursed on a current basis by the investors. Either way, such reimbursed expenses are usually deducted for the purpose of calculating the carried interest.

Exit Strategies of Investments by Venture Capital Funds

Historically, the majority of the return earned by venture capital funds results from portfolio companies either reaching the public market by way of an offering or being bought out by other companies. On average, at the time of public offering, venture capital funds hold more than 30% of the company's equity, with the leading investor holding more than 15% of the company and appointing approximately one-third of the representatives to the company's board of directors. This rate is preserved (mainly due to lock up clauses in the offering arrangement) for approximately one year after the offering.

An interesting phenomenon is that highly regarded venture capital funds have an impact on increasing the valuation of shares comparable to similar companies going public at the same time. The argument is that good venture capital funds know how to choose more successful companies and/or that the best investment opportunities are typically presented to them as well. In addition, offerings of companies which are backed by venture capital funds are often made by underwriters with more experience in the particular type of company in question, and the holdings of institutional investors in the company after the offering are higher.

After the lock up period, which is usually dictated by the underwriters, funds tend to distribute their profits from the investments among the investors. The funds may sell the shares on the stock exchange and distribute the sale proceeds, join a second offering alongside the company and sell shares to the public or, alternatively, may distribute the shares among their investors (payment in kind).

In many cases, distributing the shares among the investors somewhat complicates the measurement of the return on the investments. Since such a distribution is not an actual sale, it need not be reported to the SEC, and it is almost impossible to track based on publicly available information only. In addition, various research has suggested that the return on the shares after they are distributed to investors tends to be negative, although these findings depend on the index used as a standard for measuring the returns. The return to investors for the purpose of the "carried interest" calculation is usually measured according to the price at the distribution of the shares among the investors, since after the distribution they are free to sell the shares.

The Return on Venture Capital Funds

The large investments made in venture capital funds over the last decades resulted from a change in institutional investors' estimation of the returns and risks involved in venture capital. As a result, more resources were directed to this field.

The returns demonstrated by the venture capital industry are characterized by considerable volatility. As described previously in this chapter, the most conspicuous phenomenon in the history of the fund industry is the inverse relation between the funds' returns and the amount of money invested in them. Periods characterized by a relative shortage of capital for funds, and hence to companies, are also characterized by the highest returns. Empirical evidence points to a positive connection between the pace of investments in the field and the value of companies in the investment rounds, and hence reduced returns over time.

The IRR of venture capital funds greatly depends on the year in which the funds were established. For instance, funds established in the years 1981–1984 earned single-digit returns. Until the mid-1990s, the average return on funds which had operated for at least four years was around 14% per year, with the median fund yielding about 8% only. The prosperity in the capital market in the late 1990s, until the 2000 crisis, inflated the annual returns on funds to unprecedented dimensions. In 1999, the average return on funds was approximately 160%, but the crisis sweeping the capital market now considerably reduced the funds' cumulative returns. In the absence of stock-exchange exit alternatives, funds are concentrating on seeking mergers and acquisitions for their portfolio companies. However, as mentioned in other chapters, many companies which used to buy smaller companies suffered sharp declines in their stock prices and therefore face difficulties when contemplating acquisitions in consideration for shares or cash.

Over the years, venture capital funds have demonstrated returns which appear to be considerably higher than the returns required by investors in investments carrying a similar risk. Generally, the return demonstrated by large and experienced funds is higher than the average return in the private equity industry by about 10% per year.

Funds specializing in mezzanine-loan investments demonstrate substantially lower returns, since their investments are a blend between investments in short-term debentures and a certain equity component. The risk in an investment in debt is considerably lower than that entailed by an investment in equity, and therefore any return above 10% per year is considered good. However, it should be noted that these funds tend to suffer in times of crisis in the stock exchange, because they usually make the investment in the company shortly before the IPO, and when the IPO is postponed or cancelled, the risk profile of the company in which they invested deteriorates (or changes), and they become investors in a company which has a different risk profile from the one in which they invested.

The industry as a whole is going through one of its more difficult times in recent decades, as the opportunities for IPOs or mergers of portfolio companies have significantly been reduced. For example, during the first quarter of 2002, only four IPOs in the United States were VC-backed, raising a total of less than $400 million, compared with around $500 million in the first quarter of 2001 and over $7 billion in 2000.

Similarly, there was a significant decline in the magnitude of acquisitions of VC-backed ventures. During the first quarter of 2002, such activities constituted less than $2 billion, compared with around $5 billion in the same period in 2001, and over $7 billion in 2000. It is not clear if this decline pattern will continue, but at the current level of activity, the industry is at a shakedown, which is expected to bring the long-term returns in the industry back to their historical averages.

11

Other Venture Capital Investors

CHAPTER OVERVIEW

In this chapter, we describe other venture capital investors. Because there are many similarities between these other sources of funding and those described in the previous chapters, we highlight in this chapter the special characteristics of these non-VC funds sources of financing for entrepreneurial firms.

Private Investors (Angels)

In recent decades, the community of private investors (angels) has developed to massive dimensions. Angels are private investors who invest some of their money in the financing of ventures with the hope of gaining a high return due to the large risk involved in the investment. The angels community is obviously diverse. Some angels have extensive experience in the area of entrepreneurship; others are entirely financial investors who have no understanding of the industry and whose money is usually invested by experts in the respective fields of the venture.

In the field of technology, private investors initially financed almost every successful company. Various research has found that more than one half of successful startups relied on financing from angels in their early stages. In addition, companies that reached IPOs without financing from venture capital funds, while relying mainly on angels, usually did so in earlier stages and after securing smaller investment rounds. These companies were generally from industries that do not involve extensive R&D efforts. In the United States, angels have a particularly large share in financing early-stage companies outside California and New England. This phenomenon is explained by the relative shortage of venture capital financing in these areas.

Various research estimates the amounts of venture capital invested by angels in early-stage ventures to be in the range of $15–$30 billion per year which is invested by over 250,000 private investors.

These and other sources have recorded a substantial increase in these investments in the late 1990s and 2000, but this trend decelerated due to the crisis in the capital markets.

Private investors also constitute a considerable portion of investors in venture capital funds. Many funds allow parallel investments by certain private investors who are able either to invest large amounts of money, or can bring "added value" and a cooperative alliance, which the fund and its portfolio companies may find attractive.

Angels usually invest in less than four ventures per year and generally invest less than $1 million annually. It was found that, in most cases, angels preferred to invest in companies located in geographic proximity to them even if they were not acquainted with the entrepreneurs. Angels usually prefer to see a considerable investment by the entrepreneurs in the company, or, in other words, companies in which some of the entrepreneur's wealth has been invested. As opposed to venture capital funds, angels do not generally require strict supervision and monitoring mechanisms, but like VC funds, they assist entrepreneurs in building contacts in the industry, recruiting manpower, and planning investments.

In recent decades, the phenomenon of investment clubs that examine investments in startups together and invest in selected companies has become increasingly prevalent. In addition, many web-based virtual angel networks have emerged in recent years. These networks are sometimes founded on an acquaintance or a certain link between the angels and the potential entrepreneurs. For instance, several virtual clubs have recently been established which enable alumni of a certain university to become acquainted with companies seeking financing, the entrepreneurs of whom are also alumni of the same university. Successful angel networks provide their members with investment screening services as well as support services for the entrepreneurs. Some angel networks combine elements of incubators, leveraging the entrepreneurial capabilities of the participating angels.

As for control mechanisms, venture capital funds usually have broader representation on boards of directors than angels and are generally more involved in the daily management of the companies. Since in most cases the investment in companies neither occupies a central place on the angels' agenda nor involves large portions of the angels' wealth, angels do not usually have high expectations with respect to their involvement in the company. However, in the case of angels who are investing in companies in a field in which they are experienced, their investment could be invaluable to the company, both from the point of view of the managerial experience which the investor can impart to the company, and from the points of views of connections and reputation which the company could benefit from.

Corporate and Other Investors

Introduction

Industrial companies in the United States invest large amounts of money in R&D, most of which is invested within the companies themselves. In recent decades companies, some of which also invest in venture capital funds, have started channeling large amounts of money to direct investments in companies and to the development of in-house startups in various formats.

The high rates of return demonstrated in the 1960s by venture capital funds motivated companies to establish investment organizations within the companies. The basic idea was to take advantage of the know-how accumulated in the companies and their surplus cash to yield higher returns than the company itself could generate. A mid-1970s crisis in the capital market drove most of the investment funds which had been founded within the large companies away from the market, but with the revitalization of venture capital funds starting in the early 1980s, the number of industrial companies investing in startups and creating their own venture capital funds increased. The 1987 crisis in the capital market landed a hard blow on these programs and their number declined again. Since then, though, many companies chose to focus on seeking strategic investments for the company and to invest money in external venture capital funds to gain a high return in the venture capital market.

A widespread phenomenon in the field is companies which finance ventures created by company employees who otherwise would have retired from the company and established independent ventures. However, the company will typically prefer to have a reputable venture capital fund co-invest in the project as early as possible, since such participation signals to the company that the startup is indeed promising. In addition, since in many cases the companies have no experience in initiating startups, the participation of professional investors considerably reduces the burden imposed on the financing company.

Most companies that are involved in venture capital investments invest in fields that are related to their main business. Even if they manage a separate venture capital fund in one form or another, they often limit the funds to investments in the company's field of expertise. Alternatively, the companies establish investment funds to identify investments in fields which will enable the company to branch out in new directions.

Direct Investments by Companies in the Field

Many entrepreneurs are delighted to receive financing from companies which operate in the startup's field. There are many strategic reasons for this, including the following: The investing companies lend credibility to the company and provide a stamp of approval for the company's technological edge; cooperating with such a company, which usually supports its investment, provides the startup with much assistance in rapidly reaching the market and marketing its products; and, finally, corporate investors usually act according to technological considerations rather than just the financial considerations which guide most investors in startups.

On the other hand, entrepreneurs sometimes complain that investors which are companies in the field are often slow in their decision process and hence delay the company's financing rounds. In addition, due to the added reputation they bring with them, such companies can invest based on lower valuation than the value that would have been determined for an investment by other investors. The low valuation may be difficult to explain to future investors as well as to previous investors in the company. Furthermore, the relationship with the strategic investor may prejudice or "taint" the company's alleged independence when choosing other suitable technological partners and may bar its path to customers who are identified with the investing company's competitors. Finally, there are always issues revolving the protection of the startup's intellectual property against the investing company.

Aside from the strategic considerations in accepting such investors as well as from the economic perspective, direct corporate investments are similar to investments made by venture capital funds, both in the process of examining the investment and in the ongoing means for controlling it. Although the investments are usually made by funds which may be associated with the companies, they are typically managed as venture capital funds for all intents and purposes, except for the fact that in every investment they also weigh the added value which the investment will bring to their company as well as the added value which the investing company can contribute to the startup.

Corporate In-house Entrepreneurship and Incubators

In addition to direct investments in startups and indirect investments through venture capital funds, many companies now fund in-house startups. These startups enjoy an existing work force and infrastructure in terms of labor and know-how, and can benefit from initial in-house financing.

The main reason for the establishment of such in-house startups was the expanding phenomenon of workers departing to form their own, or join independent startups. For instance, many people attribute the decline of numerous established technology companies in recent years to the departure of workers with good business ideas to independent companies, either as entrepreneurs or as employees joining a new venture at a relatively early stage. The phenomenon resulted, among other things, from the fact that in the setting of a large organization, the share of the entrepreneur-worker in his initiative is typically smaller than the share he could obtain in an independent setting or at an earlier phase. In order to tackle this problem, many companies started in recent years to fund in-house startups to cultivate and finance workers' initiatives while allowing them to act as independently and quickly as possible. The companies give the entrepreneur-workers and the workers who join them considerable portions of the equity in their new venture, money, and financial, organizational, technological, and marketing support.

On the other hand, the operation of ventures inside an organization entails difficult issues related to the compensation of the employees and the various effects on the morale of workers who do not join the venture being developed. Many companies face complaints on the part of workers who do not move over to the startup, since they generally do not directly enjoy the success of the startup, whereas the workers who do move to the startup often continue enjoying the security provided by the parent company (the importance of which is enhanced during difficult times in the capital market), along with the possibility of benefiting from the potential success of the startup. The establishment of such startups often also involves the resolution of various issues such as conflicts between marketing channels (for instance, various pricing problems) and the recruitment of outside workers versus recruiting workers from inside the company.

Concurrently, some industrial companies have in recent years started leveraging their technological, financial, and marketing capabilities by establishing in-house incubators for outside ventures. These companies establish entities which specialize in identifying early-stage ideas and ventures in fields in which the company has an added value. Although these are not ideas which budded inside the company, as in the case of in-house startups, the principle of financial, technological, and marketing assistance is similar to that described above in the context of in-house startups.

Financial Institutions Which Invest Directly in Funds

Many institutional investors such as investment banks, insurance companies, and pension funds have increased the volume of their direct investments in startups, after years in which the majority of their investments were made through "traditional" venture capital funds.

Investment Banks

Investment banks have always filled several roles which are relevant to startups, the main ones of which are assistance in planning and executing public offerings and private placements, and assistance in monitoring and researching the fields of activity of public companies. In recent years, the volume of the investment banks' activity as managers of private equity funds which also invest in startups has increased. In their investment activities, banks operate similarly to venture capital funds. However, they can also actively assist the company in soliciting investments, either as the company's agents or within a relationship created with the company, in the hope of acting as lead underwriters when it goes public.

The capital invested by investment funds managed by investment banks often belongs to private or institutional investors which manage money with the bank, or to the bank's employees and managers. The investment is sometimes made directly from the portfolios of such investors, but is usually made through private equity funds established and managed by the bank, which also invest in startups.

Most of the investments of such funds focus on later stages and are accompanied by other services. For instance, the investment bank may structure a financing package for a company in the form of a bridge loan before an IPO, when the bank itself may act as the underwriter in the IPO, and after the bank invested in the company's second-stage financing round. Alternatively, the bank may render advisory services for a merger or an acquisition of a company in which it invested.

Holding Companies of Commercial Banks

Holding companies of banks are among the main investors in venture capital. These companies invest through outside venture capital funds or through venture capital funds established and managed by them. Similar to the case of investment banks, venture capital investments made through funds managed by the banks integrate well with other services provided by the banks, particularly providing loans and credit lines to the emerging companies, structuring financing for investments in equipment, and so forth. However, the manner in which banks examine venture capital investment opportunities and manage the funds are not materially different from that of other venture capital funds. Due to legal restrictions imposed on holdings by banks in companies, the investments are typically not made directly by the banks, but rather through the funds or through subsidiaries with independent management.

In recent years, returns on venture capital investments began having a considerable effect on the profits of commercial banks. In addition, massive profits started to accumulate on the balance sheets of the banks' holding companies through their investments. For instance, in the fourth quarter of 1999, profits from managing venture capital funds contributed about $1.3 billion to the profits of Chase Bank (and it should be kept in mind that this figure represents only the funds' share in the profits made by the investors in the funds they manage). While the funds afflicted the holding company with large losses in 2000 and 2001, in view of the remarkable past successes of the bank's funds, this fact did dissuade investors from investing in new funds created by the bank (which had meanwhile merged with J.P. Morgan) from raising new venture capital funds.

Pension Funds

As mentioned in previous chapters, pension funds are also one of the major investors in venture capital, mainly through investments in venture capital funds managed by others. Since they are usually the main investors in the venture capital funds, they sometimes pay lower management fees to the fund managers. In terms of the investment horizon, pension funds of public U.S. entities have a higher tendency to invest in short-term investments and are more averse to high risk than other pension funds. They therefore tend to invest in funds which focus on companies in more advanced stages of development.

More than 60% of pension funds have investments in venture capital funds, with a high investment commitment of more than 7% of the value of the portfolio on average.

The investments made by pension funds account for almost one-half of all venture capital investments, but the majority of this investment is conducted through investments in funds managed by others.

In recent years pension funds have been making more and more independent investments, usually through in-house venture capital funds. In most cases, these funds do not lead investment rounds. In keeping with their general profile of venture capital investments, direct investments in companies by pension funds of publicly traded companies are less frequent, and are made in the more advanced stages of the companies' lifespan. In addition, since investments by these funds are subject to lengthy decision-making processes, they are often unable to join investment rounds quickly. Venture capital funds of other pension funds invest in all investment rounds, in accordance with the investment profile defined for them by the pension fund. In light of poor returns in 2001 and 2002, numerous pension funds have decreased their involvement in the industry via their own funds, and return to the pattern of delegating money to external managers of other funds.

Insurance Companies

Insurance companies are active in the venture capital market both indirectly, though investments in venture capital funds, and directly, through direct investments in companies. They usually focus on investments in relatively advanced stages of the companies. Historically, insurance companies tended to invest in the debt market of emerging companies which carry relatively high interest rates (the "high-yield" market or "junk bonds" market). In the last decade, however, they have been increasing their investments in convertible debentures with substantial equity components (mezzanine loans). As for private startups, insurance companies usually focus on second-stage and bridge financing, with the majority of investments being made in portfolio companies of venture capital funds with whom such insurance companies had invested. In this manner, the insurance companies (or the funds they establish) gain a current deal flow after a screening process performed by investors whom the insurance companies trust. In recent years, many insurance companies have established branches for direct investments in venture capital, which are not materially different than venture capital funds in both the screening of the investments and the methods of investment. However, they are usually merely financial investors which are neither involved in managerial operations nor contribute any added value to the companies in which they invest.

Not-for-profit Organizations

Not-for-profit organizations have the optimal investment profile for venture capital investments—they have no need for quick returns and can afford to be less anxious about market volatility than other entities, such as mutual funds or pension funds, which are appraised quarterly and from which investors often withdraw money quickly as a response to market declines. The main reason for this is that the endowments of such entities are usually meant to survive indefinitely, so their investment horizon is longer than that of venture capital funds, which almost always have a limited lifespan. In recent decades, such entities have been increasing their investments in venture capital funds and some, particularly the larger ones, established entities to examine companies and invest in them directly. Other entities resort to outside advisors to decide how to allocate their money among outside venture capital funds. A notable example of this type of investors are university investment funds which exist alongside almost every leading university in the United States, such as Harvard, Yale, and Columbia.

Mutual Funds

Mutual funds sometimes invest in private companies if they are likely to go public within 12-18 months. For instance, many findings indicate that in the years 1999-2000, the majority of the return of mutual funds focusing on the technology sector resulted from investments in shares during IPOs and, more conspicuously, from investing in the companies' final investment rounds before the IPO. In most cases, the mutual funds did not lead the investment round, but join rounds led by reputable venture funds. Since the volume of investments the funds can make in the private sector (i.e., unlisted companies) is usually limited by their own investment charter, many mutual funds have been established which focus on private placements before IPOs, often limiting the liquidity available to their investors.

Other Sources of Capital

Credit Companies

One of the main sources of capital for entrepreneurs in the United States is in fact the credit card issuers. An examination of the sources of financing available to small and mid-sized companies in the United States reveals that individual and corporate credit cards finance about 50% of U.S. companies which require outside financing. This financing is provided primarily by credit card issuers, which specialize in small businesses. However, these loans are relatively small, short-term, and carry a high interest rate.

Leasing

An allotment of equity in consideration for cash is a rather expensive method of financing a promising venture. Therefore, entrepreneurs do their utmost to finance their startups by other sources.

In recent years, especially due to the fierce competition between automobile and computer manufacturers, leasing arrangements have been readily available from known companies or from companies associated with them. In practice, this is an arrangement which allows the firm to utilize equipment while making periodical payments, rather than buying the equipment upfront. As a result, these leases ease the burden on the startup's cash flow without the dilution involved in raising cash from equity investors. This is one of the only sources of debt available to startups.

Leasing has become an important source of financing for startups. Automobiles, computers, office and other equipment, for instance, are bought by the company with this form of long-term financing. In many cases, the leasing is merely operational, i.e., the equipment remains the property of the leasing company and is returned to it at the end of the leasing term without an option of purchasing at a bargain price the asset at the end of the lease. The leasing conditions have various effects on the ability to deduct its costs for tax purposes when the periodic installments contain components of payment for the equipment and components of the reimbursement of the loan which was used to finance the asset and its current costs.

There are many diverse sources of leasing financing, starting from the manufacturers of the equipment, through companies associated with them, and ending in companies which specialize in leasing financing. The latter buy the equipment for the venture and arrange for a financing package based on the venture's needs and resources.

In many cases, financing packages also include various options for equity investing by the leasing company. Disregarding the equity components of these packages, the cost of capital incorporated in various leasing arrangements is typically high and could range between 15% and 30%. This is a relatively high cost, but it is cheaper than the loss of value which results from a dilution of equity to finance such costs, especially when the value of the venture is not yet high. In addition, since leasing arrangements do not usually involve a personal guarantee, the entire risk is borne by the leasing company and its partners.

Real estate leasing is another method of debt financing, since, in practice, the company signs a long-term contract to use the property in exchange for current periodic payments. In many cases, the cost of leasehold improvements is negotiated, and in various scenarios it is loaded onto the lease and becomes part of the rent.

PART IV

Raising Capital from the Public

Part IV discusses the topic of raising capital from the public, which is an important event in the lifecycle of a venture's development. As a result, it turns from a private company with limited public visibility and financial resources into a traded company which is much more visible and has a variety of financing resources available to it.

The discussion focuses on the considerations involved in the decision to go public and in the method of executing such a decision, as well as on the general principles governing public offerings.

12

Raising Capital from the Public—Introduction

INTRODUCTION

This chapter focuses on the considerations involved in IPOs and on the company's internal preparations for such an offering. Naturally, the chapter focuses on equity offerings, although other types of securities may also be offered to the public. An in-depth discussion of the actual process of the offering, from choosing the underwriters to the commencement of trade in the share, appears in the next chapter.

As an introduction, several basic terms should be defined:

IPO (Initial Public Offering)—An issuance of stock by a private company which is raising capital by issuing securities to the public for the first time. In an IPO, it is usually only the company's shares, not the shareholders' shares, which are sold, and all of the proceeds are received by the company to ensure that the company has the capital it requires for its future growth.

Secondary Offering—This is the sale of existing shares of a publicly held company by the company's shareholders. A secondary offering can be made together with an initial or a seasoned offering.

Seasoned Offering—This is an issuance of shares to the public by a company whose shares are already listed for trade.

Private Placement—This is an issuance to a limited number of investors (usually institutional investors) which is not a public offering. There are rules which determine when an offering is not deemed a public offering. A private placement of an unlisted company (which is reviewed in Part II) should be distinguished from a private placement of a traded company.

Deciding to Go Public

As mentioned above, a public offering is a highly important event in a venture's life. The decision to go public should be weighed in earnest, and the company's readiness to go public, the advantages and disadvantages entailed by the offering, and its timing should be considered.

Is the Company Ready to Go Public?

In many cases, the company is pressured from inside (or by the investors) into going public before the company is ready for that listing. A premature IPO of a company could result in an unsuccessful offering, which is reflected in low liquidity following the offering. In other words, the volume of trade in the share is low; consequently, the share is either illiquid or a significant change in its price is caused by transactions in the stock.

When assessing the company's readiness to go public and the price per share at which the shares will be offered, the company and the underwriters examine parameters which are essentially similar to the parameters examined by entrepreneurs when they establish a company, and to those examined by the investors in each of its stages of development (as discussed in earlier chapters). The main parameters are the following:

- **Product**—Does the company have a product which is attractive to consumers? Has the product passed the stages of development and is it being manufactured? If a service is offered, what is its added value? Is there a market for such a service?
- **Market**—How big is the market? Who are the competitors? What are the market's barriers to entry? Is the market expected to grow at a high rate? Is the market expected to be crowded with competition?
- **Sales**—How big are the company's current sales volume and its future sales potential?
- **Profitability**—Is the company profitable? What is the profit potential? What is the competitive position of the company and its ability to sustain or improve it?
- **Growth**—What is the projected growth rate of the company's business? Is the company expected to have a sustainable growth rate which is attractive to investors?
- **Management**—Management's experience, credibility, quality, and its ability to successfully meet the demands of publicly held companies, whether they are legal requirements or requirements resulting from the capital market's expectation for results are important parameters in the decision to go public.
- **Financial condition**—The company's liquidity after the IPO, its current profitability, and forecasted profitability, and the financial resources which

the company will require in the future are substantial elements in the degree to which investors find the company attractive.
- **The amount to be raised**—The company's market value and cash needs are crucial considerations in determining the amount of capital the company will raise. However, issuing too small a share of the company is not customary in the capital market, since after the offering there will be too little "floating equity" in the market which will not guarantee a proper level of liquidity. On the other hand, too large an offering may cause an oversupply of securities after the offering, which could then drive prices down and therefore requires proper distribution and dissemination among many investors.
- **Investor-basis**—One of the main considerations which affects the company's value and its attractiveness as a publicly held company is the company's investor-basis. An investor-basis which includes first-rate venture capitalists is a considerable attraction for institutional and private investors since their investment in the company serves as a "quality assurance" seal. Similarly, the involvement of entrepreneurs with a good management and investment experience, and reputation enhances and contributes to the company's reputation.
- **Value in the offering**—All of the considerations listed above have an impact on the company's projected value. A market value which is too low disqualifies the company as a candidate for investment from the perspective of many institutional investors, which usually constitute the lion's share of the buyers of stock in IPOs, and reduces its attractiveness to other investors.

The Advantages of Going Public

Discussing the advantages and disadvantages of going public is very important to a developed private company which is contemplating whether or not to do so. For a startup, in which the exit is the investors' guiding principle, the discussion of the pros and cons of a public offering should be made in the context of the desired exit (IPO or sale) and of the timing of the offering.

- **Accessibility to capital**—A public offering opens up a new source of long-term capital to the company. The capital amassed in the offering, in addition to any capital gained by additional offerings, assists in the company's growth.
- **Liquidity and the rise in the company's value**—The infusion of money into the company and secondary trading raise the company's value, particularly due to the enhanced liquidity and ongoing follow-up by analysts.
- **An improved ability to borrow money**—An IPO increases the company's equity and hence its ability to raise capital from auxiliary sources (such as bank credit) at a lower cost.

- **The possibility of expanding through mergers**—Traded shares are a customary medium of exchange in mergers since their value is known (the market price) and they have a readily available market.
- **The ability to quickly realize profits**—Owners can more easily sell some of their holdings in consideration for cash.
- **An instrument for providing employee incentives**—A traded company can establish stock option plans which enable the employees to take part in the company's success.
- **Improving the level of management**—A publicly traded company usually has an experienced board of directors, and the required transparency and level of financial reporting usually forces management to adhere to higher managerial standards.
- **Public and market awareness**—A publicly traded company usually has a higher public profile than a private company. Traded companies enjoy a reputation and an image of more stable companies with better management and enhanced transparency.

The Disadvantages of Going Public

- **Loss of privacy**—The company is required to disclose a great deal of information about its business and its methods of operation and financing in the prospectus and its periodic reports. This information includes a disclosure of the directors' and managers' compensation, including their stock holdings, information about large customers and suppliers, financial information regarding sales, cost structure and profit margins.
- **Expectations of short-term results**—Shareholders and analysts monitor the company's performance from one quarter to the next and expect to see an increase in sales, profits, and market share. In addition, the company may sometimes face difficulties in explaining to the capital market an important long-term plan which impairs short-term profitability or activity volumes.
- **Reduced operating flexibility**—The need for shareholder and board approvals may slow down business processes.
- **Restrictions on sales by managers**—Regulations governing insider trading limits managers' ability to trade in the company's shares.
- **Legal exposure**—Publicly held companies are more exposed to legal suits in general and to class actions by investors in particular.
- **The cost of IPOs**—An IPO requires a vast dedication of managerial time and entails considerable costs payable to professionals such as attorneys and accounting firms, in addition to the commissions paid to the underwriters.
- **Current expenses**—A publicly held company is required to maintain a periodic reporting system which involves costs and payments to independent advisors.

- **Loss of founders' control**—Even if the founders were in charge of the company until the IPO, due to support of the venture capital investors, they may lose their control in the IPO. On the other hand, due to the dispersion of the shares, actual control can be maintained with far less than 50% of the company.
- **Dividend policy**—Shareholders may expect a publicly held company to adopt a dividend policy, and if it distributes dividends, to persist in doing so. Any change in the dividend policy affects the price of the share. This issue is less relevant in most technology companies, which do not habitually distribute dividends.

Preparing the Company for an IPO

Before contacting underwriters and putting together the team which will lead the IPO, the company must first undergo an internal process of preparing to go public.

The Managers' Responsibility

The company's managers need to undertake the commitment required for the process and recognize that they will have to dedicate much time to it. Being intimately involved in the demanding IPO process, which could last several months, while continuing to manage the company, imposes an enormous burden on the senior management.

Business Plan

The company must have a well-formed business plan enabling the company to be presented to underwriters and to the representatives of various capital markets as a company ready to go public. A detailed business plan and forecasts may also facilitate a swift drafting of the prospectus.

Legal Issues

Several issues need to be addressed before starting the actual IPO process. Among others, these issues include:

- **Rearranging the company's capital structure**—In most cases, the company is required to simplify its capital structure by creating a single class of shares only. In addition, records of ownership and transfers of securities in the company need to be updated.
- **Equalization of rights**—The company must cancel special voting rights conferred on certain shareholders, including special rights to appoint directors and adding to the corporate documents requirements for shareholder approvals before performing certain acts (negative covenants).

- **Canceling restrictions on share transfers**—The company must cancel agreements which limit the right to transfer shares.
- **"Spring cleaning"**—This means going over all the processes which took place in the company since its establishment and taking care of any matter which was performed against the law, either verbatim or in conflict with proper administrative rules, including approving transactions with related parties.
- **Drafting rules and policies on sensitive issues**—This deals with drafting directives with respect to transaction-approvals, insider trading, sexual harassment, and so on.

Accounting Issues

The company needs to ensure that its internal audit procedures meet the standards required of publicly held companies, including appointing an internal auditor and an audit committee. The internal system needs to be ready to prepare the annual and periodic reports required of listed companies. The company's financial statements need to be prepared according to generally accepted accounting principles (GAAP) and be audited by a CPA who is associated with a prestigious CPA firm (preferably one of the big four accounting firms).

Managing Investor Relations

The company needs to prepare to establish relationships with its investors. To this end, it needs to develop an appropriate investor-relations program and hence typically retains the services of an investor-relations firm (see the section on following the IPO for a further discussion).

13
The Public Offering Process

CHAPTER OVERVIEW

This chapter views the process of raising capital in the public market. The chapter describes the selection of the IPO teams, the roles of each one of the teams, and in particular the underwriters.

Stock Markets in the United States

One of the first decisions which a company has to make after deciding to embark on an IPO is in which market its shares will be listed for trade. There are two main types of securities markets: a stock exchange or over-the-counter (OTC) trading. The main stock exchange in the United States is the New York Stock Exchange (NYSE). Another large stock exchange is the American Stock Exchange (AMEX), and there are also several smaller regional and specialized stock exchanges. The best-known OTC system is the National Association of Securities Dealers Automated Quotation System (NASDAQ), which includes the NASDAQ National Market (NM) and the NASDAQ Small Cap Market. As the differences between the methods from the standpoint of an issuing firm are small, for the sake of convenience, this chapter will often refer to NASDAQ as a stock exchange, even though it is technically a system allowing trades with market makers.

Stock Exchanges Versus Over-the-Counter Trading Systems

Trade on a stock exchange such as the NYSE is performed by way of an auction, with the trade in each share being concentrated in the hands of a stock exchange member who is nominated by the exchange to be the specialist of the share. In OTC trading, each share could be traded by a large number of market makers who are connected both among themselves and with their customers by electronic media. Securities firms choose for which shares they are market makers.

There are many theoretical differences between the methods of trade, but from the points of view of the issuing company, as well as of most investors, there is no significant difference between the methods. The specialists or market makers are always involved in the trade and broker between buy and sell orders for the shares, whether the company's shares are traded in an auction-based system (the stock exchange) or a trader-based system (such as NASDAQ). The specialist in stock exchanges must ensure the continuous trade in the shares of the companies under his charge, and each of the market makers of a share in NASDAQ provide bid and ask prices for given round lots. In the market-maker method, there is no restriction on the number of market-makers for any given share. As a result of the competition among market-makers, the difference between the bid and ask prices of shares may be negligible. In the specialist method, on the other hand, one trader is responsible for bringing together all of the purchase and sale activities on the stock exchange of the share for which he is responsible. Due to concentrated volume, the specialist typically offers a small "spread" (the difference between the bid and the ask quotes) as well. These methods of trading are different from those practiced in most other Western stock exchanges, which usually bring buyers and sellers into direct contact.

In recent years, alternative trading systems (ATS) have emerged, although companies must choose either one of the stock exchanges or NASDAQ for the purpose of registration, even if a material portion of the trade in the share will be carried out through the alternative channels. To a certain extent, the existence of such channels mitigates the importance of the decision of where the share will be listed for trade.

The New York Stock Exchange (NYSE)

The NYSE is the largest securities market in the world, and most of the companies composing the Dow Jones Industrial Index are listed on it. The level of its registration requirements is considered particularly high, as are its annual and registration fees. In the past, it was customary that a company which met the NYSE's registration requirements was listed there, whereas companies which could not meet such requirements turned to regional stock exchanges or the NASDAQ. This was one of the reasons why NASDAQ prospered, since technology companies which could not be listed on the NYSE (due to size, profitability, and track record) when they went public were listed on NASDAQ, and subsequently became large and well-known companies, including companies such as Microsoft, Dell and Intel. In recent years, the NYSE has been courting emerging giants to convince them to switch to the NYSE. Thus, for instance, America Online moved to the NYSE, and the latter has been using this transition as a marketing tool when approaching companies which are considering going public.

In general, as a condition to registration, both the NYSE and NASDAQ require companies, to undertake to report information which is material to shareholders, to have material transactions approved by the shareholders, and to appoint an audit committee and independent directors, as well as other requirements which set a higher standard of corporate governance than in private companies.

NASDAQ

NASDAQ now enjoys the reputation of being the leading market for technology firms. Most technology companies are listed on NASDAQ, and in the end of the 1990s its trade volumes resembled those of the NYSE. However, it is important to distinguish between being listed on the NASDAQ National Market and being listed on the NASDAQ Small Cap Market. The former enjoys a vast reputation and bestows on the companies listed on it not only the reputation entailed by being traded on this market, but also an exemption from the requirements of state securities laws (blue sky laws), whereas the latter is intended for small companies and does not enjoy a similar reputation.

Forming the IPO Team

At first, after the company concludes its internal organization (see the section on preparing the company for an IPO in Chapter 12), an IPO team has to be established. This team includes, in addition to the company's management (CEO, CFO, and legal counsel), underwriters, outside legal counsel, CPAs, a financial printer, and sometimes also a PR firm.

The Underwriters

Underwriters play a central role in the sale of the shares in the IPO and thereafter. The underwriters are responsible for determining the IPO price, executing it, and distributing it among investors. The underwriters also play an important role in rendering advice on the structuring of the transaction, the timetables, and the manner of presentation of the information. The relationship with the underwriters does not end in the IPO, but rather begins there. The underwriters support the price of the share after the IPO (if necessary), provide coverage for the share through the bank's equity research department (which is separate from the underwriting department), and provide additional investment banking services to the company later on. The process of choosing the underwriters includes meetings with several underwriters and choosing a lead, or managing underwriter, which will be committed to the share. There is usually one lead underwriter or more (up to three) which manages the syndicate of underwriters and co-managers.

Investment banks offer companies a wide variety of financial services, including raising of capital (either shares or debt), market making and share trading, research coverage (analysts) and M&A and other financial consulting. The term underwriter refers to the underwriting, or corporate finance, arm of investment banks. The underwriters are the main players in the IPO process, and they accompany the company through the preparations for, during, and after the IPO.

Choosing the Underwriters

In most U.S. IPOs, the company undertakes a meticulous search before choosing the investment bank which will act as its group of underwriters. In some cases, the group of underwriters (the syndicate) is managed by a single investment bank, but in large IPOs it is customary to have two or three banks manage the offering. In addition, co-managers (syndicate members) are chosen, the number of which depends on the size of the IPO. When choosing the underwriters, the following issues need to be taken into consideration:

- **Reputation and experience**—The underwriter must have a good reputation in the community of investors and among companies which used its services. The underwriter serves as the gate keeper, and the market's preliminary disposition to the company is derived to a great extent from its underwriters' standing in the market. In addition, the first analyst-coverage is usually provided by the investment banks which were involved in the IPO. Lead underwriters are chosen based on the bank's underwriting reputation in the relevant field and its general underwriting expertise.
- **Commitment to the IPO**—The underwriter must be prepared to dedicate the appropriate attention and manpower to the planned IPO and to be committed to the company and the share after the IPO. A material element of the bank's role is to provide broad coverage for the share and to support it after the IPO, since without such deep commitment, it would be difficult for the company to gain recognition among investors and to increase its value. Commitment to an IPO, unlike reputation, is difficult to assess before the offering, but the experience of comparable companies with the same underwriters can nevertheless be used.
- **Distribution ability**—The underwriter's ability to successfully sell the IPO and place the shares in the hands of the right investors has a vast effect not only on the success of the IPO, but also on the share's future performance. The lead underwriter must organize a syndicate of underwriters to distribute the shares and to create the right composition of institutional and individual investors. Many underwriters specialize in different segments of the market, and it is important for the company that a delicate blend of these populations be created. That distribution will have implications on the liquidity and volatility of the share price, both immediately after the IPO and down the road.
- **Market-making and share-coverage capabilities**—An underwriter must cover the share and attract much interest to it in the secondary market after the IPO. When issuing on NASDAQ, an underwriter who will commit to act as a stock's market maker is essential. In most cases, the syndicate managers also act as the share's market makers after an IPO on NASDAQ, and they handle 40-50% of the volume of activity in the company's shares. The

underwriter's equity research department and the coverage it provides for the share are highly important. A research department which has leading analysts in the company's field of activity, together with the underwriter's commitment to cover the share, will greatly increase the stock's visibility.

The banks' regulations require that a "Chinese Wall" be erected between the underwriting and equity research departments in order to reduce the cases in which research reports are affected by the bank's underwriting relationships with the companies. Many studies indicate that this independence is not necessarily maintained, but sophisticated investors know how to neutralize these effects when making investment decisions.

- **Ability to provide additional services after the IPO**—The underwriting department is only one of the departments in an investment bank. The bank's ability to provide additional services to the company, including additional funding, M&A advisement, and finding deals should be examined.
- **Payment**—The payment received by the underwriter in consideration for its work is based on the difference between the price at which it buys the shares and the offering price. In an IPO, the standard "discount" is around 7% which is divided between the costs of preparing for the IPO, the actual IPO, and the road show. It should be understood that this figure differs from one offering to another according to the type of the company, the size of the offering, and the price at which the underwriter expects to be able to offer the shares (see the more detailed discussion of the payment structure later in this chapter).

The Underwriting Syndicate

Offerings in the United States are almost always performed by a syndicate of investment banks led by a lead underwriter. The tendency to assemble syndicates is derived from the underwriters' desire to spread the risk involved with the IPO among several underwriters and from their desire to achieve maximum distribution. Nowadays, with the increase in the size of the leading investment banks, almost every one of the leading investment banks could assume the major part of the underwriting and distribute the entire IPO alone (although this is not the common practice). The lead manager, or in many cases the co-managers or joint managers, manage the "book of orders" of the IPO. The lead manager is responsible for deciding how to divide the securities among the other underwriters. The decision of how to allocate the securities among institutional and private customers is reached in cooperation with the sales people, and the securities allotted to each underwriter are divided among the several types of target populations. When making the decision about the allotment, the lead managers take into account both short-term considerations, i.e., creating demand for the offered shares and being able to meet such demand, and long-term considerations, including creating demand for the company's shares in the long term and maintaining the stability of the share price.

Underwriter Compensation

The division of the underwriters' commission among the syndicate members changes from one offering to another, but usually follows these lines: The lead managers receive 20% of the commissions; another 20-30% is divided among the other underwriters for the underwriting risk (namely, the risk that the shares will not sell in the IPO), the division being prorated according to the underwriting commitments (i.e., the number of shares which each underwriter undertook to sell); the remaining commissions are sale commissions which are divided among the underwriters according to the actual sales of the shares and do not necessarily correspond to the underwriting undertakings. This division is determined by the order book managers. In most cases, the vast majority of actual sales are made by the underwriters' syndicate managers.

The managers' management fees are paid for preparing the IPO, which includes the following: due diligence; coordinating the road show; pricing the IPO, which involves a close scrutiny of the company's value according to its financial data and of the condition of the market at that time (see the section on pricing, signing the underwriting agreement, and registration statement effectiveness); and having the offering registered in the various states by the bank's legal counsel. The underwriting commissions do not include the company's IPO costs such as advertising, legal counseling and various marketing expenses, but only the underwriters' related expenses.

The Legal Counsel

The outside legal counsel has to be very experienced in working opposite the SEC and must be intimately acquainted with the IPO process. The legal counsel drafts the registration statement (the prospectus) and gives advice on complying with all the securities laws and regulations which govern the IPO process. The legal counsel also acts as the coordinator in the process of writing the prospectus and in the dialogue with the SEC. Choosing reputable and experienced firms which can also provide services on auxiliary issues (labor law, intellectual property, environmental law, etc.), and not only on securities issues, is advisable. The underwriters also use outside legal counsel, whose role is to draft the underwriting agreements, to ensure that the registration statement meets the securities rules, to perform the legal due diligence process, and to handle the comfort letter from the CPAs (see below).

The CPA

The CPA's functions include the following:

- **Preparing the financial statements**—The CPA, together with the company, prepares financial statements according to U.S. GAAP. Foreign companies can prepare financial statements according to the accepted accounting rules in their jurisdictions of incorporation, but these statements

must be reconciled to the U.S. GAAP either fully or partially, depending on the registration mechanism. The independent auditor also audits the financial statements included in the prospectus, and his opinion is attached to the prospectus.
- **Adjusting the registration statement to the financial statements**—The CPA also takes part in preparing the parts of the prospectus which are based on the financial statements and verifies that all the financial data in the prospectus is supported by the information contained in the financial statements.
- **Providing the underwriters with a comfort letter**—The underwriters will not sign the underwriting agreement without a comfort letter from the CPA. This letter confirms that the statements are complying with U.S. GAAP and the SEC rules; that the data in the registration statement conform to the financial statements; and that they describe any material change which occurred since the end date of the last statements attached to the prospectus.

The CPA must be approved by the SEC as one who is authorized to work opposite it. Although this is not required by the SEC's rules, companies usually choose one of the large CPA firms, since many players in the market attribute a great deal of importance to the reputation of these firms.

The Cost of an IPO

The difference between the IPO price per share and the price per share received by the company (the gross spread) reflects the management fees, the underwriters' costs, and the distribution costs. This difference averages around 7%, but it depends, among other things, on the volume of the offering. In addition, companies have to bear other direct costs related to the listing of the shares, the printing of the prospectus, the legal advice provided by the company's counsel, and the CPA's audit. Some of these costs are fixed and some depend on the size of the offering. The total cost to the company of an IPO in the United States is approximately $1 million (excluding underwriters' commissions), most of which is paid to outside advisors and to the authorities, and some of which is attributable to internal costs within the company.

The Process

Once the team is assembled and the underwriter is chosen, the actual IPO process begins. The entire process is usually composed of the following stages:

- Preparing the company (see the section on preparing the company for an IPO)
- Assembling the team (see the section on forming the IPO team)

- Signing a letter of intent with the underwriters
- Beginning of the quiet period
- Holding the organizational meeting
- Preparing a preliminary registration statement (the first draft prospectus)
- Conducting the due diligence process—concurrently with the preparation of the preliminary registration statement
- Filing the preliminary registration document with the SEC for examination
- Preparing an amended registration statement
- Distributing the preliminary prospectus ("red herring")
- Marketing ("road show")
- Holding the due diligence meeting
- Pricing, signing the underwriting agreement, and having the registration statement declared effective
- Selling the shares to the public and closing
- Trading, stabilization, and exercise of the underwriters' option ("green shoe" option)

Signing the Letter of Intent

After the underwriter is chosen, a letter of intent specifying the proposed terms of the IPO and declaring the underwriters' readiness to sign an underwriting agreement before the conclusion of the registration process is usually (but not always) signed. The letter (which is not binding) also specifies the payment to the underwriters, the type of underwriting agreement, and the underwriters' estimate of the range of prices at which they expect to be able to sell the shares (which estimate is also not binding). The projected price range may be updated several times during the road show, until the final pricing.

Quiet Period

From the moment a preliminary agreement is reached with the underwriters, a quiet period begins during which the company is subject to the SEC's rules on the publication of information. The quiet period lasts until 25 days after the effective date of the registration statement, or until all the shares are sold to the public (as is usually the case). The possibility of rousing interest in the company and the IPO is limited in order to prevent gun-jumping, namely, attracting interest to the securities other than through an effective prospectus. U.S. securities rules explicitly prohibit the publication of information on the offering in the U.S. media (other than very limited information as defined in the regulations); limit contacts with U.S. analysts and brokers during the quiet period; and restrict the distribution of reports on the company before the IPO. It should be noted that broad changes have been proposed in the method of registration in the United States (a proposal known as the "Aircraft Carrier Release"—see the discussion in the section on changes in the registration process), within which the rules governing the publication of information before an IPO would be changed. In any case, even now the rules permit publications within the ordinary course of business.

Many issues have been brought before the SEC in recent years, since many companies interview and advertise their products vigorously during the quiet period, and there are many doubts as to whether these acts constitute a prohibited promotion of the IPO. These issues are at the center of a public debate following the collapse of the prices of technology firms, and in particular Internet firms.

Organizational Meeting

After the team is assembled and the underwriter is chosen, the registration process itself may commence. The process usually begins with an organizational meeting attended by the company's managers, the underwriters, the legal counsels, and the CPAs. At this meeting, the method of the offering, the type of registration statement to be used, the timetables, and the responsibility of each participant for the various tasks are discussed. A preliminary decision of the type and scale of the capital to be raised is also made.

Preparing the Preliminary Registration Statement

The preliminary document is the first copy of the registration statement which will be filed with the SEC and is typically also used as the initial share sale document (see the section on the registration statement). The document is written jointly by the underwriter, the company, the attorneys, and the CPAs. The preparation of the document also includes drafting sessions which are held over the course of several weeks (see the section on disclosure particulars for a specification of the disclosures required in the document).

Due Diligence

The due diligence process includes examining the company's financial and business condition and perusing the disclosure documents of the offering in order to prevent the inclusion of a misleading detail or the omission of a material detail. The examination is made according to customary international standards which are based on the protection afforded by U.S. law to whomever conducts a "reasonable investigation" of the company. The need for a due diligence process derives from the U.S. securities rules, which exempt the underwriters from liability on account of a false registration statement, if they had, after judicious investigation, reasonable ground to believe that the statements therein were true and that there was no omission to state a material fact required to be stated therein, or necessary to make the statements therein not misleading.

The due diligence process is performed by the underwriters (with respect to the business portion) and the underwriters' legal counsel, together with the company's independent auditors. The process has to be adjusted to the company's industry and fields of activity and cannot be merely a general investigation. The thorough investigation includes perusing documents (including organizational documents, material contracts, etc.), visiting the company's facilities, questioning the company's managers and customers, obtaining opinions from experts and attorneys and comfort letters from the company's CPAs, and certifying the financial statements and their conformity with the registration statement.

Filing the Preliminary Registration Statement with the SEC

Every registration statement of an IPO is examined by an SEC team, which includes, among others, attorneys and CPAs. The team verifies that the document meets the requirements of the securities rules and neither contains an inaccurate fact nor omits material information. The SEC's CPAs check the statements and the financial information and their compliance with the SEC's rules, U.S. GAAP, the rules of the Financial Accounting Standards Board (FASB) and the rules of the American Institute of Certified Public Accountants. The procedure includes an unofficial process of comments and discussions between the team and the company's consultants, at the end of which an official letter addressing all the issues which need to be taken care of (letter of comments) is sent out. Foreign companies enjoy a special procedure in which they can submit the document with the SEC confidentially (confidential submission) and receive preliminary comments. Only when the document is ready and amended in accordance with the comments is it filed officially and openly.

The Amended Registration Statement

Once all of the SEC's comments are amended and updates are made following developments in the company, if any occurred, an amended statement, which also serves as the prospectus for the offering, is filed.

The Preliminary Prospectus (Red Herring)

The amended registration document is sent to brokers and potential buyers. This document is used to market the shares, and opens with a comment in red print to the effect that the information in it is not complete and may be changed, that the securities may not be sold until the registration statement filed with the SEC is effective, and that it is not an offer to sell nor seeks an offer to buy the securities in any jurisdiction where the offer or sale is not permitted. The preliminary prospectus excludes any information which depends on the IPO price. Historically, the name red herring derived from the red tape used to bind the document (obviously, nowadays, the document is often delivered in electronic form).

Road Show

The IPO is marketed by meetings organized by the underwriters with potential investors, in which the company's managers present the company (road show). The marketing process is very dynamic and requires both professional and emotional preparation. Road shows are usually 2-3 week trips, during which the managers travel through 20-30 different cities in the United States (and if the shares are also distributed in Europe, the road show will include several days in Europe). Some of the meetings are held in large groups and some are one-on-one. In these meetings, the company's management gives a presentation about the company and answers investors' questions, after which the underwriters amass orders (a process known as "book building"). Although these orders are not binding purchase offers, they serve as an important indication of the number of shares which institutional investors would be interested in buying and of the price they could bring. As mentioned above, these orders are not binding because no binding orders may be accepted until the registration statement is declared effective by the SEC.

Due Diligence Meeting

The due diligence process culminates in a meeting held before the registration statement is declared effective (which is when liability attaches to the document). The due diligence meeting is attended by the underwriters, the company's managers, the legal counsel, and the CPAs. During this meeting, the underwriters ask the managers questions about the information in the prospectus and about existing or projected developments in the company and its market, to ensure, before they sign the underwriting agreement and, in fact, buy the company's shares, that no adverse change had occurred.

Pricing, Signing the Underwriting Agreement, and Registration Statement Effectiveness

The final price and precise number of the shares to be sold are determined before the registration statement is declared effective. The price is based on financial multiples in relation to similar companies in the field, as well as on the indications received by the underwriters during the road show. If many orders were placed, the price will be in the top range of the prices determined in the red herring (or even above it), but if few orders were placed, the price will be in the bottom range (or even below it). The final quantity of shares is also determined in the pricing process; any change exceeding 20% of the quantity or the price range set out in the preliminary prospectus requires an amendment of the document (and may delay the process).

Once the price is determined, the underwriting agreement is signed (in other words, the underwriters become obliged to buy the shares at closing, subject to the terms of the underwriting agreement; see further details in the section regarding the underwriting agreement). Immediately thereafter, the information on the quantity and price of the shares is delivered to the SEC, together with a request to have the document declared effective (known as a "request for acceleration of effectiveness"). Once the document is effective (the request is approved within a matter of minutes), shares may be sold pursuant to it, and the company and all of the entities involved in the IPO become liable under the prospectus.

The pricing and distribution method enables the underwriters to determine, together with the company, the correct allocation among investors which will enable a stable trading in the share and a dispersion in accordance with criteria which will best serve the needs of the company's shareholders. Underwriters try to sell most of the shares in the IPO to "strong hands," i.e., institutional investors with a view of long-term holding who believe in the company and its management, and to minimize the number of participants in the IPO who intend to sell the shares immediately after the IPO in order to make a quick profit ("flippers"). Recently, many complaints have been heard in the United States with respect to the identity of the flippers. Surprisingly, many institutional investors—who are supposed to belong to the main investors who will hold the share for a long time—are actually the main flippers, and it is actually many of the small private investors who are the long-term investors in whom the companies are usually interested.

A customary indication of the success of the IPO is how high the price of the share rises on the first day of trading. However, this indication has no real economic significance besides expressing an additional indirect cost to the company. A more substantive standard from the company and the investors' points of view is the stability of the share price in the period immediately after the IPO. This criterion is the real test of the underwriter's ability to make the correct pricing, legally support the price of the share if needed (since underwriters are entitled to stabilize the price of the share a short period after the IPO), and successfully choose investors who will invest in the security based on long-term considerations. However, it should be kept in mind that an unusual plunge of the entire market or of the shares of comparable companies after the IPO could also cause the price of the share to be unstable, regardless of the underwriter's professionalism and ability to correctly price the share.

Selling the Shares to the Public and Closing

Closing is performed three to five business days after the underwriting agreement is signed. During this interim period, between the signing and closing of the underwriting agreement, the underwriters sell the securities to the investors who expressed an interest in them during the book building process. At closing, the company transfers the shares to the underwriters in consideration for the price determined in the pricing (i.e., the price to the public less the underwriters' discount). Various legal documents are also delivered at closing and an update (bring-down) of the comfort letter.

Trading, Stabilization, and Exercise of the Underwriters' Option (Green Shoe)

Trading in the share begins in the day following the effectiveness of the registration statement (which is one day following the pricing), in the stock exchange in which the underwriter listed the shares. According to U.S. law (Regulation M), the underwriter is allowed to support the price of the share after the IPO by creating a demand for the share. Strict limitations are imposed on the stabilization process, the main one of which prohibits the purchase of shares for more than their trading price (in order to prevent "stock running"). The stabilization is performed in practice by the managing underwriter, since only one member of the syndicate is allowed to engage in stabilization. The managing underwriter is also required to disclose the nature and scope of any stabilizing acts performed.

The purpose of stabilization is to ensure trade that is free of substantial volatility in price after the IPO and mainly to prevent unusual drops in the price. The price of the share may be supported in two ways: buying shares after the IPO in order to support the price of the share (if necessary), and selling investors, during the IPO, more shares than were actually allotted. If the share is expected to require stabilization after the IPO, such over-allotment can reach up to around 20% of the offering. However, this short position exposes the underwriters to the risk that the price of the shares will rise above the IPO price. This is one of the reasons why underwriters often incorporate into the underwriting agreement an option allowing them to buy from the company up to 15% of the offering for the IPO price, for a period of 30 days following the IPO. This option is known as a "green shoe," named after the first company in whose IPO this instrument was used. By exercising the option, the underwriters cover their short position and increase the offering according to the circumstances. Such an option may now be found in almost every IPO.

The Underwriting Agreement

The Standard Methods

The underwriting agreement is the agreement which regulates the relationship between the company (the seller of the shares) and the underwriter (which usually buys the shares). This is a complex agreement, the negotiations for which last several months, concurrently with the preparation of the registration statement. In the United States, there are two customary types of underwriting agreements:

- **Firm commitment offering**—This is the common method in the United States, according to which the underwriter buys the securities from the company for a price lower than their price to the public, with the difference being the underwriting commission. In this case, the underwriter assumes the risk that investors who expressed an interest in buying the shares during the book building process will not follow through on their orders (which are not binding, as mentioned in the section on road show, until the registration statement is declared effective). However, such exposure only exists in practice in the three to five days between the signing of the underwriting agreement (which is the date on which the registration statement is declared effective) and the closing of the transaction, upon which the shares are transferred to the buyers. Even this exposure is limited because the underwriting agreement establishes the underwriter's right to cancel the agreement if any adverse change occurs in the condition of the company or the market. In practice, however, due to underwriters' reputation considerations, this clause is almost never exercised. The underwriter usually has also an option (green shoe) to buy additional shares (up to 15% of the offering) for 30 days after the closing, in order to meet demand for the share or sale positions it had created therein. In this respect it is important to mention that an underwriter is allowed to support the price of the share (but not to regulate it) shortly after the IPO in order to prevent it from dropping under the IPO price.

- **Best efforts offering**—Under this method, the underwriters undertake to use their best efforts to sell the shares, but do not undertake to buy any shares which are not sold. The underwriters usually require an initial amount which is not reimbursed, and payment for sold shares. If the IPO fails, the company nevertheless has to pay the various consultants and does not get the initial payment back from the underwriters. In some cases, the IPO is cancelled if the underwriters do not sell the entire pre-determined amount (best efforts, all or none). This agreement is uncommon among companies which are able to choose a reputable underwriter, and use the firm commitment arrangement.

Under both methods, the underwriting agreement itself addresses the following matters: the type of offering; the company's consent to sell, and the underwriters' agreement to buy, a certain quantity of shares for a pre-determined price; representations and warranties by the company with respect to its condition and the veracity of the information contained in the registration statement; the situations in which the underwriters' undertakings are revoked (outs); indemnification of the underwriters against liability for incomplete or improper disclosures in the registration statement; conditions to the fulfillment of the underwriters' undertakings, such as receipt of a comfort letter from the CPAs and an opinion from the company's attorneys; undertakings of the company, the entrepreneurs, and the large shareholders (such as a prohibition to sell the shares (lock-up)—usually for a period of 90-270 days); the place and date of the closing.

Other Alternatives

In recent years, attempts have been made to introduce several alternatives to the customary offering method in the United States, but such attempts have so far not captured a large share of the market. The two main alternative methods are the auction method and the lottery method. In the tender method, the company allots the shares offered to the public for the highest price at which buyers may still be found for the entire supply of shares. In the lottery method (which was first promoted by Wit Capital), the shares received by the underwriter for distribution are raffled among the customers, and all the shares are sold at the IPO price. This is an ordinary offering with underwriters; the purpose of the lottery is to open the possibility of buying shares in an IPO to ordinary private investors.

The Registration Statement

The U.S. Securities Act of 1933 requires that a registration statement be filed with the SEC before the offering. The sale of securities is prohibited before the registration statement is declared effective.

The registration statement is composed of two parts. The first part is the prospectus, which must be delivered to any person who has offered to buy the securities and which contains the information required to make an investment decision: a description of the company and its business, a description of the offered securities and the use to which the sale proceeds will be put, the risks involved in buying the securities, detailed financial information (the financial statements are also attached to the prospectus), and a description of the management and board of directors. The second part contains additional information such as expenses, director indemnification, and appendices—which is not distributed with the prospectus but is available at the SEC's offices.

The registration statement has a twofold role: On the one hand, it is the sale document which presents the company to potential buyers of the securities, and on the other hand, it is a legal document designed to legally protect the company and its officers against claims resulting from omissions or misstatements of material information about the company. Naturally, these two objectives contrast with one another, and a balance is required between the presentation of the company and its future in a manner which will ensure that the securities are sold, and the need to disclose all of the risks involved in their acquisition.

There are several types of registration statements. The document used in the IPO of a U.S. company is Form S-1, and Form F-1 is used in the IPO of a foreign company (see the section on changes in the registration process for a discussion of a proposal to replace the registration forms).

Disclosure Duties

The duties of disclosure in prospectuses in the United States, as well as in other countries, are designed to achieve three main objectives: protecting investors against fraud, maximizing the market's efficiency, and ensuring the existence of a fair market for securities trade. These objectives are achieved by requiring the disclosure of all the material information needed by investors to make investment decisions (proper and complete disclosure), rather than by stating the economic value of the securities (the assumption being that when the information is readily available, the market will determine the economic value of the securities). In the past, the manner of implementation of the disclosure requirements differed from one country to another, but nowadays there is a trend to make the disclosure rules uniform in all of the main markets (see the section on disclosure under international disclosure rules). It is also important to remember that the scope of the disclosures made in the prospectus is not dictated only by statutory requirements, but also by international standards and investors' expectations.

The Disclosure Particulars

The details requiring disclosure in the prospectus are fixed in the rules (regulations) promulgated under the Securities Act of 1933 (Regulation S-K for domestic companies, Form F1 for foreign companies). In addition, there is a general prohibition on the inclusion of a misleading detail in the prospectus or on the omission of material information, but there is no sweeping requirement to disclose all the information which is material to investors. The required disclosure may be divided into four parts:

- **Business description**—What is required here is a clear description, rather than merely a technical one, of the company's business since its establishment, the market in which it operates, its competitors, customers, the company's assets, legal exposure, the offered securities, and the company's management.
- **Management Discussion & Analysis (MD&A)**—This is a review of the company from the management's point of view, including an analysis of the financial statements (which analysis has to supply investors with material information and not repeat the data which are already included in the statements) and a discussion of the company's projections—future trends, uncertainty factors, and elements which could have a material effect on the company's performance. In order to enable the company to present financial forecasts and analyses without fearing legal action in case such projections do not materialize, an amendment was enacted in 1995 to the U.S. securities laws which provides partial protection against complaints concerning future projections (see the section on liability under U.S. securities laws).
- **Risk analysis**—The company must describe the risk factors and projected problems involved in the investment, for instance, risks facing the company with respect to the protection of its intellectual property, or risks resulting from the presence of competitors with greater financial resources. The company should refrain from using general language and must describe the risks that are unique to the company.
- **Financial information**—This includes financial statements prepared according to GAAP. If the statements are not prepared according to U.S. GAAP, such as is the case for some foreign registrants, a reconciliation with these rules has to be attached: If the company is raising capital in the offering, it is required to attach a full reconciliation with U.S. GAAP, but if the prospectus is for the sole purpose of listing for trade, then a partial

reconciliation is sufficient. In addition, a financial information summary appears in the body of the prospectus.
- **Contract Exhibits**—Material contracts of the company, such as lease contracts, employment contracts for key employees, and contracts with main suppliers are attached to the prospectus.

Liability under U.S. Securities Laws

Subject to certain exceptions, the Securities Act of 1933 prohibits any public offering without an effective registration statement. The act imposes liability for the sale of securities without an effective prospectus (liability under Section 12), for non-compliance with certain requirements of the act, and for material misstatements or omissions in the registration statement (liability under Section 11). This liability is imposed on the company, its officers and directors who signed the prospectus, the underwriters, the controlling shareholders, and the experts who assisted in preparing the registration statement with respect to the parts they helped to prepare (namely, the CPAs, in connection with the financial statements). Liability is imposed jointly and severally, for any damage up to the full price of the shares sold. The liability imposed on the company is strict, whereas other liable parties can invoke due diligence defense, whereby if they had, after reasonable investigation, valid ground to believe and did believe at the time such part of the registration statement became effective, that the statements herein were true, and that there was no omission to state a material fact required to be stated therein, or necessary to make the statements therein not misleading. Underwriters usually demand indemnification from the company for any liability imposed on them (except for information they themselves had provided), although the legal validity of such undertaking is yet to be clarified. In addition, according to Section 10b-5 of the Securities Exchange Act of 1934, liability is imposed after the offering on any person employing manipulative and deceptive devices in the purchase or sale of securities. This liability has been very much expanded in U.S. case law, and now enables civil and criminal liability to be imposed for any securities manipulation, also on anyone whose involvement in the matter is indirect (such as "helpers and tippers").

From the company's point of view, any publication of incorrect material information could be used as a basis for legal action. The liability is not only theoretical, since an immense number of class actions are filed every year in the United States, often following a considerable drop in the share price. More than 90% of the claims end in a settlement in which the company and the other defendants admit no liability. Companies have often complained that such class actions are frivolous and that they are settled only because of their nuisance value. It has further been claimed that considerable amounts of the money paid under the settlement agreements go into the pockets of the attorneys, who are often involved in the actual initiation of the action. On the other hand, the importance of class actions as a tool for maintaining a high level of disclosure in the U.S. market should not be slighted.

In an attempt to reduce the number of actions, an amendment was enacted in 1995 to the U.S. securities laws according to which any information included in forward-looking statements by the company cannot, subject to certain conditions, be used as a basis for legal action based on securities laws ("safe harbor"). It is still too soon to tell decisively whether the amendment has indeed affected the number of unfounded actions. Nowadays, almost every company includes in its announcements a clause to the effect that such announcement contains forward-looking statements, which could naturally turn out to be inaccurate.

Changes in the Registration Process

In November 1998, the SEC proposed material changes in the rules governing the offering of securities in the United States. Due to the scope and significance of the change, the proposal was nicknamed "Aircraft Carrier." Five main changes were proposed: (1) The publication of information by the company and analysts' research of the company would continue regardless of the IPO (which amounts, in fact, to a cancellation of the quiet period); (2) The prospectus and any information filed with the SEC, also by foreign companies, would be transmitted in electronic form, so that investors will have access to the information via the EDGAR system (an electronic information system which includes most of the reports filed by companies in the United States to the SEC); (3) The company would be obliged to give investors information about the terms of the offering before they make the decision to invest (at present, investors make investment decisions based on the preliminary prospectus—the red herring); (4) Non-permissible free writing liability would be imposed for written information given to investors outside the prospectus; and (5) Public offerings would be given preference over private placements by giving companies more control over the IPO process, on the one hand, and canceling some benefits enjoyed by private placements, on the other hand. When the change is effected, the form of all the registration statements now used in the United States (S-3/F-3, S-1/F-1) would be replaced by a new format (Form A/Form B).

Large groups in the financial community greatly oppose the change, claiming that it will encumber and slow down the current process. The date of effectuation of the change has therefore not yet been finally determined, and modifications may be made to it during the discussions leading to its adoption.

Following the IPO

After the IPO, an effort is required to preserve and improve the company's position in the capital markets. In order to maintain a viable secondary market for the company's shares, constant interest in the share needs to be kept up by providing enhanced disclosure to shareholders and analysts, holding conversations and conference calls with analysts, and filing periodic reports. A large part of the disclosure is based on expectations which do not amount only to the reports required by law, but extend to the degree of the company's ability and willingness to answer questions by investors and their representatives, make timely reports and give warnings regarding its operating results.

Nowadays, the price of many companies is discounted due to the lack of their managers' initiative in marketing the company to players in capital markets, participating in important conventions, and so forth. Companies invest many efforts in marketing information about their financial results and their current and future product and service packages. This information is marketed to the company's existing investors, but also—and mainly—to potential investors. The information is marketed by press releases, PR firms, and various conventions, either professional or for the capital market. This field of investor relations has a material impact on the company's market value. A company's results are measured by its actual financial performance, and the market expectation of its future performance. Since these estimates are based on the information which is available to the people who make the valuations for the purpose of investments, the significance of information dissemination to the financial community is immediately visible. The impact on the share's short-term value is significant for the purposes of raising capital, recruiting employees, and for acquisitions made with the shares being a component of the price.

Alongside the information provided to the financial community to develop a positive relationship with it, periodic reporting to the SEC is also required. Following are the main post-offering reporting duties imposed by law. Foreign companies are subject to reduced reporting requirements—see the section on relief in periodic reporting requirements.

Periodic Reporting Duties

Immediately after the conclusion of an IPO, the company is subject to reporting duties under the Securities Exchange Act of 1934, which include an annual report (10-K) and a quarterly report (10-Q). The reports are also filed with the SEC in electronic form (see a later section for a discussion of the duties imposed on foreign companies).

- **Annual report**—The annual report on Form 10-K is filed within 90 days from the end of the fiscal year and includes most of the issues contained in the registration statement. Audited financial statements are attached to the report. Some of the information may be incorporated by reference to the annual report delivered to the shareholders.
- **Quarterly report**—For each of the first three quarters of the year, a quarterly report on Form 10-Q is filed within 45 days from the end of the quarter. The report includes mainly the reviewed quarterly financial statements and management's discussion and analysis of the financial results. The report also describes material developments which took place during the quarter (such as material legal actions against the firm, shareholders' votes, replacement of CPAs, and so on).

Reporting Material Events and Stock Exchange Rules

Material events have to be reported to both the SEC and the stock exchange on which the share is listed. Reporting to the SEC is made on Form 8-K within 15 days from the occurrence of the event, only with respect to the particular events specified in Form 8-K. A more material reporting duty is imposed by the stock exchanges, which require an immediate report on a list of issues specified in the stock exchange's rules (including unusual stock behavior), as well as on any other material event.

Usually, companies also publish an "earnings warning" when their financial results are materially different from previous forecasts made by the company or by analysts.

Many studies indicate that almost all of the leading companies in the United States demonstrate financial results (particularly earnings per share) which are no lower than the average projection made by analysts. The main reason for this, according to such studies, is that many companies lower the expectations before they present the actual reports by providing earnings "guiding." However, in periods of extreme market slowdown, the number of companies which announce results falling short of projections is naturally greater. For instance, during the year 2001, the number of companies which failed to meet projections was the highest in close to a decade.

In view of new regulations of the SEC (Regulation FD), companies can no longer discriminate among investors in the information they provide. For instance, companies must allow investors access to information which is delivered in meetings with analysts. It is still too soon to say what the significance of this change will be since, although the principle of an equitable distribution of information among investors is both noble and fair, various legal risks and a fear of enhanced volatility in share prices may affect the scope of the information which is now relayed to the public.

Proxy Rules

The company is required to file a detailed annual report and to deliver it to all the shareholders. This report must include most of the information contained in the annual report to the SEC (10-K) as well as information pertaining to any matter brought to the vote of the shareholders. Furthermore, whenever a shareholders' voting is required (at least once a year in the annual meeting), the company must send shareholders proxy forms, accompanied by detailed information about the topics of the vote. The annual report is usually sent to the shareholders together with the proxy form.

The Prohibition on Insider Trading

Section 10b-5 of the Securities Exchange Act of 1934 prohibits the employment of manipulative and deceptive devices in connection with the sale of securities. This section is widely used to fight the usage of inside information. In addition, the company's managers and insiders are subject to even more severe rules and a duty to report any trade in the share, under Section 16 of the same act.

Selling Shares That Are Exempt from Registration

A private placement is, in principle, an issuance to a limited number of investors who are able to "defend themselves" and therefore do not require the protection afforded by the securities rules (except for the prohibition on the employment of manipulative and deceptive devices pursuant to Rule 10b-5, which applies in any case). Shares, the sale of which is exempt from registration, are "restricted" shares, and their sale is allowed pursuant to special rules fixed in Rule 144 of the U.S. securities rules. A private sale by a non-listed company (an issue discussed in the section on legal restrictions according to U.S. law) should be distinguished from the sale of shares within an exemption from registration during or after a public offering, on which this section focuses.

Rule 144

Rule 144 regulates the sale of restricted shares which were purchased from the company or from an affiliate of the company under an exemption from registration. The rule entirely prohibits the sale of the shares for a period of one year after they are bought, other than through a registration under the Securities Act or an exemption thereof; thereafter, a limited sale is allowed. The rule states that in the second year, the larger of the following two quantities may be sold every three months: 1% of the offered shares, and the average weekly trade volume in the four weeks preceding the sale. Once the two years are up, the shares are released for trade if their holder is a non-affiliate of the company, or continue to be subject to the sale restrictions if they are held by the company itself or by an affiliate. Additional restrictions on sales under Rule 144 pertain to the requirement of full information about the company (a requirement which is usually filled anyway when the company is subject to U.S. reporting regulations), a duty to report every sale, and technical restrictions on the manner of sale (broker transaction).

Regulation S

In theory, U.S. securities rules apply to any offering of securities in which any U.S. means of communications is used; for instance, a telephone conversation in the U.S. during the process of raising capital for a French company in France.

In order to avoid this paradoxical situation, the rules of Regulation S were enacted in 1990, according to which no registration is required in offerings outside the United States to non-U.S. investors, if the company meets several criteria. A full review of such criteria lies beyond the scope of this book, but in principle, the criteria distinguish between the sale of debentures (with which we are not concerned) and the sale of equity, and between a company which has a material interest in the U.S. market and a company which has no relation to the United States. The sale is subject to various offering restrictions, designed to prevent an abuse of the exemption by way of bogus sales to foreign investors ("parking"), who would then sell the shares immediately to U.S. residents. Underwriters and legal counsel should be consulted with respect to the manner of application of these regulations for the offerings to sell shares only to foreign investors outside the United States.

An offering to U.S. investors still needs to meet the rules for an exemption under U.S. law, whether they are the rules governing the exemption for "traditional" private placements or the rules set in Regulation D (which is why it is customary to ask investors for a declaration on their status as "Accredited Investors"—see the section on legal restrictions according to U.S. law).

Regulation A

The rules of Regulation A provide an exemption from registration for offerings of up to $5 million per year. Although this is ostensibly an exemption from registration, such an offering involves fewer disclosure requirements and is known in practice as an abbreviated registration rather than a full exemption from registration. The main advantage in offering under Regulation A is that the financial statements are abridged and the costs are lower than in ordinary offerings. Foreign companies cannot use the Regulation A exemption. The main use made of this offering is for "testing the water" in terms of market demand for a full-fledged offering of the company.

Foreign Companies Raising Capital

Foreign companies raising capital in the United States enjoy several types of relief in comparison to U.S. companies, which are intended to encourage foreign companies to go public in the United States rather than on another international market. A foreign company is defined as a company registered outside the United States, provided that fewer than 50% of its shareholders are U.S. residents (the test is one of beneficial ownership and the company is required to conduct a reasonable investigation into the place of residence of its shareholders), and further provided that a majority of the company's activities and assets are managed outside the United States. Following are the main forms of relief enjoyed by foreign companies.

Disclosure under International Disclosure Rules

Foreign companies file their registration statements in an IPO on Form F-1, the disclosure requirements of which are less strict than those required of U.S. companies filing a Form S-1. The main differences concern the disclosure of managers' salaries, information about the identity of customers, and the level of specification of the company's results in various segments of operations. The disclosure rules which apply to foreign companies in the United States are fixed in Form 20-F.

Relief in the IPO Process

Foreign companies receive special treatment from the SEC, and they enjoy the assistance of the SEC's personnel throughout the IPO process. Foreign companies submit the registration statement confidentially before the official filing. The comments received after the preliminary submission are implemented so that when the registration document is filed officially, it is almost in its final form.

Relief in Periodic Reporting Requirements

Foreign companies are not required to file quarterly and annual reports (including an annual report to shareholders) nor special reports (8-K) which are filed by U.S. companies. Foreign companies are required only to file an annual report within six months from the end of their fiscal year, and the form of the report (20-F) is abridged compared to the detailed report required of U.S. companies. The reporting requirements are, however, broader if listing for trade is accompanied by the raising of capital.

Foreign companies are also required to submit, on Form 6-K, information which is circulated among all the shareholders in any form in the country of origin. In practice, many foreign companies publish their financial results every quarter by way of a press release so as to meet investors' expectations, but this is not a full report subject to the liability imposed by the securities laws. The companies are also required to file reports according to the stock exchange rules at least once every six months. In addition, many companies deliver annual reports and proxy forms to their shareholders in order to keep up with investors' expectations.

Other Exemptions

Foreign companies are exempt from the requirement of filing annual reports to the shareholders and from the other proxy rules which apply to U.S. companies according to the Securities Exchange Act of 1934. In addition, directors and officers of foreign companies are not bound by the duties of reporting and the liability set in Section 16 of the act in connection with holdings of and transactions in the company's securities.

Using ADR

An ADR (American Depositary Receipt) is a certificate issued by a U.S. depository institution, which represents shares of a foreign company (listed on a non-U.S. exchange) deposited with the bank. Foreign companies whose shares are traded in their domestic market can issue an ADR—rather than ordinary shares—in order to facilitate trading in the U.S., since every trade of an ADR is registered in the bank's records in the United States with no need for a transfer in the domestic market (which might be problematic from the point of view of trading hours and may also involve additional commissions). The bank also arranges for the delivery of reports and information to the U.S. shareholders, the distribution of dividends in dollars, and other shareholder services. The use of ADR increases the interest of U.S. investors in the share, since it turns a foreign share into a quasi-U.S. share with respect to the administration involved in holding it and trading in it.

ADRs are popular among large companies from Europe, South America, and Asia. The shares of the larger companies among them are traded in several markets and are some of the most liquid in the U.S. capital markets (for instance, the shares of Nokia, Ericsson and many of the privatized national telephone companies). Although for many firms, the majority of the trade is shifting to the United States (together with a significant increase in volume), findings indicate an increase in the volume of trade in these shares also in their countries of origin, which results, among other factors, from trade by institutional investors trying to profit from momentary price differences in the underlying asset between the markets ("arbitrage opportunities").

In addition, some institutional investors who do not invest in companies that are not listed on a U.S. exchange, can invest in firms that are listed via an ADR (although they trade the shares without such restriction). There are various reasons for this, including limitations imposed on the permissible investment charter of such investors, as well as the legal "umbrella" provided by U.S. securities laws (via disclosure and reporting requirements) to investors in the shares of companies which are listed in the United States, even if the securities were actually bought in a different country. This interesting finding is now used as a highly important factor in attempts made to convince companies that dual-listing could in fact increase trading in the firm's home country.

PART V

Mergers and Acquisitions, Bankruptcies, and Dissolution

In recent years, mergers and acquisitions (M&A) have turned out to provide many of the most successful exits. In fact, the number of exits through venture M&As exceeds the number of exits via IPOs, and hence the importance on this topic in this book.

The size and scope of the deals are also important for entrepreneurs, since there is an intimate connection between the scope and value of announced acquisitions and the amounts and fields of investments made by venture capitalists in the following periods.

As a by-product of the phenomenon, companies which are just starting out are focusing on developing their technologies with an eye to attracting leading companies to regard them as a desirable investment. The scarcity of companies which are able to achieve independently the status of world leaders in their field is another incentive to entrepreneurs to plan for the sale of the company, rather than attempt to establish a large independent company.

PART V Mergers and Acquisitions, Bankruptcies, and Dissolution

The dramatic meltdown in capital markets since the second half of 2000 had significantly affected the scope and thus the prices of M&A activities. In addition, following the general economic slowdown, it is clear that most of the acquisitions conducted in the recent years did not fulfill the buyers' expectations.

However, perhaps more than before, a thorough understanding of the various M&A alternatives and related procedures is becoming an important aspect in the investment decision, and in the venture development planning.

This part of the book discusses the strategic aspects of mergers, acquisitions, and spin-offs alongside the practical aspects of planning and executing a sale, including highlighting the primary economic and legal aspects of mergers, acquisitions, and spin-offs.

This part of the book also deals with another aspect of exits, which is more unfortunate, the bankruptcy and possible dissolution of the venture.

14

Mergers and Acquisitions (M&A)—Introduction

INTRODUCTION

Many companies undergo corporate restructuring throughout their life spans. Such restructuring may take place as part of an exit, as in the case of an acquisition or merger of the company; the creation of the company, as in the case of a spin-off; the raising of capital for divisions of the company (equity carve-out); or the sale (divestiture) of such divisions.

Mergers and acquisitions, as well as corporate restructuring, are driven by several incentives. From the acquisition side, the first is management's desire to improve the company's profitability and future cash flows, either by streamlining the company's existing activities by acquiring the technologies and skilled labor of the target, by expanding the company's activities, or penetrating new markets. The second incentive is management's desire to increase the market's awareness of the company's activities and value, i.e., enhancing its "value-revealing" activities: From the selling company side, the main incentive is of course the desire of the target's investors and entrepreneurs to exit their investment, or to increase the likelihood of such an exit (see the section later in this chapter on mergers and acquisitions for a detailed discussion of the reasons for mergers).

The Scope of the Phenomenon

Mergers and acquisitions are among the most exciting areas in the world of corporate finance. After the wave of acquisitions of the 1980s subsided, Wall Street experienced another M&A period in the mid-1990s. This wave emphasized strategic mergers and acquisitions, as opposed to the late 1980s' wave, which was characterized mainly by leveraged buy-outs (i.e., acquisitions financed with high-yield debt) by financial players.

In recent years, we have witnessed a wave of extremely large mergers and acquisitions; when such deals concerned the mergers and acquisitions of young high-tech companies, their dollar values were even higher than the amounts raised by such companies in stock exchanges. For instance, the total value of mergers and acquisitions which took place in the United States in 2000 exceeded $1.6 trillion as opposed to equity offerings of only $110 billion, as reported by the law firm Hale and Dorr. Approximately 9,500 mergers were announced, as compared with around 300 IPOs. The technology sector constitutes a principal component of this field, with around 2,500 deals executed in the computer software, supplies, and services industry. However, it is important to note that of this considerable number of deals, the largest 200 accounted for more than $1 trillion, the biggest of all being the merger of AOL and Time Warner (a merger worth $160 billion), which was approved by the authorities only in 2001.

Mergers and acquisitions are performed with compositions of various forms of payments. While most transactions are cash deals or include a cash component, the majority of the deals, from the point of view of financial volume, are either stock deals or stock and cash combination deals. For instance, in 2000 approximately 1,500 deals were made in cash in the amount of around $340 billion, as compared with around 1,400 stock-for-stock deals in the amount of approximately $750 billion; deals made with a combination of equity, debt, and cash accounted for another $230 billion.

Whereas an IPO used to be the main exit for investors in startups, in recent years the phenomenon of the acquisition of startups by large companies in early stages, often even before the development of the product is finished, has become increasingly widespread.

Starting in the second half of 2000, the scope of M&A activity related to startups had significantly slowed down, similar to the patterns observed in the IPO market. In addition, many of the transactions of recent years were written-down by the acquiring companies, in a combination of admitting over-priced transactions, and newly launched accounting rule which specifically requires the re-valuation of the price above tangible assets value paid in acquisitions (goodwill).

Types of Corporate Restructuring

Mergers and acquisitions are one type of corporate restructuring. Before starting the discussion on the relevant types of mergers and acquisitions, it is important to become familiar with some various terms pertaining to corporate restructuring:

- **Merger**—The combination of two companies (targets) or more within one of the companies (the acquirer or the surviving entity), upon completion of which all of the targets other than the acquirer cease to exist as separate legal entities.

- **Consolidation**—The combination of at least two companies, upon which all of the companies cease to exist as separate legal entities and operate as a new legal entity.
- **Acquisition**—A situation in which a company acquires full or partial ownership of the shares or assets of another company. A stock acquisition can be performed as part of a merger, an acquisition of assets, or an acquisition of shares directly from the shareholders, or by way of a tender offer for the acquisition of shares from the public.
- **Leveraged buy-out**—A series of actions in which a substantial part of the company's share capital is bought in consideration for cash raised by way of debt. In many cases, the debt is guaranteed by the company's assets.
- **Going private**—A situation in which the shares of a publicly traded company which are held by the public are bought by a group of investors who want to have the company unlisted.
- **Divestiture**—A situation in which the company sells portions of its assets (such as a certain branch of its activities).
- **Spin-off**—A situation in which the company is split into several distinct companies, with the shares in the new companies being issued to the original shareholders. This phenomenon became very common in the 1990s. A derivative of this act is the sale of the parent company's shares in the subsidiary which is already traded (equity carve-out or spin-out).

This part of the book naturally focuses on the actions which are relevant to young technology companies, i.e., mainly on various techniques of mergers and acquisitions.

Strategic Classification

Most acquisitions may be classified according to their strategic significance to the acquirer. The projected price in each type of acquisition depends on the specific characteristics of the acquirer and of the target, and on a correct analysis of the competition in the target's market (see Chapter 9 for a discussion of the impacts of mergers or acquisitions on valuation).

Horizontal Acquisitions

In horizontal acquisitions, the target operates in the same field as the acquirer, such as a merger between telephone companies which operate in the same field but in different countries. A horizontal acquisition is supposed to yield benefits such as an increase in the acquirer's market share, savings on operating costs (economies of scale), and synergy. In many cases, large companies acquire small companies which operate in a certain niche in the general field of the large companies' activity, in order to complement their line of products. Many startups now direct their plans so as to complement the product lines of such companies.

Vertical Acquisitions

In vertical acquisitions, the target operates at a different layer of the production process from the acquirer. For instance, a newspaper which is focused on media creation may acquire a company which deals with newspaper distribution.

Acquisitions of this type have been common in recent years in many fields, since many giant companies have been increasingly focusing on main fields of activity in which they aspire to become players with a relative advantage. Whereas horizontal acquisitions assist in completing a line of products in a particular field, vertical acquisitions allow such companies to create a value chain which enables their customers to receive products and services without resorting to other companies.

Conglomerate Acquisitions

In conglomerate acquisitions, the target operates in a different field from the acquirer. This type of merger may be divided into several sub-categories. One sub-category is mergers associated with the expansion of a line of products. Although the companies do not operate in the same field, they may use some parts of their infrastructure to reduce costs and enjoy higher profit margins. These mergers are beneficial also when the company has a reputation which is transferable to other fields. The Virgin group, for instance, operates in different fields (such as aviation, beverages, trains, radio), which are often united by the ability to enjoy the group's somewhat mischievous image.

Many publicly traded investment companies invest in other companies in a way which often gives the impression of a conglomerate acquisition, although they later turn out to be planned acquisitions designed to create complete packages of products and services. The boundaries between operating investment companies which create conglomerates and financial investment companies have also become vague. Investment companies, particularly those with many publicly traded subsidiaries (such as CMGI), are often trying to avoid being legally classified as mutual funds, which are subject to various investment, reporting, and supervisory rules.

Other conglomerate acquisitions are made in order to minimize the risk of bankruptcy of one of the companies by balancing out the losses of one portfolio company with the profits of another whose profitability components and sensitivity to economic parameters are different.

Numerous investment theories discuss their economic rationale for conglomerates, but in general, they have not been well-received by the financial community in the last few decades.

Why Do Mergers and Acquisitions Occur?

The M&A wave of recent years has been driven by technological changes and market conditions which forced companies to either develop technological solutions by themselves or, alternatively, buy or merge with companies which could provide them with the technological market edge or another relative advantage, such as a managerial advantage; an advantage of scale in production capacity, marketing or cost structure; a complement to their line of products or services, and so forth.

From the perspective of the acquired, merging, or selling party, the decision to make the move is often driven by the recognition that the company's operating results could improve if the company were part of a larger entity, whether in the form of an association of similar-sized companies or by being incorporated into a larger entity. In other cases, the decision to sell a business division results from the recognition that the division does not fit in well with the company's activity strategically or, alternatively, that the company has no competitive edge in its management of such division. Another main consideration is that of the investors or entrepreneurs, for whom the acquisition typically provides an opportunity to liquidate their investment by receiving cash or shares in a publicly listed company.

The main sources of value in mergers and acquisitions may be classified into several main categories, as specified below.

Reducing Development Times and Acquisition of Rapid Growth Options

Many acquisitions have a strategic value in that they enable the acquirer to gain or maintain a competitive advantage in its business environment. One of the most important strategic benefits of acquisitions of startups is the reduction of development time. Many large companies seek out companies worthy of acquiring only after they identify that a substantial market had been created. When a large company recognizes the creation of a market in which it has no leading product, there are benefits in acquiring a small company with a suitable product, which will reduce the time it would take it to offer similar products to the market and save the time and cost required for in-house development.

Furthermore, buying a product which has already undergone the "trial and error" phase enables the acquirer to choose the most suitable acquisition from among the variety of companies and products in the market, even if such products were not initially on the company's planning agenda. Cisco, for instance, acquired hundreds of companies during its growth years, which acquisitions enabled the company to enter new, high-growth fields quickly, reducing the need to set aside operating resources of the company for R&D. In that respect, acquisition costs were an integrated component of the company's R&D efforts. This is also a pattern that has been observed in the pharmaceutical industry for many years.

Operational Synergy

Most announcements of mergers and acquisitions mention the synergy phenomenon. What is meant by this is the totality of effects which a merger or an acquisition has, due to which the value of the components after the merger or the acquisition is higher than the total of such components beforehand. In fact, all operating advantages such as saving in costs and integration into a line of products are types of synergies. When analyzing the effects which a merger or an acquisition will have, we have to try to evaluate which components will create synergies. For instance, if the merger is supposed to increase the usage of production equipment, we would examine the relationship between equipment usage and profitability in similar companies.

The pooling of marketing and manpower resources may also save on the cost of many overlapping activities performed by both companies. Common duplicities exist in financial and marketing functions and, depending on the character of the companies, savings may be achieved also in development and manufacturing functions.

Vertical mergers have another advantage: The transaction costs of different entities may be reduced since some of the negotiations between independent companies become a discussion between parties to a transaction working within the same entity.

However, alongside the positive synergies, there is also much importance attached to problems which could arise after the merger, particularly on the human level. For instance, many mergers of companies, particularly those in technology, fail due to an incompatibility of the companies' management cultures. In addition, attempts to cut down on duplicate functions may lead to uncertainty and complaints among employees, which could reduce their productivity.

Where startups are concerned, operating synergies are expressed in the integration of the startup's technology with the acquirer's capabilities in the fields of research, marketing, distribution, and finance. Companies are constantly seeking technological or marketing advantages and are attempting to utilize the advantages inherent in scale. Large companies prefer to invest in young and fast companies with innovative technological solutions, whereas small companies seek large partners which will provide them with financial and marketing support. Many small companies suffer from a global access and marketing problem, and joining forces with an industrial giant provides them with fast access and presence around the world while reducing the risk of losing their technological edge to competitors. On the other hand, entities with a global presence are interested in adding products to their packages in order to offer their customers a broader range of products and streamline their usage of the mechanisms in which they invested much time and money.

Change in Market Power

In theory, two companies may sometimes merge and adopt a pricing policy which will enable them to earn more than the market average. The acquisition of a competitor could naturally reduce the competition in the market, and the prices of products may consequently rise and make monopolistic profits possible. Obviously, there are institutions which supervise such cases (such as the Antitrust Division of the Department of Justice and the Federal Trade Commission (FTC) and prevent merger agreements which could reduce competition, or at least demand clarifications for and/or changes in the agreement. Obviously, it is not an easy task to distinguish between legal and illegal agreements.

For example, there are many ways in which a merger could enable the utilization of the combined selling power by way of market segmentation which increases the manufacturer's profits. However, it should be kept in mind that the improvement in manufacturers' efficiency could compensate for the reduction in competition also from the consumers' point of view. The authorities perform economic benefit tests, which are usually guided by the interest of consumers (for more on that topic, see Chapter 17).

Ostensibly, the examination of the reduction in competition is more relevant in the merger of two companies with large market shares and less in the acquisition of startups by large companies. However, many acquisitions of startups could have the impact of reducing future competition, particularly in markets which are expected to expand (for a more detailed discussion of the reduction in competition and antitrust aspects, see Chapter 17).

Improved Managerial Capabilities

The existence of an active M&A market provides an excellent instrument of corporate governance. Companies whose performance is below the market average, if such poor performance is attributable to managerial decisions (which is almost always the case), are more likely to be a target for takeover. Managers are aware of this high probability and are therefore more sensitive to their performance. The more relevant factor for our current discussion is the improvement in the company's management following the acquisition due to the passage of management into the hands of more experienced managers in the field. If the original managers stay in office, the exposure to the management methods of a large international organization and the ability to tap into its managerial resources may also suffice to achieve an improvement in performance.

When a startup is growing rapidly, but lacks a complete internal managerial infrastructure, a merger can assist in rapidly creating an organization in which all of the necessary managerial positions are filled. Those who have reservations about this argument claim that it is usually cheaper and more efficient to recruit the necessary manpower from competitors than to merge with another company. However, it is possible to understand some cases in which the acquirer is better off merging with a target staffed by an experienced and well-accustomed-to-each-other management team since such a merger can eliminate the friction which could be caused if recruitment is performed on an individual basis.

Diversification and Capital Market Synergy

Managers and employees may benefit from diversification when a merger or an acquisition is made with a company which is sensitive to different economic parameters from their own company. This desire to diversify stems from the fact that the human capital, and often also most of the financial capital, of employees and managers is tied to the company and cannot be diversified, as opposed to the company's shareholders, who can create a diversified portfolio. As a result, one of the implications of this lack of personal diversification is sub-optimal investment decisions from the perspective of shareholders. Therefore, diversification of the company's operation which alleviates that concern may in fact be for the benefit of shareholders, in spite of the argument against conglomerate mergers.

In addition, many companies enjoy managerial reputation, reputation in the capital market, reputation in the product and service market, or reputation in the employment market. Such reputation is often transferable to other fields, and diversification reduces the likelihood that such reputation will be lost due to market volatility.

Furthermore, diversification may reduce the company's cost of debt due to the reduced volatility of the company's performance, as well as the company's tax liability over time.

A merger could also reduce the company's cost of debt by adding a stabilizing factor which results from the company's size. Furthermore, the existence of an internal financial reserve in the company could reduce its dependency on outside sources; divisions generating positive cash flows can finance other divisions in the same company while reducing the company's financing expenses. This consideration is crucial, particularly during times of crisis in the capital market when it is harder for companies to raise external funding.

Tax Advantages

When the acquirer has a cash surplus, the acquisition of other companies could replace the distribution of a dividend and in that respect is similar to stock repurchase. Thus, if the acquired company will yield for the acquiring company returns that compensate for its risks, many shareholders will reduce their tax liabilities since the tax on dividends is generally higher than the tax on capital gains imposed on the sale of shares.

Do Mergers and Acquisitions Create Value?

Although there are various methods of executing mergers and acquisitions, a few general outcomes of such transactions may be pointed out. First, a merger resulting from the combination of unrelated investments (conglomerate acquisitions) does not necessarily yield positive returns for the acquirer's shareholders. The reason for this is that the acquirer's shareholders can usually buy the shares of companies similar to the target by themselves, and the fact that the acquirer's managers compel them to participate in the investment reduces the attractiveness of the acquirer altogether. Obviously, this principle does not apply if indeed the acquirer has managerial abilities which may be implemented in different fields. However, such situations are quite rare, and among the past conglomerates, General Electric is probably the only successful one.

However, on average, companies which are conglomerates are traded at a discount compared to the sum of the values of the companies they manage, mainly due to the additional managerial and administrative costs which result from the difficulties in managing diverse and unrelated businesses.

Similarly, while mergers which are explained by the desire to reduce a dependency on seasonal sales or to reduce sensitivity to an economic situation in such or another field do indeed reduce the specific risk in the investment, they do not create value to the shareholders, who examine investments in accordance with the systematic risk they entail, as they can diversify away the firm's specific risk. On the other hand, such mergers obviously generate value if a positive synergy is created between the activities, for example, by streamlining the managerial and administrative infrastructure.

Acquisitions which create value to the acquirer's shareholders are those which utilize the acquirer's know-how, capabilities, and resources to improve the target's operating performance or, alternatively, use the target's resources to improve the acquirer's operating abilities and hence its own operating performance. The acquisition or merger may naturally generate value when it creates a company which benefits from the economies of scale in a more efficient cost structure, or when it creates a marketing power which enables it to benefit from a sustainable competitive position in the market. For instance, there is an advantage to size in the development of core technologies, which small companies find hard to shoulder.

Furthermore, acquisitions do create value through the fact that they may provide an efficient mechanism for investing the company's money. Specifically, the tax system in most countries imposes double taxation on the company's earnings: once in the form of corporate tax and again when the shareholder pays tax on the dividend paid to him or her. Even when the company buys its own shares ("share repurchase"), the payment of capital gains tax by some of the shareholders constitutes, in practice, a tax of sorts on the company's earnings. On the other hand, no tax is paid on money which remains in the company and is re-invested, until it is distributed. In practice, the acquisition, as long as it generates at least the alternative return on the money, is an efficient instrument for deferring the payment of tax on the company's earnings, which are instead invested in another firm.

Sales and Mergers Versus IPOs

A company facing a merger or a sale is often confronted with the dilemma of choosing between selling the company at an early stage or continuing the development efforts in order to take the company public. Within these considerations, the interests of the investors, who regard sales and IPOs as alternative exits, are also important.

IPOs

An IPO entails important advantages for young companies, such as the creation of a readily-available source of capital for the company; an efficient means of promoting awareness of its existence and products; credibility among potential partners, customers, and investors; liquidity for investors; the possibility for investors and entrepreneurs to continue holding the company's shares after the IPO (as opposed to a sale, in which normally the company is effectively eliminated); and maintaining their independence in management (see the section on the advantages of going public for a more detailed discussion on the subject).

On the other hand, in order to reach the stage of an IPO, there are several prerequisites such as having the status of a market leader (or reasonable prospects of becoming one), a broad line of products, and excellent and experienced management (see the section on whether the company is ready to go public for a further discussion on the subject). In addition, IPOs involve high costs and a long and exhausting process from the entrepreneurs' point of view. After the IPO, the company becomes the subject of close scrutiny by investors and analysts. This situation drives the management to focus on the company's short-term results and may divert it away from the company's long-term strategy. In addition, an IPO requires extensive and expensive preparations on the part of the company, including adjusting its control structure and accounting system. Therefore, a company limited by time and market constraints and requiring capital immediately may prefer other financing methods, including a sale.

Sales

A sale can entail many advantages to both the acquirer and the target. For a young company, a sale is an alternative to independent activity and an IPO. It is important to note that many companies are founded on a solid technological basis, but some lack experience in other keys to success factors such as marketing capabilities. Typically, in order to successfully penetrate new markets, it is beneficial to develop ties with leading companies which already operate in such markets, and merging with a larger company provides an efficient solution to such problems.

For many companies, the plunge of technology stocks from the second half of 2000 reduced the likelihood of using an IPO as an exit, relative to the likelihood of acquisitions of private companies by publicly held companies. This increase in the ratio between acquisitions and IPOs followed a sizzling period of capital raising and public listing of technology companies, using the money they raised and their shares to acquire other companies. However, as it was described in the previous chapter, the continued crisis in capital markets severely affected the M&A market as well.

In other words, there is a positive and direct correlation between the condition of the stock exchange and the number of acquisitions and mergers, and there are also certain substitutions between IPOs and acquisitions.

In many cases, it is the venture capital investors (who invested competitively in similar companies during prosperous times) who encourage mergers in times of crisis, when they join forces to reduce the chances of portfolio companies withering away. In addition, during these periods the reputation of the venture capital funds which invested in the company becomes increasingly important, since such reputable investors are sometimes the first to be contacted by potential acquirers and their network of contacts significantly increases the likelihood of an acquisition. However, since most transactions involve exchange of stock deals, such sales should not necessarily be deemed as an exit, because long lock-up periods in the case of an acquisition by a publicly traded company may postpone the actual exit or may keep the company's investors interested in the success of the acquirer.

Case Study—The Sale of Chromatis to Lucent

In May 2000, Lucent Technologies announced it was acquiring an almost unknown private company, Chromatis, for approximately $5 billion in Lucent stock. An analysis of the foundation and sale of Chromatis sheds light on and provides a practical example of some of the issues reviewed in this book, with an emphasis on issues relating to the company's sale.

Beginnings

Chromatis was founded in 1997 by Dr. Rafi Gidron and Orni Petrushka, two men who had cooperated before when they founded Scorpio Communications and sold it to U.S. Robotics for $72 million in cash in August 1996. Petrushka continued managing Scorpio under its new ownership, and Dr. Gidron worked at U.S. Robotics headquarters until it was bought out by 3Com.

Gidron and Petrushka say that after Scorpio was sold, they felt the need to experience again the sense of entrepreneurship involved in a startup. They started looking for a market in need of solutions which they were capable of offering. Gidron and Petruschka knew that after their successful experience with Scorpio, almost any initiative they would undertake would attract the keen interest of venture capital funds. Their success was not regarded as mere chance, due to their experience in corporate management and their solid theoretical background (Gidron, for instance, had been a Professor at Columbia University specializing in the area of communications).

The chosen target market was infrastructure for metropolitan communications networks ("metro"). The fundamental factors driving the market were the observations that while the volume of voice communications rises by 5–10% every year, data traffic was increasing exponentially. Consequently, without dramatically upgrading the efficiency of data communications transmissions, the existing metro infrastructure was not expected to be able to handle the data volume. A principal stimulus for the development of a market for products addressing the new congestion problem was the deregulation of the communications market in 1996, which opened the local calls market to competition. This change led to a massive wave of investments in infrastructure by existing companies, as well as by companies which wanted to enter the local markets. Obviously, the giant communications infrastructure companies such as Cisco, Lucent, Ciena, and Nortel, as well as younger companies such as Sycamore, were also interested in entering this market and capturing a significant share of it.

After concluding that communications companies were about to make massive capital investments in the metropolitan networking market, the entrepreneurs decided to examine it. First, they met with potential customers and studied their needs. This market-orientation approach, although the product was essentially technological, was different from the route Gidron and Petruschka had taken before when establishing Scorpio. This time, thorough market research was conducted before they started the development, in order to increase the likelihood of success.

Chromatis' entrepreneurs aspired to develop a full networking solution which would optimize the capacity of optical fibers by increasing the volume of traffic transmitted through them. The system integrated hardware for multiplexing several different wavelengths (DWDM – Dense Wavelength Division Multiplexing), technology for transmitting data using IP (Internet Protocol), technology for connecting telephone exchanges, and other technologies. The system was to be installed at the facilities of communications carriers, and the target market was metropolitan telephone companies. Thus was Chromatis born.

Building the Company

After deciding on their strategic direction, the entrepreneurs founded the company in 1997. The company was organized as a Delaware company with a development center in Israel, and its main offices were in Bethesda, Maryland (where several communications companies are centered and switching engineers are relatively abundant). The entrepreneurs used their own money for the initial capital. It was important to them that a leading U.S. fund participate in the first-stage financing round, which would expose them to customers and competitors in the target market. Therefore, they brought together the venture capital fund JVP (Jerusalem Venture Partners) and Crosspoint fund as their initial investors. JVP had previously invested in Scorpio, Gidron and Petruschka's previous company, and since the entrepreneurs had had a good experience with the fund, and in particular its managing partners, Fred Margalit, they decided to allow the fund to act as the lead investor in the new company in the first round, which took place in March 1998, in which Chromatis raised $7 million. In October 1998, the company raised another $5 million, this round being led by Lucent Venture Partners. All of the previous investors also took part in the second round. In November 1999, when the company was finishing its beta testing and was ready to go to market, the company raised approximately $38 million from its previous investors, including Lucent's venture capital fund, and from new investors, including the Soros and Hambrecht funds. This round was based on a company valuation of more than $100 million.

At first, Gidron and Petruschka acted as joint CEOs, but later recruited the outside CEO Bob Barron, who had approximately one year earlier declined a similar offer from Cerent, a company operating in a similar field which was later bought by Cisco for around $7 billion. Chromatis' top management team also included some former Scorpio and U.S. Robotics employees.

All along the way, Chromatis recruited first-rate employees and managers. For example, it managed to recruit Mory Ejabat, one of the best known managers in the field of communications and the active CEO of the communications equipment company Ascend Communications, a company bought by Lucent one year earlier for more than $20 billion.

Before the sale, the company employed about 160 workers. In 1999, the company launched some beta trials with telecom companies, including Quest and Bell Atlantic, but had substantially no revenue.

The Transaction

In May 2000, Chromatis announced that it had been acquired by Lucent in a stock transaction based on a value of around $5 billion. Under the agreement, Lucent allotted 78 million of its shares to Chromatis, excluding the 7% stake of Lucent Venture Partners. Lucent allotted another 2.5 million of its shares to several key employees of Chromatis, contingent upon Chromatis meeting certain performance-based goals after the sale.

The deal left almost everyone involved in the industry dumbstruck. The company was founded less than two years before the sale and had no meaningful revenues or guaranteed contracts. Apparently, a successful combination of technology, management, and strategic alliances, particularly the one with Lucent, had a material impact on the mere fact of the company's sale.

Analysis and Prologue

Confirmation that the optical networking industry had become a hot field in the capital market had already been given when Cisco bought Cerent, Chromatis' competitor, in a $7 billion stock transaction in 1998. Without any comparable self-developed technology, it was only a matter of time before Lucent, one of Cisco's most prominent competitors, would acquire a similar company. The area in which Chromatis operated appeared to be even hotter when Cisco announced that orders for Cerent's product, which integrates data flow on fiber optic networks, had risen to approximately $2 billion per year.

As it appeared when the acquisition was announced, Chromatis' price tag resulted not only from a comparison with the sale of Cerent to Cisco, but also from Lucent's relative disadvantage in the metropolitan communications market in which Chromatis operated. Chromatis offered Lucent almost a complete solution for an existing and emerging need in the metropolitan communications market, a solution with which Lucent was familiar from a relatively early stage due to its investment in Chromatis through its venture capital fund. In other words, although Chromatis had an independent market (as its beta trials with telecom companies had proven) which enabled it to keep going as an independent company, Lucent always stood in the background as a potential buyer. Thus, the need to become acquainted with one another, a stage which is necessary in any merger negotiations, was obviated. From the perspective of real options, the introduction of Lucent's venture capital fund to the company increased the likelihood that Lucent would acquire the company (as indeed was the case). In other words, introducing Lucent as an investor was tantamount to buying a partial put option. However, Chromatis paid no small premium for this option—stemming from the fact that Lucent's competitors attributed a lower probability to their possibility of buying Chromatis. As discussed in the chapter on valuation, any decision on the creation of a binding and long-term relationship with a leading company in the field can entail a cost in the form of a reduced likelihood of relationships with competing companies.

Nevertheless, it is important to note that despite its relationship with Lucent, the company also attracted the interest of other companies that considered buying it, such as the communications equipment company Sycamore.

As was apparent all along, a major key to Chromatis' success was recruiting leaders in every field. The two entrepreneurs understood that the product they were planning was needed in the market, understood how important it was to raise capital quickly, and how essential the money was, mainly to recruit the best people in the market in each field. The recruitment of such people, along with their superb product, enabled the company to demand and receive investments with the relatively high valuation of $100 million.

Lucent, on its part, had performed 33 acquisitions in the four years preceding its acquisition of Chromatis as part of its strategy of expanding into markets with faster growth rates than its traditional core business, and to complement lines of products it had had no time to develop independently in its laboratories. Starting from the point in which it entered the company as an investor, Lucent's investment in Chromatis was clearly of interest to it for strategic reasons, namely, reinvigorating its leading position in the optical networking market. Chromatis was addressing the metropolitan networking market, which was particularly attractive to Lucent since this market lacked a dominant player such as Nortel was in the long haul networking market.

How can such a high acquisition price be explained when the annual value of the equipment market targeted by Chromatis was $2 billion (even when one takes into account projected sales of around $8 billion in 2004)? The explanation lies in the valuation of companies by strategic investors: From Lucent's point of view, sales in Chromatis' target market were expected to encourage sales of other equipment sold by the company. In addition, until that time, Lucent still depended on obtaining large contracts with, among other companies, AT&T, from which it was spun off. Therefore, expanding its spectrum of products in order to appeal also to smaller clients could help Lucent in broadening its product offering and the scopes of its contracts. In the acquisition of Chromatis, as well as in acquisitions in similar markets in which there are few major suppliers, the explanation for the price lies more in the acquirer's strategic considerations than in the valuation of the target as an independent company. In addition, in stock transactions both the target and the acquirer take into account other considerations that could affect the value of the deal. For instance, the value of the acquirer's stock, as well as the ability to sell the stock received in the transaction, could affect the value of the deal. A cash transaction is not equivalent to a stock transaction with the same announced value, as the plummeting of Lucent's stock price in the coming year indicates.

In August 2001, Lucent had announced that it is shutting down the Chromatis division (originating from the acquisition of Chromatis). The potential clients for the products developed by Chromatis, the Competitive Local Exchange Carriers (CLECs), were themselves facing a dramatic reduction in sales with some of them collapsing into bankruptcy, and hence almost stopped acquiring new equipment. Lucent itself was facing a meltdown in most of its businesses, and was trying to reduce its own "burn-rate." As part of its restructuring, which included the layoffs of over 50,000 employees and refocusing on existing products, Lucent gave up on Chromatis.

The closing of Chromatis only one year following its acquisition for $5 billion signifies the dramatic shakedown in the technology area in general, and the communication field in particular. This shakedown, which started in the later part of 2000, and which people felt was associated primarily with the "Internet bubble," rapidly spread to most areas in technology. Again it was shown that the timing of investments, as well as of venture development and of exiting it, is by no means less important in determining the prospects of a venture, its entrepreneurs and its investors, than the actual strategy of the company, which includes an optimized composition of employees, technology, cost structure, "sweet spots" in target markets, innovative pricing models, and astute strategic alliances.

15

Conducting the M&A Transaction

CHAPTER OVERVIEW

Assuming that the company chooses the option of a merger or a sale, there are several techniques for realizing this goal. The discussion will focus on the techniques which are more relevant to startups: first and foremost, mergers, followed by asset sales. This classification will be followed by an in-depth discussion of how to consummate the transactions with the chosen technique. This chapter deals with the practical aspects of mergers and acquisitions, beginning with structuring the acquisition strategy through choosing the type of the transaction and the consideration, and ending with the process of its business implementation.

Mergers

Mergers are the most common form of restructuring undertaken by successful startups. A merger is by nature a statutory process, and hence its structure is prescribed by the corporate laws of the merging companies' state of incorporation.

Classic Mergers

In the classic merger, the target is incorporated into the acquirer, which is also deemed as a merging company, in a transaction which takes place at the corporate level. The consent of both companies' shareholders is usually required. The main disadvantages of classic mergers are the need for the acquirer's shareholders' approval for the transaction (which is troublesome when a large company is taking in a small company) and the legal risk involved in the acquirer's assuming all of the target's liabilities with all of the uncertainties that this entails. See Figure 15–1.

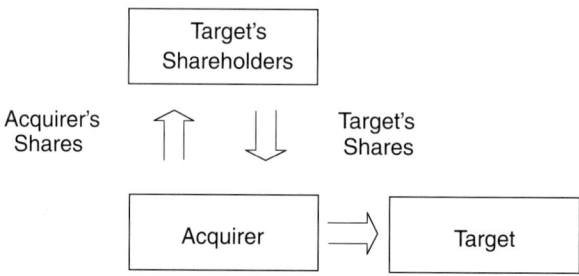

Figure 15-1 Classic Merger

Triangular Mergers

Under triangular mergers, a parent company uses a (typically specially formed) subsidiary as the acquirer. In this type of merger, only the consent of the target's shareholders is usually required. Using the triangular merger technique overcomes the two main disadvantages of classic mergers: obtaining the consent of the acquirer's shareholders and the legal uncertainty. The level of certainty rises because a "legal corporate veil" is extended between the acquirer (with its deep pockets) and the target's liabilities. See Figure 15–2.

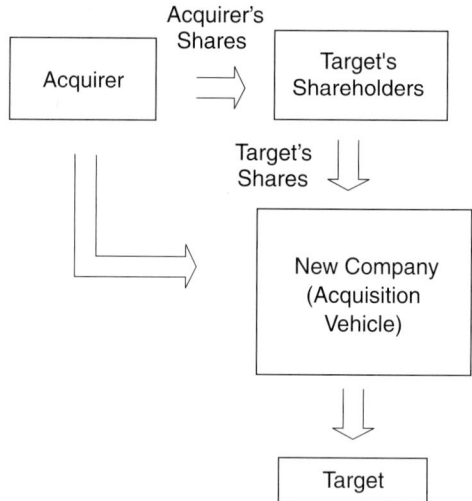

Figure 15-2 Triangular Merger

A version of the triangular merger is the "Reverse Triangular Merger" in which the target absorbs a subsidiary of the parent company. This type of merger enables the target's identity to be preserved following the merger, which is sometimes important for legal considerations (for instance, when the target has non-assignable intellectual property rights) or for marketing purposes (when the target has a known brand).

The most common mergers are triangular mergers since, as mentioned above, these transactions often significantly facilitate the process of the acquirer's approval of the transaction and create a "wall" between the acquirer and the target's liabilities. However, it is usually difficult to obtain the capital gain tax authorities' approval to defer the captial gain tax imposed on the transaction, unless the deal is made in voting stock, in which case the triangular merger may be recognized as a tax-free transaction.

From the taxation point of view, the target's tax basis in the assets remains intact even if the assets are revaluated for accounting purposes. In other cases, if the transaction is not treated as tax-exempt, the companies tend to revaluate the assets for tax purposes (and enjoy higher depreciation rates in the following periods). In such a case, the seller pays tax on the increase in the value of the assets until the transaction.

Sale and Acquisition of Assets

An alternative method available to acquirers who are interested mainly in the assets of a company (as opposed to full control of the company), is purchasing all or part of the company's assets. A transaction in which all of a company's assets are purchased is similar to a merger in that the parties in both types of transactions are the companies themselves, rather than the shareholders, and the terms are agreed upon in negotiations between the managements of the companies. There are certain main differences with mergers, which are summarized below:

- **Preservation of legal entity**—As opposed to mergers, when a company sells all of its assets to an acquirer, its legal existence is not prejudiced. After selling its assets, the selling company may choose whether to keep going or dissolve voluntarily, as is usually the case.
- **Selective transfer of assets**—In the case of asset acquisition, only the assets and liabilities which are explicitly included in the contract underlying the transaction are transferred to the acquirer. Unlike a merger, the acquirer does not step into the seller's legal shoes in its relations with third parties.
- **The proceeds remain in the company**—Asset purchases operate to transfer the ownership of the seller's assets, whereas a merger transfers ownership of its shares. In mergers, the consideration is paid directly to the shareholders; in asset purchases, the consideration is paid to the selling company, which may dissolve and pass the consideration on to the shareholders.
- **Inapplicability of the securities law**—Securities laws do not apply to an asset purchase transaction directly, whereas a merger transaction may be subject to such statutory regulation.
- **No direct effect on management**—Since an asset purchase does not include a transfer of the ownership of the company's shares, the transaction has no bearing on the control of the selling company and therefore, as

opposed to mergers, has no direct effect on the status of the seller's managers. In practice, however, if the company is voided of all its main assets, the existing management loses its *raison d'être*.

M&A Strategy

Acquirer's M&A Strategy

The company's management must determine its acquisition strategy, which needs to be part of the broader strategy discussions of the company. Such strategy typically considers the following topics, each one of them discussed in previous chapters of this book, or in this chapter: horizontal (purchasing companies operating in the same industry) versus vertical (purchasing companies with an intimate supplier-buyer relationship) acquisitions; acquisitions for the purpose of cooperating in production or management procedures versus acquisitions which do not utilize joint resources; and acquisitions of competitors versus cooperation with competitors.

Once the acquisition strategy is developed, the company builds a mechanism for screening acquisition or merger candidates. Such a mechanism may be based on a continuous examination of potential companies or, alternatively, on an examination of candidates which approach the company. Either way, management must understand the advantages and disadvantages of each company considered for an acquisition or a merger. For example, it must assess, as objectively as possible, what human and economic resources are available to the target, and its situation in areas such as business development, marketing, production, research, and finance.

Another area which management or the team responsible for acquisitions must examine is the company's organizational culture, in order to assess whether the candidate is suitable to their company from the organizational perspective. While many mergers and acquisitions are promising where cost-savings and operating synergies are concerned, lack of human compatibility between the acquirer and the target, and in particular lack of strategic fit between the companies' corporate culture is the major driver of M&As failure. Sadly though, an in-depth analysis of these issues is all too often neglected in negotiations.

Social compatibility between companies refers to the aggregate values and beliefs held by the companies' managers and employees as expressed in the daily activities of the employees and in the companies' strategic activities. For instance, following many mergers, it is found that the sales tactics of the companies' employees are incompatible, so that a merging of marketing forces will create a behavioral incongruity among the sales personnel, which naturally constitute one of the company's showcases vis-à-vis potential customers. Companies which have established a long-standing M&A reputation for themselves, such as Cisco, are known for the great importance which they attach to such managerial-cultural compatibility, so their M&A personnel emphasize this issue in all negotiations.

Finally, as mentioned in previous sections, in any examination of an acquisition, the acquirer must consider both the direct cost of the acquisition (the price paid) and its indirect cost (the effect on the competition in the market) and compare it to the cost of in-house development while taking into account the risk that a competitor will acquire the company in question. The direct acquisition cost is often high, but in-house development could cost time, resources, and the loss of a possible competitive edge.

Target's M&A Strategy

Similarly to the acquirer's M&A strategizing, if a company prefers to have another company buy it, it may choose to actively seek out an acquirer, or opt for cooperative alliances which could lead to an acquisition as discussed in previous chapters of this book. The choice between a sale strategy and continuing the independent development of the company naturally depends on the type of the company, its stage of development, the nature of its investors, and the characteristics of its entrepreneurs. The existence of potential buyers in the market must be addressed as early as possible in the company's initial business planning, as mentioned in the section in Chapter 3 on market analysis and strategic planning, since the company may choose different development paths based on such potential buyers. For example, the company may choose to emphasize efforts in R&D rather than in business development and/or sales and marketing, as those could be better handled by the acquirer. Finally, when making and implementing a sale decision, it is customary to use advisors who are experts on this topic, as specified in the next section.

The Consideration in Mergers and Acquisitions

Typical Forms of Payment

There are several typical forms of payments (a combination of several such forms is also possible) for mergers and acquisitions, which may be divided into several categories, following the classifications discussed previously in this book:

- **Cash for shares**—The acquirer pays the target's shareholders cash for their holdings.
- **Cash for assets**—The acquirer buys all of the target's assets in cash.
- **Stock for stock**—The acquirer issues its shares directly to the target's shareholders, who, in return, transfer their shares in the target to the acquirer.
- **Stock for assets**—The acquirer issues its shares to the target in consideration for the target's assets.

In recent years, a dramatic change has occurred in the customary form of payment in M&A transactions. For instance, whereas in the late 1980s more than 50% of deals above $100 million were made in cash only, this percentage had dropped to under 20% by the late 1990s. It is also possible that this fact resulted from the high stock prices, which in practice enabled large companies to use a "cheap" cash-equivalent (the target stock) to realize the acquisition.

Determining the Price

As discussed in Chapter 9 in the section on value to investors or strategic buyers, the price paid for the acquisition takes the following factors into account: the company's valuation as an independent unit, the target's effect on the acquirer's results of operations, and, ultimately, the cost in the alternative scenario in which a competitor of the acquirer buys the company. The maximum price which the buyer will be prepared to pay is the difference between the acquirer's value in the projected scenario if no acquisition (including the impact of an acquisition of the target by one of the competitors) is made, and the value which incorporates all of the synergies with respect to future cash flows if the acquisition is consummated. If this difference is higher than the company's value to the seller (in the realistic scenario in the case of an acquisition by another entity or, alternatively, in a scenario of continued independent operations), then there is a range of values in which the parties to the deal can find common ground.

The acquisition of a company by another company is an investment which is naturally associated with uncertainty. The basic principle is the same as in any business decision: Buy another company if the totality of the actions associated with it will generate a positive net present value to the company. However, valuating the advisability of the investment is more complex in the case of an acquisition than in other types of investments, since determining the acquisition value calls for an estimate of many parameters in different fields. Following are several of the main problematic parameters in such an estimate that are applicable to the acquisitions of privately held firms:

- **The difficulty in assessing strategic advantages**—The advantages of the acquisition may be strategic, and the value of the acquisition with respect to its compatibility with the company's strategy or managerial culture is difficult to quantify financially.
- **Legal and accounting uncertainty**—The acquisition of companies involves complex tax, legal, and accounting aspects, each of which has an impact on the worthiness of the acquisition. For instance, the approval of the transaction by the antitrust authorities or the conditions which such authorities may place on the consummation of the deal are clouded by uncertainties.
- **The difficulties in assessing added value**—Acquisition-analysis often focuses on the total value of the companies involved after the acquisition. However, the acquisition may change the relative weight of the companies in the totality of the added value created.

In many cases, a portion of the price of the deal is determined as a function of future performance. This component is common when the target's entrepreneurs continue to work in the company for some time. Alternatively, it is sometimes agreed that the final price will be determined after uncertainties, which may be beyond the seller's control (such as the competitive situation of the target market), are resolved. On the other hand, conditioning the price of the transaction on certain events makes it easier for the buyer to pay a higher expected price.

Additional payment arrangements may be formulated in stock transactions to mitigate the risk entailed by a change in the value of the acquirer's stock.

The Advantages of Stock-based Transactions

In a substantial part of the acquisitions made in recent years, particularly in the technology area, the payment included a large stock component. The main reasons for this are:

- **Cheap currency**—Payment in stock makes possible deals which would not have occurred under other circumstances since the buyer would have been unable to pay the price from its own financial resources. Cash financing is expensive and requires acquirers to deplete cash reserves, or borrow large amounts of money, and thereby change their capital structure or raise capital from the public. Payment in stock enables companies to use a readily available currency, which might also be at high valuation.

    Indeed, such deals are more common in bull markets. In practice, except for the incentive and taxation aspects of exchanges of stock, stock transactions are similar to the issuance of shares by the buyer and their acquisition by the target. In view of the fact that it is not always possible to issue shares in the stock exchange, one of the arguments voiced is that during times of prosperity in the capital markets, companies tend to buy other companies in consideration for a payment which includes larger stock components than at other times, since any such acquisition also effectively includes a quasi-sale of shares to the target's shareholders.

- **Tax advantages**—Economically speaking, the questions which arise in a merger are: Are the target's shareholders, who sell their shares, liable for tax on their profits? When is such tax due? And are there grounds for the payment of capital gains tax by the company on the sale of assets for a price higher than their book value?

    Generally speaking, under U.S. law, a transaction may be regarded as a reorganization and may be recognized as tax-exempt, i.e., a transaction which defers the tax liability of the shareholders of the target—until the date of actual liquidation of the received shares. The U.S. tax treatment is founded upon the concept that shareholders should not be taxed before they realize their profits. Consequently, according to Section 368(a) of the U.S. Internal Revenue Code of 1986, under certain conditions (which are met only in stock transactions), the shareholder is not taxed until actual liquidation. The tax basis for capital gains determination remains as it was, but the payment of the tax is made in accordance with only those components of the consideration which are paid in cash or by debt.

The Risks in Stock-based Transactions

When a transaction is made in the form of stock for stock, the selling party is not fully separated from its company, since the sellers effectively invest the sale proceeds in the acquirer over which they will not necessarily have control. In practice, when a transaction is made in stock, the risk it entails is divided between the seller and the buyer since both parties will bear the consequences of an unfavorable market reaction if the transaction does not yield the anticipated returns. The characteristic risks of stock transactions include:

- **A change in the acquirer's stock price**—Before they make the move in a stock transaction, both parties to the merger or the acquisition need to examine what effect a failure of the merger would have on the value of the parties' holdings. In other words, they need to examine what the value of the parties' holdings might be if the shares of the acquirer or of the surviving entity/absorbing company plummet after the acquisition. A benchmark for measuring the risk involved in an acquisition is to divide the premium paid (in either cash or stock) above the market price, if the company is publicly held, or above its value in its last investment round, if the company is private, by the acquirer's market value. This can serve as an indication, even if somewhat simplistic, of the measure of risk which the acquirer is prepared to assume, since the premium is paid for the added value expected to be received in the future in the form of residual income, as a result of the combination between the two companies. The higher the benchmark, the higher is the risk entailed by the acquisition to the acquirer, since the required future operating return is higher.

    Sometimes the parties agree that the price to be paid will be stated as a sum rather than a number of shares. In transactions of this type, the seller is protected against any decline in the value of the acquirer's shares, but it may, on the other hand, be harmed if the market rises. A customary method of handling the problem of a change in the market value of the acquirer's shares is to formulate a system of put and call options for different exercise prices. These mechanisms are nicknamed "collars." Collars guarantee, in effect, that if the price of the share drops below a certain level, the sellers will be compensated in the form of additional shares, and if the share price rises above a certain level, the number of shares which the sellers will receive will be reduced.

    On the buyers' side, it is important to understand that stock transactions are not risk-free. Even if the acquirer's managers feel that their company's stock is "over-valued" and that a stock transaction is therefore preferable, they are not necessarily selling their shares at a high price, since the selling company will demand a higher price in view of the fact that the price of the asset with which it is bought is unrealistic. One of the reasons for negative market reactions to announcements of acquisitions in stock is that the premium paid often symbolizes the seller's lack of faith in the acquirer's market valuation. Given that the seller is assumed to conduct a proper valuation of the acquirer, investors infer that the acquirer's stock is indeed over-valued.

When a company is faced with several possibilities of being acquired, it must examine the economic value of the companies proposing to buy it in order to derive the real economic value proposed by each candidate. In many cases, a company whose shares are low at that time might be preferable to a company offering a higher price but is itself traded at an unrealistically high value.

- **Departure of employees**—A stock transaction can have a material effect on the issue of employee compensation for several reasons. First, unvested stock options in the seller held by the employees are converted into shares of the acquirer, thus possibly tying the employees to a company for which they did not choose to work. In many cases, the employees demand in the negotiations that all of their options vest, so that they will be able to sell them immediately and leave the company (for example, if the new managerial culture is not to their liking). In addition, a drop in price due to a possible market disappointment from the acquisition could also have very significant effects on the acquirer's employees. It is also common to find nowadays clauses in top employees' contracts which determine accelerated stock vesting in the case of an acquisition.

The Process

When a company is considering a sale, it often relies on its investors, regular consultants, investment bankers, or other strategic advisors who are hired to examine the best route for the company's continued development. If a decision is made to follow a sale route, such advisors assist in finding and negotiating with potential buyers. Existing business partners are often possible acquirers themselves or can be intermediaries for finding potential buyers. The pace of the process is affected by the financial condition of the company seeking an acquirer.

Companies rarely declare initially that they aim to be acquired, and the negotiations often begin as various forms of cooperation, such as distribution and marketing agreements, or the granting of licenses to use a technology.

As mentioned above, companies often choose to rely on external advisors to examine sale options. The choice of the intermediary has a dramatic impact on the manner in which the solicitation is depicted in the eyes of target companies. Historically, for instance, making contact through an investment bank was usually interpreted by target companies as a solicitation of an investment, whereas an approach through strategy consultants was usually interpreted as a solicitation of business-development cooperation. However, as combinations of strategic investments and business contracts became increasingly common, the boundaries between them became obscure. Reputable intermediaries provide high added value to the parties to the transaction by assisting in the examination of the various routes for cooperation and recommending the better ones among them.

If the chosen path is to examine possibilities of a sale to or merger with business partners, then the negotiations for the business cooperation turn into a process of studying the other party. After the required confidentiality agreements are signed, the companies exchange financial information and consider the worthwhileness of the transaction. If the parties reach an understanding, the companies usually sign a letter of intent (LOI) which summarizes the principles of the proposed transaction. Although the price is an important component of this document, other important parameters are the payment method (stock, cash, or a combination of the two) and restrictions after the sale (such as the period in which the shares will be locked-up).

At this stage the due diligence process begins in which the attorneys, CPAs, and bankers play an active part. It is important to state that even at this stage, the chances of closing the deal are still unclear and about one half of all transactions are never consummated. This is one of the reasons that many agreements stipulate conditions for the termination of the negotiations and the implications of such termination. For instance, agreements often stipulate an amount which the company interested in the purchase will pay if the negotiations run aground. Obviously, various amounts may be paid in different scenarios. If the process ends well, the final agreement is signed.

Within the merger process, the target and the surviving entity prepare operating plans for the execution of the merger. These plans determine timetables and operating projections for the merger process, and typically correspond to the projections made by the parties in the process of determining the price to be paid in the transaction.

Within the acts taken after the merger or the acquisition, issues such as the replacement of officers, the division of authorities between duplicative officers whose double positions are not eliminated, or the choice of employees who will be terminated, should be handled very cautiously, in order not to undermine the internal morale of the employees of both companies. Such tender treatment is particularly crucial in companies which are based on human capital more than anything else, and is often more important than any cost-savings which the merger may generate.

Tender Offers

A tender offer is a public offer designed to convince the target's shareholders to sell their shares to the acquirer at a predetermined price and within a given time frame, subject to various conditions specified in the offer. The offer achieves its goals if the shareholders who accept it represent a sufficiently high ownership percentage to grant the acquirer control of the target. Effective control does not always require a 50% holding. On the other hand, in order to be able to coerce the minority into selling its shares in order to gain full control, it is necessary to hold 90% of the shares after the tender offer. Consummating a tender offer, as opposed to consummating a merger, does not entail the abolition of the legal existence of the company whose shares are being sold.

A tender offer is distinguishable from a merger and an acquisition of assets in that it does not require the approval of the target's organs; it is not based on negotiations between the managements of the two companies. That is, a tender offer can therefore be hostile to the interests of the target's management. On the other hand, the management's opposition to the tender offer can compromise the success of the acquisition of control.

The cordial nature of mergers enables the acquirer to execute the deal with a higher degree of certainty not only with regard to its consummation, but also with regard to its details. An acquirer which follows the path of a merger usually enjoys access to the target's internal reports, and the determination of the price is made in a more informed manner.

A tender offer entails the risk that even if it succeeds, the acquirer will nevertheless have to manage the company it controls while taking the minority shareholders into consideration, which can result in public and legal exposure through claims by a troublemaking minority.

In a merger, which is performed through negotiations between the managements, the acquisition initiative can be kept secret from the public for a long period of time, thus reducing the possibility of the development of a bid contest for the shares by the submission of competing tender offers.

There are two reasons why an acquirer might choose to pursue a tender offer: first, when the seller's management disagrees or is expected to disagree with the terms of the merger; second, when the acquirer estimates that the goals guiding it would be better achieved by acquiring effective control of the company, even if such control is not full.

Indeed, the majority of tender offers end with significantly less than 100% of the target's shareholders selling their shares. In many cases, the next stage is a merger between the target and the acquirer, which puts pressure on shareholders to sell their shares. If more than 90% of the target's shares are held by the acquirer, the company does not need the target's shareholders' approval for the merger. However, the acquirer still needs to take into account any domestic laws pertaining to the fair treatment of minority shareholders.

In the United States, tender offers are subject to an intricate set of legal rules promulgated under the Williams Act, which is part of the Securities Exchange Act of 1934. Tender offers are almost always applicable only to traded companies and have no practical application with regard to private companies (due to the many restrictions imposed on share transfers in private companies), and therefore this book does not discuss the numerous legal rules governing tender offers.

16
Additional Legal Aspects

Legal Rules Governing Mergers and Acquisitions

Applicable Corporate Laws

Corporate law in the United States—There is no single corporate law in the United States, since every state has its own domestic corporation law. The most relevant corporate law is in Delaware. For example, all mergers and acquisitions require the approval of the board of directors, but not of the general meeting, if less than 20% of the corporation's shares is offered as the consideration in the merger. This enables large companies to buy small companies without the need to go through the red tape of a shareholder approval process. Obviously, the shareholders of the target (the startup) are required to give their approval, according to both Delaware corporation law and, typically, the terms stipulated in the investment agreement.

The approval of the boards of directors of the companies has to include, among other things, a specification of the terms of the merger and a decision on which entity will survive the merger. If a shareholders' meeting is required, then it is the one which decides to approve the merger. Once the required approvals are obtained, a notice is filed by the surviving entity with the Delaware Secretary of State. After the notice, the merging company ceases to exist and its shareholders are allotted shares in the surviving entity. All of the companies' assets and liabilities become the property of the surviving entity.

Applicable Securities Rules

Securities rules are generally applicable to traded companies which are subject to reporting requirements pursuant to the Securities Law. Although the acquirer is subject to securities rules, these rules are not applicable when the offering is exempt from registration under the Securities Act of 1933 (see the section discussing legal restrictions on raising private equity). Therefore, the discussion of such rules in this book has been limited.

For transactions that are not exempt, a registration with the SEC is required in the event that such transactions include modifications, reorganizations, or transfers of control in a company, in cases in which the law in the seller's state of incorporation requires the consent of the seller's shareholders for the consummation of the transaction. Deals falling under this rule include, among others, reclassifications of securities, mergers, and asset sales.

Rule 145 also requires the delivery of a registration statement on a Form S-4, which is limited in scope compared to the Form S-1 (that is required in the case of ordinary public offerings of shares). The registration statement must be submitted to all of the company's registered security holders who are entitled to vote on the consummation of the transaction. Regulation M-A, which became effective in January 2000, regulates all the details pertaining to the consummation of various merger deals and determines the manner and scope of the disclosure required in such transactions.

Stock exchange rules—Both NASDAQ and the NYSE require the approval of the acquirer's shareholders only if it is issuing more than 20% of its shares as the consideration in the merger. Any material transaction must be reported immediately to the stock exchanges and the acquirer, if it is a traded company, also makes a press release with all the details of the transaction.

Merger or Acquisition Agreements

Purchase agreements have become rather standard over the years, and although lengthy negotiations on the terms of the agreement are still usually conducted, every U.S. law firm has a standard "boilerplate" agreement which is the starting point for the agreement. Obviously, the terms of the agreement, as well as the creativity of the economic structure of the transaction, vary from one deal to another, but in principle, each agreement usually contains the following provisions.

A Description of the Transaction

The first part of the agreement contains a general description of the transaction, including the parties and the nature of the deal (merger or asset purchase), as well as the technical details of the timing and manner of closing (place and time).

Price and Terms of Payment

When the deal is made in cash, this clause is very simple. However, when the consideration takes the form of shares, mechanisms have to be fixed for possible changes in the stock price between the date of signing and the date of closing as described in the previous chapter. There are also agreements in which the final price depends on the performance of the acquired business over time, and in such cases this provision contains the payment formulas in accordance with the terms, as well as the control mechanisms to be used in order to check whether such terms had been fulfilled.

Representations and Warranties

Naturally, most of the reps and warranties are made by the target and not by the acquirer. However, the acquirer's representations with regard to its financial stability and abilities are particularly important in a stock deal, since the medium of payment is the acquirer's shares. The target warrants a range of facts, including the veracity of its financial statements, the absence of liabilities not reflected in the financial statements, the lack of undisclosed legal claims or threatened legal action and ownership of and rights to material assets. The purpose of this section is to provide the most accurate description possible of the object of sale, namely, the company or the assets.

Covenants and Conditions to Closing

Since there is a time gap between the dates of signing and of closing of the deal due to the need to obtain shareholder approvals, complete the due diligence process, obtain approvals from the antitrust authorities, and reach an agreement with the tax authorities with respect to the amount of tax to be imposed, a contractual solution is required to bridge this time gap. The solution is twofold: undertakings with respect to the target's activity during the time between signing and closing, and other conditions which need to be fulfilled at the time of actual closing. The common undertakings assumed by the target with respect to the interim period are that it must conduct its affairs in the usual course of business, avoid irregular expenses, etc. The additional conditions include the accuracy of the reps and warranties at the time of closing, receipt of all necessary statutory approvals by such time, and the absence of any material adverse change in the target's condition. The buyer makes various undertakings pertaining to the employment of managers and employees, the conversion of options in the target into options in the acquirer, and the indemnification of directors. This part of the purchase agreement also addresses issues which are significant after the closing. Since in mergers the target ceases to exist, most of the undertakings revolve around the relationship between the target's entrepreneurs and managers and the acquirer.

Antitrust Issues

In some cases, the merger agreement must be approved by the antitrust authorities. This section reviews the basic rules for the receipt of such approvals.

Following are the main antitrust arrangements in the United States:

- **The Clayton Act** authorizes the FTC (Federal Trade Commission) to bar or qualify share or asset purchase agreements which materially reduce competition or give rise to the fear that a monopoly will be created.
- **Section 1 of the Sherman Act** prohibits any contract, combination, or conspiracy in restraint of trade or commerce which may reduce competition.
- **Section 2 of the Sherman Act** prohibits attempts to abuse or become a monopoly by, among other things, acquiring competitors.
- **The Hart-Scott-Rodino Act** imposes a reporting duty to the U.S. Department of Justice and to the FTC and a waiting period of 30 days in any acquisition of 15% or more of the voting shares or assets of a target with sales or assets exceeding $100 million. The waiting period is designed to enable the authorities to examine the effect which the merger or the acquisition will have on the competition in the relevant fields. The parties to the merger are required to notify the appropriate authorities of the intention of the transaction and to provide full economic disclosure of the proposed transaction. The government may object to the merger only during the first 30 days following the notice, unless it asks for additional information. The waiting period is reduced to 15 days in cash tender offers.

The authorities in charge of antitrust matters in the United States and Europe have been operating more actively in recent years, and a considerable part of their investigations revolve around mergers. However, examining the impact on competition is problematic. Let us assume, in the most simplistic manner, an industry in which one company controls around 40% of the market and none of whose competitors is profitable. Due to economies of scale in that industry, the dominant company wants to merge with one of its competitors. The impact of the merger will obviously reduce competition in the market. Should this plan, which is based on economic considerations other than monopolistic profits, be thwarted? Would it be better if the small companies went bankrupt?

In order to obtain approval for a transaction, the legislator requires, among other things, proof that the assets of the target will indeed exit the market without the merger and that a merger is preferable to an acquisition by other entities, even though the concentration index (see below) indicates a possible rise in market concentration.

Obviously, the element of reduction in competition is usually weighed together with other considerations which are regarded as legitimate by the legislators, and the relevant authorities take into account all of these parameters when examining deals that are brought before them.

The U.S. Department of Justice and the FTC publish detailed regulations which present various scenarios and the anticipated response of the competent authorities to different types of merger and acquisition proposals. For instance, the departments made a joint publication of regulations pertaining to horizontal mergers, which in practice concern M&A activities among competitors. The basic test is, as mentioned above, whether such a merger would create or enable a monopoly in the supply or demand in the market in question.

The directives break the analysis down into five main stages. The first stage defines the markets affected by the merger, such as the on-line ticket market only, or the entire ticket market. The second stage examines the degree of the merger's impact on the concentration in the market. One of the main tools for measuring market concentration, which U.S. authorities use as a preliminary test of concentration in horizontal mergers, is the HHI (Herfindahl-Hirschman) Index. In this simple test, the squared values of the market percentages held by each competitor in the market are added together, and a comparison is made between the values received before and after the merger between the companies.

Obviously, every merger increases the market concentration to a certain degree, which is also expressed in the HHI factor (since, in the case of positive numbers, the square of a sum of numbers is always greater than the sum of the squares of the same numbers). The real test, however, is the degree of change as a result of the merger. If the index changes dramatically, the authorities will examine whether the competition in the market is expected to actually change.

If the answer to this last question is affirmative, the authorities move on to the third stage in the analysis, examine the market reactions to the potential entry of new competitors into the market due to the merger, and assess the effect of such changes on the competition in the market. If no such changes are projected, the authorities examine, in the fourth stage of the analysis, whether the merger is justified for reasons of streamlining production and marketing processes and cost-saving, and whether a merger is the optimal method for achieving such benefits under the given market circumstances. Finally, in the fifth stage of the analysis, the authorities examine the impact of a cancellation of the merger on the parties to the merger. Their approach will clearly be different if, for example, one of the parties would go bankrupt without the transaction than if both companies are profitable.

Many argue that the market-share test, which is a central component in the decisions of antitrust supervisory entities, is no longer suitable for an examination of the absence of competition in the current dynamic business world. For instance, the fact that a company controls the computer market in a certain year is not a reliable test for the future, and acquiring its young competitors may still be its only way of staying in the game altogether for the long run.

Furthermore, an increasingly voiced argument is that the tests for market concentration should be conducted in global, rather than domestic, terms. The argument is that even if a company controls a considerable share of its domestic market, it might be still struggling in the global market and that it should be allowed to conduct acquisitions which would help it to strengthen its position in the global market.

Vertical mergers are usually not exposed to the same degree of scrutiny as are horizontal mergers. In addition, conglomerate mergers are usually not subjected to close scrutiny unless the following conditions are fulfilled: The industry in which the target operates is characterized by a high HHI factor (at least 1,800 prior to the transaction), the merger will reduce the likelihood of competitors entering the market (for example, since the target will now have the support of a larger company), and the target's market share is greater than 5%.

Fairness Opinions

Boards of directors are required to ensure that the offer is fair to the company's shareholders. When the target is traded in the United States, Regulation 13e-3 requires the board of directors to disclose the details of the transaction including the share price, the historical trade prices of the share, and the company's value as an independent company and in liquidation; to file an independent opinion of the fairness of the transaction or its value (if such an opinion was solicited); and to disclose any other proposals which were made to the company. The opinion is prepared from the point of view of a sale of control of the company, i.e., the valuation used for the opinion is based on the assumption that control of the company is transferred. This viewpoint is important when the minority shareholders could be prejudiced by the transaction. The opinion should also take into account the likelihood that alternative offers will be made to the company by other investors, i.e., a valuation in the case of other strategic investors and the likelihood that such offers will materialize.

The fairness opinion is an important tool in the hands of boards of directors of companies when approving a deal or recommending its approval to shareholders. Such an opinion is also required under the case law of many states (including Delaware) within the duty of care imposed on the target's board of directors.

The fairness opinion submitted to the company's board of directors examines the fairness of the terms of the transaction to the company's shareholders. Consequently, the opinion compares the terms of the deal to the fair value of the company soliciting the opinion. In most cases requiring the shareholders' approval, separate opinions are prepared for both parties to the transaction.

The fairness opinion also includes a valuation which relies on methods such as those reviewed in Chapter 9. In most cases, several alternative methods of valuation are used and compared. However, it is important to note that the fact that the shareholders receive a value higher than the company's fair market value does not necessarily render the offer fair to them. A possible source of unfairness is, for example, when the shareholders receive a lower price than that received by other shareholders, such as the company's managers, for their shares.

Despite the vast professionalism of reputable entities which provide advisory services for transactions (for example, investment bankers), and despite the separation of authorities between the various departments of such advisory entities, an issue of conflict of interests may arise in some cases, and the opinion may be solicited from independent outside advisers.

17

Other Restructuring

Other Types of Restructuring: Spin-offs, Split-offs, Carve-outs, and Letter Stocks

In many cases, mergers and acquisitions are performed with business units which are carved out of existing companies. In some cases, these are companies which were established as separate units within existing and well-established companies, and which are raising money in the private or public markets to continue their operations. In other cases, shares in business units within a company are distributed to the company's shareholders (spin-off). This section briefly reviews the customary spin-off options, starting from spin-offs of subsidiaries through the raising of capital for subsidiary units and ending in the creation of shares whose performance is linked to the performance of units within the company. These mechanisms are commonly used in situations where the restructured business units could be valued in the spin-offs and split-offs.

The U.S. Internal Revenue Code enables companies to distribute to their shareholders assets or shares in a subsidiary (with tax exemption) by using the spin-off and split-off mechanisms. In recent years, transactions of this type usually preceded investment rounds by the subsidiary.

Under the spin-off mechanism, the company distributes to its shareholders shares in the subsidiary in proportion to their holdings in the stock market at high valuations. Sometimes these situations can yield absurd situations. For example, when 3Com listed its Palm unit, the value of its holdings in the Palm unit exceeded its entire value. In fact, this is a dividend in kind. Under the split-off mechanism, some of the company's shareholders exchange shares in the company with shares in the subsidiary. In most cases, only some of the shareholders perform this act and not necessarily proportionately to their holdings in the company.

For a company to be able to make transactions of the said types, it must meet the following conditions: The company must have conducted business for at least five years, it cannot have been acquired in the course of the five years preceding the transaction, at least 80% of the subsidiary's shares have to be transferred to the company's shareholders, and the company must prove that the act is not motivated mainly by tax considerations, but rather by other economic considerations.

The company distributing the shares does not receive any cash as a result of the distribution and thus reduces its asset base and its ability to generate cash from the distributed assets. In many cases, following careful tax planning, when parts of the company are about to be acquired, the company's remaining assets might be transferred to a new subsidiary whose shares are distributed among the shareholders, and the parent company can conduct the sale or merger deal with a structure that is optimized to these transactions.

Various studies document higher returns on the shares of companies which perform a spin-off, in which the spun-off company is itself listed for trade. It has also been found that companies which undergo the process increase their probability of being involved in M&A activities later on. From the point of view of value enhancement, such a spin-off could be an interim stage before the acquisition of the spun-off company by another company. Furthermore, the spinning company becomes more suited to companies seeking its new activity profile, which is typically more focused.

Equity Carve-outs (Spin-out IPOs)

In this scenario, an IPO is made of some of the parent company's shares in its subsidiary. In practice, this is a sale of existing shares which are being listed for the first time. In many cases, according to the change in the ownership structure as a result of the transaction, the spun-off company may cease to be consolidated in the parent company's statements. The subsidiary's statements are now provided to the financial community separately, thus allowing it to be monitored separately. One of the direct implications is that the compensation packages of the subsidiary's employees can be more easily tied to the value of the subsidiary. The existence of a separate share also facilitates a full sale of the company's holdings in its subsidiary.

This mechanism is very similar to the spin-off in that the subsidiary's shares become traded. The main differences are in the economic nature of the actual change: In the case of a spin-off, the parent company receives no proceeds from the spin-off, whereas in this case the company receives cash proceeds; in a regular spin-off, the parent company's shareholders receive shares in the subsidiary whereas here their holdings in the parent company include a larger cash component (the IPO proceeds), but no direct holdings in the subsidiary. In most cases, the parent company also retains control of the subsidiary's assets and management. Similarly to a divestiture of parts of the company, the parent company receives cash for its shares in the subsidiary, but unlike regular sales, in which ownership is typically sold in full and control is transferred, in a spin-out the proceeds are derived from a sale made on the stock exchange, with ownership usually being retained. Spin-outs are sometimes combined with full spin-off, or are followed by a spin-off of the remaining shares to the parent company's shareholders.

Letter Stocks/Targeted Stocks

In certain cases, companies prefer to partially divest their divisions by listing a division in the company while keeping it as part of the company. GM, for instance, listed its computer company EDS separately as GME, and its subsidiary Hughes, which is responsible for satellite communications (including Direct TV), as GMH. At first, the two companies continued operating as GM units rather than as independent companies. In the case of GMH, the voting rights of the GMH shares were determined as one-half of the voting rights of the GM share, and the dividend was determined according to the division's results of operations. The results of such separate listing are: Investors in the market have the possibility of investing in a targeted share; the company is now more focused thereby the "conglomerate discount" of its shares might be reduced; the company can raise capital for a certain division separately; the company can use securities for acquisition activities in the division's fields, and the division's compensation plans can be based on the divisions' shares. The parent company does not lose control of the divisions and continues to benefit from consolidated statements for tax purposes. It also continues enjoying any operating synergies without losing all of the other possibilities inherent in restructuring.

On the other hand, the company may experience aggravated conflicts with its divisions. In many cases, the investors in the targeted shares fear that the division is not managed with their interest in mind, but rather with that of the parent company's shareholders. As a result, letter stocks will typically trade at a discount to similar independent companies.

The Rationale of Separate Listing of Units

As mentioned in previous chapters, corporate restructuring is driven by two main motivations: The first is the management's desire to improve the company's profitability and future cash flows; the second is management's desire to increase the market's awareness of the company's activities and value, i.e., to achieve value enhancement or value revelation. In many cases, the main activity is financial restructuring, for example, recapitalization by redeeming the company's public debt, changing the composition of the company's debt, and repurchasing the company's shares in the market. Another activity might be the changing of the company's asset composition, either by buying other companies or divisions of such companies, or by selling assets or divisions of the company, in order to maximize the company's shareholders' return in the short- and long-term, and to assist in increasing the capital market's awareness of the company.

The basic idea behind spin-offs is that listing business divisions separately facilitates a more optimized construction of investment portfolios by investors, their assessment of the company's value, and the compensation of employees in the unit. From the parent company's perspective, the spin-off mechanism also enables the company's management to better focus its attempts to maximize the performance of its core activities.

Similar to the outsourcing phenomenon, which calls for outsourcing of activities that are not among the core-competencies of the firms, spin-offs allow companies to focus on their core activities, and potentially benefit from favorable market valuation of their spin-off units.

The fact that many investors regard the company's value as higher after a spin-off announcement even if no operating improvements are expected in its business results is due to institutional reasons, among others. For example, analysts in investment banks often specialize in a certain field, and companies are usually assigned to the analysts whose specialty corresponds to the field of activity of the company's main division. Therefore, the activities of other divisions in the company are not priced in full. Finally, the spin-off of divisions makes it easier for the divisions to do business with competing companies. For instance, communications companies which compete with AT&T can now buy equipment from Lucent, from which it was spun-off, without many concerns.

However, it is important to note that spin-offs often raise issues with regard to the rights of the company's debt holders. Specifically, a spin-off affects the quality of the company's assets, which may be used as collateral, due to the reduction of its resources (except when proceeds are received by the company). This is one of the reasons that most loan contracts impose restrictions on the distribution of dividends and on material actions pertaining to a change in the ownership of the company's assets.

As mentioned above, one of the main advantages of spin-offs is that they increase the interest of other companies in the field in acquiring the company conducting the spin-off, or of the spun-off unit. In other words, the units become attractive to a larger number of companies since the negotiations become simpler. In many mergers, a substantial part of the negotiations pertain to plans for reorganization after the merger, whereas here the asset in which the buyer is interested may be separated from the outset.

18
Bankruptcy and Dissolution of Companies

INTRODUCTION

In any area of economic activity, many companies are established which for various reasons will cease to exist. Some companies will close down due to a portfolio of products inferior to that of their competitors, some companies will be unable to recruit workers, and some will fail to convince their potential customers of the superiority of their products, even if such products are indeed superior to the ones offered by the competition. Other companies will close down due to unfortunate capital-raising timing. Even if their product suite is good, companies may be unable to secure financing due to a temporary or long-term crisis in the capital markets, as a result of which they will find themselves at a relative disadvantage compared to similar or inferior companies which raised capital in more favorable times. From an economic point of view, dissolution is an efficient market's screening mechanism for "disposing of" second-rate companies. However, since the capital market is not always efficient, the companies which survive are often no better than those that close down.

Various studies have examined the drivers of corporate bankruptcies. The research company Dun and Bradstreet, for instance, reports that about 40% of corporate bankruptcies was due to economic reasons (including industrial weakness), 30% was due to financial reasons (including lack of sources for financing operations), and 20% was due to managerial inexperience. Note, though, that it is obviously difficult to make a clear distinction between the categories.

The same studies also indicate that only 10% of bankruptcies occurs in the companies' first year of activity. Approximately one-third of bankruptcies occurs during the first three years, and around 45% occurs during the first five years of the business.

Since a company is a separate legal entity, a legal process is required to "end its life." This process is known as dissolution or bankruptcy (we will use the terms interchangeably). It can be performed voluntarily by the company (voluntary dissolution) or be forced upon it by creditors when the company is unable to pay its debts (dissolution by the court). Involuntary dissolution usually takes place when the company is insolvent, i.e., when its liabilities exceed its assets (the balance sheet test), or when it is unable to pay its debts as they become due (the cash flow test).

The purpose of the dissolution process is to amass the company's assets, to release them from prior debts and liabilities, to liquidate them, and to distribute the proceeds among the company's creditors in accordance with the statutory priorities prescribed by law and the provisions of the company's organizational documents. Other dissolution activities include looking into the conduct of the company's officers and the connection between it and the company's collapse, and examining transactions preceding the dissolution in order to increase the assets of the company which are available for distribution.

Legal Rules Governing Bankruptcy and Dissolution in the United States

U.S. law distinguishes between bankruptcies which are governed by Federal law and winding-up procedures (i.e., dissolution of the legal entity) which are governed by state law.

Bankruptcy

Once a company declares bankruptcy, it can undergo one of two processes. In the first process (Chapter 7 bankruptcy), the company is liquidated. In other words, the company ceases to operate, its assets are sold, and the proceeds are distributed among its debt holders and shareholders according to the priorities attached to the liabilities and to the company's equity. In this process, the proceeds are distributed according to the absolute priority rule, pursuant to which debt holders are entitled to the repayment of their debt before the shareholders. Among the debt holders, secured debt holders are paid before unsecured debt holders. Holders of debt which is unsecured by assets are paid according to the priority of their debt.

The assets are usually sold under the court's supervision by a trustee who is put in charge of the assets (or a receiver). In some cases, the trustee sells the entire company as a "going concern," and in other cases the assets, if any, are sold separately. Research indicates that the consideration received in a liquidation sale is lower than the consideration received in the sale of an active company as a "going concern."

In practice, creditors with priority often agree to waive the priority rule so as to enable a faster process and prevent various claims between the creditors.

In the second process, namely, reorganization (Chapter 11 bankruptcy), the company continues operating under the court's protection and after reaching understandings with the company's debt holders. In this alternative, the debt holders and equity holders are made new undertakings by the company in lieu of the company's undertakings to them before the bankruptcy. For instance, debt holders may become equity holders, in consideration for discharging part of their debt. After the bankruptcy petition is filed, the company has 120 days to file a reorganization plan with the court, and the debt holders can either accept or reject it. If the company does not file a reorganization plan, or if it is rejected by the debt holders, the court is authorized to extend the time frame so that an agreement on the reorganization may be reached, or to ask the debt holders to propose a plan of their own. For a rehabilitation plan to be accepted, a majority vote is required for each of the various classes of debt holders and equity holders.

The court may exempt the company from the need to obtain the approval of each class of debt and equity holders if it is convinced that the plan is fair and does not discriminate among the holders of the various classes of debt and equity. In this scenario (known as "cramdown"), in which some classes of debt or equity holders do not agree to the reorganization, the holders of such classes of shares or debt have to receive, within the reorganization, at least the amount they would have received in an ordinary dissolution (under Chapter 7).

Most bankruptcies in the United States start out as Chapter 11 bankruptcies, and only if the attempts to rehabilitate the company fail is the company dissolved under Chapter 7.

Dissolution

Following is a review of the rules governing the dissolution of companies in Delaware, in which many technology firms are organized.

The law in the State of Delaware provides a broad set of rules with respect to the dissolution of companies which are organized there. The state's dissolution procedures are designed to balance between the interests of the directors and shareholders, who want to limit their exposure to claims by the company's creditors, and the interests of creditors, who want to have their claims granted. A company which operates under the state's dissolution rules provides its directors with considerable protection against claims by the company's creditors.

Dissolution usually begins with a resolution by the company's board of directors that the dissolution is desirable for the company. After the resolution is adopted, the board of directors sends a notice to the shareholders in which it specifies the content of the dissolution decision adopted and asks the shareholders to approve it. At the general meeting convened to approve the dissolution decision, a simple majority of the holders of voting rights is required. It should be noted that a decision to dissolve a company may be taken without any action by the board of directors, by a written resolution of all persons entitled to vote.

Once the dissolution decision is approved, at the initiative of either the board of directors or the shareholders, the company must file a Certificate of Dissolution for the company with the Delaware Secretary of State. The Certificate of Dissolution must include the following details: the name of the company; the date of approval of the dissolution; an affidavit with regard to the entity which approved the dissolution decision (the board of directors and the shareholders or only the shareholders); and the names and addresses of all the company's directors and officers. The date of dissolution of the company is either the date on which the Certificate of Dissolution is filed or a later date, if the Certificate of Dissolution so provides.

The company's legal entity continues to exist for another three years after the date of dissolution in order to resolve claims against the company, settle its liabilities, and conclude its business affairs. It should be noted that if a claim is filed against the company in the three years following its dissolution decision, the company will continue to exist for this purpose alone until the final resolution of the claim. In other words, no new claims may be filed against the company after the three-year period, even if its legal entity continues to exist due to prior claims.

The legal framework in Delaware enables the company's board of directors to choose one of two ways to distribute the company's assets in the dissolution: a judicial procedure or a default procedure, which is more common among Delaware companies. In both cases, the company's directors are not exposed to legal claims by the company's creditors if they follow the provisions of the law. The default procedure is faster and more flexible than the judicial procedure. In this procedure, the company's board of directors adopts a dissolution plan according to which the company either pays or arranges for sources of payment for all of the company's debts and liabilities, including contingent claims and pending contractual undertakings, which, based on known facts, are reasonably assumed to become due before the statute of limitations expires. This act has to be taken before any dissolution dividends are distributed to the shareholders.

It may appear at first sight that the default procedure is simpler and preferable to the judicial procedure. However, a close scrutiny reveals that the compliance with the demands of this procedure, particularly the demand that a "reasonable" amount be set aside to pay for any claims and debts not yet due, prior to distributing a dissolution dividend, may be put to the test and therefore places the directors at risk. Directors therefore prefer at times to enjoy the protection afforded to them by the judicial procedure.

The judicial procedure enables directors to ensure that they fulfill the requirement of meeting the company's future liabilities and therefore provides them with legal protection against personal liability. According to this procedure, the directors are required to send official notices to the company's creditors with respect to the dissolution of the company. Subsequently, the company moves the court to determine the following two items: (1) the amount and type of collateral required to pay the company's contractual undertakings, including any future liabilities not yet due; (2) the amount and type of collateral required to pay all of the company's other liabilities (i.e., non-contractual liabilities), including pending future liabilities which are likely to mature in the future.

In the judicial procedure, no dissolution dividend can be distributed to the shareholders for 210 days from the date of dispatch of the notice to the creditors. If the board of directors chooses the default procedure, the distribution of the company's assets may be commenced immediately after setting aside assets sufficient to pay the company's liabilities, including future and pending liabilities. Either way, the shareholders' debts to the creditors are limited to the amount of the dissolution dividend they received.

Additional Issues Concerning Bankruptcy of Startup Companies

The reorganization model of the U.S. Bankruptcy Code (Chapter 11) is not particularly suited to young knowledge-based startup companies. The material difference between startups and other companies is that the former lack many tangible assets which may be easily liquidated as part of the rehabilitation process. On the other hand, startups usually have intellectual property which may be sold if no restrictions are imposed on its transfer.

Investors in startups usually enjoy priority in dissolution over other shareholders, by virtue of their preference in liquidation rights (see the section on the rights attached to the securities allotted to investors). For example, investors may have a right of first refusal in the sale of the company's intellectual property.

The sale of some of the company's assets, such as customer lists or information on customers, may be challenged by the courts due to various laws protecting consumer privacy. When the toy company Toysmart.com, for instance, wanted to sell its customer list, the court objected to the sale. The Federal Trade Commission (FTC) and the Attorney Generals of more than 40 states in the United States objected to the sale of information on customers as the company promised its customers, before its bankruptcy, that it would not sell their information to third parties. The argument was that the sale of the information violated the laws of fair trade (since a representation was made to customers that the information would not be sold). In the case of Toysmart, a compromise was reached whereby the information could be sold to a company in the same field, provided that it was sold with the entire company and provided that the acquirer assumed the same privacy-protection undertakings made by Toysmart.

In another case, that of the furniture retail company Furniture.com, it was determined that customer lists could be sold, provided that customers were given the opportunity to request to be removed from the list ("opt out"). As an immediate reaction to these decisions, many companies are now modifying their privacy policy so as to explicitly state that the policy does not apply in the case of a sale of the company or of its assets.

GLOSSARY

Advisory Board
This group of experts, which typically consists of three to seven members, sits alongside the company's board of directors and is usually composed of reputable persons in the company's fields of activity. The board convenes periodically, but its decisions have no legally binding effect. Venture capital funds typically also have their own advisory board, composed of industry experts.

Agency Problem
Conflict between managers and owners of a company, where the manager (the agent) incentives, and hence actions, are not aligned with the those of the owners (the principals).

Agreement Among Underwriters
This agreement between members of an underwriters' syndicate appoints the investment bank which leads the offering as the lead underwriter, defines the underwriters' commitments according to their proportionate share in the offering, and authorizes the lead underwriter to allocate units to selling groups.

Allotment
A determination of the share of new securities issued which is assigned to each member of a syndicate, for underwriting and distribution.

American Depositary Receipt (ADR)
A security issued in the United States to represent a share of a foreign company listed in another market.

Angel
A wealthy individual investing in private companies and ventures. Angels fulfill similar functions as venture capital funds, but invest their own capital rather than manage other investor's capital.

Beta β
A parameter which reflects the degree by which the returns of a stock, mutual fund or portfolio, vary with the return of the market (usually relative to the S&P 500 index). A share with a beta higher than 1 is more volatile than the overall market, whereas a share with a beta below 1 is less volatile than the market.

Black & Scholes Option Pricing Model
A model used to calculate the value of a call option. The model takes into account the price of the share, the exercise price, the date of expiration of the option, the risk-free interest, and the standard deviation of the return of the underlying asset.

Blue Sky Laws
Laws passed by many states which require sellers of new issues to register their IPOs and to provide financial details on their company.

Board of Directors
Individuals elected by a corporation's shareholders to oversee the management of the corporation. The members of a board of directors are paid in cash and/or stock, meet several times each year, and are legally responsible for the corporation's activities.

Bylaws
The official regulations which govern a corporation's management. They are drawn in writing at the time of incorporation, as is the charter.

Call Option
The right to buy a security at a pre-determined price (or a pre-defined formula for pricing) at a given period of time, or when a certain event happens.

Capital Gain (loss)
The difference between an asset's purchase price and selling price.

Capital Asset Pricing Model (CAPM)
An economic model for valuing stocks by relating risk and expected return, based on their returns sensitivity to the market returns volatility. The model is based on the concept that investors will demand additional expected return (which is known as risk premium) if asked to assume additional risk, and that any asset specific risk can be diversified away.

Carried Interest
In the context of venture capital funds, the major part of the profits, approximately 20%, which are allocated to the general partners of the fund.

Closing
The signing of an investment contract by an investor or a group of investors.

Comfort Letter
A declaration by the company's CPA which is provided to a company preparing for a public offering. This letter confirms that the financial figures in the prospectus are based on audited statements prepared in accordance with GAAP, and that no significant changes have occurred since the report was prepared.

Committed Capital
A commitment to invest capital in a private equity fund. In venture capital funds, investment commitments are customarily not paid at once, but as required by the fund manager.

Common Stock
A security which represents an ownership right in a corporation. The stock may confer voting rights and entitles the holder to a share of the company's success through dividends and/or capital appreciation. In the event of bankruptcy, common stock holders have rights to a company's assets only after liabilities are paid to bondholders, other creditors, and preferred stock holders. This is typically the type of shares held by founders and management, and the class to which all shares are converted to before an IPO.

Convertible Security
A security that can be converted to another security under specific pre-defined conditions and terms.

Corporate Venture Capital
A venture capital fund initiated by corporation in order to invest either in companies outside the corporation or in business ventures originating within the corporation which raise external capital.

Dilution
The reduction in the rate of holdings of a company's founders and other shareholders, as a result of the introduction of new investors to the company.

Distribution
The transfer of shares owned by a venture capital fund (or cash from the proceeds of selling such shares) to the fund's partners.

Dividend
A payment declared by a company's board of directors. It is given to the company's shareholders out of the company's current earnings or excess profits. They are usually given in cash, but may also be given in the form of stock (stock dividend) or in the form of other property.

Due Diligence
A review of a company's business plan and an assessment of its management team and legal condition before investing therein.

Earn-Up
An agreement under which an acquirer of a company provides the management and investors of the acquired company with performance-based financial compensation for their sold shares.

Employee Stock Ownership Plan (ESOP)
A fund established for the purpose of granting options to a company's employees. The option plan is common in many companies and is designed to motivate employees. The plan also confers tax benefits on the company, and is also known as a stock option plan or stock purchase plan.

Endowment
A pool of assets owned by universities, pension funds, hospitals, and many nonprofit institutions, and mainly invested for long-term.

Equity
Ownership of a corporation, usually in the form of common stock or preferred stock; also, total assets less total liabilities. Hence, equity is also known as shareholder's equity, or net worth.

Equity Kicker
A transaction in which a number of shares or options are given as an additional consideration for a debt-based investment in a company.

Exercise Price
The price at which an option can be exercised.

Exit
The manner in which an investor closes out a certain position, usually by converting it to cash. In the context of a venture capital investment—liquidating the investment by an offering or sale of the company.

Financial Statement
A report which describes the financial condition of a company in quantitative terms. It usually includes a balance sheet, an income statement, a cash flow statement, and changes in equity statement.

Financing Round
The raising of capital for a company through investors. Venture capitalists usually provide the capital in stages, and therefore a typical company supported by venture capital will receive several financing infusions over several rounds which are spread out over a few years.

Form 10-K
An annual report which every traded company is required to file with the Securities and Exchange Commission. The report provides a wide variety of concise data about the company. Foreign private issuers are required to file a Form 20-F.

Form 10-Q
A document of the Securities and Exchange Commission (SEC) used to file quarterly reports, which every domestic publicly traded company in the United States is required to file. These reports include the unaudited financial statements and any other material information which the company is required by the regulations to disclose to the public.

Form 20-F
A document of the Securities and Exchange Commission (SEC). This document can be used both for the registration of shares which are already traded in the country of origin when listed for trade in the United States (Seasoned Securities), and for the filing of the annual reports of all foreign companies traded in the United States.

Form F-1
A document of the Securities and Exchange Commission (SEC) used to list the shares of

a foreign company for trade in the United States within the framework of a public offering.

GAAP (Generally Accepted Accounting Principles)
A well-known and widely accepted set of rules, conventions, standards, and procedures for reporting financial information, which was established by the Financial Accounting Standards Board.

Gatekeeper
A financial advisor assisting investors (mainly institutional) in selecting investments. These advisors play a major role in advising the allocation of institutional investors funds between venture capital funds. They may also manage funds that invests in other funds (fund of fund).

General Partner
An individual or a company managing a limited partnership, who is responsible for the current performance of the fund. The general partners are responsible for all of the fund's liabilities.

Initial Public Offering (IPO)
The sale of shares to the public of a company that has not yet been traded on a stock exchange; also, a company's first offering of stock to the public.

Institutional Investor
An entity with large amounts to invest, such as investment companies, mutual funds, brokerages, insurance companies, pension funds, investment banks, and endowment funds.

Investment Bank
A financial intermediary among whose specialties are the underwriting of securities offerings, and assisting in mergers and acquisitions.

Investment Committee
A group which in the case of a private equity fund is usually composed of general partners, which reviews the potential and existing investments, and makes investment decisions.

Lead Underwriter
The underwriter which manages the underwriters' syndicate (and which is also known as the Managing Underwriter).

Leveraged Buyout (LBO)
The acquisition of a company or a business unit through debt.

Licensee
The party which, in a licensing agreement, receives the right to use a technology, a product, or a brand name in exchange for payments.

Limited Partner
An investor in a limited partnership. Limited partners can monitor the progress of the partnership but cannot be involved in its daily management.

Limited Partnership
A business organization with one or more general partners (which manages the business and bears the legal debts and responsibility), and with one or more limited partners, which do not participate in the daily management, and are liable only to the extent and scope of their investment. The organization has a contractual arrangement that limits the term of the partnership.

Lock-Up
A condition in the underwriting contract between an investment bank and existing shareholders which prohibits interested parties in the corporation and private investors from selling their shares at the time of the offering, and for a certain period of time thereafter.

Management Fee
A payment made to the general partners, in order to cover their salaries and other expenses. The fees is typically specified as a percentage of the partners' committed capital.

Market Maker
A broker or bank responsible for conducting the bids and trade of a company's shares, and are willing and able to buy or sell at publicly quoted prices.

Mezzanine Financing
An investment in subordinated bonds which are superior to equity but subordinate to bank debt. The same terms also represent equity financing round shortly before an initial public offering.

Milestone Payments
The spreading of payments in an investment agreement. The payments are made at pre-determined times or when certain technological or business objectives are achieved.

Net Present Value (NPV)
A valuation method which calculates the expected current value of cash flows from an investment, by adjusting the nominal cash flows for the time and riskiness associated with achieving them (the cost of capital).

Non-Disclosure Agreement (NDA)
A contract in which parties to a transaction agree not to disclose certain information for a certain period of time.

Option
The right to buy or sell a security at a pre-determined price (or range of prices) in a given period of time.

Over Allotment Option, Green Shoe
The option given to an underwriter in a public offering granting it the possibility, within a period of time ranging between 15 and 45 days (usually 30 days) after the closing date of the original transaction, to purchase additional securities from the issuer (usually up to 15% of the shares sold) at the original price of the offering to the public, in order to meet over-subscriptions for the securities.

Participating Preferred Stock
A convertible share, the holder of which receives, under certain conditions, both the return of his original investment and his proportionate share of the profits generated by the liquidation of the company's assets.

Partnership Agreement
A contract specifying the terms and conditions governing the relationships between the limited partners and the general partner.

Piggyback Registration Rights
The rights of an investor to register his shares and to sell them together with the company's shares in the event that the company conducts an offering.

Post-Money Valuation
The price paid for a share in a given financing round, multiplied by the total number of shares after the round.

Preemptive Right
The right of current shareholders to preserve the rate of their ownership of a company by buying shares proportionately to their holdings in the case of an issuance to additional investors.

Preferred Stock
Stock that is given preference over common stock with respect to dividend distributions or payments in the event of the company's sale or liquidation. Preferred stock shareholders may also enjoy additional rights, such as the ability to veto mergers or replace the management.

Pre-Money Valuation
The price paid for a share in a given financing round, multiplied by the total number of shares before the round.

Primary Offering
The issuance of new securities by a company.

Private Placement
The sale of securities which are not registered at the SEC for listing. These sales are typically to wealthy individuals or institutional investors.

Prospectus
A detailed document filed with the Securities and Exchange Commission which provides a wide variety of financial and business information about the company.

Quiet Period
A period created by U.S. securities laws, which starts when a company contacts an underwriter in order to conduct a future offering, and ends 25 days after the offering. During this period, the company is prohibited from publicly disclosing any information or intimation about the company and its financial condition.

Red Herring
An early version of the prospectus which is distributed among potential investors prior to a security offering.

Registration Statement
A document filed officially with the Securities and Exchange Commission, which reviews it before the company can sell its shares to the public. The registration statement provides a wide variety of concise information about the company, as well as copies of significant legal documents.

Regulation A
A regulation of the U.S. Securities and Exchange Commission which governs offerings with a value of less than $5,000,000.

Regulation D
A regulation of the U.S. Securities and Exchange Commission which governs private placements.

Regulation S
Rules promulgated under the American 1933 Securities Law, according to which no registration (prospectus filing) is necessary in an offering outside the United States to non-U.S. investors, if the company meets several criteria which are specified in the rules, which concern the extent of the connection of the company or the public offering with the United States.

Restricted Stock
A share that cannot be sold under the procedures of the U.S. Securities and Exchange Commission or that can only be sold in limited amounts.

Right of First Refusal
A contractual provision which grants a shareholder the right to purchase assets (for example shares) before they are sold to other potential investors.

Road Show
A marketing campaign of a public offering to potential investors.

Rule 10b-5
A regulation of the U.S. Securities and Exchange Commission that generally prohibits activities with fraudulent purposes in the purchase or sale of any securities.

Rule 144
A regulation of the U.S. Securities and Exchange Commission that prohibits the sale of restricted stock for one year after the purchase thereof, and which limits the

amounts of shares sold in the second year after the purchase.

S Corporation
A form of incorporation which is recognized by the U.S. tax authorities, and which is designed for companies with up to 35 shareholders. This form of incorporation enables the company to enjoy the advantages flowing from operating as a company, while regarding the company as a partnership for tax purposes (for example, by having the company being handled as a pass-through organization).

Seasoned Equity Offering
An offering by a company which has already completed an initial public offering and whose shares are already publicly traded.

Secondary Offering
The sale of shares by existing shareholders (rather than by the company). In this type of offering, the company does not receive the proceeds from the sales of the shares.

Securities and Exchange Commission (SEC)
The federal securities authority in the United States. Its responsibility is to promote due disclosure, and to protect investors from fraud and manipulative practices in the securities markets.

Staging
The infusion of capital to companies in installments, with each installment being conditioned on the achievement of certain business goals.

Syndication
The purchase of shares by two or more private investors together. The term also refers to the joint underwriting of securities offering by two or more investment banks.

Term Sheet
A document outlining the general principles of a stock purchase agreement or of an investment agreement, to which the parties usually agree before discussing the formal language of the contract.

Underwriting
The purchase (and typically immediate resale) by an investment bank of securities issued by a company (or the promise to purchase them under certain conditions).

Underwriting Agreement
An agreement between a corporation issuing new securities and the lead underwriter of the syndicate.

Venture Capital Method
A valuation method by which the value of a company is calculated for a specific future point in time when the VC expects the exit, and then the discount of that future value to current value, by using a high discount rate.

Vesting
The period of time which an employee of a company is required to be employed thereby in order to be able to exercise the right given to him in an option and to convert the same into shares.

Warrant
An option to buy a share from the company under pre-specified terms.

FURTHER READINGS

The enclosed list is not an exhaustive list of books and articles on the topics covered in the book, but rather a list of suggested readings, for those interested in further enhancing their understanding of these topics.

Admati, Anat R. and Paul Pfleiderer, 1994, "Robust financial contracting and the role of venture capitalists," *Journal of Finance*, 49. 371–402.

Asquith, Paul and David W. Mullins, Jr., 1986, "Equity issues and offering dilution," *Journal of Financial Economics*, 25: 61–89.

Ben-Daniel D., Jesse Reyes and Michael D'Angelo, 2000, "Concentration in the venture capital industry," *Journal of Private Equity*, 3: 7-13.

Bergemann, Dirk, and Ulrich Hege, 1998, "Dynamic venture capital financing, learning, and moral hazard," *Journal of Banking and Finance*, 22:1-48.

Black, Bernard S. and Ronald J. Gilson, 1998, "Venture capital and the structure of capital markets: banks versus stock markets," *Journal of Financial Economics*, 47:243-277.

Brynjolfsson, Erik and Brian Kahin (eds.), 2000, *Understanding the Digital Economy*, Cambridge, MA: MIT Press.

Dixit, Avinash and Robert S. Pindyck, 1994, *Investment Under Uncertainty*, Princeton University Press, Princeton, New Jersey.

Fama, Eugene, 1996, "Multifactor portfolio efficiency and multifactor asset pricing," *Journal of Financial and Quantitative Analysis*, 31:441-465.

Fama, Eugene and Kenneth R. French, 1996, "Multifactor explanations of asset pricing anomalies," *Journal of Finance*, 51: 55-84.

Fenn, G.W., N. Liang and S. Prose, 1997, "The role of angel investor's and venture capitalist in financing high tech startups." Board of Governors of the Federal Reserve System, Washington DC.

Fuerst, Oren and Nahum Melumad, 2001a, "Valuing Old and New Companies," Financial Times Mastering Investments, May 23.

Fuerst, Oren and Nahum Melumad, 2001b, "Valuing Companies: Simulations, Options and Partnerships," Financial Times Mastering Investments, May 23.

Gibbons, Robert and Kevin J. Murphy, 1992, "Optimal incentive contracts in the presence of career concerns: theory and evidence," *Journal of Political Economy*, 100:468-505.

Gilson, Ronald J. and Bernard S. Black, *The Law and Finance of Corporate Acquisitions* (2d ed., 1995), University Case Books.

Gompers, Paul and Josh Lerner, 1999, "An analysis of compensation in the U.S. venture capital partnership," *Journal of Financial Economics*, 51: 3-44.

Gompers, Paul A. and Josh Lerner, 1999, *The Venture Capital Cycle*, Cambridge: Massachusetts: MIT Press.

Grenadier, Steven R. and Allen M. Weiss, 1997, "Investment in technological innovations: an option pricing approach," *Journal of Financial Economics*, 44:397-416.

Halloran, Michael, Lee Benton, Robert Gunderson, Keith Kearney and Jorge del Calvo, 1995, *Venture Capital and Public Offering Negotiation*, Englewood Cliffs, New Jersey: Aspen Law and Business.

Hellman, Tomas, 1998, "The allocation of control rights in venture capital contracts," *Rand Journal of Economics*, 29: 57-76.

Jensen, Michael and William H. Meckling, 1976, "Theory of the firm: managerial behavior, agency costs, and the ownership structure," *Journal of Financial Economics*, 3: 305-360.

Kortun, Shmuel and Josh Lerner, 2000, "Assessing the contribution of venture capital to innovation," *Rand Journal of Economics*, 31: 574-692.

Levin, Jack S., 1999, *Structuring Venture Capital, Private Equity and Entrepreneurial Transactions*, Githersburg NY Panel Publication, Aspen Publishing.

Megginson, William and Kathleen A. Weiss, 1991, "Venture capital certification in initial public offerings," *Journal of Finance*, 46:879-893.

Morck, Randall, 2000, *Concentrated Ownership*. Chicago, IL: University of Chicago Press.

Mikkelson, Wayne, Megan Partch and Kenneth Shah, 1997, "Ownership and operating performance of companies that go public," *Journal of Financial Economics*, 4:281-307.

Ohlson, James, 1995, "Earnings, book values and dividends in equity valuation," Contemporary Accounting Research, Spring, 661-687.

Penman, Stephen, 2001, *Financial Statement Analysis and Security Valuation*, McGraw-Hill Higher Education.

Penman, Stephen and Theodore Sougiannis, 1995, "A comparison of dividend, cash flow, and earnings approaches to equity valuation," Contemporary Accounting Research, Spring, 661-687.

Sahlman, William 1990, "The structure and governance of venture capital organizations," *Journal of Financial Economics*, 27:473-521.

Shleifer, Andrei and Robert Vishny, 1997, "A survey of corporate governance," *Journal of Finance*, 52:737-783.

Simesnki, Melvin, L. Bryer, Neil Wilkof, 1999, *Intellectual Property in the Global Marketplace*, New York, NY: John Wiley and Sons.

Tirole, Jean, 1988, *The Theory of Industrial Organization*, Cambridge, MA: MIT Press.

Trigeorgis, Leno, 1996, *Real Options*, Cambridge: Massachusetts: MIT Press.

INDEX

A

Accelerators, 13–14
Accounting issues
    depreciation, 40–41
    option rewarding, 80–81
    public offering, 240
    revenue, 40–41
Acquisition, 269, 285–86
ADR (American Depositary Receipt), 263–64
Agreements, 296–97
Amended registration statement, 250
American Depositary Receipt (ADR), 263–64
Angels, 118, 223–24
Annual report, 259
Anti-dilution protection, 146
Antitrust issues
    mergers and acquisitions, 297–300
    strategic alliances, 63
Assets
    accounts receivable, 30–31
    advance payments, 32
    cash, 30
    cash-equivalents, 30
    inventory, 31–32
    long-term assets, 32–33
    sale and acquisition of, 285–86
    securities, 30

B

Balance sheet, 40
Bankruptcy, 306–7, 309
Barters, 40
Benefits, 72–73
Best efforts offering, 254
Board of directors
    incorporation, 19
    incorporation in Delaware, 23–24
Bonds, 21
Bonuses, 87
Book value-based multiple, 162
Break-even point, 47–49
Bridge loans, 121
Bring along, 149
Business and market penetration, 108–9
Business cycle, 27–28
Business plan
    executive summary, 65–66
    headers, 66–67
    overview, 64–65
    public offering, 239
    structure of, 65
Business unit, weighing relative performance of employee's, 88

C

Capital, sources of
    bridge loans, 121
    corporate investors, 119
    family, 118
    financing by debt, 120–21
    friends, 118
    institutional investors, 119–20
    mezzanine loans, 120–21
    overview, 116–17
    private investors (angels), 118
    venture capital funds, 118–19
Capital market synergy, 273–74
Case study (Chromatis sold to Lucent), 277–81
Cash, 72
Cash break-even point, 52
Cash earnings, 41–42
Cash flow, 40–41
Cash flow forecasting
    cash break-even point, 52
    overview, 51–52
    profitability, scale of investment required to reach, 52–53
Cash flow statement, 40
Chromatis sold to Lucent (case study), 277–81
Classic mergers, 283–84
Closing, 252
Closing conditions, 297
Coach, 10–11
Compensation
    benefits, 72–73
    cash, 72
    incentives to tie employees to company, 88–89
    long-term compensation, 74
    methods of, 72–73
    non-monetary benefits, 73
    option rewarding, 75–83
    overview, 72
    performance-based compensation, 85–88
    planning compensation packages, 73–74
    salary, 73
    stocks and options, 72
    taxation of stock options, 83–85
    termination of employment, 89
    variable compensation, 73–74
Compulsory licensing, 97
Conglomerate acquisitions, 270
Consolidation, 24, 269
Contacting and meeting with investors, 130
Continuity, 15
Conversion, 144–45
Copyright law, 97–99
Corporate capital
    bonds, 21
    incorporation, 20–21
    ordinary shares, 20
    preferred shares, 20–21
    stock options, 21
Corporate in-house entrepreneurship, 226–27
Corporate investors, 119, 225–27
Corporate laws, 295
Corporate organs, 18–20
Corporate restructuring
    acquisition, 269
    consolidation, 269
    divestiture, 269
    equity carve-outs (spin-out IPOs), 302
    going private, 269
    letter stocks, 303
    leveraged buyout, 269
    mergers, 268
    overview, 301–2
    separate listing of units, 303–4
    spin-off, 269
    targeted stocks, 303
Corporation, 15–16
Cost of IPO, 247
Cost structure analysis and forecasting
    break-even point, 47–49
    fixed costs, 50
    market entry, costs of, 51
    network effect, costs of, 51
    outsourcing, 50
    overview, 47
    variable costs, 50
Covenants, 297
CPAs, 246–47
Credit companies as source of capital, 230

D

Decision trees used for strategic decisions, 57–60
Demand registration right, 154
Direct investments by companies in the field, 225–26
Disclosure, 262
Discount rate used by venture capital funds, 176–78
Discounting cash flows and residual income
    example, 167–69
    principles, 162–63
    projected period, estimating value component after, 166
    projected period, estimating value component during, 163–66
    valuation according to discounted residual income, 169–71
Dissolution, 307–9
Diversification, 273–74
Divestiture, 269
Documents for incorporation, 17–18
Due diligence, 131, 249–51

E

EBIT (earnings before interest and taxes), 37
EBIT-based multiple, 161

EBITDA, 41–42
Employee compensation
 benefits, 72–73
 cash, 72
 incentives to tie employees to company, 88–89
 long-term compensation, 74
 methods of, 72–73
 non-monetary benefits, 73
 option rewarding, 75–83
 overview, 72
 performance-based compensation, 85–88
 planning compensation packages, 73–74
 salary, 73
 stocks and options, 72
 taxation of stock options, 83–85
 termination of employment, 89
 variable compensation, 73–74
Employee departure, 78
Employee recruiting
 finding employees, 71
 job descriptions and requirements, 70
 screening employees, 71
Employee stock option plans, 156
Employee stock purchase plans, 84–85
Employment agreements, 155
Equity carve-outs (spin-out IPOs), 302
Exemptions, 263
Exercise price, 77–78
Expenses, 154
External advisors
 accelerators, 13–14
 financial advisors, 11
 incubators, 12–13
 legal advisors, 11
 management consultants, 11
 overview, 11
 preliminary stages, 11–14

F

Failure, price of, 7–8
Fairness opinions, 300
Family, 118
Feasibility, 8
Financial advisors, 11
Financial institutions, 227–30
Financial leverage of compensation packages, 86
Financial manager, 10
Financial projections
 business plan, 64–67
 cash flow forecasting, 51–53
 cost structure analysis and forecasting, 47–51
 credit policy, 46
 dividend policy, 46–47
 importance of, 43–44
 market analysis and strategic planning, 53–60
 overview, 43–45
 pricing, 46
 purpose of, 43–44
 sales growth, 45
 strategic alliances, 60–63
 working capital, 46
Financial reporting, 63
Financial statements
 accounting revenue, 40–41
 assets, 30–33
 balance sheet, 29–30, 40
 cash earnings, 41–42
 cash flow, 40–41
 cash flow statement, 38–40
 EBITDA, 41–42
 income statement, 35–38, 40
 liabilities, 34–35
 overview, 29
 reporting holdings in other companies and consolidation of statements, 42
Financing
 by debt, 120–21
 overview, 107–8
 sources of capital, 116–21
 value of company, 109–11
 venture capital, raising, 111–16
 venture development, 108–9
Finding employees, 71
Firm commitment offering, 253–54
First-stage financing, 113–14
Fixed costs, 50
Flippers, 252
Foreign companies raising capital
 ADR (American Depositary Receipt), 263–64
 disclosure, 262
 exemptions, 263
 IPO process, 263
 overview, 262
 periodic reporting requirements, 263
Founders, 152–53
Friends, 118
Full ratchet, 146–47
Fully diluted, 124–25

G

Group voting, 148

H

Hedge funds, 193–94
Holding companies of commercial banks, 228
Horizontal acquisitions, 269

I

Ideas
 feasibility, 8
 need for, 8
 overview, 8–9
 preliminary stages, 8–9
Incentives to tie employees to company, 88–89
Income statement
 balance sheet compared, 40
 cash flow statement compared, 40
 cost of goods sold, 36
 EBIT (earnings before interest and taxes), 37
 gross profits, 36
 net income, 37
 operating profit, 36–37
 overview, 35
 revenues, 35–36
 sample income statement, 37–38
Incorporation
 board of directors, 19
 certainty, 15
 continuity, 15
 corporate capital, 20–21
 corporate organs, 18–20
 corporation, 15–16
 described, 14
 documents, 17–18
 instrument for raising capital, 15
 limited liability, 14
 limited partnership, 16
 LLC (limited liability company), 16–17
 managers, 19–20
 normative documents, 17–18
 objectives of, 14–15
 preliminary stages, 14–21
 separation between management and control, 14–15
 separation between property of company and shares, 15
 shareholders, 19
 shareholders agreement, 18
 simplicity, 15
 tax considerations, 15
 types of corporations, 15–17
Incorporation in Delaware
 background, 21–22
 board of directors, 23–24
 consolidations, 24
 limited liability companies (LLCs), 25
 managing, 22–23
 mergers, 24
 organizing, 22–23
 partnerships, 25
 preliminary stages, 21–25
 S corporations, 25
 share capital, 23
 shareholders, 23
Incubators, 12–13
Indemnification, 154
Information, right to control and rights to, 149–52
Insider trading, 260
Institutional investors, 119–20
Instrument for raising capital, 15
Insurance companies, 229
Intellectual property
 copyright law, 97–99
 employees and, 101
 licenses, 102–4

NDA (non-disclosure agreements), 101–2
  overview, 91
  patents, 92–97
  trade secrets, 99–101
  trademark law, 99
Internal rate of return (IRR), 188
Investment agreements, 136–40
Investment banks, 227–28
Investor relations, 240
Investors
  anti-dilution protection, 146
  bring along, 149
  conversion, 144–45
  full ratchet, 146–47
  group voting, 148
  issues for, 127–29
  preemptive right, 145–46
  preference in liquidation, 143–144
  preference in receipt of dividends, 144
  prohibition of sales, 148
  right of first offer, 148
  right of redemption, 148
  rights attached to securities allotted to, 143–49
  tag along, 148–49
  weighted average ratchet, 147–48
IPOs
  described, 235
  following, 258–60
  foreign companies raising capital, 263
  issuance of options shortly before, 81
  mergers and acquisitions compared, 275–76
IRR (internal rate of return), 188
ISOs (incentive stock options), 83–84
Issuing stock to investors
  investment rounds with pool of employee stock options, 180–81
  number and price of shares allotted to investor, 179–80
  overview, 178–79
  preemptive rights, 182

J

Job descriptions and requirements, 70

L

Leasing as source of capital, 230–31
Legal advisors, 11
Legal counsel, 246
Legal issues
  mergers and acquisitions, 295–96
  public offering, 239–40
Legal restrictions on raising venture capital
  employee stock option plans, 156

employment agreements, 155
financial matters, 140–42
founders, 152–53
how to meet, 134–35
information, right to control and rights to, 149–52
investment agreements, 136–40
investor, rights attached to securities allotted to, 143–49
managers, 152–53
overview, 133
registration rights agreement, 153–55
Rule 504, 134
Rule 505, 134
Rule 506, 134
shareholders agreements, 156
term sheet, 135–36
United States law, 134
Letter of intent, 248
Letter stocks, 303
Leveraged buyout, 269
Leveraged buyout funds, 193
Liabilities
  equity, 34–35
  long-term debt, 34
  short-term liabilities, 34
  under U.S. securities laws, 257–58
Licenses
  defined, 102–3
  pricing a license to utilize a patent, 103–4
Limited liability, 14
Limited liability companies (LLCs), 16–17, 25
Limited partnership, 16
LLC (limited liability company), 16–17, 25
Long-term compensation, 74

M

Management, 108
Management consultants, 11
Management issues for public offering, 239
Management team
  coach, 10–11
  financial manager, 10
  Manager (CEO), 9–10
  marketing and business development manager, 10
  overview, 9–11
  preliminary stages, 9–11
  production manager, 10
  sales manager, 10
  technological leader, 10
Manager (CEO), 9–10
Managerial capabilities, 273
Managers
  incorporation, 19–20
  legal restrictions on raising venture capital, 152–53
Market analysis and strategic planning

decision trees used for strategic decisions, 57–60
  options, 56–57
  overview, 53–54
  target markets, analyzing, 54–56
Market entry, costs of, 51
Market power, change in, 272–73
Marketing and business development manager, 10
Material events, reporting, 260
Merchant banking funds, 193
Mergers, *See also* mergers and acquisitions
  classic mergers, 283–84
  described, 268, 283
  incorporation in Delaware, 24
  triangular mergers, 284–85
Mergers and acquisitions, *See also* mergers
  acquirer's strategy, 286–87
  agreements, 296–97
  antitrust issues, 297–300
  capital market synergy, 273–74
  case study, 277–81
  Chromatis sold to Lucent (case study), 277–81
  conglomerate acquisitions, 270
  corporate laws, 295
  diversification, 273–74
  fairness opinions, 300
  horizontal acquisitions, 269
  IPOs compared, 275–76
  legal aspects, 295–96
  managerial capabilities, 273
  market power, change in, 272–73
  operational synergy, 271–72
  overview, 267–68
  payment forms, 287
  price determination, 288–89
  process, 291–92
  reasons for, 270–74
  sales compared, 276
  securities rules, 295–96
  stock exchange rules, 296
  stock-based transactions, advantages of, 289
  stock-based transactions, risks of, 290–91
  strategic classification, 269–70
  strategies, 286–87
  target's strategy, 287
  tax advantages, 274
  tender offers, 292–93
  value created by, 274–75
  vertical acquisitions, 270
Mezzanine loans, 120–21
Multiples, valuation methods based on, 158–62
Mutual funds, 230

N

NASDAQ, 243
NDA (non-disclosure agreements), 101–2

Net earnings multiple, 161
Net present value (NPV), 187
Network effect, costs of, 51
New York Stock Exchange (NYSE), 242–43
Non-disclosure agreements (NDA), 101–2
Non-monetary benefits, 73
Non-obviousness, 94
Normative documents, 17–18
Not-for-profit organizations, 229–30
Novelty, 94
NPV (net present value), 187
NSOs (non-qualified stock options), 84

O

Operational synergy, 271–72
Option rewarding
    accounting aspects, 80–81
    advantages of, 76–77
    capital held by employees and officers, 81–82
    disadvantages of, 76–77
    fall in stock values, responses to, 80
    IPO, issuance of options shortly before, 81
    overview, 75
    spin-offs, shares in, 83
    stock option plans, 77–79
    stock options defined, 75–76
    valuation of options, 79–80
Options, 56–57
Options to abandon, 172
Options to delay, 172
Options to scope and scale, 172
Options to stage, 172
Options to switch, 172
Ordinary shares, 20
Organizational meeting, 249
Outsourcing, 50

P

Partnerships, 25
Patent pending, 94
Patents
    for business processes, 96
    compulsory licensing, 97
    non-obviousness, 94
    novelty, 94
    outside United States, 95–96
    overview, 92–93
    patent pending, 94
    period of protection for, 93
    prerequisites for obtaining, 94
    pricing a license to utilize a patent, 103–4
    Provisional Patent Application (PPA), 93
    registration, 94–95
    use of, 93
    usefulness, 94
Payment, price and terms of, 296–97
Payment forms, 287

Pension funds, 228–29
Performance evaluation, 86–87
Performance-based compensation
    bonuses, 87
    business unit, weighing relative performance of employee's, 88
    financial leverage of compensation packages, 86
    overview, 85–86
    performance evaluation, 86–87
    phantom shares, 87–88
    types of, 87–88
Periodic reporting requirements, 263
Phantom shares, 87–88
Piggyback registration right, 154
Planning compensation packages, 73–74
Post-money value, 125
PPA (Provisional Patent Application), 93
Preemptive rights, 145–46, 182
Preference in liquidation, 143—144
Preference in receipt of dividends, 144
Preferred shares, 20–21
Pre-IPO financing, 115–16
Preliminary prospectus (red herring), 250
Preliminary registration statement, 249–50
Preliminary rounds of investment, 112
Preliminary stages
    external advisors, 11–14
    failure, price of, 7–8
    idea, 8–9
    incorporation, 14–21
    incorporation in Delaware, 21–25
    management team, 9–11
    success, price of, 7–8
Pre-money value, 125
Preparation of company for public offering, 239–40
Prerequisites for obtaining patents, 94
Pre-seed financing, 112
Price determination, 288–89
Pricing
    overview, 251–52
    patents, 103–4
    real options, 173
Private equity funds
    hedge funds, 193–94
    leveraged buyout funds, 193
    merchant banking funds, 193
    overview, 191–92
    venture capital funds, 192–93
Private investors (angels), 118, 223–24
Private placement, 235
Process for raising, 127–31
Production manager, 10
Profitability, scale of investment required to reach, 52–53

Prohibition of sales, 148
Provisional Patent Application (PPA), 93
Proxy rules, 260
Public, selling shares to, 252
Public offering, *See also* public offering process
    accounting issues, 240
    advantages of, 237–38
    business plan, 239
    disadvantages of, 238–39
    investor relations, 240
    legal issues, 239–40
    management issues, 239
    preparation of company for, 239–40
    readiness of company for, 236–37
Public offering process, *See also* public offering
    amended registration statement, 250
    annual report, 259
    closing, 252
    cost of IPO, 247
    CPAs, 246–47
    due diligence, 249–50
    due diligence meeting, 251
    flippers, 252
    foreign companies raising capital, 262–64
    forming IPO team, 243–47
    insider trading, 260
    IPO, following, 258–60
    legal counsel, 246
    letter of intent, 248
    liability under U.S. securities laws, 257–58
    material events, reporting, 260
    organizational meeting, 249
    preliminary prospectus (red herring), 250
    preliminary registration statement, 249–50
    pricing, 251–52
    proxy rules, 260
    public, selling shares to, 252
    quarterly report, 259
    quiet period, 248–49
    registration process, 258
    registration statement, 255–57
    Regulation A, 262
    Regulation S, 261–62
    reporting duties, 259
    road show, 250–51
    Rule 144, 261
    selling shares exempt from registration, 261–62
    signing underwriting agreement, 251–52
    stabilization, 252–53
    stock markets in United States, 241–43
    trading, 252–53
    underwriters, 243–46
    underwriters' option (green

INDEX 327

shoe), 253
  underwriting agreement, 253–55
Purchase agreements
  closing conditions, 297
  covenants, 297
  overview, 296
  payment, price and terms of, 296–97
  representations, 297
  transaction description, 296
  warranties, 297

Q

Quarterly report, 259
Quiet period, 248–49

R

Rate of return, 188
Readiness of company for public offering, 236–37
Real options method
  options to abandon, 172
  options to delay, 172
  options to scope and scale, 172
  options to stage, 172
  options to switch, 172
  overview, 171–72
  pricing real options, 173
  types of real options, 172
Recruiting
  finding employees, 71
  job descriptions and requirements, 70
  screening employees, 71
Red herring (preliminary prospectus), 250
Registration of patents, 94–95
Registration process, 258
Registration rights agreement
  demand registration right, 154
  expenses, 154
  indemnification, 154
  legal restrictions on raising venture capital, 153–55
  need for, 153
  overview, 153
  piggyback registration right, 154
  restrictions, 154
  transfer right, 155
  types of registration rights, 154
  underwriters, choice of, 155
Registration statement
  disclosure duties, 255–56
  disclosure particulars, 256–57
  overview, 255
Regulation A, 262
Regulation S, 261–62
Reporting duties, 259
Reporting holdings in other companies and consolidation of statements, 42
Representations, 297
Research and development, 108
Restrictions, 154

Restrictions on exercise of options, 79
Restructuring, corporate
  acquisition, 269
  consolidation, 269
  divestiture, 269
  equity carve-outs (spin-out IPOs), 302
  going private, 269
  letter stocks, 303
  leveraged buyout, 269
  mergers, 268
  overview, 301–2
  separate listing of units, 303–4
  spin-off, 269
  targeted stocks, 303
Revenue, 109
Right of first offer, 148
Right of redemption, 148
Road show, 250–51
Rule 144, 261
Rule 504, 134
Rule 505, 134
Rule 506, 134

S

S corporations, 25
Salary, 73
Sale and acquisition of assets, 285–86
Sale of shares by shareholders versus investments, 124
Sales manager, 10
Screening employees, 71
Seasoned offering, 235
Secondary offering, 235
Second-stage financing, 115
Securities rules, 295–96
Seed financing, 113
Selling shares exempt from registration, 261–62
Separate listing of units, 303–4
Share capital, 23
Share price, 124
Shareholders
  incorporation, 19
  incorporation in Delaware, 23
Shareholders agreements, 156
Signing underwriting agreement, 251–52
Sources of capital
  bridge loans, 121
  corporate investors, 119
  family, 118
  financing by debt, 120–21
  friends, 118
  institutional investors, 119–20
  mezzanine loans, 120–21
  overview, 116–17
  private investors (angels), 118
  venture capital funds, 118–19
Spin-offs, 83, 269
Spin-out IPOs, 302
Stabilization, 252–53
Stock exchange rules, 296
Stock exchanges versus over-the-counter trading systems, 241–42
Stock markets in United States
  NASDAQ, 243
  New York Stock Exchange (NYSE), 242–43
  overview, 241
  stock exchanges versus over-the-counter trading systems, 241–42
Stock option plans, See also stock options
  approval of, 77
  employee departure, 78
  exercise price, 77–78
  number of options, 78
  option rewarding, 77–79
  overview, 77
  restrictions on exercise of options, 79
Stock options, See also stock option plans
  corporate capital, 21
  defined, 75–76
Stock-based transactions
  advantages of, 289
  risks of, 290–91
Strategic alliances
  advantages of, 61
  antitrust considerations, 63
  disadvantages of, 61–62
  financial reporting, 63
  overview, 60
  types of, 62–63
Strategic classification, 269–70
Success, price of, 7–8
Suppliers, credit from, 41

T

Tag along, 148–49
Target markets, analyzing, 54–56
Targeted stocks, 303
Tax advantages, 274
Tax considerations for incorporation, 15
Taxation of stock options
  employee stock purchase plans, 84–85
  ISOs (incentive stock options), 83–84
  NSOs (non-qualified stock options), 84
Technological leader, 10
Tender offers, 292–93
Term sheet, 135–36
Termination of employment, 89
Third-stage financing, 115
Trade secrets, 99–101
Trademark law, 99
Trading, 252–53
Transaction description, 296
Transfer right, 155
Triangular mergers, 284–85

U

Underwriter compensation, 246

INDEX

Underwriters
  choosing, 155, 244–45
  overview, 243
  underwriter compensation, 246
  underwriting syndicate, 245
Underwriters' option (green shoe), 253
Underwriting agreement
  best efforts offering, 254
  firm commitment offering, 253–54
  types of, 253–55
Underwriting syndicate, 245

V

Valuation of companies
  book value-based multiple, 162
  discount rate used by venture capital funds, 176–78
  discounting cash flows and residual income, 162–71
  EBIT-based multiple, 161
  internal rate of return (IRR), 188
  issuing stock to investors, 178–82
  multiples, valuation methods based on, 158–62
  net earnings multiple, 161
  net present value (NPV), 187
  overview, 109–11, 157–58
  rate of return, 188
  real options method, 171–73
  to strategic investors and buyers, 174–76
  terms, 187–88
  venture capital funds, discount rate used by, 176–78
  venture capital method, 183–87
Valuation of options, 79–80
Variable compensation, 73–74
Variable costs, 50
Venture capital
  choosing investors, 129
  contacting and meeting with investors, 130
  deciding on investment, 130–31
  due diligence, 131
  first-stage financing, 113–14
  fully diluted, 124–25
  how much to raise, 125–26
  investors, issues for, 127–29
  legal restrictions on raising, *See* legal restrictions on raising venture capital
  post-money value, 125
  pre-IPO financing, 115–16
  preliminary rounds of investment, 112
  pre-money value, 125
  preparing to raise, 129
  pre-seed financing, 112
  process for raising, 127–31
  raising, 111–16
  sale of shares by shareholders *versus* investments, 124
  second-stage financing, 115
  seed financing, 113
  share price, 124
  terms, 124–25
  third-stage financing, 115
  valuing company for purpose of raising, 126–27
Venture capital funds
  added value of, 196–99
  characteristics of, 194–95
  compensation of fund managers, 218–19
  discount rate used by, 176–78
  distribution of profits, 218–19
  exit strategies of investments by, 219–20
  how it works, 214–18
  and investors, 195–96
  organization of, 211–13
  overview, 191–92
  portfolios, 196
  raising capital for, 213–14
  return on, 220–21
  structure of, 211–13
  supervision of investments, 199–201
Venture capital industry
  crisis in capital markets impacting, 205–10
  development of venture capital industry in United States, 201–4
  future issues, 210–11
  present state of, 204–11
  United States, development of venture capital industry in, 201–4
Venture capital investors
  corporate in-house entrepreneurship, 226–27
  corporate investors, 225–27
  credit companies as source of capital, 230
  direct investments by companies in the field, 225–26
  financial institutions, 227–30
  holding companies of commercial banks, 228
  insurance companies, 229
  investment banks, 227–28
  leasing as source of capital, 230–31
  mutual funds, 230
  not-for-profit organizations, 229–30
  pension funds, 228–29
  private investors (angels), 223–24
Venture capital method of valuing companies, 183–87
Venture development
  business and market penetration, 108–9
  management, 108
  overview, 108
  research and development, 108
  revenue, 109
Vertical acquisitions, 270

W

Warranties, 297
Weighted average ratchet, 147–48

8 reasons why you should read the Financial Times for 4 weeks RISK-FREE!

To help you stay current with significant developments in the world economy ... and to assist you to make informed business decisions — the Financial Times brings you:

❶ Fast, meaningful overviews of international affairs ... plus daily briefings on major world news.

❷ Perceptive coverage of economic, business, financial and political developments with special focus on emerging markets.

❸ More international business news than any other publication.

❹ Sophisticated financial analysis and commentary on world market activity plus stock quotes from over 30 countries.

❺ Reports on international companies and a section on global investing.

❻ Specialized pages on management, marketing, advertising and technological innovations from all parts of the world.

❼ Highly valued single-topic special reports (over 200 annually) on countries, industries, investment opportunities, technology and more.

❽ The Saturday Weekend FT section — a globetrotter's guide to leisure-time activities around the world: the arts, fine dining, travel, sports and more.

The *Financial Times* delivers a world of business news.

Use the Risk-Free Trial Voucher below!

To stay ahead in today's business world you need to be well-informed on a daily basis. And not just on the national level. You need a news source that closely monitors the entire world of business, and then delivers it in a concise, quick-read format.

With the *Financial Times* you get the major stories from every region of the world. Reports found nowhere else. You get business, management, politics, economics, technology and more.

Now you can try the *Financial Times* for 4 weeks, absolutely risk free. And better yet, if you wish to continue receiving the *Financial Times* you'll get great savings off the regular subscription rate. Just use the voucher below.

---

4 Week Risk-Free Trial Voucher

Yes! Please send me the *Financial Times* for 4 weeks (Monday through Saturday) Risk-Free, and details of special subscription rates in my country.

Name _____

Company _____

Address _____ ❏ Business or ❏ Home Address

Apt./Suite/Floor _____ City _____ State/Province _____

Zip/Postal Code _____ Country _____

Phone (optional) _____ E-mail (optional) _____

Limited time offer good for new subscribers in FT delivery areas only.

To order contact Financial Times Customer Service in your area (mention offer SAB01A).

The Americas: Tel 800-628-8088 Fax 845-566-8220 E-mail: uscirculation@ft.com

Europe: Tel 44 20 7873 4200 Fax 44 20 7873 3428 E-mail: fte.subs@ft.com

Japan: Tel 0120 341-468 Fax 0120 593-146 E-mail: circulation.fttokyo@ft.com

Korea: E-mail: sungho.yang@ft.com

S.E. Asia: Tel 852 2905 5555 Fax 852 2905 5590 E-mail: subseasia@ft.com

www.ft.com

FT FINANCIAL TIMES
World business newspaper

Where to find tomorrow's best business and technology ideas. TODAY.

- Ideas for defining tomorrow's competitive strategies — and executing them.
- Ideas that reflect a profound understanding of today's global business realities.
- Ideas that will help you achieve unprecedented customer and enterprise value.
- Ideas that illuminate the powerful new connections between business and technology.

ONE PUBLISHER.
Financial Times Prentice Hall.

WORLD BUSINESS PUBLISHER

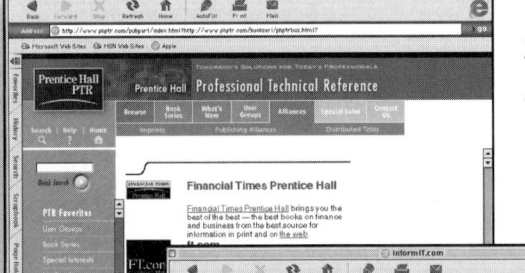

AND 3 GREAT WEB SITES:

ft-ph.com
Fast access to all Financial Times Prentice Hall business books currently available.

InformIt.com
Your link to today's top business and technology experts: new content, practical solutions, and the world's best online training.

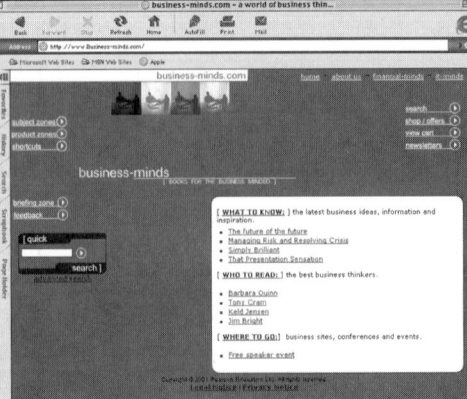

Business-minds.com
Where the thought leaders of the business world gather to share key ideas, techniques, resources — and inspiration.